THE BOOK OF TRAVELS

LETTER FROM THE GENERAL EDITOR

The Library of Arabic Literature makes available Arabic editions and English translations of significant works of Arabic literature, with an emphasis on the seventh to nineteenth centuries. The Library of Arabic Literature thus includes texts from the pre-Islamic era to the cusp of the modern period, and encompasses a wide range of genres, including poetry, poetics, fiction, religion, philosophy, law, science, travel writing, history, and historiography.

Books in the series are edited and translated by internationally recognized scholars. They are published in parallel-text and English-only editions in both print and electronic formats. PDFs of Arabic editions are available for free download. The Library of Arabic Literature also publishes distinct scholarly editions with critical apparatus and a separate Arabic-only series aimed at young readers.

The Library encourages scholars to produce authoritative Arabic editions, accompanied by modern, lucid English translations, with the ultimate goal of introducing Arabic's rich literary heritage to a general audience of readers as well as to scholars and students.

The publications of the Library of Arabic Literature are generously supported by Tamkeen under the NYU Abu Dhabi Research Institute Award G1003 and are published by NYU Press.

Philip F. Kennedy
General Editor, Library of Arabic Literature

About this Paperback

This paperback edition differs in a few respects from its dual-language hardcover predecessor. Because of the compact trim size the pagination has changed. Material that referred to the Arabic edition has been updated to reflect the English-only format, and other material has been corrected and updated where appropriate. For information about the Arabic edition on which this English translation is based and about how the LAL Arabic text was established, readers are referred to the hardcover.

THE BOOK OF TRAVELS

BY
ḤANNĀ DIYĀB

TRANSLATED BY
ELIAS MUHANNA

FOREWORD BY
YASMINE SEALE

INTRODUCTION BY
JOHANNES STEPHAN

AFTERWORD BY
PAULO LEMOS HORTA

VOLUME EDITOR
MICHAEL COOPERSON

NEW YORK UNIVERSITY PRESS
New York

NEW YORK UNIVERSITY PRESS
New York

Copyright © 2022 by New York University
Library of Congress Cataloging-in-Publication Data

Names: Diyāb, Ḥannā, approximately 1687– author. | Stephan, Johannes,
1966– writer of introduction. | Muhanna, Elias, translator. | Seale,
Yasmine, writer of foreword. | Horta, Paulo Lemos, writer of afterword.
Title: The book of travels / by Ḥannā Diyāb ; introduction by Johannes
Stephan ; translated by Elias Muhanna ; foreword by Yasmine Seale ;
afterword by Paulo Lemos Horta.
Other titles: Kitāb al-Siyāḥah English. | Library of Arabic literature.
Description: Paperback edition. | New York : New York University Press,
[2022] | Series: Library of Arabic literature | Includes bibliographical
references and index. | Summary: "The Book of Travels is Ḥannā
Diyāb's remarkable first-person account of his travels as a young man
from his hometown of Aleppo to the court of Versailles and back again"—
Provided by publisher.
Identifiers: LCCN 2022020556 | ISBN 9781479820016 (paperback) | ISBN
9781479820023 (ebook) | ISBN 9781479820047 (ebook)
Subjects: LCSH: Diyāb, Ḥannā, approximately 1687–—Travel. | Aleppo
(Syria)—Description and travel—Early works to 1800. | Paris
(France)—Description and travel—Early works to 1800. | Travelers'
writings, Arabic—Translations into English. | Travelers' writings,
Arabic—History and criticism. | Lucas, Paul, 1664–1737. |
Maronites—Syria—Biography. | Aleppo (Syria)—Biography.
Classification: LCC DS47.2 .D5913 2022 | DDC 910.9182/209033—dc23

LC record available at https://lccn.loc.gov/2022020556

Series design and composition by Nicole Hayward
Typeset in Adobe Text

Manufactured in the United States of America

10 9 8 7 6 5 4 3 2 1

Contents

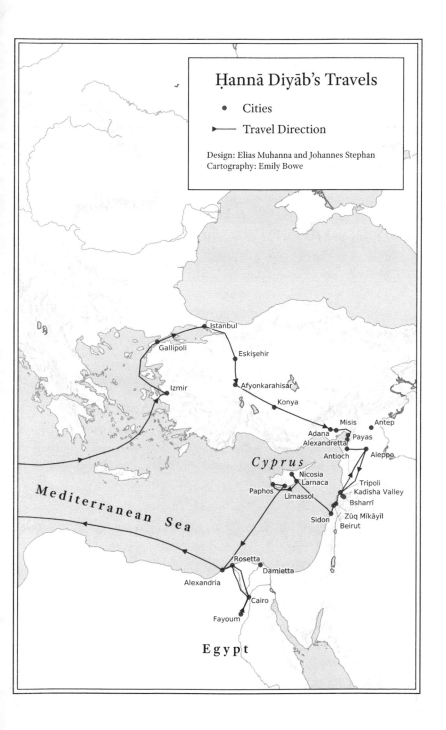

Ḥannā Diyāb's Travels

● Cities

►— Travel Direction

Design: Elias Muhanna and Johannes Stephan
Cartography: Emily Bowe

Istanbul
Gallipoli
Eskişehir
Izmir
Afyonkarahisar
Konya
Misis   Antep
Adana   Payas
Alexandretta
Antioch   Aleppo
Cyprus
Nicosia
Larnaca   Tripoli
Paphos   Kadisha Valley
Limassol   Bsharrī
Sidon   Zūq Mīkāyīl
Beirut

Mediterranean Sea

Rosetta
Damietta
Alexandria
Cairo
Fayoum

Egypt

Foreword

YASMINE SEALE

One morning in October 1708, two men walk into a room at Versailles where King Louis XIV is waiting to receive them. Between them is a cage of curious animals: a pair of honey-colored mice with giant ears and long hind legs, like miniature kangaroos. The older man, Paul Lucas, has just returned from a mission to the Ottoman Empire, where he was sent to hunt for coins, gems, and other precious things to feed the royal collection. Among the loot he has brought back are these strange, alert creatures. The king wants to know more. Lucas boasts that he "discovered" them in Upper Egypt, despite their being very difficult to catch. (He is lying: in fact, he was sold them by a Frenchman in Tunis.) And what are they called? Lucas, unable to say, turns to the young man by his side.

"I replied that, in the lands where it is found, the animal is called a *jarbūʿ*." Of how many people can it be said that their first words to the Sun King contained the Arabic pharyngeal *ʿayn*? The pharynx, and the story, belong to Ḥannā Diyāb, a multilingual monk-in-training from Aleppo who, around the age of twenty, dropped out of the ascetic life to be Lucas's assistant on his voyage—translating, interceding and, once or twice, saving his life—in exchange for the promise of a job in Paris.

It was probably through Diyāb that *gerboise*, the desert-dwelling jerboa, entered the French lexicon. At the king's request he writes down the animals' name. At the request of the king's son ("of medium height and quite rotund"), they are painted onto an enormous illustration of wild beasts. Then Diyāb is marched around the palace to be peered at, by princess after princess, until two in the morning. He peers back.

The promise is eventually betrayed; after two years with Lucas and no job forthcoming, Diyāb returns home to Aleppo where he spends the rest of his life selling cloth—and, no doubt, telling stories of his adventure. Fifty-four years after the facts, unknowably transformed, he commits them to paper.

Time is also a translator. After telling us about his encounter with the king, Diyāb adds: "Is it possible I could have retained perfectly everything I saw and heard? Surely not." It is the only moment in the memoir when he calls his own reliability into question, pointing to the half-century that separates the tale from the event. Yet *The Book of Travels*' most astonishing scene, its perihelion, is also its most believable: the royal curiosity rushing to classify, the chubby prince, the little lie.

You are reading Diyāb's true story because of others he made up: Aladdin (spelled in Arabic as ʿAlāʾ al-Dīn), ʿAlī Bābā, a dozen more told to Antoine Galland over a handful of spring nights. These encounters, among the most consequential in literature, are recorded in a cooler key, offhand. Nothing could be more normal, less worthy of note than the telling and swapping of tales— "collaborative sessions," as the editor of this volume aptly puts it.

Aladdin, readers are sometimes surprised to learn, is a boy from China. Yet the text is ambivalent about what this means, and pokes gentle fun at the idea of cultural authenticity. Shahrazad has hardly begun her tale when she forgets quite where it is set. "Majesty, in the capital of one of China's vast and wealthy kingdoms, whose name escapes me at present, there lived a tailor named Mustafa . . . ." The story's institutions are Ottoman, the customs half-invented, the palace redolent of Versailles. It is a mishmash and knows it.

Like Aladdin, like Aleppo, Diyāb's is a story of mixture. He knows French, Turkish, Italian, even Provençal—but not Greek: in Cyprus, unable to understand the language, he feels like "a deaf man in a wedding procession." Slipping in and out of personae, he is alert to the masquerades of others. Behind the European envoy's mask we glimpse a con man: Paul Lucas travels in the guise of a doctor, prescribing remedies in exchange for treasure. He treats a stomach ache with a paste made of parsley, sugar, and crushed pearls.

To meet the king, Diyāb has been encouraged to wear his native dress: turban cloth, pantaloons, dagger. But the calpac on his head is actually Egyptian, and his trousers cut from *londrin*—London or Mocha broadcloth, a textile made of Spanish wool, manufactured in Languedoc and exported to Aleppo by merchants in Marseille. His outfit, like his mind, bears a pan-Mediterranean print.

In *The Book of Travels* he is forever drawing comparisons: between Lyon and Aleppo, Seine and Euphrates, Harlequin and Karagöz. Against the clash of cultures, here is a cradle; against the border, a lattice. Here is a Syrian's view of France, a description of Europe where Arabs circulate and thrive, a portrait of the Mediterranean as a zone of intense contact and interwoven histories.

This is also an old man's account of what it was to be twenty years old, gifted and curious, somewhere new. Time has sharpened its colors. Its thrill is picaresque: a tale of high drama and low ebbs, the exuberant perils of early modern travel. At a Franciscan monastery in Cyprus, Diyāb is kept awake all night by the grunting of pigs. He is eaten alive by mosquitoes in Rosetta, by lice in Fayoum; ambushed on the way to Livorno by corsairs who cry "*Maina!*," lingua franca for surrender; abandoned to the whims of muleteers. Tobacco is smuggled in a mattress, a mummy in straw. Much energy is spent evading English pirates.

In the long tradition of Arabic travel writing, Diyāb is different: he lets us in and keeps us close. Unlike Ilyās al-Mawṣilī, whose account of the Spanish conquest of America Diyāb seems to have owned, he is not a cleric seeking to secure his reputation. Nor is this a self-consciously literary document in the vein of ʿAbd al-Ghanī al-Nābulusī's descriptions of his journeys through the Muslim world. There is no poetry in this memoir, no quotation. Its cadences are those of Syrian speech, its subject everyday emotions: fear, shame, astonishment, relief.

Some of the most vivid pages concern a storm in the Gulf of Sidra, where Diyāb and his companions nearly drown. By the time the castaways reach land, their throats are so dry they cannot speak, and their food has turned soggy with seawater. For days they eat nothing but dates, then they are reduced to eating cats. When they finally reach Tripoli, after fifteen days without nourishment, and are given bread, Diyāb is unable to swallow it: "it tasted like ashes."

Then there are the fifteen icy days in December 1708, the coldest winter in five hundred years, during which tens of thousands froze to death. "Paris was a ghost town . . . The priests of the city were forced to set up braziers on the altars of their churches to prevent the sacramental wine from freezing. Many people even died while relieving themselves, because the urine froze in their urethras as it left their bodies and killed them." Diyāb has to be rubbed from head to toe with eagle fat (another of Lucas's remedies) and wrapped in blankets for twenty-four hours before he recovers sensation in his limbs. It is in these moments of plain, precise language that hunger, thirst, and cold—untranslatable pain—come through.

Unusually for a travel writer, Diyāb is a working man. For all the pomp of the French court, his attention remains trained on those who, like him, labor invisibly: hospital workers who serve soup three times a day in tin bowls; nuns who launder clothes in the river; prostitutes whose doors are marked by a large heart made of thorns. Striking, too, is the sheer violence of everyday life. In Livorno he sees a soldier punished for desertion—nostrils slashed and forehead branded with the king's seal. In Paris he goes to a courthouse to watch the trial of highway robbers, and to the public square to see them killed.

A thought recurred as I read: you couldn't make it up. While Lucas bathes rusty coins in vinegar to reveal their inscriptions, Diyāb probes the strangeness of the world. Miracles—magical causes applied to mechanical effects—jostle with the most daily phenomena. The true colors of things take on a hallucinated quality. If the Dauphin's bestiary contains no jerboa, can his own eyes be trusted? If the remedy is bogus, but you were healed, what then?

Scholars argue over how much of Diyāb is in Aladdin, where to draw the line between fiction and truth. This memoir smudges such distinctions by showing how fantasy is woven into life, how enchantment is neighbor to inquiry. At the opera, Diyāb is dazzled by stage contraptions. Knowing how they are built does nothing to lessen their magic. Mechanical causes with magical effects: this is art.

Yasmine Seale
Istanbul

Acknowledgments

For Laila and Maya

I wish to express my gratitude to the many individuals whose contributions have enriched this book. Johannes Stephan has been all that one could ask for in a co-author, and Michael Cooperson's erudition and wit have improved our work immeasurably. I'm grateful to Paolo Horta for helping to interest the Library of Arabic Literature in the manuscript, to Philip Kennedy and the rest of the Editorial Board for their faith in the project, and to an anonymous reviewer for many helpful suggestions. Chip Rossetti, Lucie Taylor, and the production team have taken scrupulous care of our work. I would like to thank Professors Hilary Kilpatrick and Jérôme Lentin for introducing me to Diyāb's manuscript many years ago. Finally, I thank my wife Jen, whose discernment has caught many an unmusical phrase, and my daughters Laila Rose and Maya, whose love has kept me whole when, as Diyāb would say, the world seemed to crowd in upon my miserable self.

—Elias Muhanna

I wish to express my sincere gratitude to a few colleagues, notably to Elias Muhanna for his help with an early draft of the introduction to this translation. My deep appreciation goes to Reinhard Schulze under whose supervision I wrote my Ph.D. thesis on *The Book of Travels* and its literariness. My research on Diyāb's text was made possible by the support of a number of institutions: the Universität Bern and the Orient-Institut Beirut, as well as the Biblioteca

Apos-tolica Vaticana, the Forschungsbibliothek Gotha, the Bibliothèque Orientale at the Université de Saint-Joseph in Beirut, and more recently the ERC-funded AnonymClassic project at the Freie Universität Berlin, directed by Beatrice Gründler, where I hold a research post. My work is inspired through conversations with Ibrahim Akel, Bernard Heyberger, Paule Fahmé-Thiéry, Hilary Kilpatrick, and Isabel Toral, among others. Finally, my thanks go to Feriel Bouhafa for all her support.

—Johannes Stephan

Introduction

JOHANNES STEPHAN

The author of *The Book of Travels* (*Kitāb al-Siyāḥah*),[1] Ḥannā Diyāb,[2] became known to Western scholarship more than a century after his death, when his name was discovered in the diaries of Antoine Galland, the great French Orientalist and translator of the *Thousand and One Nights*.[3] Since that discovery, Diyāb, a Maronite Christian merchant and storyteller from Aleppo, has become a familiar figure to scholars interested in the textual history of the *Nights*. He has been described as Galland's muse: The informant who supplied several famous stories to the French translation of the collection, including "Aladdin" and "'Alī Bābā and the Forty Thieves."

Until the early 1990s, few scholars were aware that in 1764 Diyāb had written his own travelogue.[4] Because the first pages were missing, his work was catalogued as anonymous by the Catholic priest Paul Sbath, who came into possession of it at some point in the early twentieth century.[5] After Sbath's death in 1945, his family gave the manuscript to the Vatican Library, where it remains today. The work is an account of Diyāb's travels, mostly in the company of a Frenchman named Paul Lucas. Starting in early 1707, from the vicinity of Diyāb's hometown of Aleppo, the two journeyed through Ottoman Syria, then traveled across the Mediterranean to Paris, passing through Cyprus, Alexandria, Cairo, Fayoum, Tripoli, Djerba, Tunis, Livorno, Genoa, Marseille, Lyon, and the court of Versailles, among many other places. They arrived in Paris in September 1708 and lived there together for several months. In June

1709, Diyāb set out for home. His voyage took him first to Istanbul, where he lived for some time. After crossing Anatolia by caravan, he returned home to Aleppo in June 1710.

Ḥannā Diyāb's connection to the *Thousand and One Nights* has long tantalized scholars, and the publication of his travelogue may help shed light on that.⁶ But *The Book of Travels* is also significant in its own right. Among the topics it allows us to explore are Diyāb's relationship to his French patron, Paul Lucas; different forms of oral storytelling proper to *The Book of Travels*; and the culture of Arabic writing in eighteenth-century Aleppo.

The Aleppan Traveler and His French Patron

For the most part, *The Book of Travels* centers on the relationship between an Aleppan working man and a French antiquarian, which began as a business agreement. In exchange for serving as a translator, Diyāb was offered the chance to accompany Lucas on a journey that would span three continents. The asymmetry of this master-servant arrangement reflects, in a way, the relationship between Catholic states in the West and the Ottoman Empire during the early and mid-eighteenth century, just as it portrays an ambivalent relationship between East and West. Diyāb's relationship to his patron encompasses a combination of postures and affects, ranging from servitude, respect, and emulation to the occasional display of irony. For his part, Lucas, who also wrote an account of the voyage, does not mention Diyāb once.

Apart from a few scraps of manuscript evidence, the only available record of Diyāb's life is to be found in his travelogue, which also seems to be the only text he authored. Toward the end of the book, he indicates that he wrote it at the age of seventy-five. This means that he must have been born between 1687 and 1689, probably in the northern Aleppo suburb of al-Jdayde, a traditionally Christian quarter. The manuscript was completed in March 1764. It ends with an account of Diyāb's final adventure with Lucas after the latter's return to Aleppo in 1716. By then, Diyāb had begun a career as a textile merchant.[7] Half a century later, when he set about writing *The Book of Travels*, he enjoyed a respected social position within the Maronite community of Aleppo.[8] From the book we learn that he married a few years after his return, and fathered several children. He mentions his mother, but says nothing of his father. He does speak of his older brothers, 'Abdallāh and Anṭūn, whose correspondence with him during his travels suggests they were responsible for him.[9]

Another detail one may infer from the book's first pages pertains to the Maronite community to which Diyāb belonged. Like other Eastern churches, it was undergoing a process of catholicization that had begun in the sixteenth century. Only a few years after the Council of Trent, in the late sixteenth century, the first Catholic missionaries established themselves in Aleppo and began to reformulate Eastern Christian rites and dogma. A decade later, the Holy See opened a Maronite college in Rome. This catholicizing of the Eastern churches, which peaked in the first decades of the eighteenth century, entailed the establishment of new teaching institutions, the proliferation of books and literacy, the introduction of a printing press, and the formation of the Melkite Greek Catholic church.[10]

It was during this time of change that Diyāb set out, in 1706, for the Monastery of Saint Elishā', the main residence of the Lebanese Maronite order. The order had been established in 1694 by the young Aleppans 'Abdallāh Qarā'alī, Jibrīl Ḥawwā, and Yūsuf al-Batn, with the permission of the patriarch Iṣṭifān al-Duwayhī.[11] In founding the first indigenous monastic order based on a European model, these young men became important figures in the catholicization of the Maronite community.[12] Hoping to become a monk, Diyāb arrived at a moment when the community was still in the throes of an internal dispute over hierarchy and doctrinal direction.[13]

The experience at Saint Elishā' and his meeting with one of the founders, 'Abdallāh Qarā'alī (d. 1742), left a profound impression on Diyāb. He vividly portrays his reverence for the monks' "angelic conduct" (§1.17) and for the orderly rhythms of monastic life. He soon came to feel, however, that he did not belong in the community. When at one point he fell ill, he received permission from the abbot to leave the monastery, under the pretext of convalescing in his hometown. Failing to find a job in Aleppo, he resigned himself to returning to the monastery. On his way back, he met Paul Lucas, a traveler "dispatched by the sultan of France," and joined his entourage (§1.29).

The "gentleman" (*khawājah*) Paul Lucas, as Diyāb first calls him, was born in 1664 to a merchant family in Rouen. Two years later, after serving in the Venetian army, he embarked on his first tour to the Levant.[14] By the time he met Diyāb, he was in the midst of his third voyage to the East. Drawn by Diyāb's linguistic skills, Lucas offered him the job of personal companion and dragoman on a journey across the Mediterranean world. In exchange, Lucas promised Diyāb a position at the Royal Library in Paris. The young Aleppan was intrigued by the offer, and quickly accepted, presenting himself as a traveler interested in seeing the world rather than a humble novice returning to his monastery. After making a few discreet inquiries about the Frenchman's integrity, he agreed to accompany him on his travels.

When they arrived in Paris, Diyāb lived with Lucas, from September 1708 to June 1709, waiting patiently to be hired into the position at the Royal Library, as he had been promised. When no such job materialized, Diyāb grew frustrated. In the meantime, he had made the acquaintance of Antoine Galland, whom he describes as an "old man who was assigned to oversee the library of Arabic books and could read Arabic well" (§10.9). After Galland arranged for Diyāb to be hired by a member of the French court to work, like his former master, as a traveler dispatched by Louis XIV, he decided he would leave the French capital, but the offer of employment—like the library position he coveted—never came through. On his way home to Syria, he stopped for some time in Istanbul, where he worked as a valet and a housekeeper until he was urged by a friend to accompany him to Aleppo. Right after Diyāb's return from his travels in June 1710, his brother 'Abdallāh, with the help of an uncle, opened a textile shop for him. A few years later, Paul Lucas returned to Aleppo, sought out Diyāb, and reproached him for leaving Paris so rashly. After going on one last adventure together in the vicinity of Aleppo, the two men went their separate ways. Diyāb tells us that he worked as a textile merchant for twenty-two years, but gives no details about his life after he retired in his forties.

The encounter with Lucas had a profound influence on Diyāb. It was common for Aleppan Christians in the seventeenth and eighteenth centuries to work for (French) consuls, traders, missionaries, and travelers who formed part of the social fabric of the city. In fact, Lucas was not Diyāb's first patron; like his brothers, Diyāb had worked for a dozen years, beginning before he was ten years old, as a domestic servant in the employ of various French merchants. His contact with Europeans helped him acquire a good knowledge of French, Italian, and Turkish. His association with Lucas also helped him to attain a prestigious position within his community. In the 1760s, when he wrote *The Book of Travels*, it was important to Diyāb to assert this prestige before his extended family and larger community. Lucas is accordingly mentioned in two of the book's chapter headings. He doubtless also appeared in the now-lost first pages of the narrative, and perhaps even in the title of the book.

In the first chapters of Diyāb's travelogue, Lucas's discoveries and his acquisition of artifacts—rare precious stones, coins, books, and a mummy, among other things—are the main focus of the narrative. Diyāb describes how Lucas offered to treat people's illnesses in exchange for objects he wanted to acquire, something Lucas himself reports that he did. Diyāb mentions Lucas's expertise in astronomy, geometry, philosophy, natural history, and other disciplines. He recounts how Lucas came to his aid on more than one occasion, such as when Diyāb nearly froze to death during the icy winter in Paris, or when he was arrested by the French gendarmerie.

Given Diyāb's apparently reverential attitude toward Lucas, it is noteworthy that the latter nowhere mentions Diyāb in his own travelogue. The young Syrian cannot even be discerned among the nameless servants and dragomans that Lucas happens to mention on occasion.[15] This discrepancy between the two works can be seen in other ways. Diyāb offers a richly detailed account of the logistics of travel, of the food they consumed, and of the different types of clothing he saw. Lucas's focus is, rather, on sightseeing at ancient ruins, collecting antiquities, and describing his adventures, which include the occasional miracle.[16] He excludes from his account the countries of Catholic Europe that so fascinated Diyāb, who describes them along with the parts of the Ottoman Empire that were largely unknown to Aleppans. Thus, although the itinerary described in the two travelogues is generally the same, only a few episodes correspond well enough to be fruitfully compared.[17]

One such episode is the story of the jerboas that Lucas presented to Louis XIV and his entourage at Versailles. In his account, Lucas offers a drawing of a jerboa,[18] and claims to have witnessed a hunt for the animals in the desert in Upper Egypt.[19] In Diyāb's version of the story, we learn that Lucas had in fact acquired the jerboas at a French merchant's house in Tunis. As he reports the lie his patron told the king, Diyāb gives his readers a glimpse of his own feelings about Lucas's posturing. He also recounts how Lucas, unable to identify the exotic species for the king, turned to his companion for help. Diyāb knew the animal's name in both French and Arabic and was able to write these down at Louis XIV's request.

The jerboas—a subject of great interest to the members of the royal court—served as Diyāb's entry to the king's private chambers. As he was paraded through the palace and its various mansions, carrying the cage with the two jerboas to present them to the royal family, Diyāb, dressed in a turban, bouffant pantaloons, and a fancy striped overcoat, and wearing a silver-plated dagger in his belt, came to be regarded as a curiosity in his own right. In Diyāb's account, it is at this moment that he becomes the protagonist of his own story. By sharing with the French court his knowledge of the Orient, he outdoes his master, the supposed authority. Recollecting these events more than fifty years later, Diyāb reveals to his readers his patron's unreliability, correcting the record of what Lucas attempts to convey about his own experiences.

A further element of Diyāb's relationship with Lucas is the medical knowledge he believed he had acquired by association with him. On his journey home, Diyāb used those skills to treat people in exchange for accommodation and food. Dressed as a European, he came to be known in Anatolia as a "Frankish doctor," (§11.83) modeled on his master. Like Lucas, Diyāb recounts how rumors of his medical skill spread as he traveled through Anatolia, and that the masses flocked to him to receive treatment.[20] However, while Lucas regarded himself as a genuine master of various treatments and procedures, Diyāb's self-portrayal is decidedly less confident. He presents himself as overwhelmed by the difficulties of masquerading as a physician. His humility, confusion, and reliance on God's guidance stand in clear contrast to the self-confident mastery Lucas ascribes to himself. Setting these two accounts alongside each other, one might read Diyāb's description of his experience as a traveling doctor as a parody of Lucas's account. But it is unlikely that Diyāb meant it that way. Whereas Diyāb mentions Lucas's journaling and the fact that he had sent his book manuscript to the printer after arriving in Paris, it is unlikely that Diyāb read much of Lucas's book or earlier notes. That said, he would have known Lucas's perspectives on their shared adventures.

The relationship between Ḥannā Diyāb and Paul Lucas was one of mutual dependence. Lucas was an antiquarian with little knowledge of Arabic and other Southern Mediterranean languages and literary traditions. His dependence on local Eastern Christian guides who could move flexibly within a Western Christian context is indisputable, even if that dependence was not reflected in his own accounts. On the other hand, Lucas seems to have served both as a source of personal protection and, to some extent, as a model for the young man from Aleppo. Diyāb's interest in Lucas's professional activities during the long journey to the "lands of the Christians," as well as his emulation of his medical practices, mean he was not merely an "Oriental" servant to a French traveler, but also a Catholic familiar with global institutions such as the missionary movement and Mediterranean trade.

ORAL STORYTELLING AND *THE BOOK OF TRAVELS* AS A FRAME NARRATIVE

By the time Ḥannā Diyāb met Antoine Galland, the latter's translation of the *Thousand and One Nights* was already enjoying immense popularity in Parisian court society. The prospect of discovering new material to add to his translation must have excited the French Orientalist. Even so, Galland was scrupulous in his choice of what to publish, preferring to rely on written rather than oral sources whenever possible. At his disposal was a fifteenth-century manuscript of the *Nights* that he had received from Syria some time before meeting Diyāb. Using it and a few other written sources, he had completed eight volumes of his translation, at which point he ran out of stories. His first encounter with Diyāb, which took place on March 25, 1709, at the house of Paul Lucas, a colleague with whom he shared an interest in antiquity and numismatics, seemed promising.[21]

After this first meeting, Galland recorded in his journal a description of the young man from Aleppo as a learned person who spoke several languages and possessed a knowledge of "Oriental" books.[22] Diyāb told Galland about the existence of other tales and promised to put some stories into writing. In a note written six weeks later, on May 5, Galland reports that Diyāb had "finished the story of the lamp."[23] Titled "Aladdin and His Wonderful Lamp," this would come to be the most famous story in the *Nights*. It was only in November of the following year, however, that Galland explicitly refers to a written version of the story.[24] Whether Diyāb had written it down himself while in Paris, dictated it to a commissioned scribe, or even sent it to Galland at a later stage remains an open question. Yet there is good reason to doubt that Diyāb wrote it down himself, at least during his time in Paris in 1709. He makes no mention of writing anything during his meetings with Galland, even though he stresses his ability to write single words, letters, and also, of course, his own *Book of Travels*. As for the *Nights*, he mentions only his oral contribution to the collection of stories, and that the old man was very appreciative of his service (§10.9).

From Galland's *Journal* we learn that after Diyāb performed or wrote down the story of "Aladdin," the two met several more times. During their meetings, Galland took notes on stories recounted for him by Diyāb. These stories would become the basis of volumes nine through twelve of the French translation (published between 1712 and 1717), marking a break with Galland's previous practice of relying exclusively on written sources. One might envision these meetings between Diyāb and Galland as collaborative sessions in which the former used both Arabic and French to convey the stories to the French Orientalist. Of these stories, only the tale of "The Ebony Horse" has an attested written origin beyond Galland's notes. All the others can be identified only to the extent that they contain well-known motifs from oral folk narratives.[25] As they do not have a written source, they have been referred to by scholars as "orphan stories."[26] Of the sixteen tales he heard from Diyāb, Galland chose to publish ten. These include "'Alā' al-Dīn," the equally famous "'Alī Bābā and the Forty Thieves," and "Prince Aḥmad and the Fairy Perī Bānū."

A further link between Diyāb's *Book of Travels* and the *Thousand and One Nights* emerges from the narrative mode Diyāb adopts in his own book, one that makes ample use of embedded narratives—the central structural paradigm of the *Nights* and *The Book of the Ten Viziers*, as well as *The Book of Sindbad the Sailor*. Diyāb's travelogue contains almost forty secondary stories, most of them diegetically independent of the main narrative. Some consist of only a few lines, whereas others extend over three or more manuscript pages. The stories are a mix of historical and hagiographical anecdotes, although they also include a few tales of crime and horror. The narratives seem to stem mainly from oral sources, but a few have well-attested written origins. Among the popular early-modern motifs that make an appearance are the figure of a person buried alive, the legend of the philosopher's stone and the water of life, and reports of wonders such as the hydraulic Machine de Marly in Versailles and the Astronomical Clock in Lyon. Many of the stories are told at the point in the journey at which they were supposed to have taken place, while others are grouped according to theme.

Diyāb uses the classical Arabic categories of *khabar* ("report" or "account") and *ḥikāyah* ("story") as generic frames to indicate independent narrative units. These units are also highlighted through the use of colored ink and textual indentions. As is typical of classical frame narratives, about one third of the inserted stories are introduced not by the primary narrator, Diyāb himself, but by the characters from the story world—that is, by the people Diyāb meets during his voyages. This telling of a secondary tale by direct quotation, though common in Diyāb's narrative, is unusual in early-modern travelogues. A skilled storyteller, Diyāb drew upon a repertoire of narratives he had probably acquired from collective reading sessions in coffeehouses and elsewhere, as well as spontaneous oral accounts, and fashioned these along recognizable plotlines. It is likely that, standing in front of Galland, he performed in a manner similar to that described by Scottish doctor Patrick Russell:

> The recitation of Eastern fables and tales, partakes somewhat of a dramatic performance. It is not merely a simple narrative; the story is animated by the manner, and action of the speaker. A variety of other story books, besides the Arabian Nights Entertainments, (which, under that title, are little known at Aleppo) furnish materials for the storyteller, who, by combining the incidents of different tales, and varying the catastrophe of such as he has related before, gives them an air of novelty even to persons who at first imagine they are listening to tales with which they are acquainted.[27]

The way Diyāb employed the skills Russell describes becomes clear when we examine how he combines plotlines and details known from other narratives.[28] For example, in one passage in *The Book of Travels*, he enters the home of a nobleman and sees a stunning trompe l'oeil painting of a man holding a bird that seems to jut out of the wall it is painted on (§9.41). He proceeds to elaborate on the theme by providing a biography of the artist (who may have been a Fontainebleau painter of the Renaissance school) in three episodes. In the first episode, a shoemaker's apprentice falls in love with a princess. Her father laughs at the apprentice's proposal but says he will give him his daughter's hand in marriage if he can paint her portrait. The suitor agrees, and succeeds in painting a beautiful portrait that deeply impresses the prince. But the latter refuses to give his daughter to the apprentice, offering his second daughter instead. This breaks the young artist's heart. He leaves the prince's service, goes insane, and becomes a famous painter wandering the world. More than any other story in *The Book of Travels*, this episode exudes the spirit of the *Thousand and One Nights*.[29] The prominent role of the image recalls the motif of falling in love with a portrait, which appears in Diyāb's story of "Qamar al-Dīn and Badr al-Budūr" (omitted by Galland from his translation). Second, the motif of becoming an artist out of lovesickness appears in the *Majnūn Laylā* story cycle, which may have been familiar to Diyāb from *Khosrow and Shīrīn*, a Persian retelling popular during Ottoman times. Finally, demanding an impossible or difficult task of a suitor is a motif known from the fifth tale told during the tenth day in Boccaccio's *Decameron*, a book that itself is believed to have been inspired by "Oriental" models of frame-narrative storytelling.

In the second episode, Diyāb reports that the apprentice painter once painted on one of his master's portraits a fly so realistic that the master tries to shoo it away. Though Diyāb presents this as part of the biography of the painter whose work he had seen, the same story is told by Giorgio Vasari (d. 1574) about Giotto di Bondone (d. 1276). To this episode Diyāb adds a third episode in which the painter, now named Nīkūlā, challenges his master to a contest of realism. The master creates an image of fruits so lifelike that birds come to peck them. But Nīkūlā wins by painting a curtain so realistic that his master tries to draw it aside to see the painting behind it. This story evidently stems from the one told by Pliny the Elder (d. 79) about the contest between the painters Zeuxis and Parrhasius. Both tales include a variant of the line attributed by Pliny to Parrhasius and given by Diyāb as follows: "It doesn't take much skill to fool a few birds [. . .] Fooling a master painter like you? That takes some doing" (§9.51). Although the motif is attested in traditions other than the Greek, it may have come to Diyāb's attention in France, since it was deployed by eighteenth-century European intellectuals in their theorizations of art.[30] In his account of Paris, Diyāb mentions in passing that he had taken painting classes there.

Diyāb produces these episodes and combines them into a whole at a moment in his travelogue when he has just narrated his confrontation with the trompe l'oeil painting in Paris. He is as amazed by this painting as he is by a realistic depiction of Jesus Christ in Livorno, and by the Paris opera stage, which is populated by real animals, convincing landscapes, and royal chambers. The common theme is art that can be easily confused with reality, but Diyāb's accounts of such works appear in different places in the travelogue. Creating his own piece of art as a narrative, both in the *Thousand and One Nights* and in his *Book of Travels*, Diyāb combines motifs and known episodes, and adds new names and details to them, giving them "an air of novelty," as Russell puts it. The orphan tales, most prominently "ʿAlī Bābā," are novelistic and complex. "ʿAlī Bābā," as Aboubakr Chraïbi has noted, is a "dual composition" in which two tale types are combined.[31] Admittedly, as Chraïbi's analysis implies, Diyāb may have modeled the orphan tales on originals that were already complex. Still, tales like "The Two Sisters Who Envied Their Cadette" and "Prince Aḥmad and the Fairy Perī Bānū" have the additional feature of combining tales of two different types into one. The story of "Aladdin" may be the result of a similar process.[32]

The frame narrative structure, the modeling of new tales on old ones, and the compositional style are all features that Diyāb's *Book of Travels* shares with the *Thousand and One Nights*. Structurally, the parallels between the two books are grounded in the way the storyteller's memory functions and in his manner of refashioning existing narratives and motifs. Although some features may be unintended, in general Diyāb's storytelling in *The Book of Travels* reflects an oral practice mostly based on oral accounts. Yet, we know that Diyāb did not tell stories only from memory—he also owned books, and contributed to a new practice of travel writing that emerged in the 1750s and '60s.

Writing an Autobiography in Mid-Eighteenth-Century Aleppo

Diyāb was one of several Maronites and other catholicized Christians who composed accounts of their experiences in the Western Catholic world. Though interested in travelogues, he composed his *Book of Travels* very much as a personal narrative, and it consequently exhibits, both in plot and the perspective, specific features characteristic of autobiography.

We can get some idea of the literary models available to Diyāb by looking at his library. Besides his own *Book of Travels*, written at the end of his life, Diyāb owned at least six other books. Four are handwritten copies of devotional works:

1. a *Treatise on the Seven Deadly Sins and the Seven Virtues* (*Sharḥ mukhtāṣar fī al-sabʿ radāyil wa-muqābiluhā aʿnī al-sabʿ faḍāyil*), translated from Latin or French, and bound in a volume dated July 1753;

2. *A Useful Book on Knowing One's Will* (*Kitāb Mufīd fī ʿilm al-niyyah*), another treatise on moral theology;[33]

3. *The Precious Pearl on the Holy Life of Saint Francis* (*al-Durr al-nafīs fī sīrat al-qiddīs Fransīs*),[34] a vita of Saint Francis Xavier (d. 1552), the founder of the Jesuit order, based on the

account by Dominique Bouhours (d. 1702), and paraphrased into Arabic by a Jesuit missionary in Aleppo, dated December 1753; and

4. a four-volume collection of hagiographic tales (*Kitāb Akhbār al-qiddīsīn*) translated into Arabic by Pierre Fromage (d. 1740), dated between 1755 and 1757. The owner's name, being partially struck out, is not entirely legible, but the handwriting of this codex resembles that of the works above, as well as that of *The Book of Travels*.

The two other books are travelogues, probably copied in the 1750s or '60s, and bound in a single volume:

5. a copy of *The Book of Travels* (*Kitāb al-Siyāḥah*) by Ilyās al-Mawṣilī (d. after 1692). A struck-off name deciphered by Antoine Rabbath (d. 1913) as "Ḥannā son of Diyāb" appears as a former owner.[35]
6. an Arabic translation of the Turkish *sefâretnâmeh* by Yirmisekiz Mehmed Çelebi Efendi.

From this list, and from the way Diyāb's name appears in the codices, one can draw a few inferences about his participation in the written culture of Aleppo. First, the codices establish him as an owner but not necessarily a writer of books. Second, the items in his library, which include translations from Western European languages, represent an ideological affiliation with the Catholic world and with the Western institutions of knowledge production and power he depicts in his travelogue. Finally, although Diyāb had other travelogues at his disposal, his own adopts a different and distinct mode of self-representation.

With respect to ownership, the name "Ḥannā ibn Diyāb" appears six times as the owner of a particular text. A few volumes state, using a well-known formula, that Diyāb had "obtained the book for himself from his own money."[36] A unique inscription in the copy of

Saint Francis Xavier's vita implies that Diyāb had "copied," "transmitted," or even "translated" (*naqala*) the book.[37] It remains uncertain whether he copied his books himself, commissioned others to do so, or dictated them, along with *The Book of Travels*, to the same scribe.

The layout of *The Book of Travels* suggests that it may have been dictated. Although a large portion is presented as a finalized codex, with colored and centered chapter headings and the same number of lines per page, almost every folio contains words that have been crossed out and replaced with others. Also, the oral and colloquial nature of the text smacks of dictation. The language is a register of so-called Middle Arabic, containing many dialect features as well as many loanwords from Ottoman Turkish and Italian. Although typical of oral storytelling, as with the popular epic (*siyar*) tradition, Diyāb's language displays more variation than do other examples of Middle Arabic, notably the orthography, which is highly idiosyncratic: The same word might be spelled two different ways in as many lines. Such inconsistencies may well be the result of rapid writing that reflects actual pronunciation, and serves as a reminder of the story's initial orality.

Oral narrative, as Walter Ong has argued, displays greater redundancy than its written counterpart.[38] In *The Book of Travels*, redundancy is evident on different levels, from single words to entire episodes. For instance, Diyāb tells the story of his mother's recovery from melancholia no less than three times. He also recycles structural formulas such as "let me get back to what I was saying," a characteristic of oral performance, to link successive episodes.[39] In these respects, *The Book of Travels* resembles a performance by a public storyteller. Indeed, it may be the result of an extended performance that included some of the embedded stories.

As for the Catholic element, some of Diyāb's devotional books contain stories that resonate with the material found in his *Book of Travels*. *Kitāb Akhbār al-qiddīsīn*, a multivolume collection of hagiographies, had served as a synaxarion, a collection of saints' lives read as part of the liturgy. It had been translated into Arabic from a French composition that was in turn based on a Spanish collection of vitae, one for each day of the year. Short hagiographic stories proliferated widely in the eighteenth-century Levant. Around the time Diyāb set out for the monastery, the superior of the Lebanese Maronite order, and later bishop of Aleppo, Jirmānūs Farḥāt (d. 1732), had just completed his rewriting of a Byzantine collection of hagiographic and other edifying tales from Eastern and Western Christianity. Titled *The Monks' Garden* (*Bustān al-ruhbān*), this work garnered considerable attention.[40] Diyāb repurposed the contents of *Kitāb Akhbār al-qiddīsīn* for his own narrative, borrowing elements from the stories of Saint Genevieve of Paris and Saint Elizabeth of Hungary and merging them into one narrative. He refers to the biblical story of Saint Mary Magdalene and her fate in Marseille, and to the story of Helena of Constantinople, both of which also appear in *Kitāb Akhbār al-qiddīsīn*.

Diyāb seems also to have drawn on accounts of missionary activities, of which he was a great admirer, as he notes in several passages of the travelogue. His library included one such account, the vita of Saint Francis Xavier. A kind of spiritual travelogue, it recounts the attempt to convert Indians and Japanese to Catholic belief. Diyāb also owned a copy of the travelogue of Ilyās al-Mawṣilī, a member of the small Catholic Chaldean community of Iraq. Al-Mawṣilī's seventeenth-century journey took him across France, Italy, and other European countries, with the aim of fostering connections and collecting money from Catholics there. After arriving at the Spanish court, al-Mawṣilī was offered the opportunity to travel to the New World, where he remained through 1683. Like Diyāb, he expresses awareness of being a curiosity in the territories he visits. Similarly, he presents his readers with the picture of a world divided between Catholics and native populations awaiting conversion.[41] Both authors are interested in displays of linguistic knowledge, in acts of healing, and in the workings of charitable institutions. Each describes a meeting with an Ottoman ambassador, and each declares himself a recipient of divine guidance.

Like al-Mawṣilī, Diyāb titles his account *siyāḥah*, literally "wandering" or "peregrination." This is different from *riḥlah* ("journey"), a term used by many Muslim authors, but only rarely by Diyāb. A *riḥlah* is a journey undertaken with a clear destination or defined purpose; it also denotes a written account of such a journey. *Siyāḥah*, by contrast, emphasizes the activity of moving around, and also describes the practice of wandering that formed part of Sufi and Christian piety.[42] The term *siyāḥah* may also suggest a protracted journey. The famous Ibn Baṭṭūṭah, who traveled for more than thirty years, uses the term several times. So do al-Mawṣilī, who traveled for at least fifteen years, and Evliya Çelebi, who spent his life traveling, and even seems to define himself by that activity.[43] Yet, despite the conceptual similarities, the scope of the two books, and their strong Catholic impetus, Diyāb does not model his account closely on al-Mawṣilī's. Whereas the latter's travelogue consists of a terse listing of events and activities, Diyāb offers long descriptions and complex, embedded secondary narratives. Diyāb is a much more personal narrator who, unlike al-Mawṣilī, does not depict himself as an audacious adventurer, but rather as an inexperienced and God-fearing young man. In this respect, it is noticeable that Diyāb, especially when recounting his journey home, makes use of the relief-after-hardship motif, which is reminiscent of classical Arabic prose.

The volume containing Ilyās al-Mawṣilī's account also contains the embassy account (*sefâretnâmeh*) of Yirmisekiz Mehmed Çelebi Efendi, a travelogue by one of the most important Ottoman diplomats of the eighteenth century. His travelogue circulated in Aleppo, where it was copied several times.[44] It seems to have been translated into Arabic in the 1740s or '50s.[45] A copy of it exists as a standalone codex in the library of Diyāb's contemporary Ḥannā ibn Shukrī al-Ṭabīb (d. 1775), an Aleppan physician, who was himself the author of travelogues. In 1764 he turned the travel diary of his younger brother Arsāniyūs Shukrī (d. 1786) into a comprehensive travel account,[46] and in 1765 composed an ethnographic account of Istanbul, which he had visited the previous fall. It is quite likely that Diyāb's report of the Ottoman embassy is copied from that of Ḥannā al-Ṭabīb.

Diyāb thus appears to have been part of a culture of sharing and reading travelogues, something that must have informed his own writing. For example, upon reading Yirmisekiz Çelebi's account of his festive reception in Toulon, which included crowds of French people waving at him on the streets, Diyāb might have recalled being welcomed with great curiosity at the French court. Similarly, Yirmisekiz Çelebi's description of the opera and other festive events may have reminded Diyāb of his own visit to the opera in 1709 and his attendance at a banquet of statesmen in Istanbul.[47]

Although he writes from a Catholic perspective, Diyāb nevertheless emphasizes the importance of European-Ottoman relations. He discusses an Ottoman ambassador's visit to the French court, recounts his employment with the Venetian consul in Istanbul, and relates several stories about the cordial relationship between the governor of Tripoli (in North Africa) and a French deputy. His possession of the travelogues by al-Mawṣilī and Yirmisekiz Çelebi suggests an interest in the links between Istanbul, Aleppo, Paris, and other European centers of power—an interest he shares with his contemporary Ḥannā al-Ṭabīb.

The Book of Travels is no meticulous description of distant places. Rather, it has the character of an early-modern adventure novel with some picaresque elements. Speaking of his experiences, Diyāb often employs the term *qiṣṣah* (story). From the passages where the term appears, one can track those parts of the travelogue that relate to Diyāb's own story. These passages describe, first, the loss of his ties to his workplace in Aleppo, and his decision to travel back to the monastery; second, his encounter with Paul Lucas, who made possible the journey to Paris that takes up the bulk of the story; and third, the scheme by which Antoine Galland and a French nobleman, the Abbé de Signy, induced him to travel back to Aleppo.

These three travel episodes form the main part of Diyāb's wanderings and are encapsulated by the monastic experience at the beginning of the existing narrative and the final adventure that took place upon Lucas's return. The main episode, which fills more than two-thirds of the 174 extant folios, is the story of an unfulfilled promise. It parallels the experience that befell many other travelers from the Levant in this period, including Niqulāwus al-Ḥalabī (d. ca. 1661) and Solomon Negri (d. 1727), who were hired by Western travelers and scholars.[48] During Diyāb's travels, he encounters several such people—that is, catholicized Christians from the Middle East who somehow ended up in Europe, working as merchants, coffeehouse owners, and practitioners of other trades. Although some of these individuals succeeded where Diyāb did not, in the sense that they managed to gain employment in Europe, they too lament the difficulties of survival in their new home. By writing about them in his travelogue, Diyāb affirms his ties to these diasporic catholicized Middle Easterners.

Throughout *The Book of Travels*, Diyāb refers to his own thoughts and emotions, though he often relies on formulaic expressions to describe his state of mind. To express despair, for example, he often uses an expression that means "the world closed up on me" (see §1.28 and §10.42); of interest is the fact that such moments of despair are often followed by a radical shift in the direction of the plot. And while he often expresses his delight at the beauties of nature or architecture (see §3.7 and §3.19), the emotion he experiences most often is fear, which he expresses in many different ways.[49]

Diyāb's ability to produce a work that focuses on himself suggests that he was familiar with other autobiographical narratives. Whether in oral or written form, the autobiographies of figures such as the monk and bishop ʿAbdallāh Qarāʿalī[50] and the nun and living saint Hindiyyah al-ʿUjaymī[51] were known in Aleppo during the 1740s and 1750s. Like Qarāʿalī and al-ʿUjaymī, Diyāb describes leaving his family to start a life of his own, and in doing so creates a particular perspective on the traveling younger self.

Diyāb's narrative style merges the craftsmanship expected of a *Thousand and One Nights* storyteller with the conventions of travel writing popular among the catholicized Christians of his time. By embedding and framing personal narratives, Diyāb moves between different positions of perception. As he comments on his own actions, adds illustrative stories, and reproduces dialogue, the narrator alternates between proximity and distance to the story world. In this respect, Diyāb's *Book of Travels* has much in common with the fictional narratives that appeared in Arabic during the nineteenth century.

Like other works in Middle Arabic, Diyāb's travelogue has been marginalized in the study of Arabic literary history. Works from the late-medieval and early-modern periods, especially those in what has been termed Middle Arabic, have routinely been dismissed as illustrative of decadence and decline. But the travelogues of Ḥannā ibn Shukrī al-Ṭabīb and Fatḥallāh al-Ṣāyigh (fl. 1810, an Aleppan who traveled with Lascaris de Vintimille),[52] to name but two, deserve, like Diyāb's, to be read as Arabic literature—that is, read with attention to their oral narrative style, their patchwork character, and their autobiographical conventions, as well as their connections to other travelogues from the Arabic literary tradition. Thanks to the recent revival of interest in the Arabic textual archive of the early-modern period, Middle Arabic works are, fortunately, beginning to receive more attention. Reading them as literary constructions, rather than as examples of decadence and decline, will help us rethink the ways in which we write and understand Arabic literary history.

Note on the Text

Our aim has been to produce an English rendering of this work that captures the voice of Ḥannā Diyāb. The author's gifts as a storyteller—only tantalizingly suggested by his famous involvement with the history of the *Thousand and One Nights*—are in evidence in *The Book of Travels*, where he documents his journey across the Mediterranean with dramatic flair. The linguistic register varies across the work between a conversational Levantine vernacular and more formal varieties of Arabic. We have attempted to approximate the vernacular quality of Diyāb's language, particularly in the dialogues, without rendering it overfamiliar.

In the interest of making the translation accessible, we avoid transliterating Arabic words. Only in rare cases do we retain a word without translating it, such as when Diyāb glosses a word he suspects might be unfamiliar to his readers. With some multivalent words, we refer readers to the Glossary while translating the term differently according to the context, for instance caravansary, hostel, inn, and market for *khān*. Indeed, we have not insisted on translating a word the same way each time it is used, for instance rendering *bustān* as garden, orchard, and meadow; *sarāya* as palace, pavilion, mansion, and embassy; and *aghā* as officer and commander. Likewise, we render the term *al-sharq* as "the Orient" when it is used by Lucas and other Frenchmen. In all other cases, we translate it as "the East." We have also taken the liberty of rendering some of Diyāb's formulas in slightly different ways, for the sake of variety. For example, his favorite narrative cue following a lengthy digression is the phrase "We now return to what we were discussing" (*wa narjiʿ ilā mā naḥnu bi-ṣadadihi*), which we render as "But let's get back to our story," "As I was saying," and the like.

We confine our endnotes to points of clarification. Readers interested in additional information are referred to the fine French translation by Paule Fahmé-Thiéry, Bernard Heyberger, and Jérôme Lentin, whose work has enriched our own.

Notes to the Introduction

1   Since the first five folios of the MS of the work are lost, we based our choice of Kitāb al-Siyāḥah as the title on Diyāb's frequent use of the word *siyāḥah* (on which, see below).

2   His full name is Ḥannā ibn Diyāb (Ḥannā son of Diyāb), but Ḥannā Diyāb has become current in English.

3   Zotenberg, "Notice sur quelques manuscrits des *Mille et Une Nuits* et la traduction de Galland," 194.

4   The sole exception is Lentin, "Recherches sur l'histoire de la langue arabe au Proche-Orient à l'époque moderne," 1:48–49. After Lentin's discovery, the first comprehensive nonlinguistic studies of the text are Heyberger's introduction to Dyâb, *D'Alep à Paris*, and, from a literary perspective, Stephan, "Von der Bezeugung zur Narrativen Vergegenwärtigung" and "Spuren fiktionaler Vergegenwärtigung im Osmanischen Aleppo," both 2015.

5   Sbath, *Bibliothèque de manuscrits: Catalogue,* 1:122, previously published with a slightly different description in his "Les manuscrits orientaux de la bibliothèque du R.P. Paul Sbath (Suite)," 348. See also the reference to the travelogue in Graf, *Geschichte,* 3:467.

6   Notable are the recent works of Bottigheimer, "East meets West: Hannā Diyāb and *The Thousand and One Nights*"; Marzolph, "The Man Who Made the Nights Immortal"; and Horta, *Marvellous Thieves: Secret Authors of the Arabian Nights.*

7   Lucas, *Troisième Voyage du Sieur Paul Lucas dans le Levant,* 101–2.

8   Heyberger, introduction to Dyab, *D'Alep à Paris,* 9, uncovers a source which reveals that in 1740, Diyāb was head of a household of

twelve persons. A 1748 petition to the Maronite patriarch to protect the Aleppan monks has his signature as well as those of other family members (Fahd, *Tārīkh al-rahbāniyyah*, 147).

9   See Heyberger, introduction to Dyab, *D'Alep à Paris*, 9, on the father, who probably died when Diyāb was young.

10   See the concise overviews in Raymond, "An Expanding Community: The Christians of Aleppo in the Ottoman Era," 84; Masters, *Christians and Jews in the Ottoman Arab World: The Roots of Sectarianism*, chapters 3 and 4; and Patel, *The Arab Nahḍah: The Making of the Intellectual and Humanist Movement*, chapter 2. On the proliferation of books, see Heyberger, *Hindiyya: Mystique et criminelle 1720–1798*, chapter 2.

11   Qarā'alī, "Mudhakkirāt," 24–26.

12   Heyberger, *Les chrétiens du Proche-Orient au temps de la réforme catholique*, 110–11 and 434.

13   See the account in Qarā'alī, "Mudhakkirāt," 32ff. on this matter; also cf. Heyberger, *Les chrétiens*, 434.

14   On Lucas's family and early travels, see Omont, *Missions archéologiques françaises en Orient aux XVIIè et XVIIIè siècles*, 317ff., and Commission des Antiquités, "Note."

15   E.g., Lucas, *Deuxième Voyage du Sieur Paul Lucas dans le Levant*, 169.

16   For examples, see Horta, *Marvellous Thieves*, chapter 2.

17   Other episodes include the account of a visit to ruins near Kaftīn and of bathing at Hammam-Lif in Tunisia (§§1.35–36 and §5.94).

18   Lucas, *Deuxième Voyage*, 53.

19   Lucas, *Deuxième Voyage*, 197–98.

20   Lucas, *Deuxième Voyage*, 117.

21   Galland, *Le journal d'Antoine Galland (1646–1715)*, 1:290.

22   He later, on May 27, informs Galland about the existence of *The Book of the Ten Viziers* (Galland, *Journal*, 1:358).

23   Galland, *Journal*, 1:321.

24   Galland, *Journal*, 2:253.

25   For a comprehensive list of Diyāb's stories, see Marzolph, "The Man Who Made the Nights Immortal," 118–19.

26 Gerhardt, *The Art of Story-Telling: A Literary Study of the Thousand and One Nights*, 14–15.

27 Russell, *The Natural History of Aleppo*, 1:148–49.

28 Van Leeuwen and Marzolph, *Arabian Nights Encyclopedia*, 425.

29 Among the tales Diyāb told Galland is one about a prince who falls in love with a portrait. Here Diyāb may be reversing the motif: Instead of falling in love with the subject of a portrait, the hero paints a portrait out of love.

30 See the quotation and explanation in Görner, "Das Regulativ der Wahrscheinlichkeit: Zur Funktion literarischer Fiktionalität im 18. Jahrhundert," 92; and the study by Peucker, "The Material Image in Goethe's *Wahlverwandtschaften*," 197–98.

31 Chraïbi, "Galland's 'Ali Baba' and Other Arabic Versions," 166.

32 See Sadan, "Background, Date and Meaning of the Story of the Alexandrian Lover and the Magic Lamp."

33 Syrian Catholic Archdiocese of Aleppo, Ar 7/25.

34 Université Saint-Joseph MS BO 645. I am grateful to Ibrahim Akel, who directed my attention to this and the previous manuscript and thus helped confirm the hypothesis that Diyāb was an owner of several books.

35 See note in Université Saint-Joseph MS BO 29, fol. 2r, and in the Preface to his edition, "Riḥlat awwal sāʾiḥ sharqī ilā Amirka," 823, and further Matar, *In the Lands of the Christians: Arab Travel Writing in the Seventeenth Century*, 48. Ghobrial, "Stories Never Told: The First Arabic History of the New World," 263n8, suggests that Diyāb is the copyist of al-Mawṣilī's book.

36 E.g., Université Saint-Joseph MS BO 594, 298v.

37 Université Saint-Joseph MS BO 645, 132r.

38 Ong, *Orality and Literacy: The Technologizing of the World*, 39.

39 Ott, "From the Coffeehouse into the Manuscript," 447.

40 On the *Bustān* see Graf, *Geschichte*, 3:413.

41 Ghobrial, "The Secret Life of Elias of Babylon and the Uses of Global Microhistory," 66.

42 In the Islamic context, as shown by Touati, *Islam et voyage au Moyen Âge*, 187–91, *siyāḥah* refers to long desert journeys undertaken in

order to seek mystical union with God. In the Christian context, *siyāḥah* means being a hermit—that is, a wandering monk who lives in remote places and practices piety.

43   On Evliya Çelebi and his books, see Özay, "Evliyâ Çelebi's Strange and Wondrous Europe."

44   See Krimsti, "The Lives and Afterlives of the Library of the Maronite Physician Ḥannā al-Ṭabīb (c. 1702–1775) from Aleppo," 206.

45   The Arabic manuscripts of Yirmisekiz Mehmed Çelebi's sefâretnâmeh found in the households of Diyāb and Shukrī are falsely attributed to one Saʿīd Bāshā, very likely Mehmed Çelebi's son, Mehmed Said Paşa, who returned from Paris in 1742. A list of the gifts for the French king is attached to Arsāniyūs's travelogue (MS Gotha arab. 1549, 215v).

46   Cf. Krimsti, "Arsāniyūs Shukrī al-Ḥakīm's Account of His Journey to France, the Iberian Peninsula, and Italy (1748–1757) from Travel Journal to Edition."

47   On Mehmed Çelebi's account, see Göçek, *East Encounters West: France and the Ottoman Empire in the Eighteenth Century.*

48   Ghobrial, "The Life and Hard Times of Solomon Negri: An Arabic Teacher in Early Modern Europe," 311, 331; and Kilpatrick and Toomer, "Niqūlāwus al-Ḥalabī (c.1611–c.1661): A Greek Orthodox Syrian Copyist and His Letters to Pococke and Golius," 15, 16.

49   These include *khawf* (fear), *fazʿ* (fright), and *tawahhum* (apprehension).

50   Qarāʿalī, "Mudhakkirāt."

51   See the edition in *Al-Mashriq* by Hayek, "al-Rāhibah Hindiyyah (1720–1798)," and further Heyberger, *Hindiyya*. For an English translation, see *Hindiyya, Mystic and Criminal.*

52   See the recent edition of Al-Ṣāyigh, *Riḥlat ilā bādiyat al-Shām wa-Ṣaḥārā l-ʿIrāq wa-l-ʿajam wa-l-Jazīrah al-ʿArabiyyah.*

THE BOOK OF TRAVELS

CHAPTER ONE

¹ . . . their table were only the monks and the novices. We spent that   1.1
night at the inn, and after we'd attended mass the next morning,
the abbot summoned us to his cell. We kissed his hands and he welcomed us, inviting us to sit. Once we were seated, he asked if we had
any interest in joining the order. We confirmed that this had been
our intention when we left Aleppo.

"May God bless you and your intention!" he said. "Now that
you've spent four days with us at the monastery and gotten a sense
of our way of life and of our rules, you'll have to complete a three-
day retreat. Each of you should examine his conscience during
that time, and prepare himself for a general confession. You'll then
receive the holy sacrament, clothe yourself in novice's robes, and
adhere to the monastic rule, as spelled out in this tract."

He gave us each a booklet to study, and asked the steward of the   1.2
monastery, Father Yūsuf ibn al-Būdī, to provide us each with a cell.²
The abbot blessed us and sent us off with Father Yūsuf, who gave us
each a key for our own cubbyhole and cell, and a prayer book.

We spent three days performing our retreat. The abbot had designated a priest to offer us spiritual guidance, and when the three

days had elapsed, we made our general confessions and received the holy sacrament, which is to say, Holy Communion.

1.3   The steward of the monastery then took us into a storeroom containing the vestments of the monks. He presented me with a shirt, some drawers, a thick linen tunic, a black woolen cloak, a hempen belt, a black skullcap, two rounds of woolen turban cloth dyed a dark honey color, and black sandals with plaited cords.

"Get undressed, brother, and put on these novice robes," the steward said to me. "I look forward to the day when we dress you in the habit of an angelic monk!"

I took off my finery and put on that crude linen shirt and the rest of the clothes. I pulled on the heavy, coarse robe and attached the belt. With my robes all puffed up, I looked like a lemon seller.[3] Removing the turban and felt hat I'd been wearing, I put on the black skullcap, wrapped the honey-colored woolen cloth around it, and pulled the sandals on.

1.4   I studied myself. What a sight! At that moment, my heart turned from monasticism and I regretted what I'd done, but I was too proud to let my feelings show.

My friend Çelebi [. . .] and we left the vestry together.[4] All the monks and novices then came to offer their blessings upon us for beginning our initiation. They seemed delighted with us, and showered us with congratulations.

1.5   We each entered our cell and remained there until the lunch bell rang. We then went down to the refectory and found the abbot and the rest of the monks gathered outside it. The abbot entered first and sat at the head of the table, followed by all the priests, who sat at their places. Next, the monks entered and sat, while the novices remained standing outside. Finally, the abbot permitted the novices to come in. So we did, and each of us sat at his place, with the seniors sitting closer to the head of the table than the juniors.

There were three sorts of food on the table: a soup with lentils, wheat berries, grains, and other similar vegetables and pulses; some curd cheese;[5] and figs preserved in molasses. A bottle of wine and a glass were placed between each person and the next. Everyone drank to his heart's content.

Lined up along the shelves of the refectory were the skulls of 1.6 dead monks, each with the name of the deceased written on it. At one end of the refectory, a monk sat on a dais, reading aloud the stories of martyrs and the torments they'd suffered, whose intolerable horrors were known to all. I was shaken by this frightful scene, and couldn't bring myself to eat or drink.

Seeing that all had finished eating, the abbot would rise to his feet and everyone would stand with him and say a prayer of thanksgiving.[6] Following that, all would leave the refectory, and the cook would sit and have lunch along with the monk who'd been reciting.

The abbot would then take the monks and novices outside, 1.7 passing through the gates of the monastery into a sort of gathering space.[7] Some would sit and others would stroll, chatting about spiritual matters. They'd remain there for about half an hour, then each man would go attend to the duties appointed to him by the abbot. The tailor would go to his sewing, the cobbler to his shoemaking, the scribe to his writing, the gardener to his gardening, and so on. Only the steward was left inside the monastery.

In the evening, following vespers and compline,[8] the bell would 1.8 ring for dinner, following which all would meet again in the same gathering place and go for a walk. Then they would make their way to church, where each person would pray on his own. Finally, the abbot would repair to his cell. Each resident of the monastery would come to visit him, one at a time, to reveal his thoughts. This wasn't so much a confession as a form of guidance, so that the abbot might discern whether a person's thoughts had come from Satan or were, rather, inspirations from the Holy Ghost or one of the angels. The abbot would offer his guidance and instruct the man about Satan's devious tricks. If he perceived any sin in the man's thoughts, he would order him to perform a confession before going to sleep. That way, every monk and novice slept peacefully each night.

1.9   After visiting the abbot, each man departed in silence, forbidden from speaking to his companions until the following day. Some would go to their cells, and others, if they wished, would go for a walk in the monastery. Finally, each retired to his cell and went to sleep. At midnight, the sacristan would go around to all the cells carrying a bell. He'd rouse the monks and novices, and all would gather together with the abbot to pray the nocturne, which lasted an hour or less. Then all returned to sleep until dawn.

Each day, the large bell would ring for the morning prayer, and the mass would begin. Everyone attended mass, then went off to their designated work without any breakfast, until an hour before noon. Next they'd pray the sext prayer.[9] Afterward, the bell would ring for lunch (as described earlier). It was incumbent upon every monk and novice to confess his sins and receive communion every day of the week.

1.10   There was among the novices a tall, dignified elderly man, with gray hair and a white beard. I asked one of the monks about him. Why would a man enter the order at such an advanced age and join the ranks of the novices?

"You're interested in his story, are you now, brother?" the monk said. "Well, it seems that the old man was once a village elder, and a generous one at that. Each night, he'd welcome twenty people or more to his dinner table. Seven sons he had, all married! And married daughters too. Now, this fellow and wife had made an agreement to give up worldly things and spend the rest of their lives in orders. His wife joined a convent, and he came to this monastery. That was three years ago. He met with the abbot, Father Jirmānūs, and asked him if he could become a monk.[10] The abbot was incredulous.

1.11   "'Brother, you gave the bloom of your life to the world. And now, in old age, you choose to give the rest to monasticism?' the abbot said, trying to test the old man's resolve.

"'Yes, Father,' the old man replied. 'And perhaps God will accept me among the laborers of the eleventh hour.'[11]

"He continued to beg and plead, and finally the abbot took pity on him, but insisted that he wouldn't admit the old man to the monastery and let him join the monks until he tested his resolve.

"'Do with me what you will,' the old man replied.

"'In that case, you'll live outside the monastery without mingling with the monks, until such time as our Lord sees fit.'

"'As you wish, Father,' he said.

"Confronted with the old man's determination, the abbot ordered him to serve as a gatekeeper, and lodged him in a little hut just inside the lower gate to the monastery. He spent the next three years living in that hut, enduring the cold of winter and the heat of summer without complaint, and contenting himself with the meager scraps he received from the monastery's table. Seeing his steadfastness and perseverance, the monks and priests begged the abbot to admit the old man to the monastery and accept him among the novices.

"The abbot agreed, and they brought him in and clothed him as a novice. That was three months ago," the monk concluded. "And that's his story."

The man's story left me astonished. And yet, an even stranger thing happened some days later, when we went to the refectory to have lunch. After the abbot and monks entered the hall and everyone had sat down, the abbot admitted the novices. But when the old man walked in, the abbot rebuked him and forbade him from taking his place. The old man retreated, his arms folded and his head bowed, and remained in that posture until the monks finished lunch. The abbot, his face twisted into a furious scowl, got up from the table and strode over to him. The old man knelt prostrate at the feet of the abbot, who launched into a tirade.

"You shameless, senile old man!" he shouted, giving him a tongue-lashing as severe as any lampoon a poet ever dished out. When the torrent of abuse finally stopped, the abbot kicked him and said, "Get up, you wretch, and eat with the cook!"

1.12

1.13

The man rose to his feet, kissed the abbot's hand, and begged his forgiveness as all the monks and novices looked on. He then went into the hall to have lunch with the cook while we all filed out for our usual walk.

Witnessing this spectacle was a bitter pill to swallow. If the abbot could treat an old man so harshly, I wondered, what would happen to me if I ever crossed him? What sort of rebuke might I face?

1.14   The incident stayed with me all day, until I felt it was time to reveal my thoughts to the abbot. I went in to see him.

"Father," I blurted out, "I've spent all day thinking about what you did, and how you treated that old man so harshly! I've reproached you in my thoughts, Father!"

The abbot smiled.

"To be candid, brother, I knew he'd done nothing wrong," he said. "But my position demands that I treat the novices harshly. It trains them to be humble and it breaks down their sense of self. When it works, they grow in virtue.

"I love that man," the abbot continued. "There's something saintly about him. In fact, that's why I treated him the way I did. We have certain novices here who are too full of themselves. It'll do them good to see what real humility and resignation look like, especially since everyone knows the man had done nothing wrong."

He continued to counsel and comfort me until my nerves had steadied, and I left feeling better. I realized then that the exercise of revealing one's thoughts to the abbot was profoundly beneficial.

1.15   Another day, we got up from lunch and went out the gate of the monastery to go for our usual walk. The abbot called for a monk named Mūsā, who was in charge of procuring the monastery's provisions. The abbot would occasionally send him to Tripoli, among other places, to take care of the monastery's affairs.

When Brother Mūsā appeared, the abbot ordered him to take Brother Arsāniyūs to the village of Bsharrī and put him on a mule. He was to convey him to the village of Saydat Zgharta, where he'd hand him over to the village priest. The abbot told him to take care of Arsāniyūs and protect him along the way, and gave him a letter recommending Mūsā to the priest, asking him to treat Arsāniyūs.

The abbot sent another monk to fetch Arsāniyūs, who was ill, and hardly had the strength to walk through the monastery. He dragged himself before the abbot and knelt to kiss his hand.   1.16

"Brother, I order you to go with our brother Mūsā to see the priest of Saydat Zgharta. Obey his every word! If he orders you to eat fatty food, then do so, and accept without question the medicine he gives you."[12] When the abbot finished speaking, the monk rose and kissed his hand. He turned and started down the stairs, but the abbot shouted after him, calling him back. The man returned and knelt before the abbot.

"Forgive me, Father," he said, kissing the ground.

"Where are you going, you senseless dolt?" the abbot shouted. "Are you going to walk all the way to Zgharta just because our Rule says you should? You don't have the strength! Pride has overcome you, you wretch! Now stand up and listen carefully, and don't disobey me."

"Forgive me, Father," the monk said meekly as he stood up, head bowed.

"When you arrive in Bsharrī, get on the mule and don't go another step on foot," said the abbot, and ordered one of the monks to fetch the man's prayer book, walking stick, and outer robe. He gave them to Brother Mūsā, blessed him, and sent him off. The abbot turned to us and sighed.

"My sons, I yearn to see the blind obedience of this monk in all of you," he said. "Did you notice that he made not a single excuse? He didn't say, 'Oh Father, I don't have the strength to walk!' No, he set off immediately, obeying my orders without any doubt that he was able to walk."

The abbot continued to preach to us on this subject for the next half hour, which was supposed to be spent strolling outdoors.

I saw quite a few things in this sacred order and among the monks, whose conduct is truly angelic. What I've recounted here   1.17

are just a few stories. Even though they may reflect poorly on me, I've told these stories in order to warn others not to pursue the path of monasticism without being prepared for such a saintly vocation. Specifically, before doing anything else, you should spend a good long while asking God to reveal His calling to you. And you should train at the hand of a learned and practical guide. Then and only then will you be certain that you have indeed been called.

1.18 Shortly after I began my novitiate, I became very ill. I was ill for two months, and spent another month recuperating. During that month, the abbot freed me from the monastic rule and would send me out with the monks whenever they went to take care of the monastery's business. I'd join them and take in a walk.

1.19 One day, two monks set off for the flour mill to grind some wheat for the monastery. The abbot ordered them to take me along so I could have a walk. We headed out to a place called Rās al-Nahr, where the mill was located.[13] When we arrived and unloaded the wheat from the donkeys, the monks realized that they wouldn't be able to grind the wheat right away, as many other people had arrived ahead of them. They'd be compelled to spend the night there, waiting their turn.

"Brother, go back to the monastery and take the donkey with you," the monks told me. "Explain to the abbot why we've stayed over at the mill, so he won't be worried."

1.20 I headed out, driving the donkey ahead of me. We began to descend when we reached the valley, the donkey leading the way. As it clambered down the slope, it seemed to me as though the beast was about to slide down to the bottom! So I raced after it, grasping its tail to hold it back, but it yanked me forward, slipped loose, and galloped off while I tumbled all the way down, battering my ribs. As I recovered from my daze a moment later, I looked around. The donkey was nowhere to be seen.

My first thought was that a member of the Ḥamādah tribe must have taken the donkey and made off with it.[14] What was I going to tell the abbot? In my desperation, I forgot my aches and pains and set about searching for the donkey in the valley, but it had vanished without a trace! My heart sank. Unsure what to do next, I gave up the search and trudged all the way back to the monastery.

As it happened, on that very day, a few of the Aleppan novices I mentioned earlier had grown restless and were asking to quit the monastery. The abbot was upset about this, worried that the other novices would lose their resolve. So he summoned all the novices to him, one by one, and examined each to ascertain whether he was firmly committed or not. 1.21

When it was my turn to be summoned by the abbot, some monks reminded him that I'd gone off to the mill with the other monks, as he'd ordered.

"When he returns from the mill, send him to me," the abbot replied.

Not long afterward, I happened to arrive at the monastery, and as I came inside—feeling ashamed and frightened after the loss of the donkey—I found the monks waiting for me.

"Brother, if you will, go to the abbot," they said. "He's calling for you."

At the sound of these words, I was certain the abbot had heard about the donkey's disappearance. My terror mounted. I presented myself before the abbot and kissed his hand, and he ordered me to sit down. 1.22

"Brother, do you know why I summoned you?" he asked, frowning.

"No, Father."

"A few of the novices have asked to leave the monastery," he said. "Such an event would be harmful to the other novices, so I've been questioning each man to establish whether he's firm in his resolve or not. I do this to avoid having novices trickling out periodically, which is difficult for the others to bear."[15]

After going on at some length in this way, he finally asked if I was determined to stay or not. 1.23

"No, Father," I replied without hesitation. "I need to leave and seek medical treatment in Aleppo. When I'm well again, I'll return to the monastery."

He smiled and began to exhort me gently.

"Don't let the novitiate make you give up and return you to the world a defeated man, my son," he said. He went on speaking in the same kindly manner until at last I spoke.

"Father, let me think on it today, and see how God guides me."

1.24 The abbot was satisfied with this response, and he blessed me and sent me on my way to do some thinking. As I emerged from his quarters, I saw some of the monks waiting for me, hoping to convince me to change my mind about leaving the order.

I asked them whether they'd found the donkey.

"What donkey?" they asked, confused.

I told them what had happened, and they broke into grins.

"The monks rented that donkey in Bsharrī," they replied. "When it came back with you, it didn't run away—it just went home to its village! Don't worry, brother, it's not lost. All the donkeys returned to their stables, including the ones you took to the mill. That's what they always do."

1.25 Relieved, I went to my cell to think about what I would do. I spent all day and night until morning lost in thought. After the masses were over, the abbot gathered us all together and asked if we still intended to leave the monastery.

"Yes," we replied.

So the abbot ordered that our personal effects be returned to us. The monks had us remove our initiation robes and we put on our own clothes again. There were four of us: myself, Dāwūd ibn Jabbūr al-Kwayyis, Yūsuf ibn Shāhīn Çelebi, and Mikhāʾīl ibn Tūmā Ḥawā. Once we were dressed, we said goodbye to the abbot and the monks, and left the monastery.

1.26 At that precise moment, the superior general, Father ʿAbdallāh ibn Qarāʿalī, happened to arrive at the monastery.[16] He was saddened to see us leaving, and began to pray for us. He called me over to his side.

"Know this, my son," he said to me privately. "I've never allowed a single novice who left the monastery to return. But if you come back, I'll accept you."

He blessed me and told me to go in peace.

We set off, and made our way to Tripoli, without stopping on the 1.27 road once. In Tripoli, we found a caravan traveling to Aleppo, so we booked passage and returned home. When we arrived, each of us went to his own house; I spent the remainder of the day resting.

The next day I went to pay respects to my master, the aforementioned *khawājah* Rémuzat.[17] As soon as he saw me, he set about scolding me, reminding me of what he'd told me earlier.[18] He was so upset he could scarcely look my way, and refused to let me visit him again.

I spent three months searching fruitlessly for work. Finding 1.28 myself in dire straits, I decided I would return to the monastery and wait till a caravan was set to travel to Tripoli. When one was preparing to leave, I rented a horse from the muleteer, telling him it was for a friend. I did this so no one would find out I was leaving Aleppo and try to stop me.

The next day, I rose just before the call to the dawn prayer and 1.29 gathered the clothes I'd need: underpants, shirts, and so on.[19] I stuffed them into a satchel I'd used on my first trip and left the house for Khān al-Zayt, where the muleteer was staying. When I arrived and asked after him, I was told he'd gone to handle the luggage of a Frank who was staying at the home of *khawājah* Sauron, my brother's master.

I knew who the Frank was. He was a traveler dispatched by the sultan of France, and had arrived from Armenia, which he'd toured as a traveling doctor.[20] From Aleppo, his plan was to travel through the East—that is, Arab lands. His name was Paul Lucas.

At last I was able to load my satchel onto the packhorse. There 1.30 were a few Aleppans traveling with the caravan.

"Come on," I told them, "let's start walking while we wait for the muleteer to arrive." We set off, tugging our horses along, and soon arrived at the dome and column.[21] The muleteer still hadn't appeared, so we sat and waited.

Meanwhile, I changed my clothes and wrapped a white turban cloth around my head. I put on my boots and adjusted my satchel properly. I was ready to go. After a short while, the caravan driver arrived, followed by the aforementioned Frank. He had four or five *khawājah*s with him, each of whom would have recognized me! So I jumped on my horse in a flash and rode off alone, disappearing from view before they arrived.

1.31 The *khawājah*s finally bid farewell to the Frank, and our caravan set off. Our baggage had been sent the day before to Kaftīn. We made our way there, riding without rest even as the rain poured down. We reached Kaftīn half-drowned, and went to the muleteer's house. He quickly lit a fire for us in the stove, and we stripped off what we were wearing and set about drying our clothes.

The Frank came in with his servant, a Catholic man from Armenia, on pilgrimage to Jerusalem. After we'd rested awhile, I heard the Frank and the muleteer speaking, but neither could make sense of what the other was saying. The muleteer called for me because he knew I understood the Frankish language.

"Hey, do me a favor and ask the *khawājah* what he's after," the driver said.

I put this to the fellow in French.

"I entrusted some things to the muleteer when we were in Aleppo," the Frank explained. "And now they've vanished!"

When I explained this to the muleteer, he replied that he had the things in question tucked away in one of his bags. The Frank was pleased to hear this, and thanked me profusely.

"Are you a Christian?" he asked.

"I am, by the grace of God."

"Forgive me," he said. "I'd seen you wearing a white turban and mistook you for a Muslim."

1.32 He asked me to sit and dine with him. I declined, but he insisted, so I joined him. He ordered his servant to prepare dinner. They'd brought plenty of provisions with them from Aleppo, along with some good wine. We had dinner, followed by coffee, and the young servant then brought us a pair of tobacco pipes to smoke. We stayed up, chatting into the night.

"Which community are you from?" he asked.

"I'm a Maronite," I replied. "I heard of you when you were living in Aleppo. You were staying in the home of the Frenchman, *khawājah* Sauron. My brother works for him as a warehouseman."

"The warehouseman was your brother?" he asked me.

"Yes."

"Why didn't he tell me that you were traveling with us?" he asked in surprise.

"Because he didn't know I was leaving Aleppo."

"Why ever not?"

"If he'd known, he wouldn't have let me go," I replied.

At this, the Frank asked me where I was headed. I was too embar- 1.33 rassed to tell him the real story, so I merely said I was on a voyage to explore the world. This was a ruse meant to throw him off the scent, but as a result, he was convinced that I was indeed setting off on a voyage. Such was God's plan!

"If you're interested in travel, you won't find a better companion than me," he said, and explained that he'd been sent by the sultan of France to tour these lands and to write an account of what he saw. He was in search of old chronicles and of medallions—coins struck by kings of old—as well as particular plants to be found in this part of the world.

"Do you know how to read Arabic?" he asked.

"Yes, and French as well," I replied.

"If you come with me, I'll arrange a position for you at the Arabic Library," he offered.[22] "The king will pay you a salary and you'll spend your whole life under his protection. The king's minister has charged me to bring home a man from this part of the world who knows how to read Arabic. You'd benefit greatly from the minister's good graces. Will you come with me?"

"Yes," I said.

"Do I have your word that you'll come to Paris with me?"

"Not until we reach Tripoli," I said, thinking I should look into whether he was being truthful or not.

"In that case, while we're on the road to Tripoli, don't leave my side," he said, as he intended to have me serve as a translator. The fellow who was traveling with him didn't understand Arabic, only a little Italian.

"Happily," I replied.

I took my leave and rejoined my companions. I spent the night with them, and in the morning when we awoke, the muleteer said that he wanted to spend the day in the village, as he usually did.

1.34 When the *khawājah* heard that the caravan would be spending the day in the village, he asked the residents of Kaftīn if there were any buildings nearby dating to the period of the ancient Christian kings. They pointed out a mountain, about an hour's journey from the village, and told him there were some Christian buildings there, as well as a monastery and church: They were in ruins, but there was some Frankish writing on some of the stones. On hearing this, he called for the muleteer.

"I wish to go see that mountain," he said.

"That area is full of bandits and Bedouins," the muleteer replied. "I worry that you'll be robbed."

"That's none of your concern," the Frank replied. "Bring me some mounts."

1.35 The muleteer hired some packhorses from the village, as his own animals were tired and he wanted to rest them so they could travel the next day. They brought us the horses, and we packed some food and drink to bring along, hired four or five guards to protect us from thieves, and set off to climb the mountain.

After going a little way, we came upon the structures the villagers of Kaftīn had told us about and stopped to dismount. The *khawājah* began walking around the buildings, copying the inscriptions on some of the stones. When he finished with the inscriptions, we walked over to a tomb covered by a boulder.[23] The *khawājah* circled the tomb, looking for a place where he might enter, but all he could find was a narrow gap that opened onto the interior.

He asked for a volunteer from the guards to go down into the hole, but not a single one would dare. They told him that it might be the lair of some wild beast, perhaps a hyena or a panther, or some other ferocious beast. Who would possibly venture to go in?

While we were talking, a goatherd passed by, and the guards 1.36 asked him to go into the tomb.

"What will you give me if I do?" he asked.

The *khawājah* handed him a third of an *abū kalb*. Once the goatherd had the coin in his hand, he threw off his coat and clambered down immediately.[24] The tomb was as deep as the height of a man with outstretched arms.

The *khawājah* called down to the goatherd. "Walk around the tomb and hand me whatever you see inside."

The goatherd did as he was told, and found a human skull. He handed it to us. It was the size of a large watermelon.

"This is the skull of a man," the *khawājah* told us.

The goatherd handed us another skull, smaller than the first, and the *khawājah* said it was a woman's. He supposed that the tomb belonged to the ruler of these lands.

He threw a piece of sturdy cloth down to the goatherd. "Collect everything you find on the floor of the tomb and hand it to me."

The goatherd gathered what he found and handed it all over. Among the objects was a large, plain ring. The *khawājah* studied it and saw that it was rusty. There wasn't an inscription that he could see, nor could he tell whether it was made of gold, silver, or some other metal. He kept it.

"Feel around along the walls of the tomb," he called out to the goatherd, who did as he was instructed, and found a niche. Inside the niche was a lamp, similar to those used by the butter merchants. He didn't know what sort of metal it was made of, but he took it anyway. There was nothing left to find, so the goatherd climbed out and went on his way, and we all returned safely to the village.[25]

The next day, we left Kaftīn for Jisr al-Shughūr, and continued 1.37 from there till we arrived safely in Tripoli. The *khawājah* lodged at the home of *khawājah* Blanc, the Frenchman. I stayed at the Khān al-Ghummaydā, in the quarters of the Aleppan monks of Saint

Elishaʿ. The keeper of the hostel always held a key to their quarters, so I took it from him and brought my things in. He knew me from the time my friends and I had returned from the monastery, for we'd lodged there.

1.38   I spent the rest of the day at the hostel. The next day I went to see *khawājah* Roman, whom I'd met the first time I passed through Tripoli on my way to the monastery, when I'd brought him a letter of recommendation from my master, *khawājah* Rémuzat. After greeting him, I told him all about Paul Lucas.

"Is it true that he was dispatched on his voyage by the sultan of France?" I asked.

"Yes," he replied. "It's true."

I also asked his advice. "Would you counsel me to go to Paris with him?"

"This is your chance—take it!" he said. "Go with him and don't worry; he's a good man."

1.39   I left him and went to see Father Ilyās the Carmelite. He knew me from the time I'd spent at the Monastery of Saint Elishaʿ. After greeting him, I told him all about my time with Paul Lucas. The priest listened to my tale from start to finish, then spoke.

"Well, since you ask," the priest said, "I can tell you that I've learned that this man is indeed one of the voyagers dispatched by the sultan of France. Don't be afraid to go with him, if that's what you want to do. I'll vouch for you."

1.40   So I made up my mind to go, and went to see the *khawājah* to give him my word that I'd accompany him.

"Do you have any clothes besides those you are wearing?" he asked after I'd presented him with my decision.

"No, but I do have some other clothes in Aleppo," I said. "Some very fine clothes indeed."

"In that case, write to your brother and have him send your clothes to Sidon," he said. "If we get to Paris safely, I should like to take you with me before His Majesty, the sultan of France. You'll need to wear your native dress, and it should be elegant."

I obeyed his instructions and immediately wrote a letter to my brother, letting him know my story.

"Send my clothes right away with anyone heading to Tripoli," I wrote. "And from Tripoli, have them send the clothes on to Sidon, in the care of one of its merchants. Be sure to write to the merchant and ask him to provide me with some money, should I need it. Farewell."

As luck would have it, a messenger was departing for Aleppo that very day! I gave him the letter and told the *khawājah* that I'd sent it off to Aleppo, as he had instructed.

CHAPTER TWO

MY DEPARTURE FROM TRIPOLI IN THE
COMPANY OF THE TRAVELER PAUL LUCAS,
IN THE MONTH OF FEBRUARY 1707 OF THE
CHRISTIAN ERA[26]

2.1   After a few days, we left Tripoli in the company of a kinsman of
the al-Khāzin family known as the chevalier Ḥannā.[27] He had met
Paul Lucas in the home of the French consul, and they'd taken a
liking to one another. In the mountains of Kisrawān we came to a
place named Zūq Mīkāyīl, where the chevalier lived. He invited the
khawājah for lunch.

2.2   Meanwhile, I went off to the town square along with the servant who was accompanying us. We tied up our horses, piled up
our bags, and sat waiting for some lunch to be brought to us from
the chevalier's house, for he'd invited us as well. We'd walked all
night and were famished! But no lunch arrived, so we took out our
own food—fried fish, bread, and wine—and settled in to eat. All of
a sudden, a crowd of people formed around us!

"Are you Christians?" they demanded.

"Yes."

"Then what do you think you're doing, breaking the fast before
it's time?" they asked.

"We're travelers, and we've been walking all night," we said.
"We're not required to fast."

It was the first week of Lent. In those parts, some people would fast until noon and others until nine o'clock, and no one was allowed to break their fast publicly before the appointed time.

The same thing happened with our *khawājah*. The chevalier had tried to distract him until noon when he could serve lunch, but after a while, the *khawājah* abandoned him and joined us. Seeing us in the midst of lunch, he sat down to eat, annoyed with his host.

Eventually the chevalier appeared, apologizing for delaying our lunch. He begged the *khawājah* to return to have lunch right away, with no further delay. The *khawājah* was embarrassed, so he went with the chevalier, who sent us on a large straw tray a plate of honey and oil and two loaves of bread for our lunch. We had a few bites and sent them back. We spent the rest of the day in al-Zūq.

The next morning, we bid farewell to the chevalier and journeyed through the mountains, from village to village, as the *khawājah* foraged for plants around those lofty peaks. Eventually we arrived in Beirut, and lodged at the monastery of a Capuchin friar. He welcomed us and gave our *khawājah* a room with a bed, chairs, and other furnishings.

That same day, a fellow named Yūsuf ibn al-Mukaḥḥal, who was from our community in Aleppo, turned up at the monastery. He was a friend of mine from back home and greeted me warmly when he saw me, asking why I'd come to Beirut. I told Yūsuf the story of how I'd gotten caught up with the French traveler and asked if he would show me around, so that I might see the sights before we set off.

"Of course," he said. "Come along, and I'll take you on a tour of the whole city."

I started to swap my white turban for a blue one, but he stopped me.

"If you wanted to, you could even wrap a green turban around your head," he said. "In this town, there's no restriction on what Christians can wear."[28] But even with his reassurance, I couldn't bring myself to wear any turban but my blue one.

We set off to tour the city. After a little while, we arrived at a small palace containing an *īwān*.[29] Seated there were three or four

2.3

2.4

2.5

2.6

officers dressed in the Ottoman style. On their heads were turbans of crimped silk, the edges brocaded with gold thread. They wore long cloaks of angora wool over their shoulders, and sported jeweled daggers. Ten or fifteen young men stood before them, some wearing crimson turbans and others green ones. They too were armed with silver daggers and damascened swords.

I stopped short and took a step backward when I saw them, but Yūsuf, the young man from Aleppo, said to me, "Why are you afraid, brother? Don't you know who these officers are?"

"No," I said. "But I did think they might be the rulers of the town."

"Indeed," he said. "They're the rulers of the whole country, which is to say all of Kisrawān. This here is the customhouse, which they control. They're Maronites from the al-Khāzin family, and they've taken over the collection of the *mīrī* tax in the country."[30]

From there, he took me to see the seaport and the cave of the dragon slain by Saint George. We then returned to the monastery.

2.7 We didn't travel the next day. The *khawājah* decided to spend a few days touring Beirut, as I'd told him about all the things I'd seen the first day. When we left the monastery together, he said to me, "From now on, if anyone asks you about me, tell them I'm a doctor."

He was wearing our native dress and a calpac on his head. We went to tour the city, and he searched for old coins, the kind struck by ancient kings. We bought forty or fifty coins that day and returned to the monastery.

2.8 The next day, we set off again into the city, headed for the jewelry souk. He hunted for precious stones and engraved rings, and we found a few, along with some more coins. On our way back to the monastery, a Muslim oil presser called out to us.[31]

"I have some coins," he said. "Want to buy them?"

"Let's have a look," I said.

He went into his shop and brought out forty coins, each the size of a *thulth*, but thicker.[32] He placed them before us, and when the *khawājah* saw that they were so rusty that no writing could be made out on them, he declined to buy any. Before leaving, though, he said a few words to me in Frankish.

"Buy them from him."

After the *khawājah* left, I turned to leave as well.

"What's the matter? Aren't you interested?" the man asked.   2.9

"They're so rusty you can't read what's written on them," I said. "They're worthless."

"Name your price," he insisted.

"The doctor doesn't want them," I said. "But as a favor to you, I'll buy them myself. What do you want for them?"

"One piaster for the lot," he said. "That's one *miṣriyyah* each."[33]

I offered him half a piaster, but he wouldn't agree. So I walked out and started on my way. He called out to me again, showing me the stone from a Seal of Solomon.[34] On it was engraved a beautiful head, with some letters beneath it in some indistinguishable language. When I saw it, I turned and called after the *khawājah*. He looked at the stone and tossed it aside.

"Buy it for whatever price he asks," he said to me as he left.

"I'll take it all," I said to the man. "The stone and the coins."

After a lengthy negotiation, I brought him down to a single pias-   2.10 ter for everything, saying I could go no higher. He handed over the coins and the stone, and I gave him the piaster. I gathered everything, left, and found the *khawājah* waiting for me around the corner.

"Did you buy it all?"

"Yes, but he wouldn't sell for less than a piaster."

"Bravo!" he said. "Let's go back to the monastery."

When we arrived, he said, "Bring me a little bit of vinegar in a   2.11 bowl." He put the coins in the vinegar, and studied the stone and its engraved letters with great delight.

"Believe me, if that man had asked for a hundred piasters for the stone alone, I would have given it to him, because this stone has tremendous magical properties," he said, but he wouldn't tell me what they were. "This is the head of an ancient king," he continued. "I'll look for his name in the chronicles."

2.12 The next day when I went in to see him, he was wiping the rust off the coins. I could see that they were all pure silver, and the inscriptions were clearly visible.

"These coins were struck by the king whose image was on the gemstone we bought from that oil presser," he said.

It was evident that they were ancient coins, because when we'd asked the man where he found the coins and the stone, he said he'd discovered many of them at the base of an old crumbled wall. When he set about rebuilding it, he found them buried in the ground.

2.13 That same day, we went again to tour the city in search of old coins. Meanwhile, news had spread that the *khawājah* was a doctor, and people sent us from one place to another. He would treat some people and prescribe medicines to others, asking everyone for his fee in the form of old coins. We amassed an assortment of coins, some of silver, some of brass. A few were made of gold, which we bought, paying what they were worth.

2.14 After a few days, we left Beirut and went up to the Mountain of the Druze and roamed about looking for coins.[35] The *khawājah* would dispense medical treatment, using it as a means to have people hunt for coins on his behalf. We turned up a few, along with some mountain plants. From there, we headed to Sidon and lodged at the home of the consul, which was in a caravansary where all the foreign merchants had their quarters. The *khawājah* was treated very honorably by the consul and the merchants.

2.15 At that same time, some Franciscan friars happened to be traveling to Jerusalem.[36] The *khawājah* decided to travel with them, as he'd promised the servant who attended him during his travels that he would take him to Jerusalem. So he was obliged to accompany him, and to leave me at the consul's home while he traveled with the friars. Unluckily for me, I didn't get to go along.[37]

2.16 So I remained in Sidon. One day, while sitting by the gate of the caravansary, one of the foreign merchants who lived there called me over and asked my name. When I told him my given name and family name, he said he'd received a letter for me from Aleppo! He took me into his store, took out the letter, and handed it over.

I opened it. It was from my brother, who'd written to admonish me furiously for leaving Aleppo without telling him, and to demand that I return with the first caravan headed his way. Until then, I was to stay put, with the merchant.

"I want you on the next caravan to Tripoli, no ifs, ands, or buts!" he wrote.

As I came to the end of the letter, I welled up with sadness. How 2.17 could he have refused to send me the clothes I'd asked for?

The merchant turned to me and said, "I also received a letter from your master, *khawājah* Rémuzat. He told me to send you back to Aleppo whether you liked it or not."

"I'm not under the authority of *khawājah* Rémuzat anymore," I said, "and you can't make me go anywhere! I'll decide where I go all on my own! I now serve *khawājah* Paul Lucas, a traveler on the sultan of France's business! As soon as he returns from Jerusalem, he'll speak for me."

After much argument and back-and-forth, the merchant saw that 2.18 I wouldn't budge. So he took out a second letter from my brother, and handed it to me.

"If you don't wish to return, God grant you a smooth journey," my brother had written. "I've sent you the bundle of clothes you'd requested, in the care of this merchant. Take the clothes from him, along with as much money as you'll need. I've told him to advance you whatever you ask for. Send me receipts for the clothes and the money you've taken. Godspeed."

After reading the second letter, I was overjoyed to learn of the arrival of the clothes! The merchant took out the bundle, handed it to me, and asked how much money I wanted. I took a few piasters and wrote out receipts for everything and returned to the consul's home, as happy as could be.

2.19   I stayed on in Sidon, touring and seeing the sights. It was Easter time, and according to the custom of the Maronites, for some reason or other, one could only attend confession and receive communion from one's own church and priest. A friend of mine invited me to spend the evening of the feast at his home so that we might rise early and go to confession with the priest, attend mass, and receive communion. After fulfilling our obligation, he invited me back to his house as his guest and treated me with due regard.

2.20   I remained in Sidon until my master returned from Jerusalem, whereupon I informed him that my clothes had arrived with a letter from my brother.[38] I told him all about how my brother had instructed the merchant to send me back to Aleppo by hook or by crook.

"I'm fully committed to joining you on your voyage," I said.

"And I promise to do right by you, if we get to Paris in one piece," he replied.

The servant who'd gone with him to Jerusalem hadn't returned, remaining there so he could continue on to his own country. So it was that only I remained in the service of this *khawājah*.

We made ready to travel to the island of Cyprus.

CHAPTER THREE

MY FIRST TIME AT SEA WITH PAUL LUCAS, IN THE MONTH OF MAY 1707[39]

On the fifth of May, we left Sidon on a Greek ship headed for the island of Cyprus. The ship sailed from Sidon at two o'clock in the morning. I felt seasick from the moment I set foot on board, so I lay down to sleep by the mast. The winds were favorable and, before dawn broke, we arrived at the port of Larnaca, on the island of Cyprus. **3.1**

When I awoke from my slumber—still feeling seasick—and saw the fort and all the people on the wharf, I could scarcely believe we'd arrived in Cyprus. I had assumed we were still in the port of Sidon! By the time day had fully broken, I realized we were indeed in Cyprus, and I marveled at how easy it was to travel by sea. We'd made the journey from Sidon to Cyprus in a single night! **3.2**

We disembarked onto the dock, gathered our baggage, and went to the home of the French consul. When we walked in, the consul greeted my master warmly and had a furnished room prepared for him, with an ornate bed, chairs, and other necessary comforts. All of our things were brought up to my bedroom. **3.3**

The next day, we toured and saw the sights. The French merchants who lived in Larnaca began to invite us over. Their servants **3.4** were all Greeks, and of the Orthodox faith. I felt like a deaf man in a wedding procession: I couldn't understand their language, they couldn't understand mine. When I spoke to them in French, they understood but would only respond in Greek, mocking me, as they harbored a deep loathing for Catholics. I endured their company with much bitterness.

3.5 After a few days, my master decided to visit Nicosia, the largest city in Cyprus, just under fourteen hours from Larnaca. A priest belonging to the order of Saint Francis lived there. As we were about to set off for Nicosia, the consul gave us a letter of recommendation to present to the priest, asking him to accept us at the monastery. We hired some mounts from a muleteer, traveled all day, and arrived at the muleteer's village in the evening. We lodged at his house.

3.6 An hour after our arrival, I heard a great racket coming from the surrounding countryside. I went outside to find out what was going on and saw several herds of swine returning from the pasture. One herd came to the muleteer's home, where we were staying. The pigs went into a corral by the house, and we couldn't sleep a wink all night because of their grunting and snorting.

3.7 In the morning, we set off again. The abundance of trees and the water coursing everywhere made it seem as though we were strolling through a garden! Everything was green, even the ears of grain shooting up out of the earth. All the stone was white and blue and of fine quality. To say nothing of the lush vineyards found in those mountains, with no owners to tend them! That's when I knew that everything I'd heard about Cyprus was true. It was indeed the Green Island!

3.8 In the afternoon, we arrived at the city and lodged at the priest's monastery. He welcomed us most generously and gave us keys to the cells, telling us to settle in anywhere we liked. We spent the night there and attended his mass the next day. A little while later, a messenger arrived from the abbot who lived in Larnaca. The priest was ordered to go see the abbot as soon as he received the message, and not delay for an instant. The priest showed my master the letter, apologized, and explained that he had no choice but to set off right away, as the abbot's orders had to be obeyed. He did, however, give us the key to the cellar and told us it was fully stocked with butter, oil, old and new wine, salted pork and ham, olives, cheese, and so on. The only thing missing was bread. The bread of Cyprus, by the way, is delicious and has no equal. We bought it fresh each day.

The priest bid us farewell and went to see his abbot. We remained   3.9
at the monastery that day, as we couldn't find anyone to guide us on the roads. A Frankish man named Callimeri, born in Nicosia, heard we were in town and came by to offer his greetings to my master and to welcome him.[40] My master was pleased by the arrival of this fellow, as he was a local who knew his way around. They sat and chatted.

"Would you be kind enough to take me around the city tomorrow to see the sights?" asked my master.

"It would be my pleasure," Callimeri replied.

My master took him by the arm and insisted he stay for dinner, which   3.10
he did. Afterward, the *khawājah* asked him what his occupation was.

"I'm a doctor," he replied.

"Are herbs to be found in your mountains?" the *khawājah* asked, showing him a book illustrated with various herbs that he was always on the lookout for in the mountains.

"You can find them on a certain mountain, about a day's journey away," Callimeri replied. "There are some ancient buildings there—churches, monasteries, and settlements, all of them in ruins. If you're eager to visit these places, I'll go with you."

My master agreed, and advised him to hire a muleteer that night so they could set off early in the morning. The next day, he sent for the supplies they needed, and enlisted a local fellow to work as a servant. My master directed me to remain at the monastery, since the priest had left it in our care.

"It wouldn't be right for us to leave the monastery untended," he said. "We wouldn't want anything to happen that might cause the priest any trouble."

3.11 So I alone had to stay behind in the monastery. After they left, I too went out, to tour the city and see the sights, but I didn't stray far so as not to get lost, and soon returned. There was an elderly man there. He was too old to move about anymore. The priest had entrusted him to our care, and asked us to share with him our lunch and dinner. He had a small house in the monastery courtyard. I took him some lunch, filled his tankard of water, and kept him company. He started to address me in Greek, but when he saw that I didn't understand him he switched to Turkish and asked me where I was from.

3.12 "I'm Aleppan, from the Maronite community," I said.

"Ah, a fellow Maronite! Welcome!" he responded in Arabic.

"Are you a Maronite?" I asked.

"Yes, I'm one of the last remaining descendants of the Maronites who lived on this island when it was under Venetian rule," he said. "There used to be more than five hundred families here. Some of their descendants remain to this day, but they don't make their presence known because they're afraid of the heretic Greeks. I've taken refuge with this priest. He's shown me charity, and provided me with a little food so I can live out my days. I worked at the monastery a long time, but I don't have the strength for service anymore."

3.13 I stayed around to chat with him and raise his spirits till evening came, when I left to cook some dinner. After I ate and brought him his food, I packed my pipe and went for a walk in the courtyard. Coming upon some stone steps, I climbed up to the terrace. When I reached the far end of it, I came to a parapet. Curious to know what was beyond, I peered over and saw a courtyard. In it were some women, along with a man who seemed to be the owner of the house. When he saw me, he began to curse in Greek and Turkish! I immediately turned away the moment I saw the women, even as the man continued to shout and curse, and I retreated downstairs to the monastery courtyard to resume my stroll. Suddenly, I heard someone hammering on the monastery door with a rock! I walked over to the door and asked who it was.

"Open the door, you son of a bitch!" he replied in Turkish, cursing me. "If you don't open up, I'll fetch one of the pasha's magistrates. Then we'll find out why you're spying on people's women!"

"Please forgive me, my lord!" I called out, terrified. "I'm a stranger here, and only arrived yesterday. I didn't know there were women behind that wall!"

But the more I begged his pardon and tried to mollify him, the more he cursed and shouted and hammered on the door with the rock.

It so happened that a Greek man was passing by at that time—a Catholic—whom God sent to save me from the nasty neighbor. He began to converse with the neighbor in Greek, sweet-talking and soothing him until he managed to send him away. After the man left, the Catholic fellow spoke to me in Italian.

"Open up," he said. "There's no need to be afraid; I'm a friend. And I've gotten rid of that other man. He's gone now."

Still terrified, I didn't dare open the door.

"Go on, open up," he repeated. "Never fear, I'm a Catholic like you."

When I heard this, I opened the door right away to let him in and slammed it shut immediately, for fear that the short-tempered neighbor would return. My Catholic friend counseled me not to go up to the roof or near the wall.

"If you go back a second time and peep in on him, he'll shoot you," the man said. "That's what he swore he'd do. And don't think that this is all about him jealously guarding his wives from your sight! No, it's because he hates the priest and the monastery like the very Devil. The Greeks, you see, are working like mad to abolish the monastery, because they're afraid it'll draw their children to the Roman Catholic faith. They always say, 'Better Muslims than Romans!' There isn't a family here that doesn't have a Muslim or two in it, sometimes even three. They marry their girls off to the janissaries, you know. That way, they're protected from the authorities. They have no honor! And no religion either."[41]

3.17   Struck by the man's friendly demeanor, I begged him to visit me each day until my master returned. He politely consented and said goodnight. Left alone, I was terrified that my irate neighbor would set upon me in the night and kill me. I retreated to my cell, locked and bolted the door, and spent the whole night lying awake in fear.

3.18   When morning came, the young man came by for a visit. He was kind enough to keep me company and chat with me to take my mind off my predicament, and his affectionate manner led me to ask if he'd be willing to take me out to see the city before I traveled away. He agreed, and we left the monastery together.

3.19   As he guided me through the streets, I could see that Nicosia was a grand city but that most of its buildings were in ruins. We passed by a vast open space surrounding a tall mosque with broad columns, a towering minaret, and a large, magnificent dome. Around the base of the dome were statues of angels in white marble. The portal of the mosque was made of precious white and black marble, and alongside it were two statues carved from white marble. One was Saint Peter and the second—also in white marble—was Saint Paul. I contemplated the splendid building in amazement.[42]

"What is this place?" I asked the young man.

"A mosque."

"But how can it be a mosque, with statues of angels and saints?" I asked him. "That's forbidden to the Muslims."

"There are many more statues inside the building, which are part of the structure itself," he said. "If they wanted to remove them, they'd have to destroy the whole church. So they've left them in place to prevent the whole thing from collapsing."

3.20   We left and he took me on a tour of the town. I saw women selling wine in the streets, each with a wineskin in front of her. They extolled the wine they were hawking as delicious and well-aged. A draft cost a single 'uthmānī. Some women sold pork, and one had loaded a wineskin onto a donkey, and would go around to people's houses, selling it. None wore veils, so all had their faces exposed.[43]

"What about all that talk from the fellow who scolded me for spying on his women?" I said to the young man, when I saw such immodesty on display. "Just look at all their women, shamelessly exposing their faces! And sitting in the street in front of all the passersby!"

"You're right," he said, "but as I explained before, what that bully did had nothing to do with you looking at his wives. It was because of his hatred for the priest and the monastery."

"Why do the Muslims who live in this city allow people to sell wine and pork in the streets?" 3.21

"The people have permission from the governors of the country, so they can pay the *mīrī* tax they owe," the man explained. "They continue to pay the same tax they did when the country was prosperous. It's ruined now, and yet the governors continue to levy the same old tax. These oppressive conditions are worsening, which is why so many on the island have fled."[44]

We finished the tour and returned to the monastery, where I 3.22 spent the night. The next day, my master arrived with the doctor who'd accompanied him on his trip. They'd brought back some of the herbs that were illustrated in my master's book. I told the *khawājah* about what had happened with the nasty man during his absence. When he heard the story, he was furious and immediately dashed off a letter to the consul, informing him of the situation and asking him to send a dragoman right away so that he could lodge a complaint with the pasha, seeking restitution against that man. His intention was to make an example out of him so people would stop threatening the monastery and the priest.

He hired the muleteer they'd taken on their excursion to the 3.23 mountain and gave him the letter to deliver to His Excellency the consul in Larnaca. But then the doctor came forward and, having learned of my master's intentions, tried to dissuade him from following through with the whole affair, as it would just lead to trouble for the priest and the monastery at the hands of the Greeks living in the city. It was only through flattery, civility, and charity that the priest had managed to live among these people. Otherwise, he wouldn't have lasted a single day in the monastery! When the *khawājah* heard this, he changed his mind and took back the letter.

3.24 We stayed at the monastery until the priest returned, at which time we returned it to his care, bid him farewell, and traveled back to the home of the consul in Larnaca, where we remained until a French ship bound for Alexandria was ready to depart. We booked passage, boarded the ship, and set sail for Egypt.

CHAPTER FOUR

OUR VOYAGE TO EGYPT AND WHAT HAPPENED TO US IN THE MONTH OF JUNE 1707[45]

A day after leaving Larnaca, we arrived at the port of Paphos, which   4.1
is also on the island of Cyprus. The ship laid anchor there, as the
captain aimed to load the ship with bitumen and tar from the port.
There was a bitumen deposit in the mountains, which the mountain
folk would gather and sell, using the revenue to pay the *mīrī* tax.
We went ashore and found the port in ruins. There was no one to
be seen except for the tax official and his men, and a few peasants
harvesting the bitumen and tar.

The sailors went off to hunt in the mountains, and returned to the   4.2
ship in the evening with three goats and a cow, which they'd shot
with a rifle. I rebuked them for doing this. Hunting other people's
livestock was wrong; how could they do that? In response, one of
the sailors insisted that the goats and cow didn't belong to anyone,
as their owners had left them in the mountains when they had fled
their oppressors. Many goats, cows, and pigs had been abandoned,
and the grapes remained on the vines year after year, with no one
around to harvest them. All because of how badly they'd been
treated by their own neighbors.[46]

4.3   Once the captain had loaded the bitumen, we set off for the port of Limassol. We arrived, laid anchor, and went ashore. We found a prosperous port city, full of people and commerce. The main thing for sale was wine, five piasters for a *qinṭār*.[47] They stored the wine in cisterns, each of which held twenty *qinṭār*s or more. This abundance was on account of the many vineyards in the mountains. The captain loaded fifty casks of wine—each the size of an Aleppan *qinṭār*, costing, as I said, five piasters—to sell in Alexandria. From there, the wine would find its way to the rest of Egypt.

4.4   After the loading was complete, the captain prepared to sail with the first favorable wind. That evening, two hours after nightfall, we were strolling along the deck of the ship when we spotted a man swimming in the sea! He approached the side of the ship with his tunic wrapped around his head. As he climbed aboard, he put it on, covering himself up, and came over to us. He asked to see the captain.

"Who are you? What's your business here?" the captain demanded as he strode toward the man.

The fellow threw himself at the captain's feet and begged to be taken to Alexandria.

"Where are your travel papers?" the captain asked.

"I don't have any travel papers," said the man. "I'm on the run from the tax official."

"You know I'm not allowed to let you board without clearance from the tax office, don't you?" the captain asked.

"Yes."

"Well then, how am I supposed to let you onto my ship?"

4.5   He ordered the sailors to put the man into a rowboat and drop him off at the port. When the sailors seized him he began to weep, imploring us to intercede on his behalf with the captain. My master took pity on him and prevailed on the captain to bring him along. Out of respect for my master's wishes, the captain was bound to take the man, but on condition that they shave the man's beard, dress him in sailor's clothes, and give him a wig and a hat so that he wouldn't be recognized as a Greek.

The man agreed to the terms, so they shaved his beard and mustache on the spot. The sailors gave him threadbare clothes, a wig, and a cap, and he stayed on the ship, working alongside the sailors.

After two days, fair winds began to blow and we sailed for the 4.6 port of Alexandria, reaching it in twenty-four hours. Just as we were about to enter the harbor, though, a gale blew out from the land, and we had to retreat to sea. Twelve days of tacking later, a favorable wind blew out from the sea and we managed to enter the harbor safely.

Once we disembarked, we headed for the residence of the 4.7 consul, who welcomed my master warmly and ordered his servants to bring our things from the ship. They prepared some furnished rooms for us and brought over all our bags without the customs official inspecting them. There we stayed, treated in the most honorable fashion, and the French merchants began inviting us to their homes, displaying their due regard for my master.

A few days later, the merchants escorted him outside the city to 4.8 show him a column as tall as a minaret standing by the sea.[48] On it were carved birds, reptiles, gazelles, and other animals. According to those informed about the subject, the column was made of baked brick. It couldn't possibly have been made of rock, as there were no mountains in those parts, nor any kind of rock to speak of. What's more, the column's thickness and immense size meant it couldn't have been dragged on a cart or carried. No one could have budged it! The length of column buried in the ground was as great as its height above ground. It was clear, for all of these reasons, that it was made of brick.

My master stood by the column, copying all the images inscribed 4.9 on it. When they asked him why he was copying the images and what they meant, he replied, "These pictures represent letters and words—secret signs containing mysteries that engaged the Greek philosophers long ago."

Beside the pillar was a cave known as the Cave of the Slave.[49] It 4.10 was a hollow in the rock, and open to the sea, so it roared with the pounding of the waves. Very few swimmers could reach the cave;

those who had managed to do so said it was huge. It was so vast and the waves so turbulent that no one had ever reached the end of it.

4.11   Next, we went to see the forty cisterns the people of the city had once built to store their drinking water.[50] According to the astrologers of the time, the appearance of certain stars had a polluting effect on the spring water. They believed that the polluted water caused those who drank it to go mad; that was the reason they built the cisterns. The astrologers would observe the skies shortly before the appearance of those stars, then divert the water of the springs toward the cisterns and fill them. They drank the cistern water until the effects of the stars passed. At least, this is what we heard about the construction of the cisterns, but God knows best.[51]

4.12   We toured many other ancient sites and buildings. The city of Alexandria is one of the world's great ancient cities, just as the chronicles record. We returned to our house and stayed in the city a few more days, and were treated honorably and hospitably.

4.13   Each day, I'd go down to the harbor and gaze at the fish caught in the sea, whose waters mixed with the waters of the Nile. It was something amazing to see! I'd never seen or tasted such delicious fish in all the lands I'd toured.

In the harbor, they'd built some corrals in the water to catch fish. Inside each corral was a device that prevented the fish from leaving once they'd entered. In that way, they could be caught in the corrals without any effort at all. You'd see the fish piled up in heaps along the edge of the harbor. From some fish, they'd harvest the roe; others would be salted and dried. A great quantity was exported to many countries. All this is to say that the livelihood of the working people in that country came mostly from those fish and Asyūṭī fabric, meaning linen.

4.14   My master prepared to travel to Cairo and see its sites. We booked passage on a *ma'āsh*—which is a large riverboat that travels along the Nile.[52] We left the consul's home in the morning, went down to the riverboat, and sailed in the sea till we arrived at the straits of the Nile. Every now and then the sand would pile up on one side of the straits, blocking the entrance, so there were always people there to guide riverboats in, pointing out which side to enter through.

As we passed through, I studied the way the Nile flowed into the sea. It was something wondrous! It poured into the sea, but didn't mix with it at all: I could see a line between the two bodies of water, as the Nile waters headed to the seabed. This was something I'd observe again during my voyages at sea. I saw white lines on the seabed when the waters were calm, and when I inquired about them, I was told they were the freshwater rivers that entered the sea without mixing with the salt water. Some people claimed that the clouds would absorb water from these rivers.   4.15

I also witnessed this at sea on rainy days, when a rain cloud would descend to the sea and the water would churn and boil beneath it. It would split the sea open and reach down to those rivers, soaking up the fresh water. Here's one proof of this: When a ship's fresh water runs out while sailing on the ocean—the Indian Ocean, I mean— the sailors lower a copper bucket into an undersea river that flows below. The bucket fills with fresh water, and a mechanism inside the bucket closes the lid tightly so no salt water can get in. And that's how they get their fresh water, according to those who've traveled the Indian Ocean.   4.16

Let me return to my account. We entered the Nile on that riverboat and traveled the whole day before arriving at Rosetta, one of the two access ports to Cairo; the other is Damietta.[53] When we arrived, we disembarked and went to the home of a French merchant named *khawājah* Durand.[54] We entered his house, ascended some wide stone stairs, and arrived at a spacious, paved walkway. At the end of it was a salon overlooking the Nile and the surrounding emerald-green fields of rice. It was a sight that truly warmed the heart!   4.17

Khawājah Durand came up to meet us and greeted my master most effusively. He ordered the servants to carry our things upstairs and had a room prepared for my master with all the necessities. We remained there the rest of the day, till it was time for dinner. They dined together while I ate with the rest of the servants, staying up   4.18

late to chat with them until it was time to sleep. One of the servants offered to show me the room they'd prepared for me to sleep in, but I declined.

"I'll sleep here, on this walkway," I said. "Who could possibly sleep inside in summertime? In this scorching heat?"

He advised against it, and tried to insist, but I wouldn't listen, so he left me to my own devices. There I stayed, all by myself on that walkway, strolling back and forth. I set up the camp bed we had brought with us and lay down to sleep. I had no sense of what was about to happen to me that night.

4.19   As I lay down on the bed, I heard a loud buzzing noise and my face was suddenly covered with mosquitoes—the insect found in the stagnant waters of the rice fields in that region. My face swarming with them, I jumped up from the bed like a madman and tried, unsuccessfully, to bat them away from my face, arms, and legs. In the end, I lit my pipe and the smoke of the tobacco drove them away, so I strolled for a while along the walkway with the pipe in my mouth. Eventually I felt sleepy, and went back to my bed. But the mosquitoes came for me again, just as they had the first time! So I got up again and walked and smoked so that the mosquitoes wouldn't come near me.

4.20   I did this until just before daybreak. Then I remembered that the servant had told me he'd set up a mosquito net for me in the room. I went around, quietly trying the doors one by one till I found a door that opened. Inside, I came upon a bed with a mosquito net—a light drapery covering a bed dressed with two sheets of the finest linen. I was certain that this was the bed intended for me and, unwilling to look a gift horse in the mouth any longer, I threw myself down on the soft mattress and slept until they came and roused me for lunch.

4.21   When I got up and put on my clothes, I felt dizzy and weak, and had no appetite. So I sent away the person who'd come to wake me, and stayed in the room feeling all muddled, and unable to open my eyes properly. I saw a mirror hanging on one side of the room, so I went over to look at myself. My complexion was hideous, and my proportions so exaggerated that I didn't even recognize myself. My face had swollen up, and it appeared as though I had cheeks on top of my cheeks, and eyelids over my eyelids! My lips had swollen, my mouth was engorged, and I felt terrible. All thanks to those mosquitoes!

I stayed in the room all afternoon without eating, too ashamed to let myself be seen by others. Finally, my master noticed I was absent and asked where I was. They told him I was hiding in my room and wouldn't come out, so he assumed I was ill. 4.22

He came by to visit me.

"Whatever happened to you?" he asked, when he found me in that sorry state.

I told him what had transpired overnight with the mosquitoes, and how I'd not taken the advice of the servant.

"Don't you worry," he said, and brought me some ointments right away, daubing my face with them. The swelling subsided that same day and my face returned to normal. Let this be a warning to anyone who might go to Rosetta. Don't sleep without a mosquito net!

The next day, my master and I toured the town, observing its buildings, streets, and caravansary. We passed by a tenement inhabited by Jews and their families. Their women sat working in the covered arcades, without veils or scarves. They didn't withdraw from anyone's sight—it was as though they were living in the land of the Franks! I saw similar things in other parts of the countryside around Cairo. 4.23

The coffee shops were on the banks of the Nile, and they'd remain open all day and night. One was free to walk around at night without being stopped by the authorities or anyone else—unlike other parts of Egypt. It was a wonderfully pleasant and safe town. There wasn't a single thing wrong with it, except for the mosquitoes. We were so happy and relaxed in Rosetta that we spent twelve days there, but it felt as though only a single day had passed.

We booked passage on the riverboat and traveled to Cairo along the Nile.[55] We arrived at Būlāq, the port in Cairo, and had some 4.24

donkey drivers load up our bags. We straddled a pair of trotting donkeys and rode into Cairo, having ordered the drivers to take us to the Mouski quarter, where all the French merchants lived. The French consul's house was in that quarter, and news of our arrival sped ahead to the consul as soon as we reached it. He sent some servants, who brought us to his home.

When the consul set eyes upon my master, he embraced him and greeted him most cordially and honorably. He'd heard about my master's arrival in Alexandria, and knew he'd been dispatched on a voyage of exploration by His Majesty the sultan of France, so he treated him with great deference and prepared one of his finest rooms, going so far as to order his domestics to put themselves at my master's service—something that other consuls had not done.

4.25   We remained in the consul's home for three days, receiving all the merchants and paying our respects. Then the *khawājah* asked the consul's permission to let him tour Cairo and see the sights, and the latter appointed a *ghuzzī* in his service to accompany us and take us around the city. The man came along each day and gave us a tour of a different quarter of Cairo, showing us the pharaoh's palace, the Citadel, Ramliyyah Square, the residences of the *sanjak*s, and other sites. We toured with the *ghuzzī* for three days, and learned our way around all the lanes and alleys and avenues.

4.26   My master wished us to tour on our own, without a guide, as he wanted to hunt for the things he typically sought out in every town: old medallions, old chronicles, diamonds, rubies, emeralds, peridots, and other such precious stones. He was also on the look-out for stones with medicinal properties, which few people knew about in the lands of the East. My master had a vast knowledge of the region's valuable stones and obscure minerals, whose properties I will discuss in the appropriate place.

4.27   As far as I could tell, this man was familiar with just about every science. He was especially skilled in medicine. Just by looking at a person's face, he'd know what his illness was, without asking about it! He was proficient in astronomy, geometry, philosophy, natural history, and physiognomy, and knew all the medicinal properties of the different herbs and plants, and other such things related to medicine. I witnessed many proofs of his skill, which I will recount in the appropriate place.

After our tour with the aforementioned *ghuzzī*, my master 4.28 decided to visit the home of Our Lady the Virgin Mary in Old Cairo. It was three miles from New Cairo, more or less. When we arrived, we stopped at the Monastery of the Holy Basil.[56] From there, the priest took us to the Virgin's house, which is now surrounded by a Coptic church. We entered that noble place, where the Virgin and Saint Joseph and the baby Jesus lived for seven years, as the Holy Gospel recounts.[57]

We attended that priest's mass at the temple of the Virgin, inside 4.29 the house. Following the mass, the priest invited us to have lunch with him at the monastery, after which he took us out and gave us a tour, showing us all the ancient sites and ruins, including the storehouses of grain Joseph the Fair had built, as the Holy Book recounts.[58] There were forty storehouses whose traces could still be seen. Those that had been completely demolished had left no trace.

We toured and saw the sights, and returned to our lodgings at the 4.30 consul's home. From then on, we began to tour on our own, with no guide. We'd go through the souks and coffeehouses, and sit and chat with the shopkeepers. It soon became common knowledge that my master was a doctor, and many people would come to see us to be treated. He'd see them for free, asking only that they hunt for medallions—that is to say, ancient coins—and they'd bring great quantities to him.

One day, a Coptic man brought us a Torah on a roll of parch- 4.31 ment. It was written in Estrangelo, which is derived from the Syriac language.[59] He claimed that this Torah had been copied during the time the Israelites lived in Cairo, in the days of the pharaohs. Paper didn't exist at that time, he explained, and people wrote on parchment. When my master saw it, he wanted to buy it from the man, but on condition that he could first study it for a few days. The man agreed, and gave it to us. We settled on a price of forty *riyāl* piasters, if it was indeed a genuine Torah.

4.32   My master showed it to the priests, who examined it to determine whether it was in fact a copy of the Torah. After studying it, some people with a knowledge of the language concluded that it was truly a Torah, and that it contained the Book of Genesis. Convinced of its authenticity, my master paid the man the forty *riyāl* piasters for it, as we'd agreed.

"To me, that Torah is worth four thousand piasters," he said, and was very pleased with his purchase.

4.33   We bought old chronicles written in the various languages from those and other lands. We continued to tour the streets of Cairo, and at the jewelry souk my master bought many valuable stones, and an especially large quantity of peridots. Because of the abundance of this stone, we bought it cheap in bulk. In Frankish lands, this stone is worth as much as an emerald!

4.34   One day, a Jewish man came to see us and asked me if we wanted to buy valuable stones.

"Yes," I replied.

"Follow me," he said.

We followed him to a *wikālah*, a sort of guesthouse or caravansary, and went up to the top floor with him, where he took us into a room and shut the door behind us. He opened a Frankish steel trunk, and began taking out valuable stones: diamonds, rubies, emeralds, and other precious jewels.

My master selected a few stones and, after they had settled on a price, said to the man, "Follow me to the home of the consul, so I can pay you." My master had an order from the French realm to all the consuls in the lands of the East, stipulating that they were to grant the *khawājah* Paul Lucas all the money he asked for.

4.35   As we prepared to leave, the Jew said, "I'd like to show you something, on condition that you swear to keep it a secret." My master assured him that he would keep the secret safe, and that he had no reason to worry. The man took out a bejeweled belt worth a fortune, and told us that it had once belonged to a Turkish king.

My master studied it and saw that it was worth a great deal of money. Although he wasn't interested in buying it, he made the fellow an offer.

"If you pry some of those stones out of the belt for me, I'll buy them."

The Jew refused. He took a box out of the trunk. Inside was a 4.36 black diamond weighing twenty-four carats, a true rarity. My master set his heart on acquiring it.

"This stone has been dyed," he said to the Jew. "This is not its natural color."

They disputed over it for about an hour. The Jew swore it was authentic. My master had every intention of buying the stone, but was afraid the Jew would become greedy and refuse to strike a deal with him. So he pretended he was ignorant of the stone's value and had no knowledge that it was a real diamond.

"Come with me to the consul's home," he said to the man. "I'll examine the stone there and settle on a price with you."

The Jew refused, fearing that if people found out about the 4.37 stone, one of the *sanjak*s would seize it. We promised him that we wouldn't tell anyone about it and that he had no reason to be afraid. After much back-and-forth, we convinced him to come with us to the house. Inside the consul's chambers, he met privately with the consul, a translator, and my master for three hours. Finally, the Jew emerged and went on his way. I had no clue how much my master paid for the stone, and the matter remained between them.

On another occasion, it happened that one of the French mer- 4.38 chants had bought an engraved stone for one hundred *miṣriyyah*s from a peasant. The merchant showed it to my master, who, upon seeing it, wanted to buy it. But the man didn't want to sell. My master tried to tempt him by raising the price, to no avail. He offered him 250 piasters, and the man still didn't want to sell! Exasperated, he complained to the consul, insisting that he force the man to sell the stone.

"Everything I buy, gemstones or otherwise, is for the treasury of the sultan of France!" he told him. So the consul sent for that *khawājah* and forced him to sell the stone. Powerless to refuse, he handed over the stone and accepted the money.

4.39   Around that time, a peasant from the countryside came to the Mouski quarter, where the Frankish merchants lived. Speaking in confidence to one of the consul's servants, he told him that he'd found a mummy. There was a ban on selling mummies, and he was afraid that if the authorities found out about it, they would confiscate it for the royal treasury.

Whenever a mummy was discovered, the peasants would hide it away so they could sell it to a trader for a high price. Mummies could be found near the pyramids—the tombs of the pharaohs of Egypt—but they were rare, as the tombs were covered by sand dunes. Only after a few hundred years might it come to pass that a windstorm would blow away the sand, revealing the tombs, and the sharecroppers would go looking. On rare occasions, they might find a tomb containing a preserved body. When they did, they'd hide it, selling it to the merchants a while later.

4.40   When my master learned about the mummy from the servant, he immediately relayed the news to the consul and insisted that no effort be spared to obtain it. A mummy turned up so rarely, and the sultan of France would be enormously pleased to receive one.

The consul had the peasant brought to him in secret, and interrogated him to determine whether he had indeed found an embalmed body. The peasant replied that he had. They settled on a price of 250 piasters, on condition that the peasant bring the mummy to him without anyone seeing it. Once they had agreed, the peasant went on his way.

4.41   A few days later, the peasant returned with some loads of straw. He brought them into the consul's stable to sell to the stableman, asking a higher price for the straw than it was worth; that way, there would be no risk of the stableman unloading it and accidentally discovering the preserved body. Leaving the straw in the stable, the peasant went outside and found the servant with whom he'd first shared the news about the mummy, and told him to inform the consul of his arrival.

When the consul heard that the peasant had arrived, he sent for him and asked if he'd brought the object of interest. But the peasant apparently had bad news.

"The people who told me they had it went back on their word and canceled the deal," he said. "So I gave up. I did bring some loads of straw to sell you, but now your stableman wants to bargain me down. Could you please tell him to pay what I ask?"

As the peasant approached the consul to kiss his hand—imploring him to permit the stableman to buy the straw for that price—he signaled that the mummy was inside the straw, and made a gesture indicating which sack it was in! Catching his meaning, the consul dismissed him.   4.42

"Off you go," he said. "I'll tell the stableman to pay your asking price for the straw."

The peasant went out to the stable and sat by the straw. Meanwhile, the consul summoned the stableman and ordered him to deliver a message to Rosetta, but to pay the peasant first and have the straw unloaded while he was away. The stableman did as the consul bade him: He paid the peasant for his straw and ordered a servant to unload it during his absence, and left.

After the stableman departed, the consul sent one of his servants to lock the stable door and bring him the key, telling him to unload the straw only after the stableman returned from Rosetta. The servant did as he was told and brought the consul the key, promising the peasant that he could return the next day to get his empty sacks.   4.43

The consul waited until midnight, when all the servants were asleep. He and my master then went down to the stable and opened the sack the peasant had indicated. In it they found a body wrapped in strips of Egyptian linen. They brought it up to the consul's house, left it in a room, and locked the door, the consul pocketing the key.

4.44 This all happened without me knowing a thing about it! It wasn't until after we'd left Cairo that my master told me the whole story about the mummy and how they'd hidden it without anyone finding out—not even the servant who'd first heard from the peasant.

4.45 A few days later, the consul sent for a carpenter and gave him the dimensions for a trunk. He ordered him to make a partition in the middle using a strong board, and to leave off the top and bottom, only marking the spots for the nails. The next day, the carpenter brought the trunk, fashioned precisely as the consul had ordered. The body was placed in the middle of the trunk, and various fine fabrics—sheets, handkerchiefs, fine linen, and other expensive goods—were laid on top of it, until one side was full, and the first cover was nailed down over it. The trunk was flipped over, some more fabrics were placed inside, and the cover was nailed down just like the first one.

4.46 The consul did this so that if the trunk was opened from either side in the customhouse, they would only find the fabrics. The trunk, along with all of the things we'd bought in Egypt—including coins and jewels and books, and many other things besides—were to remain with the consul until he forwarded them to the French port of Marseille.

My master secured a receipt and an inventory from the consul for everything he'd handed over to him, and registered them in the chancellery (that is, the consul's court in Cairo). This was in accordance with their customary practice. This is what the *khawājah* did with every consul we visited. That way, when we arrived in Marseille, we'd find everything we'd purchased from those places.

4.47 We toured all of Cairo and saw everything: caravansaries, markets, the homes of the *sanjak*s, the Citadel, the Gate of the Janissaries, al-ʿAzab Gate, and other places too. What got us in everywhere was the medical treatment my master provided. Instead of asking for money, he treated people in exchange for the opportunity to look around. By doing this, he made himself welcome everywhere.

My master decided to visit Mount Sinai, and began preparing for a trip to the holy mountain. When the consul learned of the plan, he didn't look kindly upon it. He related to my master all the difficulties of the journey to the mountain and the perils on the road. 4.48

"You'll have to ride an *'ashrāwī* camel,[60] which is so fast that a rider has to be tied onto its back to keep from falling off and getting killed," he said. "There's no water along the way, and nothing to eat. You'll have to bring enough food and water for four or five days, depending on the camel's pace, because it travels seven or eight days' distance in a single day. Trust me, you won't last long traveling like that!"

Hearing this, my master changed his mind about traveling to the holy mountain, afraid he might perish. He decided instead to travel to Upper Egypt, to the headwaters of the Nile and into Abyssinian and Sudanese lands. He consulted some people who had traveled there and they, similarly, discouraged him from going. 4.49

"*Khawājah*, you can't travel through those parts," they said. "The natives are nasty brutes who cast spells, the trip is dangerous, and there's no guarantee that you'd return alive. People have disappeared before, mark our words! But if you insist, then go to the city of Fayoum. From there, you'll be able to learn about those places and people without putting yourself in danger."

My master resolved to go to Fayoum. He asked the consul for approval, and received it. 4.50

"Father Ḥannā is the only priest there," the consul said. "I'll give you a letter of introduction so that you can lodge with him at his monastery. You'll be safe in his hands: He's a physician who gets along well with the city governor."[61]

We prepared for the journey and embarked on a riverboat bound for Fayoum. It was the flood season then. When we left Old Cairo, we saw that the Nile waters had reached towns and territories four days' journey away. The villages within those areas were 4.51

little hamlets surrounded by water not more than a handspan deep. When the villagers would see us pass by, they'd come out stark naked—both boys and girls—to beg for a scrap of bread or some hardtack.

Since we were traveling against the current, four men hauled the boat forward. Often the riverboat captain would lose his way and the boat would become mired in sand. With great effort, they'd manage to push the boat back into the current. Every evening, we would tie up on the side of the river, and go onto dry land to spend the night. In the morning, we'd return and set off again.

4.52 We traveled for four days, arriving on the fifth at the dam of Joseph the Fair, who summoned his father Jacob to Egypt during the days of his rule and built the city of Fayoum for him, as the Holy Book recounts. Joseph built the dam in order to channel some of the Nile waters to irrigate those territories. For that reason, it was named Joseph's Dam, as recorded on a stone that marked the date of its foundation.

4.53 When we arrived, they tied the riverboat to a mooring and transferred its freight to a second boat on the other side of the dam. We spent the day there, waiting for the freight to be loaded, eating fish caught from the top of the dam. The fishermen would dangle their nets without letting them touch the water that flowed down. The water fell with such force that it would hurl the fish into the air, and they'd fall into the nets! In that way, the fishermen would catch them and sell every three or four for half a piece of silver, which is to say a single *miṣriyyah*. The fish fryers seated there would fry a fish for a *jadīd*, in other words for a *fils*.

4.54 The next day, we traveled on the second riverboat (the one on the other side of the dam). We reached Fayoum in the evening and asked for directions to the home of Father Ḥannā.

When we arrived, my master presented him with the consul's letter, which asked the priest to lodge its bearer with him, put himself at his service, and show him around the city. After reading the letter, the priest welcomed my master warmly and prepared a place for him to sleep. He did the best he could, as his home was very small and cramped.

We spent the night. The next morning, after we attended mass and had some coffee, the priest urged us not to leave his home before he could introduce us to the *sanjak*, who was the governor of the town and the surrounding villages and countryside up to the frontier of Upper Egypt. The priest was very well liked by the governor and served as his personal physician. Were this not the case, he wouldn't have been able to live in Fayoum, as the residents in those parts were wicked and wild. Some were Copts and others were country peasants.[62] They wore nothing but tunics over their naked flesh and went barefoot and bareheaded. Their faces were misshapen and ugly, and one couldn't tell a Copt apart from a peasant! The women spun flax, and the men wove Asyūṭī fabrics. They made *samānī* straw mats and other such handicrafts.[63]

As I was saying, the priest went off to see the governor and told him that a doctor had arrived who was deeply skilled in all the sciences and arts.

"Would it please Your Excellency to be introduced to him?" he asked.

"Bring him here, so I may see him," the governor replied right away.

"With pleasure," the priest said. "But seeing as how you're about to head off to the Palace of Justice, why don't I bring him with me tomorrow morning for Your Excellency to meet him?"

The priest returned to his house, where he told my master about the conversation he'd had. The next morning, we went with the priest to the governor's palace, and were ushered into a place between his private chambers and the government house. The governor emerged from his private chambers. We rose to our feet and kissed his hands. He sat down and invited us to have a seat on either side of him. He ordered a servant to bring us marmalade and coffee. The governor and my master began to converse, with the priest acting as translator. Things continued in this fashion for two hours.

4.55

4.56

4.57

Finally, we asked permission to take our leave, and the governor told the priest to ask my master to come by for coffee every morning, with no obligation or fuss.

"It would be my pleasure," my master replied.

4.58   The governor, you see, was well-versed in astronomy and geometry. When he asked questions about these subjects, my master would reply with convincing and pertinent responses. The governor was eager to converse with him, so we'd visit each morning and have coffee together. The two men would converse and I translated, until the time came for the governor to depart for the Palace of Justice. Then we'd take our leave and proceed to tour the city fearlessly, hunting for old coins. We found a great many of them, and also bought statues of idols (some made of silver and some of copper) and books on parchment written in Hebrew and Estrangelo, dating to the days of the Israelites.

4.59   One day, while we were out on a walk, we passed a man selling wares by the side of the road. He'd laid out some pieces of iron, some nails, colored beads, ring stones—agate, or perhaps tinted glass—and other odds and ends. My master inspected the wares and told me, in his own tongue, to buy the whole lot from the man. Personally, I questioned the wisdom of this proposal, so I spoke up.

"What do you want these odds and ends for?" I asked. "They'll make us a laughingstock."

He repeated his request and departed, annoyed with me. Left with no choice, I negotiated a price of thirty pieces of silver with the man, unfurled a handkerchief, and gathered everything up. I followed my master back to the priest's house.

4.60   "Did you buy it all?" he asked.

"Yes."

"For how much?"

"Thirty *miṣriyyah*s."

He laughed and said, "You paid too much."

He took the handkerchief from my hand and went into his room. After a few moments, he returned the handkerchief and some of its contents.

"Throw it out," he said.

Now, I was bewildered by all this, but my master knew what he was doing. Among the odds and ends we'd purchased was a rough stone worth a tidy sum. Later on, I'd learn exactly what it was, as he registered it in his diary on that date, referring to it by name as a certain type of rare and precious gem. My master was knowledge-able about rough stones. In this case, he may have bought a stone unknown to anyone else! (I was personally ignorant of this subject, and wouldn't learn about it during our travels.)[64]

Strangest of all, he knew all about the medicinal properties of stones. I'd once told him that my mother had been suffering from melancholy for the past twenty years.[65] So, he went to the jewelry souk and purchased a certain stone for two *miṣriyyah*s. It looked like a piece of agate, and was pierced. Handing it over, he explained that I was to thread the stone and put it around my mother's neck, letting it hang down to her chest. When I returned to Aleppo and placed the stone around her neck, she immediately recovered from her long illness. Before that, she hadn't been able to sleep, speak, or eat in her usual fashion, but when she put the stone on her chest, she returned to her usual healthy self. We'd spent a lot of money on doctors and medicine, but nothing helped except this stone that my master bought for two *miṣriyyah*s!

4.61

But let me get back to what I was saying. Each day, we visited the governor so that he and my master could chat together. One day, the governor said to me, "Ask the good doctor to come dine with me this evening."

4.62

When I relayed what His Excellency the governor had proposed, my master looked pained and said nothing.

"What's wrong, doctor? You don't want to eat my food?" the governor asked.

"Tell His Excellency that I would be honored to do so," my master told me, "but we can't eat without having a proper drink."

I translated this response for the governor, and begged him not to take offense.

"Not to worry, doctor!" said the governor, who was himself a drinker. Turning to me, he said, "Tell him that I have what he wants."

4.63   They laughed and agreed to have dinner together. The governor went to the Palace of Justice and we returned home. In the afternoon, he sent two of his attendants to escort my master over. We went with them to the palace, where we took our seats in the area between the private chambers and the government house. When the governor entered, we rose to our feet out of respect and he invited us to join him in the harem.

4.64   A salon with sumptuous furnishings awaited us. Delightfully sprawled out before it, extending as far as the eye could see, was an orchard full of orange, lemon, and citron trees, and other trees besides. The governor invited us to be seated, and a handsome and elegant young servant boy emerged from the harem bearing a cup of coffee, which he presented to the governor. He brought some coffee for my master and me, as well as some pipes packed with agarwood-scented tobacco. They sat and conversed for an hour, then the governor ordered the servant to prepare dinner.

4.65   The boy set the table, placing on it a silver platter ornamented with gold. He wrapped a cloth napkin around it, on which he laid some loaves of bread. He brought some good wine and a gold cup, and began to carry in plates of food from the harem, placing them off to the side. There were twenty plates of food in all, not counting the desserts.

The boy set about serving us one delicious plate after another. The governor pronounced the name of God and reached forward with his hand, eating a couple of morsels from the plate. My master and I did the same, each of us taking a couple of bites. The servant boy took away one dish and presented the next, and we continued in this way, eating a couple of bites from each dish before the boy served the next one.

He presented us with a dish of chicken, from which wafted a ravishing aroma. Its Turkish name was *kazan kebabı*.[66] My master tasted it and found it delicious. The boy was about to remove the dish and bring another as he had been doing, but my master held on to the platter, complaining in French about this manner of eating, which was contrary to the customs of the Franks. I burst out laughing at this sight, and could hardly speak as the governor asked what was the matter.

"My lord, please don't hold this poor etiquette against him," I said, kissing the hem of the governor's robes. "These Franks have the custom of placing all the food on the table at the same time, and each person eats from the dish that he likes. My master enjoyed the chicken dish that was just brought to the table. That's why he grabbed it and stopped the servant from taking it away." 4.66

The governor laughed, and ordered the servant boy not to take away the dishes from the table until they were finished. So they sat eating and drinking that good wine until all the dishes were finished. They had dessert and fruit—which had no parallel in all of Egypt—and finally some coffee. We strolled out into the orchard, whose meadows, streams, and brooks filled us with a great sense of contentment. We remained there until evening fell and the time came for us to go. 4.67

We left the orchard and went back to where we'd been sitting. The governor ordered two of his servants to accompany us to the home of the priest, and my master heaped praise on the governor, thanking him profusely, and we headed home with the two servants. 4.68

We continued to visit the governor every day. Soon enough, everyone knew we were under his protection, and we no longer felt threatened by the townspeople. 4.69

One day, we were told by a Copt that an hour from Fayoum there was a tall, stout black column with images drawn on it.[67] No one knew how such a column had come to be built in this sandy region, where there wasn't a single pebble to be found, let alone any large stones. When my master heard about this column (such things were of great interest to him), he immediately set about preparing for the trip. Without consulting the priest, he ordered me to rent a donkey so he could go see the column. He paid no mind to the dangers in those places, secure in the thought that he was in the good graces of the governor and that no one would harass him.

4.70   We gathered some food, drink, and other necessary provisions, and set off with the donkey, eventually arriving at a towering column, which was both tall and stout—like the column we'd seen in Alexandria, but even taller and thicker. It also had birds and other animals inscribed on it: gazelles, panthers, dogs, lions, and other such wild beasts. According to my master, these images were all secret signs that contained meanings, which were explained in chronicles held by the Franks.

4.71   After we'd rested for a while and had some breakfast, my master set about copying the inscriptions on the column. All of a sudden, we were surrounded by a crowd of two hundred men! They were locals—barefoot, bareheaded, and ugly—and they began to talk among themselves as they glared at us.

In the days of their ancestors, I heard them say, there had been two columns in this spot. Their fathers had been told a story about a European who turned up, muttered a spell over one of the columns, and made it vanish. He took the gold that was buried under it and disappeared.

"Let's kill this one and get the gold that's under the column before he disappears with it!" they shouted.

"No, let's take the gold from him first, and then kill him!" others retorted, and began, mouths agape, to stride up to my master one by one to address him.[68]

"Give us the gold under that column, or we'll kill you!"

4.72   My master couldn't understand what they were saying. Trembling and near senseless with terror because of those savage brutes,

I rushed over and told him what they'd said. My master was certain we were going to die.

"What shall we do? How can we escape? What will happen to us?" he cried.

"Let me talk to them," I said, turning to speak to the men.

"Be patient so that he can extract the gold and give it to you—and save a share for me while you're at it," I said. "Let's have him bring the gold out, then we can take whatever we like." Hearing this, they settled down and stopped shouting.

Just then, God saved us from our predicament! Out of the bowels 4.73 of the earth a great dust cloud rose, then lifted to reveal a horse and rider heading toward us. The men saw him and fled like bees from smoke, disappearing without a trace. A few moments later, the horseman arrived and, when he saw us, dismounted from his steed and came over to greet my master, whom he recognized from the governor's palace.

"What's wrong? The two of you look terrified!" he said. "Did someone harass you?"

We told him what had happened with the wild men, and how they'd threatened to kill us.

"They'd have put us to death, no doubt about it, had God Almighty not sent you!" I said.

He reassured us that we were safe, and explained why he'd come. 4.74 It seemed that he'd been in the nearby village where he served as magistrate, and was sitting on top of a hill with a view of the column.

"I was surprised to see a large crowd gathered around the column, and I wanted to know what was going on," he said. "So I got on my horse and rode here, and found you. You can relax now. No one will trouble you again."

We calmed down, our fright subsiding. My master went back 4.75 to copying the inscriptions on the column. The soldier stayed with us until my master had finished his work, and then we set off all together. As we drew close to the soldier's village, he invited us to visit it. Soon afterwards, we arrived at the soldier's house, and climbed up to the spot he'd mentioned. It was furnished, and had windows that looked out over the countryside in every direction.

He ordered his servant to prepare some fried eggs and cheese for lunch, and we also took out our own provisions and wine. After we'd had lunch and some coffee, we got up to leave, but the soldier protested.

"Stay a little longer until the weather cools off, then I'll take you back," he said.

4.76   So we stayed until the afternoon, then rode off together. The soldier delivered us to the priest's house, went on his way, and we thanked God Most High for saving us from those savages!

That's when my master decided against going to Upper Egypt, what with its dangerous territories that he'd been urged not to visit, as I've already mentioned.

4.77   We stayed with the priest and never set foot outside the city, touring and enjoying ourselves within its confines instead. The city was like a garden, full of orchards, abundant water, delicious fruits, and flowing breezes, but the people were like wild animals, as I've said.

Lice teemed in the city like maggots.[69] There were so many that they even scaled the walls, something I've never seen in any other country! They seemed to be a species of ant, and had completely infested the priest's house. My description doesn't do it justice— I had to change my shirt three or four times a day when we first arrived, and I'd still be covered with them. Soon enough, I couldn't bear it any longer.

4.78   "My lord, let's get out of this place!" I said to my master one day. "The lice are eating me alive! I'm on my last legs!"

"Have you ever seen a single louse on me?" he asked.

"That's the strange thing," I said. "They never touch you, but they've feasted on me."

"I'll get rid of them for you," he replied, opening his trunk. He took out something I couldn't identify, wrapped it in a piece of linen, and tied it up with string.

"Hang this around your neck, and put it under your shirt against the skin," he said. "You won't see any more lice." I did as he told me, and not one louse came near me for the rest of the trip.

The priest with whom we were staying claimed to be a healer   4.79
of bodies, but his real purpose was to treat the soul. Men, women, and children would seek him out—Copts and peasants too—and he would teach them the correct path to faith. He treated their illnesses in a strange manner. He'd build a fire in a stove and place some irons inside, and use them to cauterize the patient—some on their foreheads, some on their necks, others on their chests, thighs, and elsewhere.

"Father, doesn't your heart break for these people?" I asked him one day. "You torture them with hot irons and inflict such pain on them!"

"My son, these people have the nature of wild animals," he replied. "Ordinary medicines have no effect on their bodies, and provide no benefit. I've been compelled to treat them in this way, with the methods used on animals."

This is what I saw in Fayoum, of which I've related only a small portion, so as not to go on too long and bore my reader.

We decided to return to Cairo. Saying our goodbyes to the gover-   4.80
nor and the priest, we boarded a riverboat and traveled to Joseph's Dam. There we transferred to a second boat on the Nile side of dam. Now we were sailing down the Nile—an easier ride than the first journey, as we were traveling with the current. In no time at all we arrived in Old Cairo, loaded up our things on donkeys, and went off to the consul's house in the Mouski quarter, where we'd previously stayed. A few days later, we traveled by boat to the port of Rosetta, and from there back to Alexandria, where we lodged at the consul's house again. We remained there a few days until a ship bound for Tripoli of the West was ready to sail.[70]

It was a French ship. A soldier from Tripoli had hired it and   4.81
loaded it up with coffee, Egyptian fabrics, and other commodities much in demand in the Maghreb. When the hold was packed to the

gunwales with goods, the soldier sealed over the entrance with wax to keep the water out. In the Frankish tongue, this sort of vessel was known as a *pinco*, a small coastal boat with a single hold. The soldier rented out space inside to people returning from the hajj, heading for Tripoli. Among them were two Maghrebi women and their husbands. There were forty of us, not including the sailors.

4.82   My master had decided we would travel with the ship. The consul and the foreign merchants, however, declared this to be out of the question.

"It's a small ship, there are many passengers, and space is tight," they said. "The other passengers are all from Barbary, and a man like you wouldn't be able to abide their company."

"This is a time of war, and there are many pirates on the seas," my master replied.[71] "If we travel with this ship, in the company of Muslims, we'll have no reason to fear any English pirates. Plus, this kind of ship sails close to the coast, so the pirates won't spy it."

"Do as you wish," they said.

Chapter Five

Our Travels to the Maghreb
in the Year 1708[72]

We boarded the ship headed for Tripoli. It was the month of February, and we sailed in painfully cramped conditions in the company of those Barbary natives. Eventually, we arrived at a place called the Gulf of Sidra, where the sea extends inland, forming a gulf about two hundred miles in both length and width.[73] This is called a *dīl* in Turkish. Because our boat couldn't stray from the coastline, it entered the gulf.

On our second night in the gulf, two hours after sundown, half of the sailors went to sleep. The other half stayed awake to stand watch, as was their custom. I was strolling along the deck of the ship with the captain's first mate when, lo and behold, we saw what looked like birds flying out of the sea! Some of them landed in the ship, and I dashed over with the first mate and some sailors to pick up a few. They were fish with wings like birds! We were amazed by this strange creature, and our shouts woke up the *rayyis*, the captain, and everyone else on the ship. The *rayyis* was the overseer of the ship, an old man who'd been a sailor for many years. When he saw the fish, he immediately ordered the sailors to haul in the large sail and to keep the small one (which was called the trinket)

5.1

5.2

at half-mast. He also ordered them to tighten the lines attached to the sails, and to carry out all manner of other procedures that take place on ships at sea.

5.3   I was surprised to see all this activity, because there didn't seem to be any reason to take such precautions. The weather was serene, the sea was calm, and we were sailing with a good wind. I asked the first mate why they'd brought down the sails, pulled the ropes tight, and secured all of the fastenings on the anchors. They'd even lashed down the rowboat inside the ship, though the weather was pleasant and the sea was peaceful.

"The *rayyis* has been a sailor for a long time," the first mate replied. "He knows all about the sea and its fickle ways, and he says these fish are a sign of a big storm. Apparently, when the sea becomes agitated and the waves get bigger and more turbulent, the fish start flying."

When I heard this, I thought the *rayyis* was being foolish. Paying no heed to the mate's words, I lay down to sleep in the rowboat. There I remained until midnight, when I woke to find the sea rolling and the waves rising higher and higher. There were waves breaking over the ship, and the water on deck was half an arm deep! The drains couldn't keep up, so the sailors had to bail using pails. They kept this up until morning, but the situation worsened, the waves swelling like towering mountains and raising the ship up on the crests, then sending it plummeting toward the ocean floor!

Every man clung to his spot—some at the ropes, some at the masts, some by the anchor chains—each afraid that the might of the wind and the waves would throw him into the sea. The thunder, lightning, heavy clouds, and heavy rains only added to our despair!

5.4   We endured that punishing ordeal for two days and two nights, with no food, drink, or sleep. We were on the verge of being capsized and sunk, and we begged God Most High to save us from drowning. On the third day, we saw a great column descending from the clouds to the sea. As it descended, the sea split open and a great chasm formed within. As I recounted earlier, this was the sort of cloud that soaks up water from the rivers flowing along the ocean floor. I didn't believe such a thing could be until I saw it with my own eyes.[74]

When the *rayyis* and the captain spotted the cloud, they were terrified. If the ship fell into the chasm, they knew it would certainly sink, because the sea would close in again when the cloud rose back up to the sky. Any ship trapped inside would be pulled down to the seabed, with no possibility of escape.   5.5

The captain ordered the first mate to pray to the Virgin Mary and to all the saints, for they'd lost hope of being saved. As the sailors fell to praying, the Maghrebis on the ship, now certain that they would soon drown, began to wail and bid each other farewell, promising to pass on their goodbyes to each other's children and families if they were saved.

Seeing the sailors take hold of barrels, planks, and so on, waiting for the ship to sink, I stared death in the eye and lost my senses.   5.6

As I clung to the rowboat where I sat, I heard a small child crying out. I was bewildered to hear such a sound, and felt sure the child had emerged from the sea or fallen from the clouds. That's when I fainted, tumbling into what seemed like a deep slumber.

Suddenly, I was roused again by the child's voice ringing in my ears. It was the ship's cabin boy, calling out and waving that he could see land!

At that point I came to my senses, and all the Maghrebi passengers did too. Overjoyed, we learned that after the captain saw the cloud and the chasm, he had lost hope of being saved and ordered the helmsman to turn the wheel and make for land.

"Better we wreck on land than sink at sea," he'd told himself.

That was an inspiration from God, and it saved us from sinking. When the ship turned landward, the captain sent the cabin boy to the top of the mast to keep a lookout. When the ship was a few miles off the coast, the sun began to set and the sea had subsided a bit. And the cabin boy spotted land! He came down immediately to tell the captain and passengers. With this good news, we were   5.7

ourselves again and were overcome with happiness. We thanked God Almighty for the grace He'd bestowed on us! In less than half an hour, we saw land with our own eyes, and after a short time, the anchors were lowered and the ship moored.

The passengers rose from their places like the dead from their graves. They looked like they'd emerged from a hole in the ground or a cesspit, their clothes soiled with filth. Over the course of those three days, they'd answered the call of nature in their own pants and shirts, making them filthy and miserable. They washed themselves and changed into clean clothes.

5.8 By then we were suffering from hunger and thirst, and our throats were so dry we couldn't even speak. When we managed to find our provisions, we discovered that the hardtack, rice, and butter were all soggy with seawater. Seawater had, in fact, gotten into all of the food, and the brine had made everything inedible. We went without food or drink till morning.

5.9 Come morning, we learned that the sailors had thrown overboard everything that had been on deck. The barrels of fresh water, the cooking stove, and the firewood were gone, along with all the supplies belonging to the sailors and the captain. Our provisions, too, had been lost. The passengers appealed to the captain, asking him to give them some of his own stores, if there was anything left. He took pity on them and brought out a sack from his cabin, containing about four or five *raṭl*s of hardtack, meant for his breakfast, and half a barrel of fresh water, which had been set aside for his own consumption.

5.10 When the soldier who had stocked the ship saw the captain's sack and half barrel of water, he commandeered them and ordered one of his servants to draw his sword and stand guard next to the barrel of water to prevent anyone from drinking it all at one go. He gave each of us part of a hardtack biscuit to stave off certain death, and a small cup of water to wet our throats. When the full extent of this predicament dawned on the passengers, we lost all hope of survival.

"God saved us from drowning; now we'll die of hunger and thirst instead!" we all cried.

We were at a loss for what to do, because the land that lay before us was a deserted wasteland. There was neither man nor beast nor bird to be seen, as there was no water to drink and nothing to eat there. It was nothing but a sea of sand.

An old man among the ship's passengers spoke up. "This country 5.11 is inhabited," he said. "The people here harvest *qaṣab* dates. They dry them and sell them in the Sudan."[75] We agreed that a group of us should form a search party, in hopes of finding someone to sell us enough food to keep us alive.

The captain and passengers agreed. They lowered the rowboat into the water, and the first mate and I boarded it along with some passengers. Once ashore, we started walking and soon spotted some palm trees, which augured that there were indeed people living in the desert. When we reached the trees, we spied in the distance some tents that looked like Bedouin dwellings. In our excitement, we quickened our pace. After a half hour of marching through the sand, we were gasping and stumbling from exhaustion, our legs sinking ankle-deep into the sand with every step.

After much effort and toil, we arrived at the tents, and split up to 5.12 check them all. The first mate, a Maghrebi man, and I went into a tent together. Seated inside was a man who looked like a demon: He was black-skinned, with eyes like a monkey's, and he had wrapped himself in a dark blanket. The sight of him was terrifying!

We asked if he had any bread to sell us.

"Bread? What's that, you wretches?" he sneered, and we told him our story.

"What do you eat?" we asked.

"*Bsīsa* and dates."

We asked the Maghrebi with us what *bsīsa* was, and he explained that it was millet flour.

"When they come to these parts to dry the dates, each person brings along a sack of flour and a jar of butter," the Maghrebi explained. "He puts a little flour in his palm and some butter, and mixes them together. That's what they eat, along with the dates."

5.13   After conferring with each other, we agreed to buy some dried dates. Negotiating a price of one piaster for two baskets of dates, we loaded them onto a camel and sent them back to the ship with one of our companions, telling him to bring back a couple of barrels on the camel, which we'd fill with water from the camp's supply. When the two barrels arrived, we told the Bedouins to fill them with water but they refused.[76]

"We don't have enough water for you and us both," they said, and showed us the spot they'd dug in the sand, which contained a little bit of water. When we drank some of it, we found it brackish, hardly distinguishable from seawater. But we had no choice but to bring some back. Only after strenuous bargaining did they let us fill one barrel for a piaster. They filled a second barrel with some sand to act as a counterweight, loaded them onto the camel, and we headed back to the ship.

5.14   We arrived at the dinghy and unloaded the two barrels, got in ourselves, and rowed out to the ship. We all dug in to the dates and drank that brackish water, which did nothing to quench our thirst. We lay anchored in that spot for three days until, finally, the sea grew calm and the waves subsided. The crew weighed anchor and unfurled the sails, and we set off. But on the second day, a strong gale picked up around noon, and the captain ordered the sailors to turn landward so we wouldn't be battered again. As we approached the shore, it became apparent that the water off the coast was shallow, so we had to drop anchor three miles from land. We spent the night there.

When morning came, we awoke to find our ship mired entirely in sand! We couldn't believe our eyes. What a calamity! How had the ship come to be beached on the sand, we asked the *rayyis*, with the sea now a mile or more away?

"It's just the tide," he explained. "It's a natural thing, which you'd know about if you were sailors. No reason to worry."

We spent the day and night with our ship anchored in the sand, and the next morning the sea had risen again. But the ship remained lodged in the sand. The *rayyis* and the captain were surprised. They promptly ordered the sailors to dive into the water and swim under the ship and have a look.

It turned out that the ship was caught on a reef. Using all of their strength and skill, the sailors tried to push the ship to deeper water, but it wouldn't budge an inch. As we stood on the brink of disaster yet again, God delivered us from our predicament. Another ship appeared, which we hailed as it passed. When it drew near, our captain and the passengers begged the other captain to order his men to jump in and help our crew push us out to deeper water. The sailors jumped down from their ship and added their efforts to those of our crew, but weren't able to wiggle it loose. We spent the whole day locked in a fruitless contest. 5.15

Perhaps the ship was damaged, they suggested, only adding to our sorrow, fear, and despair. But by God's providence and inspiration, the two *rayyis*es held a consultation and decided to transfer us all to the other ship so ours would become lighter and rise up from where it had settled. They ordered us to take turns crossing over to the other ship in the rowboat. After we'd all disembarked, the women, who had been kept behind in the captain's chambers, began to cry and beg us to take them along as well. 5.16

Suddenly, I heard a baby crying, and I remembered that when we were stuck in the maelstrom I had heard the same thing. At the time, I was utterly mystified, ignorant as I was that someone's wife had given birth during the storm. She delivered it safely, thanks to Almighty God, and the child lived! I later saw him in the arms of his father, in one of the quarters of Tripoli. They'd nicknamed him "Man Overboard." 5.17

But back to our story. After we'd all disembarked and boarded the other ship, our sailors and their sailors went in to push our ship toward deeper water. We aided them with our prayers for an hour or so, until the ship was finally clear of the reef and bobbed up to the surface of the water, with no damage anywhere! We thanked God Most High for His beneficence, unfurled our sails, and set off. 5.18

5.19   After two days, the *rayyis* discovered an old moorage and dropped anchor, hoping we might find people there who had food and drink. But the place was deserted. It was an old quay that had been abandoned years before and was now in ruins. We remained there that day, eating dates and drinking brackish water until our throats were dry and our strength sapped. The sailors went so far as to eat the cats that were on the ship. Were it not for the dates, we would have been forced to eat each other. This is to say nothing of the itch we got from eating all those dates! We patiently endured God's will, waiting for Him to deliver us.

5.20   We spent the night on that quay. Everyone fell asleep, including the party of sailors whose turn it was to keep watch. At midnight, a loud noise jolted us awake. It was the captain, who'd woken and seen that the ship had drifted close to the shore and was about to be smashed to bits! Seeing the sailors still asleep, the captain lost his mind. Seizing his cane, he began to beat them mercilessly.

"Get up! Hurry! She's running aground!"

5.21   The sailors all jumped up like madmen and began hauling on the line tied to the outer anchor, in order to pull the ship out to deeper water. But the rope had come loose from the anchor, so they had no way to pull us to safety!

All ships, you see, drop an outer anchor half a mile from a harbor. As the anchor line plays out, the ship advances into the harbor. The rope is then tied down so that it can't unravel further. That's how the ship remains in place, with the outer anchor holding it fast so it can't go any closer to land. When it's time to sail again, the sailors pull on the outer anchor line until the ship returns to the spot where the anchor was dropped. The spot is marked by a buoy—an empty barrel tied to the anchor by a rope. The sailors heave it up with the rope and tie it securely to the starboard side of the ship. When they arrive at another harbor, as I've said, they drop it half a mile out again.

This was why our ship had drawn so close to land: The rope of the outer anchor had been severed by the rocks on the seabed!

Back to the story. The *rayyis* ordered the sailors to get into the rowboat, rig a towline, and row toward deeper water. They did as he ordered, and with the help of God Most High, pulled the ship clear. They raised the sails and made for the open sea, reaching a point about twenty miles from the harbor. We'd been saved.

In the morning, the ship returned to where the buoy was floating on the surface of the water, as I described, and we pulled up the anchor from the seabed. After tying it to the side of the ship, we sailed off. The sea and wind were fair, and we were able to make up eight days' journey in a single day. According to the *rayyis*, we were to arrive in Tripoli that very evening. We were overjoyed and congratulated each other on our safe arrival, forgetting the perils that had befallen us, the hunger, and all the other tribulations. Our ship was like a bird, flying over the surface of the water. We sailed all day and half the night, lit brightly by the full moon.

"Are we approaching the harbor?" we asked the *rayyis* (this is what he'd told us, after all).

He seemed perplexed, trying to work out how his calculations about our arrival had been wrong. Checking the water's depth, he found that it was not, in fact, the Sea of Tripoli, as he'd thought! Immediately, he ordered the sailors to take down the mainsail and leave the trinket sail at half-mast until morning. He'd then be able to see whether he had taken us off course or not.

Our ship slowed to the pace of a small child. When morning broke, we spotted land in the distance, and a towering mountain.

"That's Old Tripoli," the Maghrebis said to the *rayyis*. "It's sixty miles from New Tripoli."

The *rayyis* realized we'd sailed right past Tripoli harbor on account of those high winds. He'd thought that in the course of a single hour the ship would cover an eight-hour journey, but it was even faster than that, covering a ten-hour span in just one hour! So he had to turn the ship around and go back the way we'd come.

But now the winds were against us, and it took ten hours to cover a single hour's journey. We continued in this manner for three days and nights before finally arriving at the harbor of Tripoli.

5.25 As we were entering the harbor, a great gale rose up from the land and prevented us from advancing. It was only with great effort and the help of two dinghies that came out to pull us in that we were able to gain the harbor, where the crew dropped anchor and furled the sails as usual. We couldn't wait to reach dry land.

5.26 A rowboat appeared carrying food—fruits, and a round wooden platter bearing loaves of bread. The captain bought the whole platter and gave it to the sailors. I took a loaf myself and bit into it. I wasn't able to swallow it—it tasted like ashes! I threw it aside and cursed this place and its inedible bread!

"What's the matter?" my master said when he saw me toss the bread aside.

"We've finally arrived safely, after all that suffering and exhaustion, only to find that the bread here is disgusting!" I complained. "It tastes like dirt!"

"The bread is delicious," he said, laughing at me. "Your sense of taste has changed because you haven't eaten bread in a long time."

5.27 We brought our baggage down into the rowboat and went ashore, heading for the house of the French consul in the city. His name was Lemaire, and he had a splendid house. We arrived as he was having lunch. When he saw my master, he leapt up to greet him most graciously and insisted that he join him for lunch. My master demurred, and told him the story of everything that had happened to us, from the moment we left Alexandria until our arrival in Tripoli.

"We spent fifteen days without proper food," he said. "And for ten of those days, we ate only dates and drank only brackish water."[77]

When the consul heard this, he immediately ordered his cook to boil four fat chickens and prepare a broth, advising my master to have only chicken broth for a few days, until our throats had relaxed and our intestines opened up again. We spent eight days consuming only broth and Cypriot wine that had been aged seven years, until our strength returned and our throats returned to their former state.

We began to tour Tripoli, with no need to worry about our own   5.28
safety, since the consul was in the good graces of the bey, the ruler of the city and the surrounding countryside. He was, in fact, like a brother to him. It seems that during his youth, the bey had been taken prisoner in Malta. A French cavalier bought him and took him to Marseille, where he began working as the cavalier's servant. At some point, he became severely ill, and his master sent him to the hospital.

One day, the consul *khawājah* Lemaire went to the hospital to visit the invalids, in keeping with the laudable custom of his people. As he passed by this particular prisoner, who was lying in a bed, he stopped to sit with him and chat. The consul comforted him, raising his spirits and encouraging him to be steadfast in the face of his adversity, for recovery would surely come.

He asked him which country he was from, and who his people   5.29
were. The prisoner replied that he was a Maghrebi from Tripoli, that he was from a good family, and that his relatives were among the country's notables. Lemaire felt sorry for him, and ordered the director of the hospital to put the prisoner in a chair and carry him to his house, where he had his own servants prepare a bed and change the young man's clothes, telling them to serve him just as they served their master. Lemaire sent for a doctor and engaged him to treat the prisoner as he saw fit, without sparing a single medicine or distillate, no matter the cost.

The man remained at Lemaire's home, attended by servants   5.30
and the doctor until his health returned and the severe illness that afflicted him had abated. Eventually, he rose from his bed in perfect health, thanked the consul, and asked his permission to return to his owner. Lemaire, however, decided to see his act of charity through to the end. So he bought him from his master and put him on a ship bound for Tripoli. He paid the captain for his passage and meals, and entrusted the man to his care. He bid him farewell and sent him off to Tripoli, where he arrived safely.

5.31   The young man remained there for many years, serving the bey at the time. Because of his excellent service, he became one of the bey's close advisors, and was placed in a high-ranking position as governor of the lands under his rule. He governed righteously, and the whole country rejoiced in his rule and loved him dearly. Eventually, after a short illness, the bey died, whereupon the nobles and the generals chose his servant to be their bey, pledging allegiance to him in accordance with their ancient customs.

5.32   It was around that time that *khawājah* Lemaire happened to be appointed consul of Tripoli. He had no idea that the prisoner he'd bought and sent home had become a bey and assumed power. When Lemaire arrived in Tripoli, he went to meet with the bey after a few days, in keeping with the customary practice of consuls. When the bey recognized Lemaire, he rose from his seat, embraced him, and kissed him, doing him the greatest possible honor.

"This man saved me from captivity and death," he said to all the nobles present. "Honor him as you honor me!"

When the consul left the palace, the bey had surrounded him with all the members of his court and his servants. He heaped more honors on Lemaire than he had on any previous consul, and always referred to him as "my brother," for he loved him deeply.

5.33   This is the story of the bey and the consul, which I heard from trustworthy sources. And I myself can testify to the many wonderful attributes of this blessed consul: his cordial manners, his modesty, and his love for the poor and the prisoners of that city. Just inside the door of his house was a room set aside for distributing alms to the poor and the wretched. He appointed one of his servants to stand there at all times, handing out bread and biscuits, which never ran out.

5.34   He was very pious. Each night, before going to sleep, he would gather in his chapel his three children—two boys and a girl—and all his servants. He would turn to face them as we waited for everyone to arrive. They would then say their prayers and the Litany of the Virgin. After all the prayers were complete, each person would go to his bed, and the consul would follow them to his own bed. Similarly, all would attend mass with him early in the morning.

The consul made a great effort to buy back prisoners and send them home to their countries, using the alms he received from Christian countries for this purpose. In short, he devoted his whole life to virtuous acts.

One day, while we were in Tripoli, the bey received news from the Bedouins that a large Venetian ship had run aground on the shore, three days' journey from Tripoli by land. The Venetians were always at war with the Maghrebis, so the bey sent five hundred soldiers on the march to seize the ship and all its property, and to bring the passengers to Tripoli to be imprisoned. He summoned his "brother," the consul Lemaire, and asked him to send a vessel from the harbor to load up the goods carried by the Venetian ship, along with the cannons and the munitions. The consul acceded immediately to his request. 5.35

He left the bey and sent for a captain whose ship was moored in the harbor, ordering him to sail to that spot and load up everything on board the Venetian ship—money, cannons, and people—and bring it all back to Tripoli harbor. This, at least, was the apparent nature of the consul's order; God only knows what he secretly told him to do! The ship sailed, headed for the Maghreb, and the bey's soldiers arrived first. In the meantime, however, those on the Venetian ship had emptied the vessel of all that was on board, except for the contents of the hold. It was full of wheat, which they'd loaded in the Province of the Islands[78] before sailing for Venice. 5.36

While they were on their way, however, the ship began to take on water. It grew so heavy that it began listing dangerously, so the captain made for land. They happened to be near the North African coast. Afraid the ship would sink, the captain ran it aground on the sand. They unloaded everything on board except for the wheat and left the ship stricken at sea. Meanwhile, the bey's soldiers arrived, led by of one of his commanders. They tried to seize the Venetians, but the ship's guards wouldn't surrender. Instead, they turned their cannons and rifles on the bey's men, putting them to flight. 5.37

5.38   Soon after, the ship sent by the consul of Tripoli arrived. Its captain dropped anchor and went ashore to meet with the soldiers from the Venetian ship. It soon became clear to him that they weren't willing to surrender.

"I've been sent on behalf of the French consul in Tripoli," he told the captain of the Venetian ship. "I have orders from the bey and the consul to transfer all the goods and people on your ship to my own, and to bring you to Tripoli."

"We won't be taken prisoner," they replied. "We'd rather die here than surrender."

5.39   The captain recognized that neither he nor the bey's soldiers had enough men to subdue them, as the Venetian ship had two hundred soldiers in addition to its sailors and passengers.

"If you do what I say, I can save you from these people," the captain urged. "I'll take you back to Venice, on the following conditions. You must swear to me, in writing, that if we reach Venice safely, you'll protect me from the French. I don't want them coming after me to take revenge. Also, you'll have to provide for my livelihood until I die."

They immediately agreed and wrote out a contract, guaranteeing his demands. You see, the ship was a vessel of the Venetian Republic, and there were important people on board, including some cavaliers, by which I mean spahis, along with some army officers and other similar high-ranking officials.[79]

5.40   After settling matters with the Venetians, the captain went to find the commander of the bey's soldiers, and reassured him that the ship's passengers and soldiers had surrendered, as they had no means of escape. The commander and his soldiers returned to the scene, and the commander ordered them to load the Venetian ship's goods onto the bey's ship. When all was complete, he told the captain to transfer the Venetian passengers to his ship, with the exception of the two hundred soldiers. The captain obeyed.

5.41   The commander ordered his five hundred soldiers to shackle the two hundred, and march them to Tripoli to be paraded before the bey. After sending them off, the commander tried to board the French ship but the captain stopped him.

"Let me go and put the passengers in the hold first, as I'm worried that they'll raise a mutiny against us while we're at sea," the captain said. "Once I've prepared a decent room for you, I'll send the dinghy back for you and your servants."

The commander agreed, and the captain hurried off to his ship. This was a wise move on the captain's part; he did it so the bey wouldn't blame the consul for the capture of the commander and his coterie.

When the captain arrived at the ship, he quickly ordered the sailors to weigh anchor and pull the ship to the outer mooring. Finally, they were able to unfurl their sails and head out to sea. As he watched the ship sail away, the commander suddenly realized he'd been tricked! He was forced to chase after his soldiers and make the journey with them back to Tripoli. As for the French ship, it sailed for Venice carrying all of those passengers, saving them from captivity.

5.42

After a few days, the commander arrived in Tripoli with the two hundred Venetian prisoners. They made quite a spectacle as they entered the city, all bound in ropes. They were paraded before His Excellency the bey, who had them imprisoned. He then sent for the consul and told him what he'd heard from his commander, about how the captain had left him behind and sailed off.

5.43

"He still hasn't come back to Tripoli," the bey said to the consul. "Do you think he took them back to their country? Believe you me, if that's what happened, I'll kill every last one of these two hundred soldiers! And if it weren't for my friendship with you, I'd sequester every French ship in my harbor until my own ship was returned to me!"

At this, the consul made a show of insisting that he too would be furious if that were the case, and set about trying to placate the bey. He promised that the ship would return, adding that he'd write to the king of France asking him to dispatch some envoys who'd be responsible for bringing the ship back to Tripoli. The consul also

5.44

beseeched the bey, for the sake of their own friendship, to free the prisoners without harming them, for they'd done nothing wrong: "The ones to blame are the ones who kidnapped the captain!" he said. "And it was the commander who showed a lapse in judgment by letting all those people board the ship. They must have overpowered the captain and crew, and taken control of the ship."

5.45 "You're right, brother," the bey agreed. "It's all the commander's fault. I'll take my revenge on him instead!" And he ordered that the two hundred soldiers be freed.

"Set the prisoners free, as a favor to my brother the consul, and bring them before me!" he commanded.

When they were brought before the bey, he declared, "I've pardoned you for the sake of my brother the consul." They kissed his hands and left in peace. The consul rose, thanked the bey, and returned home. As it happens, I was present at the time and witnessed this whole scene from start to finish.

5.46 Here's another story we heard about the bey's affection for the consul. It so happened that when the ships of the principality of Tripoli were plying the seas and marauding in their usual way, they came upon a ship belonging to the principality of Genoa. They followed the ship, harassing it, and eventually managed to lay hold of it and its crew. They brought it back to Tripoli, and, after anchoring in the harbor, informed the bey about the ship they'd captured.

5.47 The bey ordered them to parade before him the men who'd been aboard. There were more than two hundred in all, including the captain, his guards, the sailors, and the passengers. Studying the prisoners, the bey saw that there was a young boy among them. He was radiantly beautiful, and wore fine clothes that were a testament to his wealth and good breeding. The boy was the son of a prince of Rome, and his father had sent him to visit his aunt in the town of Messina, by way of a pleasure cruise.

The bey was drawn to him, and felt such strong feelings of affection welling up deep within that he called him over to put him at ease, and ordered his dragoman to calm the frightened boy.

"Tell him this," the bey said to the dragoman. "'His Excellency the Bey has taken a liking to you and would like to make you his beloved son.'"

The boy wasn't put at ease at all, and instead began to cry. As his 5.48 crying grew louder, the bey realized that the child was inconsolable, so he sent him to the harem, where the women could try to soothe and distract him. He selected two other young prisoners and ordered them to serve the boy and keep him company, and sent the rest of the men off to prison.

With each passing day, the boy felt increasingly at ease. He began to come out of the harem and appear before the bey, comporting himself most courteously. The bey's love for him grew more intense, and he would often hug him to his chest and kiss him. Out of regard for the bey, all the members of his court showed the boy every possible favor.

Time passed, and the boy continued to be held in high esteem. 5.49 One day, a French ship arrived in the harbor. The captain went to see Lemaire, the consul. He gave him a letter from one of the dukes of France.

"This concerns the boy taken captive in Tripoli—whose name is such and such," the letter read. "The boy's father has written to us, begging us to urge you to spare no effort to liberate his son from captivity, whatever the price may be, and to send him to us. We've sent you two trunks full of expensive gifts in the company of this ship captain, because money alone may not be enough to set the boy free. Present these gifts to the bey who rules over the city. If it's necessary to offer him money on top of the gifts, don't hesitate; you are so authorized. In other words, make sure the boy returns. We look forward to a favorable reply, and, indeed, will accept no other. Salutations."

When the consul finished reading the letter, he felt utterly at a 5.50 loss. He knew of the bey's great love for the boy, and that he'd never let him go. In any event, the consul went to see the bey, as was his usual custom, whether or not he had a favor to ask. He presented himself, and the bey invited him to sit down. They began to chat amiably in their regular way, and the consul asked the bey if he would promise to grant a certain request. If not, the consul said, he wouldn't make the request at all. The bey couldn't imagine that the consul would ask for the boy, so he responded immediately.

"Speak, brother! Far be it from me to deny your request, no matter what it is."

The consul hesitated, and the bey repeated his exhortation.

"Brother, do speak up! Don't you know that your requests will never be denied, even if they're at my own expense?" the bey said, so the consul told him about the letter he had received from the duke.

5.51   "He has asked me to send the boy back to his parents," the consul explained. "They've sent Your Excellency gifts worthy of your station," he said, as he called for the gifts and had them brought before the bey.

But the bey didn't even glance at them. His face was full of anger and sorrow. He didn't say another word to the consul and stormed off to his harem. He was furious, as this affair had put him in a real predicament. On the one hand, he'd promised not to refuse the consul's request. On the other, the prospect of losing the boy filled him with grief.

Meanwhile, the consul realized that his plea had failed to hit the mark. With his hopes dashed, he returned to his house, despondent. But the bey's thoughts continued to dwell on the consul. He loved him dearly and didn't want to put him in dire straits because the request hadn't been granted.

5.52   The next day, the bey sent for the consul so they could patch things up. When the messenger came by with the summons, the consul suddenly thought of a trick to save the boy. It went like this. The consul had a young son named Nicholas, and the bey loved him as dearly as his parents did. Whenever he accompanied his father on his visits, the bey would hug and kiss him, and grant him whatever he asked for, never denying him any request.

Now, this Nicholas was a bright, precocious, chatty child, and his father said to him, "When we're about to leave the bey's house, grab hold of the boy and cling to him. Don't let go! If they try to take him away from you, cry and beg the bey to let him stay with you, so that you can spend the rest of the day playing together." And the consul added, "Whatever you do, don't let go of that boy, even if I tell you to!"

Having given his instructions, the consul took his son and went to see the bey, who welcomed the consul as soon as he arrived.   5.53

"I've been so worried," the bey said soothingly. "I hope I haven't put you in a difficult spot by not accepting your request. If only I'd known that you were going to ask me for the boy, I'd never have made that vow! Ah well, what's done is done. I hope you won't hold it against me."

When the bey saw the gifts the consul had brought him from the boy's father and his poor mother, his own anger subsided, and he and the consul sat chatting in their usual way, having some drinks and coffee. An hour or so passed, while the consul's son played with the young boy, as children do. Finally, the consul rose and asked the bey's permission to take his leave and go home.

At that, Nicholas grasped the boy's hand and began pulling him   5.54
along. The bey's servants tried to stop him, asking him gently to let go of the boy's hand. But he wouldn't, and instead began to cry and plead with the bey to let him take the boy home, just as his father had taught him.

Oblivious to the trick that was being played on him, the bey tried to distract Nicholas by sending for a pony that he could ride along-side his father. But Nicholas refused, insisting that the boy come with them.

"Let go of his hand!" the consul chided his son, who only cried more and kept on pleading. Seeing how determined Nicholas was, the bey decided not to upset him any further, if only for his father's sake and his love for him. So he permitted them to take the boy along and keep him at their house for as long as Nicholas wanted.

Delighted, Nicholas ran to kiss the bey's hand, and the bey hugged the boy to his chest and kissed him. Then he let him go and gave permission to the boy to accompany Nicholas, as if he'd been the one to offer in the first place. The two boys happily left together.

5.55 The young boy remained at the consul's house for a few days, and the bey didn't come looking for him. It was as though he'd reconciled himself to losing him. Concluding that the bey had given the boy to his son Nicholas, the consul sent for the captain who had brought the gifts, and ordered him to make ready to sail.

5.56 In the middle of the night, he sent the boy to the ship, which set off as soon as he was aboard. Some time later, letters arrived from the duke and the boy's father, the prince. They thanked the consul as well as his son Nicholas, who had facilitated the boy's escape. The prince had included among the letters a document that read as follows:

"I hereby bestow upon Nicholas, son of the French consul Lemaire, one of my own properties, whose income is one thousand piasters per year, which no one may deny him or his offspring, in perpetuity. May this signature testify to my statement."

So Nicholas would receive one thousand piasters from an agent in Rome each year, a practice that continues to this very day.

5.57 That's the story of the bey's affection for the French consul. I heard it from the man who served as the consul's dragoman at the time, and who knew him intimately. I know that his account was faithful, as I heard the same story from others.

5.58 We remained at the consul's home in the utmost comfort and ease. One day, when the Jesuits living in Tripoli were celebrating one of their holidays, I decided to attend their mass to obtain some indulgences. I put on the fine clothes that I'd sent for from Aleppo, and something told me to put on my turban and felt cap, my native dress. The consul was very happy to see me dressed in this way, as my outfit delighted him.

5.59 I set off for the Jesuit monastery and attended the mass. On my way back to the consul's house, I encountered four janissaries.

When they spotted me, they stopped short, pausing to take a good look. Shaking their heads, they began insulting me in their language, and growled as if they were going to kill me. I was terrified! Suddenly, one of them lunged forward, as though he were about to attack, snatched the turban from my head, and went off with his friends. I stood there, bareheaded and senseless with fright! Once they'd gone off a little way, I collected myself and started walking in the other direction, looking behind me to make sure that they weren't coming back. I arrived at the consul's house in that sorry state, my head bare and my wits scattered.

Nicholas, the consul's son, was standing at the door with his 5.60 sister, Margarita. When they saw me in that condition, they ran off to tell their father. He and my master came down to see me as soon as they got word. The consul was astonished and demanded to know what had happened. Who had taken my turban? I told him the story from start to finish. The consul was furious and immediately summoned the dragoman.

"Go find the people who snatched the turban and cap off the head of our guest," he ordered the dragoman when he appeared. "And bring them here at once!"

The dragoman set out. Soon after, he sent someone to ask me where I'd been robbed.

"Near the alleyway by the Jesuit monastery."

He left, and a short while later called for me again. 5.61

"May I ask why you were wearing a turban and cap?" he inquired. "No one is allowed to wear such things in this country—no one, that is, except the pasha sent from Istanbul to serve as the sultan's ambassador. Yes, only the pasha may wear a turban and cap, and the men who took yours won't return them. Now, I worry that this is going to cause some trouble, and it'll have been your fault. If the consul asks you about the turban, just tell him that it was returned. That way, we'll nip this in the bud. The soldiers here are a tough lot, you know. They're split up into regiments, and protect each other. They certainly don't fear the bey when they get up to mischief."

5.62   As I listened to the dragoman, I didn't let my true feelings show,[80] and promised to tell the consul that I'd gotten the turban and cap back. If he told me to wear them, I'd beg off by saying that wearing them was forbidden in this country, so I'd rather not wear them if he didn't mind, to avoid any trouble. The dragoman and I agreed on this response, and I kept my calpac on until the consul came down for lunch.

"Did they bring you the turban?" he asked.

"Yes," I replied.

"Why aren't you wearing it?" he asked, and I replied as I'd agreed with the dragoman.

"Go put them on, and don't be afraid," the consul said. "No one will harm you while you're staying with me."

He went in to have lunch with my master, and when I failed to follow them in, he sent one of the servants to summon me to the table.

"What's the matter?" he asked. "Why aren't you wearing the turban?"

"I'll put it on tomorrow."

"I'd like you to put it on now."

"Obey the consul's orders," my master said.

5.63   What was I supposed to do? I was afraid that if I told him I hadn't gotten it back, I'd cause a lot of trouble. But if I told him I had gotten it back, he'd ask me why I wasn't wearing it. I was compelled to take my master aside privately and tell him that I hadn't received the turban. Meanwhile, the consul awaited my reply, and when my master realized that the consul demanded an answer, he was forced to explain the circumstances. Hearing that the dragoman hadn't gotten the turban back after all, the consul summoned him. This dragoman had once been a prisoner who'd converted to Islam, and the consul had taken him into his home in order to bring him back to the faith. When the dragoman appeared before him, the consul rebuked him, cursed him, and ordered him to go to the bey.

"Tell him that I want him to seize that soldier, flog him with a hundred lashes, and take back the turban and send it to me immediately!"

The dragoman left the consul's presence, unsure of what to do. If 5.64 he went to the bey—who'd never refuse the request of his brother, the consul—the soldier would be summoned and flogged. The soldier's regiment would revolt and it would cause an unspeakable mess!

So he didn't actually follow the consul's orders. Instead, he went to the senior members of the janissary corps and told them the whole story. Upon hearing it, they ordered the soldier's commanding officer to have the turban and cap sent immediately. He followed their orders, and they handed the turban and cap over to the dragoman.

"Please convey our regards to His Excellency the consul, and tell 5.65 him that the senior janissaries insisted that His Highness the bey should not be troubled with something so trivial," they said to the dragoman. "The consul may rest assured that we'll ensure that his rights are respected, and will take care of the matter ourselves."

The dragoman returned to the consul with the turban and cap. He told him what happened, and how the senior janissaries had prevented him from going to complain to the bey about something not worth complaining about.

"They send you their greetings, and assure you that they will discipline the soldier as you've requested."

The consul ordered me to put on the turban in front of him, so I did. But I was afraid that I'd run into those soldiers again while I had it on. They'd surely kill me without giving it a second thought! So, whenever I left the consul's house, I'd always take off the turban and wear the calpac instead.

After I returned from my travels, I saw the consul Lemaire 5.66 in Aleppo, along with his children. I went to see him and his son Nicholas. He welcomed me warmly and treated me most honorably. He told all the *khawājah*s about me, how I had stayed with him in

Tripoli, and about the things that had happened while I was traveling in the company of Paul Lucas, my master.

5.67   Back to our story. We remained in Tripoli at the consul Lemaire's house for thirty days, eating and drinking and enjoying ourselves. We saw many things, but I've decided not to mention them all so as not to make this account too long.

5.68   My master decided to journey by land to the city of Tunis next, so that we could tour its sites and territories. He told the consul about his plan, then went to see the bey, from whom he received a firman—an order—written in his own hand, recommending my master to all the governors under his jurisdiction whom we might encounter along our route.

5.69   The bey had ample provisions prepared for us and summoned a muleteer who was trustworthy and of good character. He placed us in his care and ordered him to take us at our preferred pace, and not to protest at any of our requests. These lands were safe enough to transport gold through them, and one could travel without fear.

At last the consul bid us farewell, and we set off from Tripoli, headed for Tunis. We traveled the roads and crossed the deserts for five whole days, but went at our own pace. Each time we passed a village, we'd stop and observe the peasants, the organization of the village, its farmland, and so on and so forth.

5.70   Finally, we arrived at the city of Djerba. The people scrutinized us when we entered their city as they could see that we were foreigners. They asked the muleteer about us.

"This man is a doctor who was staying with the bey of Tripoli," he said. "He's on his way to Tunis to treat people there."

We asked for directions to the governor's palace, and they pointed the way for us. When we arrived at the palace, we asked permission to enter and meet His Excellency the governor. We were admitted into his presence, and my master presented the order the bey had given him.

5.71   When the governor read it, he smiled broadly and welcomed my master. I served as their interpreter.

"Who is this man?" the governor asked me. "Which community is he from?"

"He's a Frankish doctor, of French origin."

"Why did he come here? What is he looking for?"

"He's a traveler, my lord, searching for certain medicinal herbs found in this country," I explained.

He invited us to sit down, and ordered the servants to bring us something to drink, along with some sweets and coffee, as was the custom there. He told my master that he'd developed a severe stomach pain, which made it difficult for him to eat. Whenever he ate something, he'd immediately vomit. I told my master what the governor had said.

"Not to worry. I'll concoct a paste for you. If you use it for three days it will strengthen your stomach," my master said. "You'll be able to eat five times a day, and still won't feel full!"

The governor was overjoyed to hear that he would soon be cured, and he ordered that we be provided with furnished lodgings, food, and drink, and dismissed us. We went to our quarters and my master set about cooking up the paste. It was made of essence of parsley, thickened with sugar, to which he added four *mithqāl*s of crushed pearls and some other ingredients. He put it into a porcelain cup and sent it to the governor.

After just two days the governor's stomach settled, and he began to eat as well as he ever had. Seeing that he was now cured, the governor sent for us and showered my master with gratitude and treated him most honorably for ridding him of his stomach pain and returning his appetite to its previous state. He asked my master to prepare a jar of the paste to keep for times of need.

"It would be my pleasure, but I'll need fifty dirhams' worth of pearls," my master replied. "They can be broken, or small in size," he added, and the governor immediately sent a quantity of pearls, along with a number of dirhams. My master refused the money, but we took the pearls and returned to our lodgings to prepare the paste for him.

5.72

5.73

5.74   We took to touring the city and seeing the sights. One day, while we were out and about, we happened upon a square. There were three tall towers in the square, each built in the shape of a sugar cake, and made entirely of human skulls.[81] We were astonished by this dreadful sight.

An old man passed by.

"What's the meaning of these towers of skulls?" we asked him.

"When these lands were ruled by the Christians of Spain, Ismāʿīlīs from the Maghreb[82] waged war on them and seized these territories by fair means and foul," he said. "When they reached this city, the inhabitants resisted them, and so were placed under siege for three months. The armies only conquered the town by starving its inhabitants, and the prince who waged the war on the city swore that when he took it, he'd kill every last man, woman, and child. And in fact, when the town fell, he ordered his soldiers to kill everyone and not spare a single soul. They built these towers out of the heads of the dead, as a reminder to later generations. In the towers are the corpses, surrounded by the skulls, which were used like building stones, set in gypsum so that the towers wouldn't come apart and would last for years."[83]

When we heard this sad tale, we felt sorry for the people of that region, which is known as Ifrīqiyah. It comprises eighteen bishoprics, its history well known from the chronicles.

5.75   After touring the city, we went to see the governor and obtained his permission to depart, and bid him farewell. He offered us a letter of introduction to the governor of Sfax, which we brought with us. On our way, we passed various hamlets and villages, many with ruins, and didn't stop till we reached Sfax, a prosperous city with lofty fortifications, and with many orchards, streams, and gardens.

5.76   When we entered, we asked for directions to the palace of the governor, where we were admitted. We presented him with the letters of the bey and the governor of Djerba. He read them, welcomed us, and invited us to sit down. Coffee and other beverages were served, as was the usual custom, and the governor asked my master about the medicinal paste he'd made for the governor of Djerba.

"Do you have any left over?" he inquired.

My master had kept some of the paste in a container, and promised the governor that he would send him a small jar of it. The governor ordered his servants to give us a place to stay, and we rested there that day.

The next day, we went to see the governor and presented him with the paste. He was pleased, and ordered the servants to treat us as honored guests and to put themselves at our service. We thanked him and set off to tour the city and see its ancient sites, which included the churches, monasteries, and schools of the Christians who had once lived in those lands. They were all in ruins, but there were dates inscribed on some of the stones, which provided information about them. My master copied these down. We bought many old silver and copper medallions, which had served as currency there, along with other antiques: history books and chronicles about the Saracens, some in Arabic and others in Latin, and other such things. 5.77

All of this was made possible by my master's medical practice. He would treat people and ask them to search for such objects, which he'd purchase at a generous price.

We stayed in Sfax for seven days. We then paid a visit to the governor to bid him farewell, and asked him for a letter of introduction to the other governors who were on our route. 5.78

"A day's ride from the city, you'll enter the jurisdiction of the bey of Tunis, and my letter won't be worth anything to you," he said. "But don't worry—the road is safe."

We said goodbye and went back to our lodgings to gather our provisions for the road. We set off, together with the muleteer who'd come with us from Tripoli. We traveled for about eight days, passing many ruined buildings along the way and other traces of civilization. We also came upon petrified olive trees, their olives turned to stone, and petrified watermelons as well. Breaking one open, we 5.79

found yellow seeds inside, similarly transformed into stone. We also saw a dried riverbed with petrified fish lying among the river stones, and the shapes of fish stamped onto the surfaces of rocks. We were amazed by these sights, and asked the muleteer about them.

"This was once a prosperous place, full of people," the muleteer explained. "Then one day, God grew angry at the people, and kicked up a great storm that leveled the town and buried it in sand! After years under all that sand, you see, all the trees and plants were turned to stone." Pointing to a nearby hill, he continued, "Eventually, God sent a strong wind to blow the sand away, and that's where that hill came from."

5.80 We took some of those olives and watermelons with us, as well as some of the rocks with the shapes of fish pressed into them, and set off again, continuing on until we reached Sousse. But the muleteer held us back from entering the city.

"This town is full of horrible heretics," he said.[84] "They're so hateful that they won't have anything to do with Sunnis, Christians, Jews, or people of any other community."

So we had to make camp outside, at the base of the city wall, where we spent the night.

5.81 When morning came, we prepared to depart, and sent the muleteer into town to buy provisions and some meat for the road. After he got everything we needed, he hired a mount from one of the townspeople to travel with us. The muleteer had two beasts of his own, and in every town we entered he would hire a third, along with its owner, to travel with us. He loaded all of our things on the hired beast, as he usually did, freeing his own two mounts for my master and me to ride. The hired beast would carry our luggage.

Once the muleteer finished loading it up, though, the other man was not pleased to see that his beast was carrying all of the luggage, while the other two had no load at all.

"That's why I hired that beast of yours," the muleteer said. "To carry the baggage!" They began to quarrel.

Striding over to his beast, the man took hold of the baggage on   5.82
its back and dumped the whole load on the ground. Among the
baggage was a case of twenty-four bottles of good wine, which the
consul of Tripoli had given us. There was no wine to be found anywhere along our route, you see, and my master was incapable of
drinking water without mixing it with wine. When he saw the man
dump the load—including the case—onto the ground, he was sure
the bottles had broken and his wine was gone.

Flying into a rage, he began screaming and cursing in Turkish
and Arabic and French. He knew how to say "dog" in Turkish and
Arabic, having learned the words *köpek* and *kalb*. Striding up to the
man, he shoved him so hard that he nearly knocked him down. The
next thing we knew, the man had dashed off toward the city gate,
shouting to the townspeople, "For the love of the Prophet, help me!
A Christian has attacked me!"

A crowd burst through the gate like a swarm of locusts, heading   5.83
right for us. When the muleteer saw them coming, he was terrified
something might happen to us.

"Run!" he said to my master. "Save yourself, or they'll kill you!"

Taking to his heels, my master found a place to hide in the nooks
and crannies around the rampart towers. When the mob arrived,
they found only me standing there, so they seized me, meaning to
kill me! But the man whose beast we'd hired pushed them away.

"This isn't the one who cursed me," he said.

I begged and pleaded both with him and them. Eventually he   5.84
pried me out of their hands, and they went off in search of my
master. But he'd happened upon a crevice to hide in, covering himself with some straw he'd found, so they never saw him.

Meanwhile, the muleteer and I were pleading with the man we'd
hired. I promised him that we wouldn't load up his beast with anything at all. I would ride it myself with no luggage. I also promised
him that I'd give him two gold pieces on top of his regular fee. When
he heard about the two gold pieces, he became more agreeable. He
rounded up everyone and said to them,

"I'll lodge a complaint about him in Tunis with the bey, and I'll have him burned!"

5.85   With that the crowd broke up, and we put our luggage back on the muleteer's beast. When I inspected the trunk, it turned out that not a single bottle had broken and none of the wine had spilled.

After we'd loaded everything up, we set off along the wall so we could spot the *khawājah*. Seeing no one, we stopped, uncertain what to do. He spotted us from under the straw, came out of the crevice, and joined us. He was terrified and all the color had drained from his face.

"Don't worry, the crowd's gone; we're safe," I reassured him. "And none of the wine bottles broke!"

I told him what had happened in his absence and how I'd barely escaped.

"If that man hadn't stopped them, they would have killed me for certain," I said. "And you too, if they'd spotted you."

We thanked the good Lord for saving us from that pack of savages.

5.86   We mounted and rode for two hours. When we came to a green field with a spring, we unloaded the beasts so we could have lunch and rest for a while. After eating and resting, we set off across that desolate landscape, pressing on until the evening without seeing any villages or a single person—not even a bird—and had to spend the night out in the open. In the morning, we mounted again and rode all day, arriving that evening at a place known as the Valley of Lions. There were some people encamped there, so we set up camp alongside them.

5.87   For fear of the lions, no one dared cross the valley without a company of twenty or thirty men. We spent the night there, and set off in the morning through the valley, accompanied by fifteen people rounded up from some local villages. After a day's journey, we arrived in the evening at a large clearing. It was surrounded by fires that remained constantly burning, day and night. Every convoy that entered the clearing would cut down some trees and throw them into the fire, to prevent the lions venturing in and killing the people and their mounts.

We passed the night in the clearing, listening to the sounds of the lions roaring and slapping their tails against their bellies, and of the horses snorting—because they could see the lions in the darkness.

In the morning, we set off through the valley again, emerging from it at midday. We pressed on until evening and came to a plain covered in snow-white salt as far as the eye could see. We spent the night at the edge of the plain, and the next day began our ride across it. There was no other road. We covered our faces with blue scarves and turban cloths so our eyes wouldn't be dazzled by all that glaring whiteness.   5.88

It took about three hours of walking to cross the salt flat. From there we continued on till we came to a village called al-Ḥammāmāt, which was prosperous, and whose inhabitants were people of good character. We entered the village and spent the night there, and the next day went sightseeing. We met some people from Tunis, who treated us kindly when they learned that we were on our way there to visit the consul. We told them about the man from Sousse whose beast we'd hired and how he'd brought all those people together to kill us.   5.89

When they heard this, they rose up against him and were going to kill him on the spot.

"Heretic! You deserve to die!" they shouted.

But my master interceded on his behalf and paid him, and we sent him away. He didn't dare ask for the two gold pieces I'd promised him!

After a day in the village, we left the next morning for Tunis, stopping at a caravansary three hours' journey from the city. The merchants in our caravan didn't want to enter Tunis in broad daylight, as they intended to hide some of their goods from the customs agents. So we stayed at the caravansary.   5.90

There was a *qablūjah* nearby, a place where hot water comes out of the ground. I went off to have a look, and entered the building where the hot spring was located. Inside, I found a large pool, a hundred feet in length and the same in width, covered by a vast,   5.91

towering dome. All around, people were bathing. Some were in up to their knees and others to their stomachs. Some were in all the way up to their chests. The steam rose as high as the top of the dome. There were people watching over the clothes, and whenever a man came out of the water, he would hand the attendant an *'uthmānī* coin.

5.92   I took off my clothes, sat down beside one of the bathers, and stretched out one of my feet to touch the water. When I felt how hot it was, I jerked back, certain I'd scalded my feet from the intense heat! The bather invited me to sit beside him again.

"Why did you pull away?" he asked. "Sit here next to me, and I'll show you how to bathe."

I sat beside him.

"Dip one foot in slowly until it goes numb," he said. "Then dip the second one in slowly."

I did as directed. My foot came to rest on a step, the water up to my ankle. I remained there until the heat made my foot go numb and I could no longer feel it.

5.93   The man told me to put my feet on the second step, which I did. Then I went down to the third step, and so on, until the water reached my chest, while my feet remained planted on the steps.

I stayed in the water for about half an hour and stopped feeling the heat. But I could feel the dampness trapped in my limbs dissipating in the sulfurous water, which had wondrous healing properties for all manner of ailments and illnesses. Many people with leprosy and other afflictions would seek it out, some of them coming from faraway lands for a cure. The pool was always full of water, overflowing day and night. It continues to do so to this very day.

5.94   I came out of the water, put on my clothes, and went to see my master. I told him about the water and the pool and its beneficial properties. When he heard about it, he wanted to go bathe there as well. We returned to the building, and when my master saw the boiling water, he asked me how I was able to step into it. I explained the method that I and others used to go in, so he dipped his hand into the water to feel, but found it unbearable! He refused to go in, and we went back to our lodgings, even as he continued to marvel at how people could bathe in such hot water without being scalded.[85]

We stayed at the caravansary until the middle of the night. 5.95
When the merchants and drivers got up and packed their loads and left the inn, we followed them. While we were in the desert, my master looked up at the stars and determined that it was midnight, and decided he didn't want to follow the caravan. So the two of us remained alone in the wilderness. Meanwhile, our muleteer had gone ahead with the caravan, his beast carrying all of our baggage. He didn't realize that we'd split off from the caravan and stayed behind. After spending the night in the wasteland, we mounted our horses and rode toward the city. But we took a wrong turn and wandered off the main road.

Meanwhile, the caravan had arrived at the city, and the muleteer, 5.96
not seeing us anywhere, had turned back to search for us. But we were on the wrong road. On our way we passed a peasant going to his village and asked him if we were close to Tunis.

"You've passed it," he said. "It's off to the left. Go back the way you came. When you arrive at a wide road, follow it till you reach the city."

"If you come with us and show us the way, we'll pay you," we said to him.

So he led us to the road. After walking for about an hour, we 5.97
came upon the muleteer, along with two Maghrebis from Tunis. They'd come with him because he'd taken our things to the consul's house and was asked where we were.

"They fell behind and didn't arrive with the caravan," he replied.

When the consul heard this, he sent two men with the muleteer to fetch us and bring us to his house. They left the city, assuming we had to be nearby, but didn't see anyone. So they set off in hurry, arrived quickly at the place where we'd lodged, but didn't find us. The muleteer was baffled, and he worried that something had befallen us.

On the way back, they spotted us in the distance and the mule-teer began to call out. We responded and headed over to meet them. When they asked about the reason for our delay, we explained what had happened and how we'd wandered off the road.

5.98 We rode back to the city together, and headed to the consul's house.[86] It was inside a large caravansary, and the French merchants resided there together. We went up the stairs to the consul's residence. He came out to meet us and welcome my master. The two men greeted each other. The consul had received a letter from his opposite number in Tripoli, notifying him about my master's arrival, explaining that he was an envoy sent by the sultan of France. The consul of Tunis welcomed him with great cordiality and made available his own sumptuous bedroom for my master to use. They also gave me a room, and brought our things in from the caravansary to our rooms.

After a little while, the merchants came to the consul's house to greet my master and congratulate him on his safe arrival. We remained there that day to meet with all the merchants.

5.99 The next day my master went to pay visits to all of them, as was the custom. Three days later, the consul invited my master to come with him and meet the bey of Tunis, who was the ruler of the city. My master agreed, and a carriage was prepared for them. My master climbed in and the consul sat next to him, and a few merchants rode alongside on their horses. I rode with the servants, and we all went together to the bey's palace, which was called Bardo.[87] It was an hour and a half away from the city.

When we arrived, I beheld a sight beyond description: a grand palace surrounded by verdant gardens with springs flowing everywhere. The palace had towering columns and lofty, intricately constructed pavilions, with crystal windows on all sides.

5.100 We passed through a first gate into a pavilion with open salons, pools overflowing with water, and other exquisite structures. We then entered a second gate, and passed into the private residence of the bey. This was even larger than the previous one, and its construction even nobler and more opulent. We climbed a tall, graceful set of wide marble stairs, and arrived at the palace courtyard, which was paved with white marble. On each of the four sides of the courtyard a pavilion had been erected. There was one for each of the four seasons of the year. The bey was sitting in the spring pavilion.

Once he was informed of the consul's arrival, the bey ordered that 5.101 he be brought in. We entered the pavilion and presented ourselves before him. The consul and his entourage bowed deeply before the bey. He welcomed us and invited us all to sit down. We were brought beverages and coffee, as was customary. The consul briefed the bey on the reasons for my master's journey to his country.

"He came with us today to have the honor of meeting you," the consul concluded.

My master rose from his place and bowed before His Excellency the bey, who welcomed him and congratulated him on his safe arrival. He asked him about the things he'd seen on his travels and the cities he'd visited, and my master replied to all his questions. The consul's dragoman served as a skillful interpreter, embellishing my master's words and helping the bey understand them perfectly.

The bey was pleased with my master's replies, and particularly 5.102 the praise of his beautiful country and of the elegant design of his palace. My master said that he'd never seen its equal in any of the other Ottoman kingdoms.

"My palace pleases you, then?" the bey asked.

"Yes indeed," my master replied, "but no more so than your luminescent face, your genial qualities, and your graceful words," adding other such sweet pleasantries to his praise of His Excellency the bey.

After a lengthy discussion, the consul rose and asked permission 5.103 to depart, and it was granted. The bey had the dragoman tell my master to come back and visit him as long as he was in Tunis.

"With pleasure," my master replied. "It would be my great honor."

The bey ordered one of his finest horses to be kept ready for my master, which he could ride whenever he wanted to visit the palace.

My master thanked him warmly and we headed back to the consul's house in Tunis.

5.104 The next day, we went out to see the city in the company of one of the consul's servants. Its design and organization seemed to us to have no parallel. We toured its avenues and souks. The merchants sitting in their shops looked like princes, such was the elegance of their clothing, their graceful manner of conversation, and their habit of cordially greeting whoever approached them. Some insisted that we stop and join their company, putting themselves at our service and affably offering to help us with anything we needed. All in all, the people of Tunis seemed to us to be unlike those of any other town in the Maghreb.

During our time there, whenever someone would ask me about my master I'd tell them he was a doctor. News of the Frankish doctor spread throughout Tunis, and everywhere we went people began to seek us out for treatment. My master would offer treatments and prescribe medicines, and he cured many people of painful ailments.

5.105 We passed by a lodging reserved for prisoners of war. It was full of people, each occupied with a particular task, and there was a church where Capuchin monks held mass. In Tunis, there were three similar lodgings, each with a church and monks from the four monastic orders.[88] We visited these as well, and I found that the captives led very pleasant lives, unlike in other places. This was all thanks to the bey's clemency.

5.106 We were taken on visits to the homes of the notables, to treat those who were ill. And we toured other places as well, leaving no spot unvisited. The buildings, souks, and general layout of the city seemed to me like Aleppo, though Tunis is smaller. Every few days, we would go see His Excellency the bey. When we arrived, he would have sent people to bring us up to his pavilion, as he could see us coming from the moment we left the gates of the city.[89] My master would sit with him and they'd converse, while I translated for them.

One day, the bey asked my master if he was interested in jewels 5.107
and precious gems.

"Yes, absolutely," my master replied.

So he took us into the ancient royal treasury and presented some
of his finest gems and jewels. My master, knowledgeable about
gemstones, began to appraise these stones for the bey, pointing out
the rubies, emeralds, diamonds, and other gems. There were some
stones in the treasury with which the bey was unfamiliar, whose
names he didn't know. My master identified each one, along with its
properties and value. The bey was delighted with him and his expertise, and they remained in the treasury until the evening.

Eventually they emerged and went up to the pavilion. From the 5.108
window, the bey spied a priest walking out of the gates of the city.

"Go on," he told the prisoners of war who were standing before
him. "Receive your priest."

This particular priest would come to the bey's palace every Saturday night and sleep over with the prisoners who were in the bey's
service. The next day, with the bey's blessing, he would hold mass
for them, and the prisoners would spend all day with the priest,
returning to service Monday morning.

My master was astonished at the remarkable civility and clemency of the bey, which could scarcely be believed. That too was
my impression of this noble man. What a charming, dignified, and
decent ruler! My description does not do him justice, so I leave the
reader to infer the best description.

We sought the bey's leave, and returned home.

Another day, a merchant invited us to his house to see a sick man 5.109
who was staying with him. Off we went to the house, where the merchant received us most honorably. My master examined the invalid,
and the merchant had a fine breakfast prepared for us. We ate, and
drank coffee, and the merchant showed us around his palace. As
we passed an outdoor salon, we saw a cage with two small wild animals. My master scrutinized them, finding them most peculiar in

appearance, yet beautiful to look at. Their form was marvelous and bizarre; I might describe it as follows:

Each was the size of a small rabbit, with long hind legs like a crane's. The forepaws, which were beneath the jaw, were short; each resembled a human palm with five fingers, which they used to eat.[90] A long tail, like a lion's, stood high over the back, and two-thirds of it was covered in striped white and black plumage. They had the eyes of a gazelle, the snout of a pig, and the coat of a deer. All told, they combined the traits of four or five different wild animals!

5.110 My master was astonished by their strange appearance, and told the merchant that he'd never seen such a creature though he'd spent his life traveling all over the world. He implored the man to sell him the animals.

"These were sent to me by a friend living in Upper Egypt," the merchant said. "As a favor to you, I'd be happy to write to him and ask if he'd send me a few more. You can have them for free if I receive them from him; and if he doesn't have any more to send, I'll give you these."

"Are there many such animals to be found in that region?" my master asked him.

"Yes, but they're very difficult to catch. It's impossible to chase down these creatures; no person, not even a dog, bird, or horseman, can do so, as they're very nimble, swifter than birds. So, they use a particular ruse to hunt them. The hunters know where their dens are, and when the animals come out to graze, the hunter reaches into the den and blocks it up on the inside. When an animal returns to its burrow, the hunter thrusts his hand in and seizes it. That's how they catch them."[91]

The merchant promised he'd write to his friend and ask him to send a few of the animals. My master thanked him for this, and we returned home.

5.111 One day, two Jesuit priests arrived in Tunis and took up lodging in the consul's house. These monks would visit once a year to purchase prisoners of war, using alms collected from the Christians. One of them was a preacher skilled at giving sermons, and one day the consul begged him to preach a sermon that would stir people's souls.

"Gladly," the priest replied, "if you let me preach two hours a day for seven days." The consul agreed, for he was a Christian man who feared God and loved charity and good works.

The priest began the first sermon on a Monday after mass, two hours before noon. He went into the church and closed the door, the windows, and the skylight. He blew out the candles. We were engulfed in almost total darkness in the church. He made the sign of the cross upon his face and began his sermon by saying that it would exercise our intellects. We were to close our eyes and accompany him in spirit throughout all the parts of the sermon, following him to all the places he entered spiritually. 5.112

In the first part, he began by recounting how God created the world, the sun and moon, the stars, and the angels, and how He brought all the water into the seas, and created everything on the face of the Earth. The second part of the sermon addressed how God created Adam and Eve and put them in Paradise, and how Adam fell and was expelled from Paradise. He then moved on to the life of Our Lord Jesus Christ, and other stories from the holy books.

He next explained to us the four final stages of the human being: death, the final judgment, hellfire, and Paradise. With each one, we walked with him in spirit, until we descended together to Hell. At each station of Hell, he would ask the souls of those who were there what sins had damned them to this infernal place, mercilessly enslaved and cut off from all hope for eternity. 5.113

Later, we rose with him to the Kingdom of Heaven, where he asked the assembly of saints about their salvation. How did they come to enjoy this eternal bliss? The preacher continued in this way, stirring our souls with his words, and concluded his sermon here on the seventh day. We emerged from this retreat feeling giddy, dazed, and disoriented, as if in a trance.

One day, while I was kneeling in the church after mass in a state of contemplation, I fell into a similar kind of stupor and remained 5.114

insensible until lunchtime! When they came looking for me, they found me kneeling in the church, out cold. They had to wake me from my witless state.[92]

5.115   Anyway, at the conclusion of the preacher's sermon, each of us went to confession to receive the Holy Communion. It was around that time that my master became gravely ill. He was practically on the brink of death, and we'd lost hope of his recovery. That night, I lay down to sleep beside his bed, feeling a profound sorrow about his looming death. I plunged into the ocean of my own thoughts.

"What will happen to me after he dies?" I fretted. "Here I am, a stranger in a strange land, with no one to turn to, far from home."

After half the night had passed, I heard the sound of his cane rapping the board we'd placed beside his cushion so he could summon us if he needed anything, as his voice was too weak. When I heard him strike the board, I hurried over to see him.

5.116   He ordered me to fetch his doctor's trunk and place it beside his bed. I brought it over and put it on a chair in front of him. He told me to take his purse from under his pillow and find the key to the trunk. I did what he asked and opened the trunk.

Inside, I found a smaller chest made of ebony and plated with brass. It was closed, and seemed as though it were made of a single piece of wood, with no place to insert a key. My master showed me the mechanism that opened it: There was a rivet that looked like all the others on the chest. When I pressed it with my thumb, the chest popped open. Inside, I found yet another small chest, inside which was a crystal flask with a brass stopper.

5.117   My master told me to bring him a glass with two fingers' worth of wine in it, which I did.

"Turn the stopper in the mouth of the flask," he told me. I did as he said, and the mouth of the flask opened. Inside was another stopper, made of crystal and covered in light-brown wax. I took everything out of the trunk.

"Put your thumb over the mouth of the flask and measure out three drops of the liquid—just three!" he said. He told me to put everything away, close the trunk, and put the key back in his purse.

After I finished doing everything he asked, he took the glass from my hand and I held his head in my hands and helped him drink it. He rinsed the glass with a little more wine and drank that. He lay back down and fell asleep, and I went to my own bed and slept until morning.

The next day, he summoned me without rapping the cane. I got up hurriedly and came and stood before him.   5.118

"What do you need?" I asked.

"Bring me some clothes so I can get dressed," he said.

I brought him some clothes, and he sat up by himself in bed, without my help. I was astonished to see that he'd managed to sit up, and that his strength had returned! I began to strip off his clothes, which were soaked through with sweat. It took some effort to peel off his shirt. After I dressed him in fresh clothes, he took hold of my hand, got out of bed, and sat on the chair.

"What else would you like?" I asked.

"Change my blankets and flip the mattress over." They were soaked through with his sweat, which had seeped down as far as the third mattress.

I did as he asked, and he got back in bed and slept for two hours.   5.119 When he woke, he ordered me to bring him a bowl of broth. I went to the kitchen to fetch some broth, a napkin, and a spoon, and brought it all back to feed him. I found him walking around the room! My delight at this sight was mixed with astonishment. How had he managed to stand up after being on his deathbed the night before? I hadn't yet realized that those three drops he'd drunk were the reason for his recovery from that terrible illness. Later, he told me how he'd been cured by those three drops.

"But sir, why didn't you take them earlier?" I asked. "You could   5.120 have saved yourself all that pain and suffering, to say nothing of the rest of us!"

He laughed.

"I wouldn't have taken them had I not known that I was near death," he said. "I spent twenty-four years traveling around the world before I was fortunate enough to acquire a unique plant, the elixir that wards off all ailments and illnesses from human beings."

5.121 "I once came upon a story by a traveler," he continued, "which was recorded in a chronicle of the Monastery of Saint-François in Paris. On the feast day of that saint, the people who come to confess their sins and receive Holy Communion are granted indulgences. One day, while a priest sat in the confessional, a handsome young man bowed down before him and asked him to hear his confession.

"The priest made the sign of the cross over him and said, 'Confess, my son. How long has it been since your last confession?'

"'Sixty years, Father,' the young man replied. The priest was taken aback.

"'Think you're funny, do you?' he said. 'Don't you know that confession is no place for jesting or lying?'

"'Why would you say that, Father?' the young man said. 'Do you think I'm crazy enough to lie to you, or to God for that matter?'

5.122 "'Fair enough, my son,' the priest replied, 'but how can I believe that you haven't confessed in sixty years, when you can't be a day older than thirty? Run along and give your confession to someone else. I won't accept it unless you can prove your story is true.'

"'Come with me,' said the young man. 'Let's go up to the monastery and I'll tell you my whole story.'

"The priest agreed and the two of them went up to the monastery. The priest went into his cell and invited the young man in. Sitting there, alone together, the priest asked the young man to tell him the truth of the matter.

5.123 "'Father, I was born in this country, and embarked upon my travels when I was forty years old. I spent sixty years voyaging in faraway lands, searching for certain plants and drugs described in ancient texts. I found the herb that I was looking for, the elixir—which the books of Greek philosophers call *bīrū filūsūfa*, "the philosopher's stone." I composed a medical powder from this herb, and when I finished testing it, I found that its effect was just as the books described: If a man consumes just a bit of it, he's protected from all ailments and illnesses for ten years, his health remaining sound throughout, just as it was in his youth.

"'I began to take a single pill every ten years, and have remained 5.124 in the youthful state you see me in today. This is what led me astray. It made me forget about death and pay no heed to my soul's salvation. But now, God has shown mercy on me and touched my heart with His grace. I've awoken from that evil slumber, realizing that I will inevitably die, for God—whose name be praised—has ordained death upon every human being. Indeed, the philosophers who made use of this herb eventually perished. So I have returned to my country and seek to confess my sins and repent before I die.'

"When the priest heard the young man's words, he was amazed. 5.125

"'The elixir you mentioned,' the priest said. 'Is there any of it left?'

"'Yes,' the young man replied. 'In fact, I have some with me here.'

"'Would you give me a little to try, so I can see if you're telling the truth or not?'

"'Certainly,' the young man said, and brought out a silver box from his satchel, from which he took ten pills. He gave them to the priest.

"'If you take one every ten years, you'll live a hundred years past your present age,' he said.

"The priest took the pills from the young man, and heard his confession. He made him repent for his sins, absolving him and imposing a penitence upon him, then sent him away.

"For a while, the priest pondered how he might test the effect of 5.126 the pills. He recalled that in the monastery there was a decrepit old dog that didn't have the strength to walk. The monks would bring it a little bit of broth in a dish and it would drink without rising. The priest took a pill, dissolved it in a bit of broth, and put it before the dog, who lapped it up as usual. The priest then returned to his cell to read his breviary.

"After his prayers, the priest returned to see the dog, and found it running around the courtyard of the monastery, invigorated, its strength restored! Convinced the young man's story was true, he wrote down an account of the whole affair in a notebook.

5.127 "'If you don't believe me, go look at that decrepit dog,' he wrote in conclusion. 'See how its strength has returned!'

"The priest left the notebook on his desk and vanished without a trace.

"When the monks noticed his absence, they asked the abbot for permission to break open the lock of the priest's cell. They found the notebook on the desk, read it in amazement, and hurried off to see the dog, who was just as the priest had described.

"The news of this event spread rapidly through the city of Paris. People rushed to the monastery to see the dog, and the story was recorded in the monastery's chronicles."

If you don't believe me, consider this: My own master was over sixty years old, yet looked a man of thirty![93]

5.128 Let me get back to what I was saying earlier. My master recovered from his terrible illness, and his good health returned. We began touring the streets of the city as was our custom, and sometimes went to Bardo to visit the bey. We would stroll through his gardens and orchards, and His Excellency continued to honor my master and treat him affectionately. Eventually, the day came when my master decided to leave Tunis. He went to see the bey and bid him farewell, wishing him all the best.

5.129 We set out for our lodgings and, just before arriving at the consul's, happened upon the merchant who'd promised my master he'd send away for those wild animals we'd seen at his house. He greeted my master and gave him the good news: The animals had arrived, five in all! My master was delighted, and we went with the merchant to his house and found the creatures in a cage made of palm branches. My master tried to pay the man for the expenses of obtaining them but he wouldn't accept any money, and even told one of his servants to carry them to our house. My master thanked him and returned to the consul's home. When we got there, we found the servant waiting with the cage.

My master gave him a tip of about ten piasters, and sent him 5.130
away. He immediately sent off for a carpenter and explained that
he wanted a cage with separate compartments to keep the animals
apart. We put them in the cage and watched each disappear into
its own chamber. We gave them some almonds and hazelnuts and
other nuts to eat. In fact, they ate everything we gave them, other
than meat.

After they'd eaten, they'd sweep the floor of the cage with their
tails, expelling all their waste and refuse. Their appearance and
manner of eating and cleaning were striking. They would eat standing upright, picking up the nuts with their hands and putting them
in their mouths as humans do. Each would then disappear into its
chamber. We placed some pieces of raw wool in the cage, which
they would shred into lint, clean, and burrow under for warmth.
The lands they come from are very hot, and the merchant had
warned us not to let them get cold, and to give them pieces of wool
for warmth.

After we'd prepared the cage, my master put me in charge of it 5.131
and of the animals. He told me to guard it carefully and keep it out
of the cold, so the animals wouldn't die.

"If they're still alive when we get to Paris, you'll be glad to have
them," he told me. "They'll open doors for you that never open for
anyone." Hearing that, I suggested to him that we cover the cage
with a horsecloth, and we did.

A few days later, a small English ship came into the port of Tunis. 5.132
It was carrying wheat to sell in Livorno. When the consul heard about
the ship, he suggested that my master consider sailing aboard it.

"The English corsairs won't seize it. And if French corsairs do,
they won't harm you because you're a Frenchman and have connections to the sultan of France."

My master appreciated the wisdom of the consul's words, so we
booked passage with the English captain to go with him to Livorno.

After a few days, the captain gave us notice to send our baggage 5.133
to the port of Carthage, once famous for its vast size. It was ruined

when the sea level rose around it. When this region was seized from the Saracens, they built the city of Tunis, which is three or four miles from the harbor.[94]

We transported our luggage to the port. In the meantime, the consul had prepared ample provisions for us, including wine, chickens, a sheep, and other necessities for a sea journey.

CHAPTER SIX

OUR JOURNEY TO THE LANDS OF THE FRANKS IN THE YEAR 1708

We left Tunis at the beginning of June. We boarded the ship and set **6.1** sail the next day, making for the island of Corsica, which was ruled by Italy. The ship dropped anchor in the harbor, and the captain asked the locals if they'd heard anything about a French corsair in nearby waters.

"Yes," they replied. "There is indeed one cruising in the area," and they advised him not to set sail because the ship was large, with twenty cannons and two hundred armed men on board, not counting the sailors. So the captain decided to remain on the island until he received word that the pirates had left the area.

We spent the day in the harbor, chatting with the islanders aboard **6.2** our ship. Traveling with us were eight prisoners whose ransom had been paid by the Jesuit priests. One of them was an old Corsican man who'd been held prisoner for twenty years. He inquired after his wife and children, asking the local people whether they were still alive.

They were brought to him. When the man saw his wife and chil- **6.3** dren alive and well with his own eyes, he began to cry tears of joy. His wife and children also wept, and begged him to come down from the ship and go into quarantine, a place where travelers would remain for forty days, whether coming from the east or the west. After that period, they would be fumigated and allowed to enter the city.

But the old man didn't want to leave the ship.

"I just need to go to Livorno to take care of a few matters," he said. "I'll return home soon enough."

His family begged us to force him off the ship but he wouldn't listen to anyone. It was his misfortune to remain on board.

6.4 We spent the day in the harbor. At sunset, a favorable offshore breeze rose up. When the captain felt it, he said to himself, "There's sixty miles between me and Livorno. If I set sail now, we'll reach the harbor by morning and escape the corsair."

Putting this plan into action, he ordered the sailors to weigh anchor, unfurl the sails, and shove off. They did as he ordered, and the ship sailed with those favorable winds for thirty miles.

6.5 Then a dead calm settled over the sea and the winds died. The sails went limp, and the ship stood as still as though it were anchored in a harbor. In the face of this disaster, the captain was terrified. He told his men to pray, asking God Most High to send even a little bit of wind to help us cross the remaining distance. Alas, this was not what God had willed.

6.6 The ship remained motionless all night. At dawn, the captain ordered one of the sailors to climb to the top of the mast to see if he could spot any ships. The sailor mounted the mast, then descended, reporting that he'd spied something dark in the west—one of the mountains of Italy perhaps? The captain wasn't convinced, so he sent the first mate up the mast to investigate. Was it a mountain or a ship?

The first mate climbed to the top of the mast. In the meantime, morning had broken. He climbed down and told the captain he'd seen a large ship headed in our direction. What's more, they'd spotted us before we'd seen them!

The captain took the spyglass and trained it on the ship being   6.7
rowed swiftly toward us. It had thirty-six blades—that is, oars—
rowed by two hundred young men. Our captain was forced to put
our own six oars into the water, and begged the passengers to start
rowing! Then he turned the ship back toward the island we'd sailed
from the night before. We all started working together, rowing to
escape the other ship while they too threw themselves into their
pursuit of us.

After a short while, the other ship drew close, and our captain   6.8
ordered the sailors to drop the ship's rowboat into the water. They
tied it to the bow of the ship, and the first mate jumped in along with
four sailors to row ahead, helping to pull the ship along.

But the captain actually had a different plan in mind. He had four
trunks of coral, which he'd bought from locales where it's harvested
from the sea. Coral grows on the seafloor, just like trees planted in
sand. He also had a quantity of gold *riyāl* coins. While we were busy
trying to escape, he put the four trunks of coral and the coins into
the rowboat without anyone noticing.

After a short while, the corsair drew up alongside us and fired   6.9
a cannon. The cannonball flew just over the mast. We kept up our
efforts to escape, refusing to surrender, so the pirates fired a second
cannon. This time, the cannonball passed overhead at half the
height of the mast. Still we wouldn't surrender, and the captain was
urging us to make good our escape. Then they fired a third cannon,
and the cannonball passed right over our heads. At the sound of
it, we all hit the deck in terror. Had it struck its target, none of us
would have been spared!

We got to our feet and shouted at the captain, and forced him to
surrender. A few of us hurried to lower our flag, which was the sign
to cease fire. As soon as the flag came down, the corsairs called out
with their bullhorn:

"*Maina* to France, *maina*!" which means: "Surrender to France,
surrender!"[95]

6.10   We lowered the sails. Meanwhile, the first mate—who was in the rowboat, as I mentioned—saw that the captain had surrendered. There was no longer any hope of being saved, so he cut the rope tying the rowboat to the ship, and fled in the direction of Corsica. God would see to his safe return.

As for the corsair, it paid no mind to the rowboat. Instead, it lowered its own large rowboat into the water and fifty armed men jumped in to come over and seize our ship.

6.11   I stood watching from the side of the ship. Beside me was that Corsican prisoner I mentioned earlier, who saw his family after twenty years and refused to leave the ship and join them. In his hand was a waist purse stuffed with money. He was about to throw it into the sea, but I snatched it from his hand.

"Why do you want to throw it away?" I asked.

"Let me do it!" he pleaded. "I'd rather throw it away than let these people steal what I've toiled for the past twenty years!"

"Why don't you leave it with me?" I said. "Perhaps God Almighty will keep it from falling into their hands."

I went and placed it inside a sack that contained a pot, a frying pan, some plates and spoons, and other cooking supplies we'd brought with us.

6.12   Meanwhile, the other prisoners gave my master their own traveling sacks to place in his trunk, as they knew he was a Frenchman; the corsairs surely wouldn't rob him. When the rowboat arrived at our ship, the corsairs boarded and pounced on us like rapacious wolves! They brought us down into their dinghy, and the armed men who had come over stayed aboard our vessel while the sailors took us to the pirate ship.

As soon as we'd climbed aboard, my master spotted the pirate captain, and recognized him! His name was Capitaine Brémond, and he also recognized my master. They embraced and exchanged affectionate greetings.

6.13   "Where have you come from, and why are you traveling with this ship?" the captain asked.

"I was in Tunis, and the consul advised I sail with it," my master replied. "He was afraid that the English privateers would rob me."

"You did just the right thing," the corsair captain replied. "Let me have your bags brought over to my ship so nothing is lost."

My master thanked him and ordered me to return to the ship, gather our things, and load them into the dinghy.

The captain told the sailors to fetch our things along with those of the prisoners, and not to leave anything behind. They did as he ordered. We went to the ship and our baggage was brought down first, then the prisoners' baggage. When we returned to the pirate ship, all the bags were brought on board and put in the captain's chambers. Then they brought the other ship's sailors over and confined them in the hold.   6.14

The corsair continued to cruise the area until the next day. It was the second Thursday after the Feast of Corpus Christi, so the priest on board held a mass for us. Following the mass, we had breakfast, and the captain gave the order to have our luggage placed before him along with the prisoners' bags.   6.15

He opened the prisoners' trunks and baskets and made a list of their contents. When they brought our bags to him, he began to take whatever he wanted! We had a four-shot rifle with a single hammer, and a pair of pistols, each also with four shots and a single hammer. There was a two-shot rifle with a single hammer, a very valuable old damascened sword, a dagger, an expensive Frankish rapier, and other weapons too. The pirate took everything.

Then he opened my bags and took what he wished, including my turban with the gold stitching on its borders!   6.16

"You won't need a turban in the Frankish lands," he sneered.

Fishing through my master's trunk, he found some sacks full of silver coins and a packet of Tunisian fezzes. He deduced from the sacks and the fezzes that they belonged to the prisoners, and took them as well. My master was enraged. He drew himself up before the corsair captain.

"Are you going to strip me of all my luggage? Perhaps you're not aware that I've been sent on this voyage by the sultan of France!" he said, taking out his royal edict of appointment, which recommended him to all the French consuls residing in the eastern lands.

"On my ship, I am sultan!" the pirate replied. "And seeing as how I found you aboard an enemy ship, why shouldn't I rob you? Go soak your edict and suck on it."[96]

6.17   The other captain and the officers from our ship testified to the truth of what my master said, but the corsair captain paid no mind, seizing everything. So my master let him do as he wished, biding his time until the ship reached Livorno.

Early the next day, we entered Livorno's harbor and dropped anchor. A little while later, the rowboat that had fled the corsair Brémond—with the trunks of coral and *riyāl*s—arrived at the harbor. Brémond got word that it had managed to escape with the most valuable merchandise on the ship! When the corsair saw it, he was furious, but what could he do? The bird had flown the coop.

6.18   The corsair captain gave an order to have the English captain and his people put into the rowboat and taken to the quarantine house. The rowboat dropped them off and returned to the ship. Then the corsair brought out our things—besides what he had taken for himself—and had them loaded into the rowboat. My master and I got in, and off we went to the quarantine house, where we were given a room. The place was open to the elements and surrounded by a wide canal filled with seawater, like an island.

6.19   We spent the day there. Early the next morning, my master wrote a letter and sent it to the French consul in Livorno, who served as an ambassador, representing the sultan of France. When the letter arrived, the consul made some inquiries about the identity of its sender.

"Who is this fellow?" he asked the people in his palace. But the corsair captain had already spoken to the consul's entourage, telling them that my master was one of those people who traveled around the world, pretending to be someone they weren't.

"If he complains to His Honor the consul, don't listen to him," the captain said. "He's a liar with a counterfeit edict from the king."

They told the consul what they'd heard from the captain and he believed them, so didn't bother responding to the letter. Meanwhile, my master waited patiently all day for the consul's reply, which didn't come. The next day, he wrote to him again, and again the consul paid the letter no mind. Another day passed without a response.

I spent the day strolling about near our lodgings. As I walked, I spotted, some distance away, the prisoner whose waist purse I had snatched while on the ship! He was also out for a stroll. Reminded of the waist purse, I went to rummage through the sack in which I'd placed it. There it was, where I'd left it, between the pot and the plates. I took it out of the sack and went outside again, waving at the man and calling out to him. When he approached me and saw the purse, he sank to the ground in happiness, unable to stand back up. 6.20

I walked over to him and clasped his hand to help him up, and he rose, kissing my hand and thanking me. 6.21

"Brother, you should thank God Most High, who kept the pirates from spotting your purse," I said. "Did you see how they searched our luggage, including the sack where it was hidden? Somehow they didn't see this! God showed mercy on your family."

The man began to open the purse to give me some of what was in it, but I refused to take anything from him, and sent him on his way.

The day passed and still no response arrived for my master, who was now furious. 6.22

"Just you wait," he said. "You'll see what happens to that captain and his crew tomorrow."

On the morning of the third day, my master wrote another letter to the consul, issuing him a direct order on behalf of the king of France to come to the quarantine house and hear his complaint about Capitaine Brémond. He included some royal formulas in his letter to prove to the consul that he was indeed an envoy of the king.

Less than an hour had passed when I saw a large gathering of people emerging from the city gates. It was the consul in his carriage, 6.23

accompanied by his entourage and all the French merchants. They entered the lazaretto, crossing the canal.[97] The captain of the lazaretto came out to meet the consul, welcoming him and bringing out chairs for him and his company of merchants. They sat down while their servants stood before them, their hats removed in deference.

His Honor the consul then ordered the captain to summon *khawājah* Paul Lucas, the Frenchman, who was presently in the lazaretto. The captain, in turn, ordered the man responsible for guarding those who'd come from Capitaine Brémond's ship to summon *khawājah* Paul Lucas to appear before His Honor the consul.

6.24 The guard came to see us and issued the invitation. My master rose, put on his fur pelt, and brought along his royal edict.

"Follow me," he said.

We walked out together to meet the consul.

When he appeared before the consul, the first thing he said was, "My lord, I hope this visit does not represent an onerous imposition. It would have sufficed for you to send your lowliest servant to attend to my suit against Capitaine Brémond. But since it also now concerns His Majesty the king, God preserve him, you must adjudicate it yourself and inform His Majesty of your decision."

"What is the nature of your suit, and your charge against Capitaine Brémond?" the consul asked.

6.25 "In the first place, he robbed me of my property, even though he recognized that I was a Frenchman," my master replied. "When I told him that I was an envoy of the sultan of France and that I had a royal edict of appointment, he said to me, 'On my ship, I'm the sultan, and I don't recognize your letter. Go soak it and suck on it!'" My master added, "The ship's officers are my witnesses."

He took the edict from his cloak and held it out to the consul, who ordered it to be brought over to him so that he could read it. His men held out toward my master a length of cane with a slit in its end. They pulled the edict out through the slit and fumigated it before giving it to the consul.

Upon reading the edict, the consul bounded up from his chair, 6.26 removed his hat, and began apologizing to my master.

"Please forgive me!" he cried. "They told me you were someone else!"

He ordered his attendants to go to the harbor immediately and to bring the captain and his company to the lazaretto. Shortly thereafter, the captain and his men arrived and presented themselves before the consul, who asked the captain if he'd indeed said what Paul Lucas claimed. The captain denied it.

My master turned to the witnesses, who couldn't deny what he'd 6.27 said. After all, this had all transpired in the presence of those on board. They reported what the captain had said, word for word, and once their testimony had been verified, the consul ordered that the captain be imprisoned in the lazaretto, and sent the crew back to their ship. The trial was set for the next day. The consul then bid my master farewell and went off to his house. We too went to our lodgings.

The following day, the consul returned with his attendants and the merchants, as he had the previous day, and they established a tribunal. The consul summoned Capitaine Brémond, and issued an order to have all of my master's things brought from the ship to the lazaretto. The luggage was brought over, and the consul invited my master to come forward and recover the property the captain had seized from him on the ship.

When my master appeared before the consul and the assembly, everyone got to their feet.

"Is it all there?" the consul asked. "Look and see."

My master instructed me to take delivery of our property. I went 6.28 through every last object, one by one. When I was finished, he spoke up again.

"I'm missing four pouches of money and a red pouch with two hundred and twenty antique coins," my master said. "There's also a silver ring with a seal of Solomon, and six dozen Tunisian fezzes."[98]

The consul ordered the captain to go to the ship and bring the pouches he'd taken from my master's trunk, as well as the fezzes. The captain argued that the pouches didn't belong to my master, but rather to the captives.

"Did you find them in the captives' baggage?" the consul asked.

"I saw them in Paul Lucas's trunk," the captain replied.

"So how could you know who they belonged to?" the consul scolded him. "Didn't you take them from this man's trunk? Go get them and bring them here at once!"

6.29   The captain went to his ship and brought the pouches of money and the hats, but not the pouch of antique coins. My master demanded the last pouch.

"This is all I took from your trunk," the captain said. "I saw only these pouches."

My master turned to the consul.

"The pouch with the antique coins was registered in the chancery of Tunis, and was specifically acquired for His Majesty the king," he said. "In all my travels, I never saw the like of those coins. I'd allow Capitaine Brémond to take all of my things if he only returned that pouch to me."

6.30   This was a trick by my master meant to vex the captain! The pouch he'd described was real enough, and did in fact contain a ring, but the coins had been left with the consul of Tunis along with other things we'd brought with us from the tour in the East. This was my master's regular practice in every city with a French consul: He'd entrust to his care all of the coins, books, engraved stones, precious gems, and other such things, registering them with the chancery. The consul would issue him a receipt and send everything to Marseille, where my master would pick them up and take them on to Paris.

6.31   On hearing my master's offer, the consul was convinced that there was a pouch after all. He ordered the captain to return to the ship and search for it.

"I beg you, sir," the captain implored. "Send some of your men with me and tell them to search the ship from top to bottom. They might find that pouch, but I've never laid eyes on it or heard of it!"

The consul kindly asked my master to go to the ship, sending the chancellor with him along with two of his attendants to search the captain's chamber and trunk, as well as the trunks of everyone else on the ship, in hopes of finding the pouch.

Off they went to the ship, and upon searching the captain's 6.32 chamber, they found the pouch with the ring. All then returned to the consul with the sack in hand.

"The pouch has been found," the consul cried, turning to the captain. "Now, where have you hidden the coins meant for the sultan of France? Or do you deny seeing them too?"

The captain began pleading and swearing on his life that he had no knowledge of the coins, nor any idea of their whereabouts. The consul was stymied, and felt at a loss about how to proceed.

The merchants advised him to summon the company of the 6.33 pirate ship and question them. Might that, perhaps, shed light on the coins? On their advice, the consul summoned all who had been on board, including the seamen. When they assembled before him, the consul asked them one by one if they had any knowledge of the coins. All denied it. Furious, the consul ordered that they be imprisoned, and threatened to torture all who had had access to the captain's cabin if they didn't produce the coins! Threatened with imprisonment, the sailors began to talk among themselves.

"None of us have done anything wrong!" they said to each other. "It's all the fault of the sentinel," meaning the man in charge of guarding the captain's chamber and the gunpowder storeroom. "He used to let his friends pilfer the prisoners' belongings."

When the consul's men heard what the sailors were saying, 6.34 they reported it to the consul, who brought the sailors before him and asked them to explain themselves. They told him what must have happened: It was surely the captain's guard who had acted treacherously. So the consul summoned the guard and asked him if he'd stolen anything from the captain's chambers. The guard denied it, swearing that he hadn't taken anything. But the sailors testified against him, and the consul sentenced him to hang if he didn't produce the coins. The man was seized, bound, and marched to the gallows.

6.35 Realizing that it was now a matter of life and death, my master began to fear that his stratagem would drive the consul to execute an innocent man.

"Let's not rush to judgment," he said to the consul. "Leave this man in prison until we can question the rest of the ship's company. Perhaps they know something. In the end you'll do as you see fit."

Afraid that he'd provoke a complaint and a rebuke from the minister, the consul kept the man in custody, and had everyone else sent to prison as well. Then he called for the harbormaster, telling him to remove the ship's rudder, sequester the vessel, and await further instructions. He also took the pouch and sealed it in everyone's presence, telling my master that he would send the pouch and the trial proceedings to the minister, and then do whatever the minister ordered. Meanwhile, the ship's passengers and the captain were to remain in the lazaretto.

6.36 The consul, his attendants, and the merchants left. We too returned to our lodgings, and the trial was concluded. We stayed at the lazaretto until the end of the twenty-day quarantine. The chief doctor came to the lazaretto and summoned all of us before him. He examined us each individually to make sure that none of us was afflicted with any disease. After scrutinizing us, he told each of us to strike our armpits and groin with our hands.[99] Then they fumigated us and let us go.

6.37 We went into the city. After we passed through the gates, the governor's men appeared and searched through our things to make sure we had no tobacco, salt, or arak, for those things were assessed import duties. Anyone caught smuggling them would be sent to do hard labor in the galleys, and have his tobacco confiscated.

I had forty packs of good strong tobacco with me from Tunis. The night before, I'd learned that anyone who smuggled tobacco would be sent to the galleys, and that those who declared it would have to pay a tax of four piasters on each Aleppan *raṭl*. They'd instituted this practice to prevent people from bringing in tobacco from elsewhere; instead, the government would import it from other countries, to benefit the treasury. They'd pay just one piaster for three or four *raṭl*s, and sell each *raṭl* for four piasters. The same went for salt.

When I heard about this, I didn't know what to do! I began to   6.38
think of a way to smuggle the tobacco without worrying about the dangers involved. I slit open the mattress we had brought with us, ripped out the wool inside, and began stuffing the packs of tobacco into the mattress, placing wool above and below the packs. Then I sewed up the mattress and reattached the buttons. There were five packs of tobacco left. I couldn't bring myself to give them to the guard who was in our service at that time. Then an idea came to me. I opened our trunk with the bottles of wine in it, and took the bottles out as well as the lint padding at the bottom. I took the packs of tobacco, put them under the padding, and replaced the bottles. Then I locked the trunk.

The governor's men approached to search our things. The mat-   6.39
tress was wrapped in a carpet and tied up with a rope. They untied it and removed the carpet, finding the mattress and a small pillow inside, but nothing else. So they left it alone.

"Open this trunk," they said to me.

I did as they asked. Inside were the bottles of wine, which they left alone as well. They searched the rest of our baggage and purses, but didn't find a thing, so they permitted us to pick up our belongings and go. We handed our bags over to some porters and made our way to the home of a Frenchman who had married in Livorno, and who was a friend of my master's.

He welcomed us warmly when he arrived at his house and   6.40
told his servants to take our things upstairs. For my master, they

prepared a room with a fine bed, chairs, and furnishings of the sort found in luxurious quarters. They gave me my own room and put the luggage there as well.

The man's wife came and welcomed us and congratulated my master on his safe arrival in Christian lands. The greetings out of the way, my master went up to change out of his traveling clothes and put on something that wasn't the clothing of my country. A barber showed up to give my master a shave, and my master told him to shave me as well.

6.41 I sat in the chair and he washed my face and beard. Then he took the razor and ran it over my beard, and in so doing took off half my mustache. When I realized what he'd done, I shouted out, and he got a fright.

"What's the matter?" the barber cried in confusion. "I didn't cut you!"

"If only you'd cut me instead of shaving off my mustache!" I replied. "Don't you know that we men from the East don't shave our mustaches as you do?"

I reluctantly allowed him to shave off the second half. In that country, every man shaved his beard and mustache, even the priests, except the Capuchins.

6.42 We spent the rest of the day at the man's home and were treated most hospitably. Some of the merchants came by to see my master and congratulate him on his safe return. They begged him to forgive Capitaine Brémond, and to prevent the suit from reaching the minister's desk.

"It's out of my hands," my master told them. "I filed my suit against him in your presence, and in the presence of the consul. Now it's up to the minister. There's nothing anyone here can do about it, so there's no need to get involved."

For three days, the merchants continued to come by and plead with him. Finally, after the third day and much strenuous supplication, he promised them that he'd pardon the captain. They thanked him for his benevolence and went to tell the consul that *khawājah*

Paul Lucas had pardoned the captain, asking him to notify the minister.

The consul made preparations for a banquet and sent his steward 6.43
to invite my master to his house the following day for lunch. My
master accepted, and the following day the consul dispatched his
steward again to accompany my master to the palace. They greeted
each other and the consul asked my master if he'd consented to have
the captain and his crew released from prison.

"For your own sake and the sake of the merchants, I'll bear the
brunt of this matter myself," my master replied. "Let them go."

The consul thanked him for his benevolence and immediately 6.44
sent for the captain and his crew.

"You must thank this *khawājah*," he ordered the captain, "for had
he not pardoned you, you'd have stayed in prison along with your
gang until I received a response from His Excellency the minister,
ordering me to send you to him—or to have your ship and property
impounded in order to make an example of you! Instead of honor-
ing the king's letter and its bearer, you treated them both with contempt; a contempt that extends to the source of the letter, meaning
of course His Majesty the king!"

The captain threw himself before my master in gratitude. Then
he kissed him and begged for forgiveness, and they were reconciled.
Sitting at the table together, they drank happily to each other's
health, and went their separate ways.

The following day, I went out to stroll the streets of the city. I 6.45
was utterly stupefied, never having encountered such sights before.
It was the first city I'd visited in Christian lands. I saw women in
shops, selling and buying goods as though they were men. They
strolled down the streets with their faces unveiled. I felt as though
I were dreaming.

As I was walking down one street, someone suddenly called out
to me in Arabic. I turned around and saw a man in a coffeehouse. I
walked over to him.[100]

"Ho there, countryman!" he said. "Come inside and give me a whiff of home!"

6.46 I obliged, and the fellow continued to greet me with salutations in Arabic, which I returned.

"Who might you be, brother?" I asked. "Which country are you from?"

"I'm from Aleppo," he responded. "A Maronite."

"I'm from Aleppo too!"

We embraced and shook hands, and he invited me to sit with him. He treated me as an honored guest, served me some coffee, and brought me a pipe to smoke. We chatted away. We soon became fast friends and I'd visit him every day to quiz him about the country's customs and to learn about their ways.

6.47 One day, I was out for a stroll by the seaside and came upon a man wearing my native dress. He stopped and asked me where I was from.

"I'm from Aleppo," I said, and he greeted me with great warmth and affection.

"Have we met?" I asked.

"To be honest, I have no idea who you are, but I like the look of anyone from my part of the world," he said. "Let's walk together, brother, and I'll tell you about my troubles."

6.48 "I'm from Damascus myself," he continued. "I'm a churchgoing Syriac Catholic. Heretic Syriacs persecuted me and stole half of my property. Once I realized I couldn't stay in Damascus any longer, I came up with a plan. I paid off my debts and collected all the money that was owed to me, without anyone suspecting anything. I left my donkey and my house with one of my relatives to take care of, and pretended I was taking my family on a pilgrimage to Jerusalem. With my wife and three children—two girls and a boy—I set off in the company of some other pilgrims and made the pilgrimage. Then I returned by ship to Sidon.

6.49 "I stayed in Sidon for a few days, waiting for a ship bound for Christian lands. My plan, you see, was to take my family to Rome.

Soon enough, a French ship bound for Izmir appeared in Sidon harbor. 'You should take that ship and buy some goods in Izmir,' I told myself, as I had a certain sum of money with me—'goods that people in Christendom will want to buy,' so I made up my mind to travel with that ship.

"We arrived in Izmir after a few days, and I started looking into what sort of merchandise would sell well in Frankish lands. An honest man advised me to deal in Persian products, like Isfahani printed textiles, rhubarb, wormseed, and other commodities from that part of the world.

"After completing my purchases, I bought a few expensive Per-　6.50
sian carpets made in Khorasan, as well as a few *qinṭārs* of beeswax to bring to Rome, for the churches. The total value of all the goods was more than five thousand piasters. I had a thousand Venetian gold piasters left over for travel expenses.

"I stayed in Izmir for a few days until a ship was ready to sail to Marseille. It was a large vessel loaded with the merchandise of Izmir's traders. I paid for passage and brought aboard all the goods I'd bought. A few days later we set sail for the port of Marseille.

"When we neared the island of Malta, the captain saw a ship in　6.51
the distance. He feared that English pirates might have entered the port. We remained anchored in place for ten days for fear of the pirates. Finally, the captain received word that their ship had sailed east and that the sea was free of pirates, and he decided to sail on. We left Malta by night with a favorable wind. But when morning broke, we saw before us a warship with forty cannons! Ours was equipped with only twenty.

"The two ships made ready for battle and began to fire their can-　6.52
nons! I took my family down to the ship's hold. We were absolutely terrified—especially my wife and children. Can you imagine? A man's wife caught in a battle like that! We lost all hope. The mother began to cry over her children and the children cried over their mother. And I was near senseless with fright.

"When the captain of the other ship saw that we weren't going to surrender, he began to fire upon us directly. Many on board were killed or injured. One of our masts shattered and was completely ruined. Our captain could no longer put up any sort of resistance to the bombardment, so we surrendered to the warship.

6.53   "They seized us and brought us here, to Livorno. We were marched off the ship and taken to the lazaretto and our property was confiscated. Everything, that is, except for my wife's trunk, which they didn't touch because it belonged to a woman. Mercifully, they returned it to her. Inside the trunk was her purse, containing the sum of a hundred piasters, and her jewelry, which was worth five hundred piasters. That was all the money we had to live on, so I put the children to work in different trades.

"My wife, though, hasn't left the house for the past three months. She can't bear to go out without a wrap or a veil,[101] and I've given up trying to persuade her. Could I prevail upon you to speak to her, seeing as how you're one of our countrymen? If she hears it from you, maybe she'll put aside her funny ideas and come out of the house for some fresh air."

6.54   "I'd be happy to," I replied. "I'll come by whenever you like."

"Tomorrow is Sunday," he said. "I'll wait for you at the church and we can go to my house. Perhaps she'll come with us for a walk outside the city."

We agreed on the plan, and the next day, after attending mass, we went to his house. Once inside, I saw that his wife had hidden herself behind a curtain. I greeted her and she responded from behind the curtain, refusing to come out while I was there.

"What's all this foolishness?" I demanded. "Come out and see for yourself! All the women walk around without veils, and no one cares. This is a Christian country, and no one can make you wear one."[102]

6.55   Even after a lot of back and forth, she still refused to go out without a veil. So I asked her if she had a *khimār* instead.[103]

"Yes," she replied.

"Put it on and come out with us."

She agreed, and took out a fine dress and an embroidered *khimār* from her trunk. She put the dress on, wore the *khimār* covering, and joined us and her children for a walk outside the city gates.

At that hour, there were plenty of men and women heading out 6.56 for a stroll outside the city. When they spotted this woman all covered up, every last one of them came up to us, craning their neck to catch a glimpse of her face, and asking us why she was covered. We were at a loss as to how to respond—especially to the women! The crowd of men and women that gathered around us grew so large that we couldn't stay on that path any longer. We had to veer off and take refuge in a hillside cave near the sea.

Once we were safely in the cave and out of sight, I turned to the 6.57 woman.

"If you want me to keep walking with you, then take that veil off your head!" I said. "Dress like other women do, and no one will glance twice at you."

She refused. So, faced with her stubborn determination, I left them and returned to the city. I don't know what became of them. It became clear to me, from this experience, that women from back home could never learn to behave as women do in this country, as they've been raised never to show themselves to strangers.

One day, while I was visiting with my friend, the Aleppan coffee 6.58 man, a young fellow came in. He was tall and handsome, clearly prosperous, but modest and humble nonetheless. After having some coffee, he went on his way. I took a strong liking to the young man, drawn as I was to his fine appearance and good manners. I asked the coffee man who he was.

"He's the Dead Woman's Son, and his story is a strange one," he replied, and began to recount it to me.

"The boy's father was a merchant, and a wealthy one at that. He 6.59 married the daughter of another merchant, and gave her a diamond wedding ring worth five hundred piasters. According to the marriage traditions in these parts, the husband and wife exchange rings.

After the wedding ceremony, the woman moved into her new husband's house along with a group of her relatives. There she lived, and with each passing day she began to grow plump, until eventually she'd become enormously rotund.

"One day, the man looked at his wife's hand and saw she'd grown so fat that her ring had sunk deeply into the flesh of her finger. He tried to remove the ring so that it wouldn't hurt her, but was unable to pry it loose.

6.60   "He sent for a jeweler and ordered him to break the ring and take it off her finger. When the wife learned that the jeweler had arrived to break the ring, she wouldn't consent! Instead, she went to her husband and begged him not to allow the jeweler to break the ring, insisting that it didn't bother her and that she was very happy with it.

"'But I've told the jeweler to refashion it for you after he takes it off,' her husband explained.

"'If you love me, leave the ring on my finger,' she said, 'even if I die wearing it.'

"Her husband loved her very much and didn't want to go against her wishes, so he sent the jeweler away, and the ring remained on her finger for a good long while.

6.61   "One day, while she was seated, she suddenly lost consciousness and was dead within two hours. There had been many sudden deaths of that kind in the country in those days. Once her death was confirmed, they held a funeral service, and removed her clothes. But they couldn't pull the ring off her finger. They consulted her husband about whether to cut her finger off. He remembered her words—'Don't take this ring off my finger, even if I die wearing it'— so he forbade them to remove it: 'Leave it on her hand.'

"In the end they draped her in a burial shroud and put her into a casket. Then they placed it in a mortuary house, as was their custom, and left.

6.62   "Now, one of the people who'd attended the woman's shrouding noticed that the ring had remained on her hand. So he spent that night hiding in a thicket within the cemetery. At midnight, he opened the door of the mortuary house and went inside. The man had brought along a candle, a flint, and some matches. He lit the candle, placed it upright on the ground, and removed the lid of the coffin. He reached under the shroud and pulled out her right hand, which had the ring. Knowing in advance that the ring wouldn't just slide off, he pulled out a knife and started to cut off the finger with the ring.

"As soon as the blood began gushing out, the dead woman regained consciousness!

"'Where am I?' she screamed.

"When the man heard her, he was terror-struck. What if she recognized him? So he left the candle and knife behind and fled.

"The woman came to her senses and realized she was in a coffin, 6.63 shrouded, and lying among the dead in a mortuary house. She began to howl and wail, and woke the sacristan of the church with her screams. He rushed over to the mortuary house to find out who was making all the noise. The door was open and there was a lit candle inside! Baffled at this and at the sounds that were coming from the corpses below, he ran off to wake the abbot and the monks, and told them what he'd seen and heard.

"Everyone rushed to see what was happening in that place. It was 6.64 just as the sacristan had described. Terrified by the dreadful scene, they began to urge one another to go down into the mortuary house to find out what was going on. The only one courageous enough was the sacristan.

"'Pray for me, Father,' he said to the abbot. 'I'll go down.'

"The abbot blessed him. After securing him with a rope, they lowered him into the pit. When he reached the bottom, he saw the lit candle beside the coffin that held the woman who'd risen from the dead. She was still weeping and wailing.

"He approached the coffin, shaking with fear. Steeling himself, 6.65 he cried out, 'Who are you, O dead body?'

"The woman identified herself and repeated her plea. 'For God's sake, help me out of here! If you don't, I'll die!'

"The monk went over to her and pulled her out of the coffin. The blood was streaming from her hand and there was a knife beside the coffin. He was astonished by this, and unable to comprehend what had happened to the woman.

6.66   "When she was finally brought out of the mortuary house and the people got a good look at her, they recognized her as the woman they'd buried the day before.

"'Who cut your hand?'

"'All I remember,' she said, 'is waking up and finding myself in a coffin, bleeding from this cut on my hand!'

"Upon examining her hand, they determined that one of her fingers was half cut off and that the ring was still attached to her little finger. That's when they realized she hadn't, in fact, died at all. Instead, her heart had been congested with blood, which made her lose consciousness. Then, when her finger was cut, the blood began flowing again and she woke up. The ring was what had saved her!

"They sent word to her husband and her relatives, who came and took her home, now the very picture of health. Following this calamity, the woman went on to have three children—two boys and a girl.

"The young man you just saw here was one of the three," the coffee man said.[104]

6.67   Another day, as I was strolling through the streets of the city, I saw a troop of soldiers marching by, as though preparing to set off on a journey. Each soldier was carrying a full complement of weapons. The soldiers were organized into companies, each marching to the sound of its own fife and drum, and led by its own captain.

"Who are these soldiers?" I asked someone.

He explained that at the beginning of each month, the troops would gather in a certain square. It was a large, open space, used for the purpose of drilling soldiers for war. I headed to the square and joined a group of others at an elevated spot. I saw, at one end of the square, an impressive-looking man splendidly dressed, and seated upon a dais. He was the commander-in-chief.

Each company passed before the commander. Whenever he 6.68
saw a soldier carrying a piece of equipment that wasn't clean, or if
anything was missing, the commander would order that the man be
given a hundred lashes on his buttocks, as an example to the others.
After the companies passed inspection, they lined up in formation,
one after the other. They marched in unison, without a single foot
out of place! Twelve ranks formed, the first company of six separated slightly from the second. The drums of the six forward companies began to beat, and the rhythm indicated that the troops were
to raise their muskets high with their right hands.

Then the beat changed, signaling that they were to raise their 6.69
muskets and tuck them against their shoulders, as though aiming
at a target. They moved as one, holding their weapons in precisely
the same way. Their feet, too, were perfectly aligned, not deviat-
ing in their symmetry by a hair's breadth. The rhythm of the drums
changed, and the soldiers turned to the right. It changed again, and
they swung to the left. Then they took up their original stance, with
their muskets aimed and ready to fire. Finally, the trumpet blew and
all of the drums beat, which was the signal that they were to unload
their muskets, which they did in the highly organized fashion I've
described.

The beat changed again and the company commanders cried 6.70
out. Suddenly, the rear companies marched straight ahead, moving
between the ranks of the forward companies. In an instant, they had
switched places, and the second group performed the same actions
as the first. Meanwhile, the first group knelt to load their muskets as
the other group discharged theirs.

Alas, words don't do justice to this display: I simply can't explain
or give an accurate account of the maneuvers I saw during that drill!
Nothing like it exists in the East; it's simply unheard of.

Another day, I saw the soldiers marching down the same street, 6.71
so I followed them to the square. They lined up all around it. In the
middle was a man on his knees with his hands shackled in front of
him, holding his hat. The executioner stood by, in possession of a

document that registered the charges against the man. When the companies finished lining up, the executioner began reading out the register. The man had deceived his commanding officer and had fled, and so deserved to be hanged.

6.72 Following some appeals for mercy, however, his sentence had been commuted to three years of labor in the galleys. And so that all would know that he was a traitor, the law ordered that he should have his nostrils slashed, and his forehead and temples branded with the king's seal. After he finished reading the register, the executioner slashed the man's nose and branded him with a burning iron. Then all the soldiers passed before him and offered their sympathy before he was handed over to the captain of the galley. They then all dispersed and went their own way.

6.73 Another day, I climbed up to the citadel with a friend, who served as one of its caretakers. He showed me the various parts of the building one by one. We saw cannons that had been polished so they shone like mirrors. There was a sheet of lead covering each cannon's touchhole, which was tied fast and covered with a seal.[105] Each cannon's carriage moved so swiftly on its wheels that a small child could have easily pulled it along.

6.74 My friend then took me down to the arsenal, which consisted of four rooms in a cruciform arrangement. Each room contained a different type of weapon. These were arranged along two sides of the room and placed on thin wooden hooks, lining the walls from floor to ceiling. There were muskets, pistols, double-edged swords, rapiers, bayonets, and other types of weapon. In one of the rooms, there was steel-plate armor, chainmail, steel helmets, and steel shields. I even saw steel-plate armor made specifically for women, with space for their breasts. It is reported that in ancient times, in the days of idol worship, women used to fight in battle.

In the arsenal, I saw twelve men at work, polishing the weapons with oil so that they wouldn't rust. When they finished with one set, they'd begin another, continuing in this way until they finished polishing them all. Then they'd go back to the first room and start all over again. These twelve men had all they needed in that place, which was where they lived. When one died, he was replaced with someone else.

I thought back to the citadel of Aleppo, which has no equal in the whole world. But its cannons are buried in the ground, their carriages broken and rusty. When you enter the arsenal tower, you wade ankle-deep in dust. The weapons are strewn in a heap and left to rust, unoiled and unpolished, for generations. As a result, they've degenerated completely and are useless, all because no one has cared for them! My point is not to criticize the citadel or the arsenal, but those who are responsible for maintaining the royal treasuries.   6.75

We climbed to the top of the city's ramparts, where I saw some small masonry structures, each with a window. Some faced the land and others looked out to sea, a hundred paces separating one from the next.   6.76

"What are these?" I asked the man.

"Turrets for the guards."

Each company of soldiers stationed in the city had to stand watch every night. A soldier would go into a turret and remain on watch there for four hours. Then someone would come relieve him. After the next soldier's watch was complete, he too would be relieved, and so on and so forth, till morning.

Inside every turret hung a bell. Every hour on the hour, the guard in the first turret would ring his bell. Upon hearing it, the guard in the second turret would ring his, followed by the third, and so on, until the ringing made a circle of the city walls. The purpose of this practice was to keep the soldiers from falling asleep. If their commanding officer passed by and saw one of them sleeping, he'd wake him up and give him a few lashes with his whip to rouse him. This system was put in place to prevent an enemy from hiding outside the walls at night and attacking the city when the gates were opened in the morning.   6.77

6.78   One evening, I was walking by the seashore beyond the gates of the city with that Syriac man from Damascus I mentioned earlier. We stayed out until sunset.

"Shake a leg!" he cried. "We need to get back before they close the gates!"

We hurried back to the city. Upon our arrival, I saw about fifty armed soldiers, pointing their muskets out the gates, looking as though they were about to fire. I was afraid, and began to retreat in panic.

"What's the matter?" my friend asked. "Go on in, don't be afraid. I'll explain."

We went past the soldiers into the city. Once inside, I asked him why they had been standing there with their muskets.

"It's an old tradition of theirs," he replied. "Whenever the gates of the city are opened or closed, the soldiers line up as you saw them, just in case there is an enemy lying in ambush. That's why."

6.79   A peculiar story was recounted about one of the notable Jews of Livorno in those days. It so happened that the Grand Duke—who was known as the Duke of Tuscany, who ruled those lands, and who resided in the city of Florence—was in need of a loan. He had to pay the salaries of his soldiers and some other expenses, and found himself in the position of needing to borrow money from some town notable. The duke consulted the officials in his kingdom to find out whom he might ask for a loan.

"There's a Jewish gentleman in the city of Livorno with a vast fortune," they replied. "Summon him, and he'll provide you with whatever you need."

6.80   The duke took their advice and ordered the man to be brought before him. When he appeared, the duke welcomed him cordially and invited him to sit down. After exchanging some pleasantries, the duke got to the point.

"I need eighty sacks of silver," he said.[106] "I'd like you to loan me the silver till I can collect some taxes from the kingdom and pay you back."

"Happily," said the sly swindler. "What's mine is yours, my lord! I am at your service."

The duke thanked him and ordered the secretary of the chancery to draft a document guaranteeing full repayment. The Jew threw himself at the duke's feet.

"What is this, my lord? How could a servant accept such a document from his master? The money is yours, just as I am your servant!"

"I have no wish to cheat any of my subjects," said the duke. "If you won't accept the guarantee, then I won't take a loan from you. Go in peace."

The Jew then came up with a devilish scheme, the likes of which 6.81 had never been heard of before.

"Sire, I know all too well that a master is surely not obliged to fulfill the wish of his servant," the Jew began. "Which is why I might suggest that your lordship sell me some property you are free to dispose of, for this very sum."

The duke agreed, and asked him what he had in mind.

"Sell me the sun for this price, and I'll give you eighty sacks of silver each year," the duplicitous Jew replied. "You may draft a document stating that I've consented to provide you with this sum on that condition."

The duke was baffled, and believed that the man must have lost his mind.

"Fool! How am I supposed to sell you something I don't own?" 6.82 he asked. "Can the sun be bought and sold?"

"You're right, my lord," the Jew replied. "But indulge me, even if everyone has a laugh at my expense."

The duke's officials, who were present at the meeting, turned to him and said, "Sire, give him what he asks, and let's see him try to take hold of the sun!"

The duke took the advice of his officials, as he wanted to see where this strange matter would lead. He ordered the secretary of the chancery to draft an edict giving the Jew free disposal of the sun, as well as a document requiring him to provide eighty sacks of silver to the treasury each year—equivalent to forty thousand ecus, or piasters. The secretary drafted the two documents for the Jew, who was then sent on his way.

6.83   Neither the duke nor the officials of his court caught on to the Jew's cunning scheme. Instead they mocked him, underestimating his intelligence. The Jew, meanwhile, returned to his home in Livorno, and immediately registered the duke's edict at the courthouse. Three days later, he summoned all of the landowners who grew wheat and other grains on their properties, and read them the edict that His Excellency the duke had given him, which granted him authority over the sun.

"Your crops depend on the sun," the Jew said. "Therefore, I ask that you pay me such and such an amount in tax each year. If you refuse, I'll farm the lands myself and pay the tax to His Excellency the duke."

6.84   At a loss as to what to do, the men felt compelled to draft a document agreeing to pay what he demanded. The Jew then summoned the orchard owners and came to an agreement with them. He drafted a document and sent them away. He did the same with the launderers and the dyers, and everyone else whose livelihood depended upon the sun. The news of the Jew's actions—authorized by nothing less than an edict from the duke himself—spread throughout the city.

6.85   The notables of Livorno convened and held a council, to which they summoned the city's judges, bishops, and clergy. They all agreed that this whole affair was unacceptable. After all, God made His sun shine down upon the virtuous and the wicked alike, and no one had the right to administer the gift God had given to His servants! Unanimously agreed on this position, they drew up a petition testifying to their refusal of the duke's order. Everyone signed the petition, and they elected a few distinguished members of their assembly to visit the duke.

6.86   The representatives went to the duke and presented themselves before His Excellency, greeting him with the salutations befitting his station. They presented their petition, which contained over two hundred signatures. These included the names of bishops, priests, and the abbots of monasteries. The petition read: "His Excellency, our master and gracious benefactor, has been cheated by a Jew, an enemy of our religion. By means of this swindle, he has laid hands on an immense fortune surpassing three hundred sacks of silver." They explained how the man had imposed a certain tax upon every person whose livelihood depended on the sun.

Once the duke read the petition, he became furious, realizing the mistake he'd made. How could he have given this swindler a sword with which to smite his subjects?

The duke summoned one of his court officers and ordered him to 6.87 bring the deceitful Jew before him as quickly as possible. The officer left, and soon after returned with the man in tow.

"You've deceived me and led me astray, you traitor to God and king!" said the duke to the Jew when the latter appeared before him. He took the edict back from him and seized all of the debt contracts he'd drawn up against the duke's subjects. Summoning the executioner, he ordered the Jew to be hanged and his properties confiscated.

Such is the punishment of those who swindle kings![107]

Another strange affair involving a Jewish man occurred back 6.88 then. In his youth, he had sought to convert to Christianity and be baptized. After having spent three years completing his novitiate, during which time he was subjected to a profound examination, he was determined to be firm and unwavering in his conviction. So the bishop ordered the priest to baptize him, to hear his confession, and to administer Holy Communion. Following his conversion, the man remained faithful to his decision, growing more pious with each passing day, even electing to join a monastic order. For several years, he devoted himself to piety and virtuous conduct, so it seemed only fitting that he would eventually be vested in the sacred habit of the monk. Shortly thereafter, he was ordained as a priest, and recognized by all for his good deeds. He spent many years as a deeply virtuous and pious priest.

6.89   One night, while the city guards were patrolling the streets, they passed beneath the windows of the monastery where the Jewish priest lived. They saw clouds of smoke billowing from one of the windows, as well as the flicker of fire, and suspected that the cell was in flames. Some of them rushed up to the monastery and pounded on the door until a servant woke up and hurried over to open it.

"We're here to tell you that one of the cells is on fire!" they exclaimed. "Go and put it out, quickly!"

The servant went off to wake the abbot and monks, and told them about the burning cell. They made a round of all the cells until they reached the Jewish priest's room. Smoke was pouring from the spaces around the door. They assumed that both the cell and the monk were on fire.

6.90   The abbot ordered the monks to pull the door off its hinges and rush inside to help the monk. They obeyed and entered the cell. They discovered that the wretched priest had emptied out the mattress that was under the bed of its clover hay stuffing, which was what they usually used. Flames leapt from the hay, and a crucifix lay in the center of the fire! And yet the flames had had no effect on the crucifix, which remained untarnished. The monks yanked it from the fire and kissed it. Then they turned to the unfortunate man and asked him why he'd done what he'd done.

"I wanted to burn the crucifix you worship, since I'm a Jew and an enemy of the cross!" he spat at them, foaming at the mouth in his rage.

6.91   The abbot and the monks were baffled by the insolence of this wretched, miserable man. The abbot ordered him to be seized and kept in confinement. The next day, they told the bishop what had happened, and he demanded that the man be brought to him. His Holiness the bishop asked the man if he had performed this act while of sound mind, or if he'd been seized by a bout of melancholy or madness. He asked him this question to determine the man's intentions.

"I'm a Jew, and an enemy of the cross," the cursed man replied. "That's why I tried to burn it."

The bishop sent the man to the governor of the city and explained what had taken place. When he appeared before the governor and the details of his case were read out, the governor sent him to the tribunal—that is, the courthouse. His case was examined and he was sentenced to be burned alive for his crime.

Following the sentencing, he was taken before the governor to have the sentence carried out. But the governor was a tenderhearted man, and hesitated as he did not want to put the offender to such a cruel death. He was wary of the people's response should he controvert the law, so he sent the Jew to Florence to appear before His Excellency the duke. That way, he would let the duke make the final decision, sparing himself from doing so. When they brought the man before His Excellency the duke and read out his sentence, the duke immediately ordered him to be burned. And thus, his body burned in this world and his soul burned in Hell. What a terrible fate! 6.92

One Saturday morning, I saw some women and men of our neighborhood preparing to visit the Church of the Virgin Mary, which stood on the Black Mountain,[108] about three miles from the city. I'd heard about this noble church, which was named for the Virgin Mary, and about all the miracles that had taken place there. I very much wished to visit it, so I asked my master for permission to go, and he consented. The mistress of the house ordered one of her servants to accompany me on the route. She also gave me a hat made of palm leaves to wear. It was as large as a sieve and yet, despite its size, weighed less than half a pound. 6.93

"Wear it as you climb the mountain, and it will protect from the heat of the sun," she told me. It was August at the time, and the weather was hot.

The servant and I set off and soon arrived at the foot of the mountain. I saw many people, both men and women, climbing up the mountain. Some were barefoot, treading upon the black rocks, which were sharper than knives! Others, demonstrating their deep piety, climbed the slope on their knees, as they addressed their 6.94

requests to the Virgin Mary, worker of miracles. Others walked with their heads bowed, asking for her intercession.

6.95   We finally arrived at the summit of the Black Mountain. From it one could see the sea below, crashing against the mountainside. Before me stood a splendidly built church with tall columns, alongside a large monastery. We entered the church just as a mass was beginning, in praise of the Virgin of the icon. This icon was covered by three lavish screens. During the first third of the mass, they would draw the first screen back. During the second third, they would remove the second screen, and during the final third, the last one. The icon of the Virgin Mary would then be fully revealed, and the people would receive her blessings. This took place every Saturday, year round.

After attending mass and receiving the benediction at the altar, I was taken around the church by the servant who'd come with me to the mountain. He showed me the miracles the Virgin Mary had performed for those who had sought her help in times of need or peril. Each miracle was represented by a statue and a written account placed beneath it.

6.96   Among these miracles was one about a man who'd been shipwrecked while traveling at sea. He called out for the help of the Virgin Mary of the Black Mountain, and she saved him by sending him a fish called a dolphin, which carried him to safety and cast him onto dry land. In gratitude, the man gave the church a small ship made of silver, beneath which was a fish, also made of silver. Another miracle regarded a man who'd fallen from a tall ladder. He too called out for the Virgin's help, and escaped unharmed. He offered the church a silver ladder, writing beneath it a description of the miracle performed for him by the Virgin Mary. The church was packed with countless miracles of this kind. It seemed to me that if I spent three days there, I still wouldn't be able to count all of the miraculous stories hanging in that church!

6.97   One of the miracles had taken place in Habsburg lands, where there was a castle guarded by a company of soldiers and their commander. It came to pass that two soldiers hatched a plan to flee the castle by night, without the permission of their commanding officer. The next day, when the officer learned of their flight, he flew into a rage, and swore he'd hang the both of them if they were found. He dispatched a few sharp-eyed soldiers to search for them, and ordered them to do whatever was necessary to bring the runaways back. The soldiers set out in pursuit, asking around if anyone had seen them. Two days later, they caught the deserters and brought them back before the officer who, in a wild fit of rage, ordered them both to be hanged.

One of the men began to plead for his life. "Have mercy on me, my lord," he cried. "I'm not to blame! My friend got me into this mess!" 6.98

The other man joined in with the same pleas, claiming that he wasn't to blame. The officer was unsure of what to do. Which of the two deserved to be hanged?

"We'll cast lots," he said to the men. "Whoever draws the short stick will hang."

So the officer cast lots and one of the men drew the short stick. The officer ordered him held until the morning, as the hour had grown late, and he was cast into prison.

The man fell to weeping and cursing his fate. By and by, the 6.99
friend he'd fled with came and joined him, doing what he could to distract him and alleviate his suffering. In the prison cell hung an icon of the Virgin Mary.

"Don't be afraid, brother," the condemned man's friend said to him. "Turn to the Virgin Mary of the Black Mountain, and she'll save you. No one who seeks her protection is ever disappointed."

So the prisoner knelt before the icon of the Mother of Mercy, hot tears streaming down his face, and begged her all night long to save him. When dawn broke, the officer summoned the prisoner and ordered the executioner to hang him immediately.

The executioner led the man to the gallows, dropped the noose 6.100
around his neck, and sent him up the ladder that lay against the side of the gallows. Then he pushed him off the ladder.

"Virgin Mary of the Black Mountain, save me!" the man cried. At that instant, the rope snapped and he fell to the ground, very much alive.

The officer ordered a stouter rope to be brought. Again they put a noose around the man's neck and made him climb the ladder, and the executioner kicked him off. But the man's faith in the Virgin Mary was strong, and as she had saved him before, so he again cried out as he fell, "Virgin Mary of the Black Mountain, save me!"

6.101 Again the rope snapped, and the man tumbled to the ground. Exasperated, the commanding officer ordered them to use a very strong rope made of linen.

Soon the preparations were complete. "Let's see if your prayers help you now," said the witless fool of an officer, who didn't believe in the power of the Virgin and wouldn't admit that she had worked a miracle by breaking the rope twice. Meanwhile, the condemned man, confident in his faith, had climbed to the top of the ladder. When the executioner pushed him, he cried out at the top of his lungs, seeking succor from the wonder-working Virgin of the Black Mountain. Just like that, the strong rope snapped—and this time it had been cut to pieces!

6.102 "Can't you see it, sir?" the assembled men shouted, after witnessing this miracle. "Have faith in the miracles of the Virgin Mary taking place before your very eyes!"

The officer accepted the miracle and repented of his cruelty and lack of faith. He summoned the condemned soldier, embraced him, and pardoned him. The soldier rose in his esteem.

"From now on, you're exempt from conscription," the officer told him, "and you have a place of honor with me!"

But the man had another wish.

"Give me leave to spend the rest of my life serving her, as she saved me three times from death, and performed this great miracle for my sake!"

Hearing this, the officer consented and sent him off with a tidy sum of money and ample provisions for his journey. The man traveled to the Black Mountain and gave thanks to the Virgin Mary. He then joined the monastery there and became a monk, spending the rest of his days engaged in fasting and prayer and devotion to Our Lady.

When I returned to Aleppo after my own travels, it so happened 6.103 that I was speaking to some groups of Christians and told them the story of the miracles of Our Lady of the Black Mountain. I explained to them that no one who'd ever sought her help had been refused, and described the testimonies to all the miracles I'd seen in the church, as I recounted earlier. Well, not long afterward, a man from one of those groups I'd spoken to came to see me.

"Brother, I heard you speak about the miracles of the Virgin 6.104 Mary of the Black Mountain," he said. "For several years, I'd been having some serious troubles and could find no way out. But then I followed your advice: I asked the Virgin Mary for help and pledged a votive offering. The next thing I knew, I was saved."

"And here's my votive offering to the Virgin," he continued. He handed me twelve gold Venetian ducats and asked me to send them to the church.

"Follow me," I said, taking the coins. We went off to see a French merchant named *khawājah* Guillon, who had business interests in Livorno. I implored him to send the votive offering to his business partner there, and to ask him to forward it to the Church of the Virgin Mary of the Black Mountain. The man agreed, and he placed the coins in an envelope and wrote on it: "Deposit in trust for the Virgin Mary of the Black Mountain." We thanked him for his kindness and left.

Soon thereafter, another man came to me with twelve Venetian 6.105 gold ducats, which he had vowed to give to the church. Our Lady had aided him when he asked her to deliver him from a false accusation that would have ruined his life.

As for me—writing this account fifty years later—I too once lost something, worth 1,100 piasters. After it had been missing for forty days, I lost all hope of recovering it and felt certain I was on the brink of ruin. One day, it occurred to me to ask the help of the Virgin Mary of the Black Mountain. That very night, the person who had taken my property went to see a priest and confessed to his crime! With the help of a close friend of mine who acted as an intermediary, the priest shared the good news that the lost item had been found, without letting me know who had taken it. My friend brought it to me the next day. Nothing was missing! I gave thanks to the Virgin Mary, Mother of Miracles, for her beneficence.

6.106 Let me now recount what I heard from some trustworthy people about that noble icon and the founding of the church. There was once a shepherd who lived on that mountain. One day, as he was walking along the mountainside, he came upon that very icon of the Virgin Mary hidden among some boulders. The shepherd stared at it and was struck by its magnificence. He lifted it from its spot among the boulders and hung it from a tree.

Later, when the time came for him to leave the mountain, he said to himself, "I'm going to bring this icon into town and give it to the bishop. Maybe he'll give me something for it."

6.107 In the evening, he went to see the bishop and gave him the icon. Studying it carefully, His Holiness the bishop recognized it as a rare masterwork, the product of an expert artist.

"Where did you find this beautiful icon?" the bishop asked the shepherd.

"I spotted it on the Black Mountain, discarded among the rocks, so I brought it to Your Holiness."

The bishop thanked him, gave him a few coins, and sent him off. And that was that.

6.108 The next day, the shepherd took his sheep up the mountain, as usual. When he passed by the same spot, he saw very same icon of Mary, lying among the boulders where he'd found it the first time! Amazed, he picked it up and took it to the bishop.

"And where did you find that icon?" the confused bishop asked when he saw it.

"It was in the same place I found it yesterday, among the rocks," the shepherd replied.

The bishop was astonished, and sent his disciple to go and check whether the icon was still in his chambers, where he'd hung it. The disciple returned and reported that it had vanished. The bishop grew even more bewildered, gave the shepherd a token of his thanks, and dismissed him. He hung the icon in his cell once again, in the very same spot.

On the third day, the shepherd passed the same place and saw 6.109 the icon yet again. Stunned, the simpleminded shepherd told himself that someone must surely be stealing the icon from the bishop's room and discarding it here. So he picked it up and hurried back to see the bishop.

"My lord, one of your servants must be stealing the icon and leaving it in that spot!" he said. The bishop raced up to his room and saw that the icon was missing again. Finally, it dawned on him that this was a miracle worked by the Virgin Mary, who wanted a shrine on that mountain.

The bishop immediately summoned all the curates and priests, 6.110 the abbots of all the monasteries, and the rest of the clergy, ordering them to gather at the bishopric. Wearing their ceremonial vestments, with the deacons carrying candles and censers, they were all to march in a jubilant, festive procession. The next day, they convened as His Holiness had requested, and once all were present, the bishop raised the icon above his head in a gesture of deep respect and veneration, and the procession set off for the mountain.

They summoned the shepherd and asked him about the exact spot where he had found the icon, and he led them there. The bishop then came forward and indicated where the church was to be built. Skilled builders were summoned, and they set about constructing the church, which included a chapel dedicated to the icon of the Virgin Mary.

From that moment until the present day, the Mother of Mercy 6.111 has continued to work her dazzling miracles. All who seek refuge with her and make their requests faithfully obtain what they ask for.

This is what I saw and heard about Our Lady of the Black Mountain.[109] Her story is so renowned throughout Christendom that whenever a ship sails past the church, regardless of which nation it belongs to, it signals its submission to Our Lady by firing its cannons. Any ship that fails to do so is inevitably beset by misfortune and ruin, as experience has taught. And anyone who doesn't believe that my story is true should ask others who have been there themselves.

6.112   Following my own visit to the Black Mountain, I fell ill. For two weeks I was overcome with chills and fevers. It was during that time that we received word from Genoa that three galleys belonging to the French realm had arrived from Messina. Aboard the galleys were some princesses who had gone to Messina to pay a visit to another princess, herself the daughter of one of the members of the French royalty. My master was overjoyed to receive this news, and decided then and there to travel to Genoa to meet up with the galleys. From there, he could travel with them to Marseille without fear of encountering any pirates.

6.113   "You're ill," the *khawājah* said to me as he prepared to travel. "You can't come with me. Stay here and rest, and I'll wait for you in Marseille."

When I heard these words, I felt miserable. Being so far from home and in my sorry state, I turned to the Mother of Mercy, the Virgin Mary, beseeching her to help me. Just then, an old philosopher came by to bid my master farewell. My master and I used to visit him, so he knew who I was.

"What's the matter with you?" he asked when he saw me.

I told him about my illness, and how my master was going to leave me behind when he left.

"Don't worry. God willing, you'll go with him," he replied, adding, "Come by my house this evening at four o'clock. I need to see you."

He left, and I waited patiently until four o'clock then headed to 6.114
his house, where I found him waiting for me.

"When do you get the chills?" he asked.

"They begin at nine o'clock in the morning and continue until noon," I said. "Then I have a fever until sunset. Only after that do I experience some relief."

He took a crystal flask out of his cabinet and poured a thirty-dirham measure of distilled water into a small bottle.

"Drink a third of this before you go to sleep," he said, handing me the bottle. "Drink the second third when you get the chills, and the last third before you go back to sleep. And if you ever have the chills again, you can blame me."

I did as he instructed, and my chills went away. I'm now seventy-five years old and haven't felt a chill since, all thanks to the beneficence of the Virgin Mary, whom I called upon when I was ill.

The next day, we departed Livorno in a small sailboat. Fearing 6.115
pirates, the boat didn't stray far from land. We arrived at the port of Genoa, disembarked, and took our baggage with us into the city. We arrived at an inn, but when we tried to enter, the innkeeper refused to let us in until we brought him a document from the governor's palace. This was one of their peculiar customs. By order of the governor, no one was allowed to host a foreigner without permission from the authorities. This was so that the governor knew how many foreigners were in the city at any given time, and no potential enemies could infiltrate it.

My master and I went to see the governor. When we arrived, we 6.116
found a man seated in his own room, whose sole occupation was to deal with such cases.

"Which country are you from?" he asked. My master explained that he was a Frenchman and that I was from the East.

"What's your purpose in coming to this country? And what's your destination?"

My master recounted the reasons for our arrival in Genoa and our intended departure to France. The man wrote out a document of safe conduct, dated it, and handed it over. We took it to the inn and presented it to the innkeeper. We were finally allowed to bring in our things, and they gave us rooms. We remained there, waiting till we could leave on the galleys. Three days later, the innkeeper asked us to renew our travel papers with the man who had issued us the first document, so we were compelled to return to get a new, freshly dated document.

6.117   We spent fifteen days in Genoa, which I spent touring the city and seeing all those magnificent buildings and lofty palaces built out of white marble, and visiting its splendid churches. One day, as I was walking down an alleyway, I saw some houses in ruins. Surprised by this sight, I asked some people how these sumptuous dwellings had fallen to pieces, and they told me the story.

6.118   It so happened that the sultan of France once had an ambassador in this city, representing his illustrious name. It is the custom of kings to send their ambassadors to principalities such as these to offer them protection against their enemies. But the people of this principality are proud—hence its nickname, Genoa the Proud. They looked down on this ambassador and didn't see fit to treat him with the respect he deserved, nor indeed the king who sent him. Now, the ambassador endured this affront patiently because he was a God-fearing man who didn't wish to cause any trouble or animosity. But modesty only invites treachery.

6.119   One day, the ambassador's servants found the door of his residence stained with filth, as well as the insignia of the French king that hung above it. They told His Excellency the ambassador what they'd seen, and he went to verify their report with his own eyes. Thereupon he was seized by a desire to avenge the honor of his sovereign against the Genoese for this act of vulgarity. He felt honor bound to leave the city, so the very next day he gathered what he needed, boarded a ship, and sailed to Marseille without anyone being the wiser. From Marseille, he and two of his officers traveled by coach to Paris.

The ambassador went directly to see the king's minister and told   6.120
him the entire story. The minister took him to see His Majesty King
Louis XIV. The ambassador submitted a report of what had taken
place in Genoa to the king, recounting the vulgar insult proffered
by the city's people and their disrespect for His Majesty the king of
France. After reading the ambassador's report, the king grew very
angry. He immediately summoned the commander-in-chief and
issued an edict ordering him to take forty galleys along with a number
of troop ships and sail to Genoa. He was to bomb it to pieces, leaving
not a single stone standing, even if every last resident perished.

The commander-in-chief set off as His Majesty had ordered.   6.121
When he was outside Genoa, he ordered the captains of the troop
ships to drop their anchors far from the harbor, and instructed the
galleys to anchor closer to the city and on the other side, so as not to
fall prey to the citadel's cannons. Genoa's inhabitants, in the meantime, didn't know why the French had arrived, and it didn't occur
to them that they intended to destroy the city. At least, not until the
bombs began raining down on them like a shower of embers falling
from the sky, landing on buildings and leaving them in ruins. The
people were stunned, and feared that they and their families would
perish beneath the bombardment.

The doge of Genoa went to the seashore accompanied by the   6.122
city's notables, the bishop, and the priests. Flinging themselves
before the French commander, they begged him to stop bombing
the city, lest all of its inhabitants be killed.

"My lord the sultan of France has ordered me to destroy this city,
and to not leave a single stone standing," the commander said. "If
you're worried about the people of the city and their families, order
them to leave the city and stay well away so they don't perish. Far be
it from me to disobey an order from the sultan of France to reduce
this city to ruins."

They begged him to hold off, to give them an opportunity to
visit the king and seek a pardon. The commander consented, and

ordered the bombardment to cease pending further orders from His Majesty the king.

"We will await your return," he told the Genoese.

6.123   The doge selected twenty of Genoa's nobles and sent them to Paris with gifts for the sultan of France. They went immediately to meet with His Excellency the minister and begged him to ask the king to receive them. The minister consented to their request, and asked permission for them to enter. When they appeared before His Majesty the king, they threw themselves at his feet, imploring him to pardon their city and its people, as his fury had placed them in grave peril!

The king took pity, pardoned them for their infraction, and granted clemency. He ordered the minister to welcome them as guests and treat them honorably. This the minister did. He prepared a grand reception for them and took them on a tour of all the buildings and gardens in the king's palace, which has no equal in the entire world.

6.124   Once the Genoese had finished their tour and partaken of the food that was offered them, they prepared to depart. At that moment, the minister—instructed by the king—turned to them and asked,

"Are you pleased with the order and beauty of His Majesty's palace? I trust you are now happy and content?"

"My lord, we found the palace to be exquisitely composed and surpassing all in perfection," they replied. "In fact, the only thing to detract from it all was the sight of the notables of Genoa throwing themselves at the feet of the king of France!"

They spoke these words proudly and arrogantly, for they'd found the prospect of death easier to bear than the act of humiliation and contrition they were forced to carry out against their will. The minister scolded them harshly for their haughty and insolent rejoinder, and praised the wisdom and mercy of the king. Disgraced and remorseful, they were promptly dismissed.

The nobles left Paris and traveled directly back to Genoa. They presented the French commander with the order they'd received from His Majesty the king. He was to lift the siege and return to France. However, because of the insulting words the nobles had spoken, the king's minister had also dispatched a messenger by land, carrying a letter for the commander.

"Do not depart without making them pay for the cost of sending our ships and galleys, the soldiers' salaries, and all other associated expenses," the letter read.

The commander sent a message to the doge asking for a specified sum to cover the expenses of his fleet, and refused to leave until he'd received the full amount. He then returned to France and gave a full report to His Majesty the king.

Chapter Seven

Our Voyage to France

7.1 We eventually left Genoa aboard the French galleys, headed for Marseille. We were given space on the captain's ship along with the princesses, and my master was treated with great honor due to his royal connections.

The galley was like nothing I'd ever seen before. It was over a hundred cubits in length. Aft there was an elevated area where the captain's cabin was situated.[110] Outside his cabin was a space resembling an outdoor salon, with windows overlooking the sea and tables on both sides, all exquisitely painted in beautiful colors. Above the captain's cabin was a deck, over which hung a large crystal lantern. There were two heavy cannons beneath the captain's cabin, each with its own porthole facing out to sea.

7.2 I ventured into the captain's cabin. It was like a royal palace! Its ceiling was covered with crystal mirrors. Arranged along all four walls were weapons fit for a king, gleaming like silver. The room was painted in dazzling silvery and golden hues. At the stern of the galley were two more stout cannons, each with portholes looking out to sea. Above the cannons sat a large deck as wide as the ship itself, which was where the soldiers were gathered. The kitchen was belowdecks and contained an iron stove and a small iron oven, which was used for baking fresh bread each day. All around the captain's cabin and the outdoor salon were planters full of herbs, for salad. In the hold, there were chickens, pigeons, pullets, and sheep, to provide fresh meat every day. Everything was laid out in perfect order.

When I explored the central part of the galley, I found twelve benches on each side, separated from each other by a space of two cubits. On each bench sat six convicts, completely naked, who operated the ship's oars. Patrolling the aisle between the two sets of benches were soldiers carrying bull-pizzle whips. If a soldier saw one of the rowers slowing down out of fatigue or laziness, he'd strike all six rowers across their backs with his whip, leaving them covered in blue bruises. It was truly a sorry sight, a living hell where they were flogged and tortured by demons. 7.3

When I saw this awful spectacle, I turned to the ship's priest, standing next to me. 7.4

"Father, how can Christians treat men so cruelly? Why is that allowed?"

"I don't blame you for being ignorant of these matters, since you're a foreigner," the priest replied. "But since you ask, my son, let me tell you that each of these men deserved to be put to death for his crime. But the law decreed, for one reason or another, that they should be treated with mercy. So each was sentenced to serve in the galleys for a specified length of time, depending on the seriousness of the offense. Some will spend three years here, others five, and others will serve a life sentence. They've become an example to others, a warning not to commit such heinous and manifestly flagrant crimes."

I was persuaded by the priest's response, and realized that my own life was a heavenly paradise compared to that hellish existence. May God protect us from such an awful fate!

A few days later, we entered the harbor of Marseille to the sound of cannons from the two citadels that stood at the mouth of the 7.5

harbor. Entering the harbor required passing through the straits between the two fortified citadels. As a ship approached, it would lower its sails, and dinghies would tow it through the straits and into the harbor to be tied to a mooring. The reason for this was that the harbor was within the city, which is to say that the sea flowed into the city itself. It was absolutely enormous, and could accommodate all the ships as well as the galleys. A thick iron chain lay across the straits, extending from one fortress to the other. After sunset, the chain would be stretched taut by means of a wheel mechanism located in one of the fortresses. Once it was pulled up to the surface of the water, even a little dinghy wouldn't be able to pass through the straits. When morning came, the chain was loosened and it would sink into the sea, opening the way again to maritime traffic.

7.6   I saw that they'd fashioned a sort of machine to dredge the harbor. It was a large, broad dinghy that held a great wheel. Two convicts were put to work, turning the wheel with their hands and feet by climbing rungs inside it. In this way, they remained in the same place while the wheel turned around them. As it turned, it would cause two iron scoops to emerge from the water. One scoop would go down to the seabed and dredge up the sediment, then rise to the surface and empty it into another dinghy. Then the next scoop would descend, dredge up some more mud, and rise to empty it. It was all mechanized, such that the scoop would come to the surface and empty its contents without anyone having to touch it. It operated every day of the year.

7.7   When the princesses disembarked from the galley, a festive parade was held in their honor. They were taken to the palace of the commandant—that is, the governor of the city—accompanied by a grand, honorable procession befitting their station as the daughters of royalty. The reception lasted for eight days, and all manner of entertainments were brought before them.

The entertainment included a young man who'd been on board the galley. He was the son of a prince, and had once committed a crime worthy of a death sentence. Some other princes, who were friends of his father, tried to arrange a pardon for him but were unsuccessful. They did manage to have his punishment reduced to a life sentence of labor on the galleys. Now, this young man was handsome, and a superb dancer. In all of France, his skill and agility had no equal.

It occurred to the governor of Marseille to have the young man 7.8 dance for the princesses. He sent a group of soldiers to meet the captain of the galley, ordering him to free the man and bring him to the palace. I happened to be at the party when the young man entered and presented himself before the princesses, greeting them with due deference. The governor then ordered him to dance and to put all of his skills on display. And so, accompanied by musical instruments, the young man began to dance, revealing a ravishing mastery of the craft. All the spectators were stunned. When he was finished, he rushed up to the princesses and, with hot tears streaming down his face, pleaded with them to use their royal authority to set him free.

"Whatever you desire will be granted, young man, except your freedom," said the eldest princess. "This is your legal punishment, and we have no power to annul it. Go in peace."

Hopeless and dejected, he left in tears, and everyone present felt sorry for him.

Let's return to our story. Once we entered Marseille, we checked 7.9 into an inn called Petit Paris, which means "Little Paris." The mistress of the inn welcomed us most cordially and prepared two furnished rooms for us, decked out with all the necessities. A couple of hours later, I felt the need to answer the call of nature. I went downstairs to search for a toilet.

"What are you looking for?" one of the servant girls asked me, and I told her.

"You'll find it upstairs," she replied.

I returned upstairs, and began hunting for the toilet, opening 7.10 one door after another. No luck! I went back downstairs and asked the servant girl to show me the toilet herself, as I was unable to hold it any longer.

"What you want is in your room, under the bed," she replied.

I went back upstairs to my room and lifted the blanket that covered my bed and saw a large chamber pot. It then dawned on me that they had no latrines! I had no choice but to leave the inn right away.

Once outside, I began asking people about the quickest way out of the city, and they gave me directions. Once I'd made my way to the orchards on the outskirts of the city, I found a secluded spot and did my business. Then I went back to the inn.

7.11 Puzzled about the mystery of the chamber pot, I asked a man from Aleppo (whom I'd met at the inn) for an explanation.

"There are no latrines in this city because it is close to the sea, which makes it difficult to dig in the ground," he replied. "So each person answers the call of nature in his own room, just as you saw, in a chamber pot. At night, they empty it out the window into the streets, and the garbage collectors come early in the morning to pick up all the filth. The city streets all have central gutters. Water is constantly running through them, flowing down from a high point in the city. Each person also cleans the feces off his doorstep using that water."

7.12 In the middle of the city, there was an open space between the Gate of Rome and the Gate of Paris, which was called Le Cours. Trees were planted at either end, with a bench set between each two trees. A canal of running water flowed there, day and night. The notables of the city, as well as many ordinary folk, strolled along the wide path that ran through the center. It was a delightful place, a sort of garden, shaded from the sun by the trees.

There was another place called the Hôtel de Ville, a large building with tall columns. That's where all the merchants and brokers would meet and conduct their business, buying and selling from ten o'clock in the morning till noon, and then again from two o'clock till the late afternoon. The consul's residence was upstairs. From there, the consul would oversee the affairs of the merchants, acting as a sort of overseer.

There was another place called the chamber of commerce, where the consul supervised the affairs of the merchants of India and the East. He served as a sort of judge over all who traded in the two regions. In order to conduct business or become a merchant, one had to receive permission from these people. They'd look into a person's background and secure a guarantee of a certain sum of money from other reputable merchants before allowing the new person to do business in the lands of his choosing. Similarly, the brokers in the port had to be endorsed by others. They purchased the right to this occupation with a security deposit of three thousand piasters, since they handled all the merchants' goods, after all. They took possession of their merchandise on the strength of their own integrity. The merchants relied upon them in all their commercial dealings, allowing them to act as though they were the proprietors themselves. No one ever stood in their way. This is what I saw of the commercial system in France, which I duly record here.

I wandered the city of Marseille, taking in the sights and visiting churches and monasteries. One day, I followed directions to the Cave of Mary Magdalene, where she had lived with her brother Lazarus when they were cast out of Jerusalem by the Jews. They had been put in a boat without mast or rudder and left to float out to sea. Our Lord saved them from drowning and brought the boat to Marseille, whose inhabitants at that time worshipped idols.

Mary and her brother went into the city and took refuge in a cave. They were reduced to begging for food. Over time, however, they performed so many miracles that the people of the city began to have faith, all thanks to them. Eventually, the apostles arrived there and baptized the people. The whole story is too long to tell here.[111]

Anyway, I went to visit that holy cave, which was on the opposite side of the harbor, close to the merling storehouses.[112] Anyone who has visited the city has heard of this place.

I also visited the Church of the Virgin Mary of Marseille. It stood on the summit of a mountain called "Madame de Garde" in French. It was associated with many miracles. I climbed up the mountain

7.13

7.14

7.15

with a group of pious people from Marseille, all devotees of the Virgin Mary. At the foot of the mountain, I came upon a chapel with a window. Inside was a statue of Jesus on his knees, praying.[113] It was a representation of the scene of Jesus praying in the Garden of Olives.[114] He was fashioned to look like he was covered in sweat and anguished, just as the Holy Bible describes him—a picture of sorrow. The scene was placed there to encourage people to contemplate the suffering of Jesus.

Climbing a little higher, I came across another chapel. In this one, there was a Jesus tied to a pillar, and soldiers carrying switches of thorns and whips, looking as though they were about to flog him. Beyond that was another chapel with a Jesus and some soldiers placing a crown of thorns upon his head. Higher up was yet another house, in which Jesus was being made to carry the wooden cross.

7.16 In the final chapel, farther up, Our Lord the Messiah lay upon the cross as the executioners pounded nails into his hands and feet. The hammer in the hand of one of the cruel executioners seemed poised to strike the heavy nails into the limbs of the Messiah. A boy stood beside the soldier, carrying a basket of nails. All of this was fashioned so perfectly that the onlooker felt he was present in the very places where these five sorrowful mysteries occurred. Passing by these five painful stations before coming to the church, a person felt a profound sense of humility and remorse.

I finally arrived at the church. It was perched high up on the summit of the mountain, with a view that extended three miles out to sea. Sentinels surveyed ships entering the port of Marseille from that spot, always on the lookout for enemy vessels coming across the sea.

7.17 I entered the church, attended its holy mass, and headed back to the inn. On the way, I came upon a merchant from Marseille.

"Aren't you that fellow from Aleppo?" he asked, studying me carefully.

"Yes."

"Don't you recognize me?"

As I looked more closely, I did indeed recognize him! It was *khawājah* Rimbaud, who had been my master when I was a boy. We greeted each other, and he asked me how I'd come to Marseille. I related my whole story and explained that I was headed to Paris with my master. At this news, *khawājah* Rimbaud became very concerned on my behalf. He asked me to accompany him to his house.

When we arrived, he ordered his servant girl to bring us some breakfast. We ate together, and I then asked permission to return to the inn. But he refused.

"Why don't you stay here, at my house?" he asked. "I think too much of you to let you go off with some stranger!"

"Would you do me the honor of inquiring about this man? I have my heart set on going to Paris with him," I replied. "He's promised to do right by me."

Khawājah Rimbaud consented, and dispatched one of his attendants to invite my master over for lunch.

He arrived soon thereafter, and the two men stood face to face. 7.19

"Would you believe that I raised this young man when I was in Aleppo, and now here he is!" *khawājah* Rimbaud said. "I'd like him to stay here with me."

My master introduced himself and explained that he was one of the king's travelers.

"I've been ordered by His Excellency Minister Pontchartrain, Minister of the Orient, to bring back a man from the Orient who can read Arabic," my master said. "He'll be put in charge of the king's library of Arabic books, and I promise he'll be rewarded handsomely."

Khawājah Rimbaud was persuaded by this, and consented to have me go with my master to Paris. However, after they finished lunch and my master left for the inn, *khawājah* Rimbaud spoke to me privately.

"Go with him, but in the event that he does not keep his promise, I will give you a letter addressed to one of my friends in Paris," he said. "It will ask him to keep an eye on you, in case you need anything. And he can send you back to me, if need be."

I thanked him for his kindness and left.

7.20   I began to receive invitations from all the merchants of Aleppo who knew me. All of them treated me honorably: *khawājah* Bazan, *khawājah* Simon, *khawājah* Bonifay, *khawājah* Roux, and *khawājah* Samatan, who was my dearest friend in Aleppo.[115] They all would take me for strolls through their orchards and show me various interesting things. They invited me to their homes and treated me with great affection and generosity.

7.21   We spent ten days in Marseille, during which my master went to the chamber of commerce to pick up all the baggage he'd sent from the East through the consulates. There were seven locked trunks in all. In order to avoid having the trunks opened by a customs agent along the way, my master obtained a certificate from the customhouse of Marseille, stating that no duty was owed on these goods. They also placed a lead seal bearing the royal insignia on each trunk. With that done, my master handed over the trunks, along with the rest of his property—which was all locked up—to the carriage man, who would travel with them to Paris and deposit them at the customhouse.

In that country, carriage men would transport passengers in long carriages. The people would sit on top of the carriage, which was pulled by six strong horses. My master gave the trunks and our other baggage to the carriage man, and we were left with nothing cumbersome besides our clothes and the cage with the animals. Two were left, as three had died along the way.

Chapter Eight

Our Journey from Provence to France and the City of Paris[116]

We departed the city of Marseille in March of 1708.[117] The first city   8.1
we encountered on our way was Āzāy, a city of beautiful buildings and columns.[118] A French king had given this city to one of the
ancient popes during a visit by His Holiness. Today, it falls under
the jurisdiction of whoever sits upon the Apostolic Throne. The city
is known for jurisprudence, and all the courthouses and tribunals
follow its rulings with respect to legal matters.

A day later, we left that city and headed out, passing various
cities and villages along the way. While on the road, we would have
lunch at one inn, then have dinner and spend the night at a different
inn. As a result, the entire voyage passed quite gloriously.

When we arrived in the city of Lyon, we checked in to one of its   8.2
inns and stayed there five days. I spent that time touring the city and
seeing the sights. It is a large, populous city with high walls and tall
columns, elegant buildings, opulent palaces, magnificent churches,
and a great river flowing through it. Every trade is plied in Lyon.
Foremost is the production of silk and other luxurious fabrics, such
as silk brocade embroidered with silver and gold thread—which
costs ten piasters per cubit—and other costly luxuries. This is also

where they cast the wheels used to spin gold thread. The city has various other industries also found in other countries. This impressive city is about the same size as Aleppo.

8.3   There was a large church there, the Church of Saint-Jean, which I went to see. After visiting its altar, I walked around inside the church and came upon a tall clock made of hardened steel.[119] It was the height of a man with his arm outstretched, and was topped by a brass dome. Sitting on top of the dome was a brass rooster. Below the dome were angels, with church bells in front of them, and beside each church bell was a . . . .[120] The clock had four faces. The first face was solemn—that is, long and thin. It had an iron clock hand, which made a complete rotation once every hour, marking each minute. As it turned, the clock's hand would lengthen or shorten according to the radius of the clockface. When it reached the middle, for instance, the hand would shorten, all on its own, to the narrower dimensions of the clockface. It was made of a single piece of iron. It was an astonishing sight to see!

8.4   On the second face, the clock hand made a complete rotation every twenty-four hours. The third face's clock hand made a full rotation once a year, displaying the almanac for the year—that is, the feasts and fasts, the opposition of the solar and lunar eclipses, and other such astronomical matters. On the fourth face, the clock hand rotated once every hundred years, announcing such things as only scholars with a specialized understanding of astrology could grasp. And on each saint's day, the saint would appear in a little window, their names inscribed above them.

8.5   Upon the hour, the rooster on top of the dome would flap its wings and crow three times, just like a real rooster. Then the angels beneath the dome would strike the church bells in front of them in a way that resembled a musical melody. A kneeling Virgin Mary would emerge alongside the angel Gabriel, who saluted her, followed by the Holy Spirit, which circled above them in the shape of a white dove. When all these movements were done, the clock would strike.

From the moment this clock was set in motion to the present day, 8.6
this has all taken place every hour, day and night, without missing
a stroke, and without a person making it run. The travelers all said
they'd never seen anything like it in the whole world. That's why
the man who fashioned the clock was blinded after he completed it.
His eyes were filled with kohl so that he would never create another
clock, ensuring that this one would remain unique.

This is what I witnessed with respect to that wonderful clock. I
saw many other things in Lyon, but for the sake of brevity I have not
recorded them here.

After five days in Lyon, we set off again, passing many villages 8.7
and towns and inns, stopping each night to sleep at a different inn,
and enjoying the heights of esteem and comfort. Every service and
accommodation was made available to us. We pressed on, and eventually arrived at a grand, towering bridge called the Bridge of the
Holy Spirit.[121] It had two gates. At each stood a royal guard, who
inspected the passengers entering and leaving. This was the first
entry point to the interior of France.

After the inspection, we left the bridge behind us and arrived at 8.8
a large, prosperous village nearby, where we checked in at an inn to
spend the night. There were twelve men in our traveling party.

"Would you like to have dinner together?" the mistress of the
inn asked.

"Yes," all replied.

"And what might you like your dinner to be?" she asked.

"Something delicious," one of our companions responded.

"Right away."

She disappeared and sent one of her servant girls to us with a
pitcher of wine. She poured a glass for each of us in turn, and we all
had a drink.

The table was set with all the necessities: plates, clean napkins, 8.9
silver forks and spoons, and soft bread. She then placed a large platter before us with a turkey and twelve grilled chickens on a large
skewer. There were two plates of chicken wing fricassée as well as

pieces of beef, and two plates of lettuce salad. We sat at the table to eat, and two servant girls appeared with cups in their hands, and continued to fill our glasses with good wine throughout dinner. Afterward, they cleared all the plates away and brought out some French cheese, two plates of olives, and two plates of apples. Following dinner, we all washed our hands and they cleared the table. They brought out a large basin of Frankish porcelain filled with water. Around the edges of the basin, sitting in the water, were six glasses and two carafes of wine.[122] Whoever wished to have a drink could pour some wine for himself at his leisure.

8.10   When it was time to sleep, we were invited to repair to our beds. The mistress of the inn opened a large cupboard containing about two hundred clean white sheets. She ordered the servant girls to take two sheets for each man's bed and lay them on top of each other between the blanket and mattress, so that there were three layers on the bed. They did as she asked then retired to their own rooms. Each of us got into his bed and stretched out on a soft mattress. Beside each bed was a cushion set before an icon, in case one wished to pray, and a white linen nightcap lay on the pillow. We all fell into peaceful slumber and slept till morning. We rose from our beds, headed out to attend mass, and returned to the inn.

8.11   Soon after, breakfast arrived. There was cheese, soft bread, and a pitcher of wine. We finished breakfast and asked the mistress of the place what we owed her for room and board. She asked for four piasters in all, charging each man a third of a piaster. They protested that her price was too high, and offered her three piasters instead. She accepted, thanked us kindly, and we set off.

If you were to ask me if we'd encountered such reasonable prices throughout our travels, I'd have to say certainly not! The lands of Provence were expensive, unlike the lands of France, which were cheap due to the abundance of its harvests, particularly in the countryside and the villages.[123]

8.12   We passed into the region of Bourgogne, a land rich in fruits and vines. According to what I was told, it was a four-day journey from one end of the region to the other—in both length and width—and all of it was covered with grapevines. Bourgogne was known as "the fount of wine," and produced the finest wine in all of France, similar to the wine of the Jurd district in Lebanon. From there, we pressed on to Paris, arriving at that magnificent city in the evening.

As we approached the city, I saw a vast expanse extending as far as the eye could see, so crowded with lights that it shone as bright as day. 8.13

"What's that great blaze of lights?" I asked my master.

He told me it was the city of Paris, which had no walls to hide it from view. As we entered the city and traveled down its little lanes and broad avenues, I saw that all of the shops on either side of the street were lit by two or three candles. Every twenty or thirty feet there hung a glass lantern with a tall candle burning inside.

How marvelous Paris was, in all its immensity! There were countless houses. Next to each one was the shop belonging to the master of the house, with his workshop inside. Every trade was represented, and every shop was grouped with others in the same trade. From one's own shop, a person could climb up to his house on the second story. All of the houses had five floors, each being five or six steps above the lower one. On the second floor was a threshold and a door, beyond which was the family home, with various bedrooms, a sitting room, and a kitchen. The rooms all had large windows overlooking the street. The third, fourth, and fifth floors all had the same arrangement. 8.14

As for the lanterns, they were installed by the city authorities. Candles were distributed to the residents of the quarter, who would place them in their lanterns. Each lantern was equipped with a locker nailed to the wall, and every resident of the quarter was responsible for lighting the candles for a whole month.

Each homeowner is also required, by order of the governor, to sweep in front of his door each morning. An hour after sunrise, the inspector appointed to this task by the governor makes his rounds. Anyone who hasn't swept is fined a piaster, to be paid by the person 8.15

responsible for sweeping, whether a male or female servant, or indeed the owner of the property. As for the rubbish that piles up in the streets, it's collected by people who put it in a bin atop a wagon, and dump it outside the city. In other words, an hour after sunrise, one finds the streets of Paris cleanly swept and free of dirt and rubbish. This was just the first example of orderliness that I saw in the splendid city of Paris.

8.16 But let's go back to our story. After reaching Paris, we spent half an hour walking to the house of one of my master's friends. We were staying with him because my master's hometown, Rouen, was a four-day journey from Paris. We were welcomed most honorably by the friend, who had our things brought inside and had rooms and fine beds prepared for us.

OUR ARRIVAL IN PARIS, IN OCTOBER 1708[125]

We remained at the home of my master's friend for a few days, until my master had sorted out his affairs. He had an expensive suit tailored for himself, and sent his book off to the printer. The book described in great detail the journey he had undertaken, the lands he had visited, and all the stories and sights he had seen and heard, which he had recorded every day. And he had a fine cage built for those animals I mentioned previously, of which only two remained.[126]

9.1

Once my master had secured all that he needed, he told me to put on the clothes I'd sent for from Aleppo. They included a short reddish-brown overcoat made of Damascene *alājah* fabric, some *jakhjūr* trousers made of *londrin*, a fine belt, a silver-plated dagger, a turban cloth and cap, and other such pieces of Eastern clothing. I put on all the clothes, but instead of the turban I wore a calpac similar to the ones made of sable fur my master had purchased for me in Cairo. It was a beautiful calpac.

9.2

We climbed into a carriage and set off for the town of Versailles and the king's palace. It was an hour and a half from Paris. As we

9.3

approached Versailles, I perceived something glittering in the distance, so bright it dazzled the eye.

"What's that I see?" I asked my master.

"The king's stables," he replied.

As we drew near, I saw that it was a splendid, imposing building, roofed with those black stones that people write on.[127] The chimneys had gilded funnels, and when the sun shone it was impossible to fix your gaze upon them, as they gleamed so brightly. We spent half an hour driving by those stables before arriving at Versailles.

9.4   As we approached the king's palace, I could see that there was a vast open space before it, surrounded by an iron fence as tall as a man with his arm outstretched, and topped with points as sharp as spears. At the center was a gate that opened onto the space, flanked by tall soldiers carrying battle-axes and spears, and snarling like panthers. They allowed no one to pass except those they recognized to be known at court. When we approached the gate, the soldiers tried to turn us away, but my master gave them a password and they let us through.

9.5   We entered the square and walked across it to the gates of the king's palace. There were soldiers there just like the ones we'd seen earlier, along with a seated chamberlain wearing an ornate uniform. He was a handsome man of dignified bearing, attended by a group of servants. When my master stepped forward and introduced himself, the man welcomed him in most cordially. We climbed a grand set of stone stairs, then headed to the pavilion of the minister known as Pontchartrain, who was minister for the Orient. We received permission to enter, and presented ourselves before His Excellency the minister, accompanied by the chamberlain.

9.6   My master bowed ceremoniously and announced that he'd returned safely to Paris from his voyage. He presented the minister with an inventory of the seven trunks' worth of goods he had purchased for His Majesty the king during his travels. The minister read the inventory and repeated his greetings, congratulating my master on returning home safely despite all the frightful things he'd surely encountered during his voyage. I stood at some distance from the two men, holding the cage with the animals inside. The minister spotted me.

"Who's that, and what's he carrying?" he asked my master. 9.7

"This young man served as my dragoman during the voyage," he replied. "When we were in Upper Egypt, I discovered some peculiar animals, which I'd never seen in all the lands I'd visited. I managed to procure seven of them, despite the fact that it's very difficult to catch them. I put them in a cage to transport them home, but five perished along the way and only two survived. If Your Excellency would like to see them, they're in this cage."

The minister gave an order to have me brought before him, and 9.8 the cage was taken from me and presented to His Excellency.

"I'm going to show these animals to the king tomorrow," he said when he saw the curious creatures. "It's too late to go now, since he's already left for the hunt."[128] The minister then ordered some lodgings to be prepared for us at the palace. We were taken to a furnished residence, and offered food and drink of the finest kind.

We remained in that residence until the next day. Two hours 9.9 before noon, the minister summoned us, and took us to the king's council room. The minister entered first. We remained outside and waited for the king to emerge from his pavilion and enter the council room. Once he had, the minister informed him of my master's arrival and asked permission for us to enter. We were brought into the room, and I saw the king standing there, with the notables of his realm lined up to his right and left looking extremely prim and proper.

The king was tall and splendid to behold. His presence inspired such awe that it was impossible to fix one's gaze upon him for long. My master presented himself before the king and saluted him with due reverence, praying that his reign would endure, and expressing all the formulas appropriate for the greeting of kings. I heard the king address my master tenderly and affectionately, thanking him for the effort he'd expended in his service.

9.10   The minister then stepped forward and asked if the king would like to see the animals, and the king ordered them to be brought forward. They took the cage from me and set it before him. When he saw the creatures, he was astonished by their appearance and asked my master where he'd found them.

"In Upper Egypt," he replied.

"Is there one female and one male?"

"Sire, there were originally seven, both male and female," my master explained.[129] "At present, however, I no longer know whether they're female or male."

"What are the animals called in their country?" the king asked.

My master, who didn't know the name, or perhaps had forgotten it, looked embarrassed, and turned to me.

"Your Majesty, the young man who accompanied me knows what they're called."

9.11   The king and all his nobles turned to face me. Someone asked me what the animals were called. I replied that, in the lands where it is found, the animal is called a *jarbūʿ*.[130] Then the king ordered his attendants to give me a pen and paper so that I could write the name down in my language. I took the paper and wrote the name in Arabic as well as French, for I knew how to read and write in French. After I'd written the words and they'd showed them to His Majesty the king, he studied me carefully.

"Who is this young man?" he asked my master. "What country is he from?"

"My lord, this young man is from Syria, in the Holy Land," my master said, looking down. "He belongs to the Maronite sect, which has been part of the Church of Saint Peter since the time of the apostles, from which it has never diverged, even to the present day."[131]

9.12   At that moment, Monseigneur the Dauphin, the king's son, entered the room. He was of medium height and quite rotund. People liked to point out that although both his father and firstborn son were kings—the latter being the king of Spain—the dauphin was not a king himself. He came forward to examine the animals and was amazed. He had an enormous drawing in which all the animals in the world were represented, with the exception of these particular ones. He summoned the king's physician, Monsieur Fagon, a learned man whose knowledge of medicine, natural science, and other such disciplines was unrivaled in all the world.

Monsieur Fagon appeared and looked at the animals, and the king's son asked him if he knew anything about them.   9.13

"Are they mentioned in any books of natural science?" he asked, and the physician replied that he'd never heard of such creatures, nor seen a drawing of them. Monseigneur the Dauphin called for an artist to add them to his illustration of wild beasts, and the king ordered the minister to hold the animals and their keeper in a place where they wouldn't be seen, until such time as Madame de Bourgogne returned from the hunt. She was the king's daughter-in-law—the wife of his son, the Duke of Bourgogne[132]—and the king loved her like a daughter.

That was the first time I had the great honor of seeing King Louis XIV, the sultan of France, in his council room, and I've faithfully recounted everything that took place, without any additions or omissions. But I've also been brief about it, so the reader won't suspect that I dreamt all of this up. After all, I witnessed many things on my journey that I didn't write down, and which haven't remained in my memory over these past fifty-four years. As I now write this account of my voyage, it is the year 1763. I visited Paris in 1709. Is it possible I could have retained everything I saw and heard in perfect detail? Surely not.

Let's get back to the story. We left the king's council room with   9.14 the minister and went to our chambers. The minister told the chamberlains not to let anyone enter, royals or otherwise, so that they wouldn't see the animals before the king's daughter-in-law did, as His Majesty the king had ordered. We remained there until ten—that is, until two hours before midnight, at which point the minister summoned us. Once we'd joined him, he set off with us in tow, preceded by four men carrying candles. We arrived at the residence of Madame de Bourgogne, the king's daughter-in-law.

9.15 The minister knocked and asked for permission to enter. A few moments later, two attendants emerged and invited the minister in. He went inside and spoke to Madame de Bourgogne, telling her about the animals, and how the king had ordered that no one was to see them before she did. She ordered us to enter.

Her attendants emerged from the room and brought us inside. As we entered, I saw the princess seated on a chair. Before her sat all the young princes, playing cards. Each had a pile of gold coins before him. The princes were surrounded by attendants as radiant as moons, wearing sumptuous clothes embroidered with gold thread. We presented ourselves before the princess, who surpassed everyone in beauty and finery, and she turned to observe the animals. All the princes also got up to come and look.

9.16 Then they turned to study me and my costume. They lifted the hems of my outfit, and one reached out to touch my chest, while another took the calpac off my head. No longer interested in the animals, they gazed upon me and my clothes instead, laughing.

"Who is this young man and what country does he comes from?" the princess asked my master. He explained who I was.

"Why does he have a beard?" she asked, meaning a mustache.

"This is the custom of their country," he replied. "The men do not shave their mustaches."

9.17 We stayed with the princess for half an hour, then left with the minister. On our way, we encountered a beautiful young girl wearing a royal cloak of embroidered silk. On her head was a spellbinding crown, encrusted with fine jewels like diamonds, rubies, and emeralds, and her entourage consisted of four beautiful attendants wearing sumptuous clothes. It struck me that she must be the king's daughter. When the minister saw her, he halted in his tracks and saluted her most cordially. The girl asked him who we were, and he explained the matter of the animals we had with us. She wanted to see them.

"With pleasure," he replied.

The attendants took the cage from me and placed it before the princess, and the minister removed the cover to show her the animals. When she saw them, she took fright and ran. The minister strode off in pursuit, encouraging her to come and see them, but he was unable to persuade her to return.

When the minister returned, he invited us to his residence. **9.18** We hadn't taken more than a few steps in that direction when we received a summons from His Majesty, borne by two of his personal attendants. They ordered the minister to send the cage with the animals to the king, along with their bearer. So we turned around and headed back to the king's palace. Standing before it were forty tall, strapping men: the king's palace guards. Eventually we arrived at the king's bedroom. The attendants took me inside with them while the minister and my master remained outside the bedroom.

I saw the king seated on a chair. Before him were two candles, **9.19** and he held a book in his hand, which he was reading. On the other side of the room was a bed surrounded by embroidered silk drapes. A princess was reclining on it; beside the bed stood the young girl I'd seen earlier. The attendants ushered me forward to the princess and placed the cage on a chair for her to see. The king rose, came over to us carrying a golden candelabrum, and showed the animals to the princess.

There I was, standing beside the king. Not knowing any better, I reached out to take the candelabrum from his hand. The king was magnanimous and handed it to me, knowing all too well that I'd acted out of inexperience, unaware of what I was doing. For it turned out that I had done something most extraordinary! Who would dare to reach out and take something from the king's hand? Later on, my master would tell everyone in Paris that this young man once took a candelabrum out of the hand of the king!

Once the princess had finished observing the animals and the **9.20** king returned to his seat, they gave me the cage and I took my leave. I found the minister and my master waiting for me. We went back to our residence with the minister and found two attendants waiting there. They had been sent by Madame d'Orléans, a princess. The attendants asked the minister to send the cage with the animals to her, along with their keeper. The minister told me to go with them. Once I arrived at the palace, I saw that there was a gathering of princesses. They'd all come to see the animals and their keeper!

When they were done scrutinizing the animals—and me as well—they sent me off to see another princess, and from her to yet another one. I kept being taken from place to place until two o'clock in the morning! Finally, they took me back to our residence, where I found my master waiting, and we passed a most comfortable night.

9.21   It so happened that Madame de Bourgogne, the daughter-in-law of the king, had woken up that morning feeling unwell, following the strenuous efforts of the previous day's hunt. So the wives of the princes all gathered at her residence to keep her company while she lay in bed. Among them was a princess who'd heard about the animals and wanted to see them. She begged Madame de Bourgogne to have the animals brought in. So they sent off a servant right away to find the minister, asking him to send the cage with the animals, along with the Oriental porter. The minister accordingly sent for us. When we appeared, he ordered us to go with the servant.

9.22   When we arrived at the princess's palace, they brought me alone with the cage to her private residence and bedroom. I went in and saw the royal bed draped with fine brocade curtains. Reclining on it was the princess, whose beauty was without peer among all the women of her epoch. Seated around her were the wives of the princes, as radiant as moons, wearing dresses that glittered luminously from all the jewels set in them. The sight was simply indescribable.

9.23   They ushered me forward toward the princess reclining on the bed. I presented myself, put the cage down, and bowed deeply, greeting the princess with the deference my master had taught me. As I was leaning forward, one of the princesses noticed the point of the silver-plated dagger I'd slipped into my belt. She reached out and grasped it.

"Come and see the Muslim's sword!" she cried to everyone in attendance.[133]

Hearing these words, I drew back the tail of my coat and said, "No, my lady. What you see here isn't a sword but a dagger."

Upon hearing me utter the word "dagger," she drew back from me and the color of her face changed. But she paid the dagger no more regard, and the other princesses gazed upon the animals and at my clothes.

Eventually, they let me go and I picked up the cage and left. My master, who arrived after I did and had seen what happened, was waiting for me. As I approached, he glared at me furiously and was so angry that he refused to say a word to me. Once we'd arrived at our residence, he reached out to my belt, seized the dagger, and threw it to the ground, attempting to break it!

Then he turned to me and began scolding me for my actions and my heedlessness. "First, you have the audacity to swipe a candelabrum right out of the king's hand!" he said. "I've never heard of anyone behaving so outrageously! Thank goodness our king is so magnanimous, and deigned to permit you to take the candelabrum from his hand. But now you've gone and done it again! You told the princess that this isn't a sword but a dagger! Don't you know that there's an absolute prohibition—which applies even to the king himself—which states that anyone found carrying a dagger or a poniard will be sent to the galleys, where he'll spend the rest of his life? Some have even been sentenced to death if they were merely suspected of being criminals."

My master explained, "It's often said that daggers and poniards are a hidden enemy, unlike a foil, which is there in plain sight, after all. You can always be on your guard when someone is carrying a foil, but a dagger or poniard? They give you the element of surprise against your enemy. That's why the authorities have forbidden anyone from carrying them!

9.24

9.25

"With this prohibition in effect across all of Paris, who would have the nerve to march right into the palace, into the king's bedroom no less, brandishing a pointed blade?" he demanded. "Somehow God saved you—and saved me as well—from a real predicament!"

He broke off the blade of the dagger and took it away.

"But I didn't know!" I offered by way of apology.

"It's only because you didn't know any better that God saved you, and that His Majesty didn't hold you to account!"

9.26   I asked him about the various places we'd visited and about the princess I'd seen in the king's chamber, as well as the young girl standing beside her whom we'd met on our walk with the minister. Was she perhaps the king's daughter?

"No," he replied. "It's a long story, but let me tell it to you so you know what you're talking about when you tell the story yourself. The princess in the king's bedroom is called Madame de Maintenon, and is the wife of the king. The young girl you saw is the ward of the queen, who raised her as her own daughter and educated her."

"*That* was the king's wife?" I asked my master. "But she wasn't beautiful or majestic at all, and she wasn't wearing any royal tokens."

9.27   "Hers is a long and peculiar story," he replied. "The king took her as his wife because of her remarkable intelligence, which has no equal in the whole kingdom. That's why, in fact, he fell in love with her. She'd been an attendant of Madame d'Orléans, the princess with whom the king was in love.[134] He would visit the princess often, and would find this young woman with her. Her conversation skills, fine manners, and keen wit delighted the king."

9.28   One day, the king sent a letter to the princess, summoning her to visit him.[135] The princess, who was feeling quite unwell at the time, could not accept the invitation, but had no idea how to decline it politely. So she ordered her attendant Madame de Maintenon to reply to His Majesty the king, begging his forgiveness for delaying her visit. The young woman set about fulfilling her mistress's request. She wrote a letter conveying her regrets, which began with an overture to the king, followed by a grand, versified apology composed in beautiful language and using refined expressions. The king was dazzled by the letter, and his love for the princess's attendant grew. He wished to bring her to his court and elevate her station. But his wife, the queen, wouldn't consent. She was a saintly woman who feared God, and didn't want any suspicions to arise from the matter.

After a few years, the queen passed away. A great funeral was held for her, and all the church bells of Paris tolled, including the great bell, whose sound can be heard in places as far as seven hours away from the city. The queen's body was transferred to the Church of Saint-Denis, which houses the mausoleum of the kings of France—I myself visited her tomb, as well as the tombs of all the French kings there. 9.29

Forty days after her death, the king's ministers held a council to discuss the matter of the king's marriage. Because Christian kings are anointed by God, they're not permitted to remarry. The ministers had to seek the permission of the pope to sanction the marriage, an action necessary to preserve the royal lineage. Once they received the pope's permission, the ministers went before His Majesty and asked him to consider remarrying. They had in mind a splendidly beautiful princess whose lineage included kings of great nobility. But when they suggested her to the king, he refused. 9.30

"I will take Madame de Maintenon as my wife."

Baffled, the ministers threw themselves at the king's feet in protest. 9.31

"Sire, how could you consent to marry a serving girl, and a foreigner to boot?" they asked. "We don't know anything about her except that she comes from Savoy, a country hostile to your realm. And what will all the other kings say when they learn you've married a servant?"

The king glowered, and told them to keep their advice to themselves. The ministers threw themselves down at his feet once again, begging him to reconsider. But the king refused. When the ministers saw that he wouldn't change his mind, they addressed him once again.

"Your Majesty, you are our king and benefactor," they began. "Yet, even if Your Majesty should consent to let this woman be your wife, we will not accept her as our queen!"

Furious, the king threatened to send them into exile if they did not accept his decree. They then left to consult with one another about how to respond.

9.32 The ministers felt they had no choice but to turn to the king's son, the dauphin, hoping he could dissuade his father and reconcile the ministers with their king. So Monseigneur the Dauphin went to see the king and begged him to change his mind about this scandalous matter.

"Go back to your palace and stay there!" the king retorted, putting him under house arrest.

After that, the dignitaries of the city of Paris gathered to draft a statement declaring that they would never accept the stranger as their queen. Seeing that the townspeople, the military officers, and the nobles of the realm were all of the same mind, opposed to his marriage to the foreign girl, the king reversed course and made it clear to them that he'd decided not to marry her after all. Things then settled down, the gossip ceased, and everything went back to normal.

9.33 The king remained unwed for a whole year. During that time, he initiated the construction of Versailles, building a palace unequaled in any part of the world. He decorated it with all sorts of indescribable gardens, parks, and promenades. The palace is renowned among all the Christian kings.

A curious aspect of Versailles's construction concerns the fact that the River Seine, a great river like the Euphrates, passes behind Versailles, separated from it by a tall mountain. The king wanted to bring the river to Versailles, so he gathered all the engineers and ordered them to channel the river into the gardens surrounding the palace. The engineers consulted among themselves, and agreed that the only way to achieve this was to cut a channel through the mountain.

9.34 They presented this idea to His Majesty the king.

"What would be the point of the river flowing from the *base* of the mountain?" he said. "I want the water to descend from the *top* of the mountain onto the gardens and grounds!" The engineers were baffled, and told the king such a thing was impossible.

"There's nothing we can do," they said, cowering meekly before him. At this, the king grew angry. Suddenly, one of the engineers came forward and kissed the hem of his robe.

"Sire, I'll bring the water down from the top of the mountain," he said. "But it'll cost you a pretty penny."

When the king heard this, he ordered an edict to be drafted, granting the engineer the necessary funds. "If you are true to your word, I'll give you whatever you wish," said the king, signing the edict. "Name your price."

The man kissed the ground before the king and set off to embark upon this wondrous construction.[136] First, he ordered some long iron pumps to be cast, in the style of cannons. He also called for some steel waterwheels and pistons. Once they'd been fashioned according to his design, he summoned some builders and ordered them to dig a deep trench alongside the river. A second trench was then dug beside the first, and this was repeated all the way to the summit of the mountain. He then had a wall built on either side of each trench, installed the first waterwheel, and placed a pump beside it. 9.35

The water flowed through the waterwheel and, as the wheel turned, the piston would enter the pump, fill it with water, and push that water into the second trench, which was two fathoms higher than the first. When that trench, which sloped downward like a millrace, had filled up with water, it would spill onto the second wheel. When the wheel turned, it would work the piston in the pump, pushing the water into the third trench. From there, it flowed into the fourth, and so on and so forth until it reached the summit of the mountain, whereupon the water coursed down copiously into the king's gardens. 9.36

The king ordered the construction of some large pools and stone fountains resembling terraces, and the water flowed down over 9.37

them. They also erected tin fountains in the shapes of various fruit trees, such as orange, lemon, and citron. Water flowed to each tree through a pair of pipes, and spouted out of every leaf![137] Beneath each tree was a meadow with a couple of thin pipes that also sprayed water. There was a broad walkway, as wide as four men walking side by side, and two hundred cubits in length. Water spouted over the walkway from both sides: The fountains on the left side sprayed water to the right side and the fountains on the right side sprayed water to the left side. The streams met in the middle, forming a watery vault! And yet, those who walked beneath it didn't feel a single drop, thanks to the power of the water descending from the top of the mountain.

9.38 The excess water flowed into a small river that ran through the gardens and then left Versailles and rejoined the river running behind the mountain. In addition to all of this, a great number of trees were planted in a dense fashion, creating a sort of forest. On its borders, there was a hedge formed out of a certain species of tree that coils endlessly upon itself, sprouting so many leaves and tangled branches that even an arrow shot at it wouldn't pass through. Inside the forest, they let loose rabbits, gazelles, and other wild animals to be hunted. The forest extended for a day's journey by foot from one end to the other, and the animals soon proliferated throughout.

The waterwheels continue to work to this day, and the water still comes down that mountain. The glories of the place are simply indescribable. I haven't done them justice with this humble account.

9.39 Let us return to our story. Once the construction was complete and the plans had come to fruition—the splendid and lofty palaces, the garden, the watercourses—the king ordered all his things transferred from his palace in Paris to the palace in Versailles.[138] He placed his throne in Versailles in a suitably august setting and brought all the dignitaries of his realm, the ministers, and the courtiers to Versailles, in order to punish the people of Paris for not accepting Madame de Maintenon as their queen. That was why he brought her to his palace in Versailles and married her there in a Christian wedding, all of its conditions fulfilled.[139] The king remained in Versailles until his death, and never returned to Paris.

This is the story my master told me about the queen I saw reclining in the king's room.

I spent eight days at the king's palace, during which time the 9.40 cage ordered by the king's son, the dauphin, was completed and the animals were placed inside. During those eight days, I toured the palace freely; no one prevented me from going wherever I wanted. Finally, I returned to Paris, where my master had rented a house at his own expense. We resided in that house, which was above Pont Saint-Michel. We were visited by many of Paris's dignitaries, and my master would also visit them, bringing me along to see their lavish mansions and well-designed properties.

One day, we visited the home of a prince. At the rear of the 9.41 salon, I saw a painting of a man holding a bird in his hand. From the onlooker's perspective, however, it seemed as though the man's hand and the bird protruded out of the picture. I studied the painting and was convinced his hand was outside the frame, but those present told me it was nothing but a picture. I wouldn't believe it until one of them rose and touched the painting with his hand. Finally convinced, I praised the master who had produced that remarkable painting, which, I was told, was a copy of an original by the artist Pietro.[140] It had been purchased for five hundred piasters.

The story of that artist is extraordinary indeed. During his youth, 9.42 he was a cobbler's apprentice, and an ugly one at that. One day, he spied the daughter of a prince, whose beauty was unrivaled by any other maiden. She was out for a walk with some other royals, and as he stared at her, his heart was overcome with love. So much so, in fact, that he followed her from one place to another until she arrived at her father's palace and disappeared from sight. The youth began to lie in wait near the palace, waiting for her to emerge every now and then when she would go for a walk, as was the custom in those lands. When she did, he'd follow her and gaze at her.

This happened several times without the girl taking any notice. But then the children of the other princes who accompanied her on her walks began to congratulate her on having such a charming and handsome admirer.

9.43   This made her angry, and so she went to speak to her father about the young man, telling him how he followed her everywhere, staring constantly, and making her into a laughingstock among the prince's other descendants. The prince was furious and had the young man brought before him.

"Who do you think you are, following my daughter the princess wherever she goes?" he asked angrily. "What do you want with her?"

"I love her," the young man replied.

Hearing these words, the prince laughed aloud at the boy's ignorance.

"Would you like to marry her?" he asked sweetly.

"Yes."

"And what will you offer as her dowry?"

"Ask what you wish," the young man said.

To this, the prince said, "I wish for you to paint her portrait. If you do that, I'll let you marry her, on the condition that if you continue to follow her, I'll have you hanged."

9.44   The young man agreed to this condition, and left the prince's house in a state of elation. He set about scribbling on walls, trying to sketch the girl's portrait, but failed to make any headway. So he was compelled to work for a period as apprentice to an artist, grinding paints while he studied the master at work, learning his techniques of drawing and his methods for composing different paints. Eventually, he set about drawing the portrait of the girl from memory, as her image was emblazoned in his mind, so deep was his longing for her.

9.45   At last, the young man perfected the portrait. He went to see the prince and presented him with the painting. The prince studied it and was astonished by its fine craftsmanship. He couldn't believe it was the work of that young man.

"Who painted this?" he asked him.

"This is the work of my own hand," the young man replied. "Just as you stipulated."

The prince refused to believe him and wanted to hear the truth. He summoned four master artists and showed them the painting.

"Do you know the artist who painted this?" he asked them.

"No one could paint a portrait like this," they said. "Not in this country, and not in India either. No human being painted this. It must have been an angel or a demon!"

Faced with this evidence, the prince now realized that the painting had to be, in fact, the young man's work. So he summoned him once again, and asked if he was indeed the true painter of the portrait. 9.46

"My lord, why not investigate the matter?" the young man replied. "If any other artist can produce a painting like this, then I'm a liar."

"You've spoken well, my son. But I've already married my daughter off, because I never believed that you could produce her portrait," the prince said. "As for my vow, I offer you her sister instead."

When the young man heard that the girl was married, he lost his senses and began to hallucinate. He fled the prince's house like a madman, his passion for the girl having stripped him of all reason. He set about wandering through wilderness and wasteland. Eventually, tormented by his hunger and miserably bedraggled state, he stopped in a city and found work as an artist's servant, grinding paint in exchange for food. 9.47

At that time, the artist was at work on a glorious portrait, which he hoped would win him recognition as the finest of all painters. When it was finished, he set the painting in a place of honor and went to invite all the master artists to come see his work and to declare him a great master. After he left, the apprentice—whose name was Nicholas—stood up, painted a fly on the nose of the person in the portrait, then sat down again and went on grinding paint.

A little while later, his master returned in the company of the other artists. They sat down on some chairs and the master 9.48

presented his portrait to them. Seeing what appeared to be a fly on the surface of the painting, he reached out to shoo it away, but it didn't budge. Scrutinizing it carefully, the master realized that it was in fact painted on! He whirled around to face his apprentice, embarrassed at having been fooled.

"Who came in here and painted this fly?" he demanded.

"Nobody came in besides Crazy Nicholas, your apprentice," he said. "It was *he* who painted the fly!"[141]

9.49   When the assembled artists heard that the painter was none other than Nicholas—who had acquired no small amount of notoriety in those lands—they rose to their feet in his honor.

"As a master of this art, why are you treating yourself in this way?" they asked him. "Come join us, and we'll be *your* students!"

But he didn't accept, nor did he pay them any mind. He turned to leave.

"Why don't you stay here with me now, and we can explore the subject of painting together?" his master persisted.

"Why?" the apprentice Nicholas asked. "What's your purpose in keeping me around?"

"I'll paint a picture, and then you paint a picture," his master proposed. "Whoever paints the finer one, in the judgment of these artists, will be the master."

9.50   Nicholas agreed to the challenge. The artists all went on their way, and his master began to paint. When his painting was complete, he invited the artists back to show them his work. It was an image of fruits and grapes hanging from a trellis. He hung it outside, and the birds were fooled, flocking around and pecking at the painting as though the fruits and grapes were real! Witnessing this scene, the assembled artists attested to his mastery, for he had managed to deceive the birds.

"Now it's your turn," they said, turning to Nicholas. "Paint us a picture so that we can judge them both accurately."

"Give me a room to myself so that I may paint alone," Nicholas replied. "No one may come in until I'm finished, one month from now."

The artists agreed. They gave him a room and some painting supplies, and left him alone.

Nicholas began his painting, and completed it within a day. His plan, though, was to give the artists the impression that he'd taken much longer to finish it because of the great craft it demanded. After a month had passed, the artists hurried over to see the painting, convinced that it would be a unique masterpiece. 9.51

"Open the room so we may see the painting!" they demanded.

Nicholas handed the key to his master. Opening the door, they spied a painting at the back of the room, covered by a draped cloth. Nicholas's master reached out to lift the cloth, but his hand struck the wall: The cloth had been painted directly upon it! The master was embarrassed, as he'd been fooled a second time.

"It doesn't take much skill to fool a few birds," said Nicholas, turning to his master. "Fooling a master painter like you? That takes some doing!"

He turned and walked away, leaving them all flabbergasted by the cloth and its artistry.

Whenever this fellow would check into an inn, he'd stay for two or three days, eating and drinking his fill. And when the innkeeper would ask him to settle his bill, Nicholas would tell him to bring him some paper to draw on. 9.52

"Take this paper to a master painter and offer to sell it for five gold pieces," he told the innkeeper. "If he doesn't pay you, bring it back to me."

The man would go off and present the drawing to one of the master artists, asking for five gold pieces. The artist would offer three, so the innkeeper would return with the drawing to consult with Nicholas, who'd grab his work and rip it in half. Then he'd make another drawing, this one even more sublime and masterful.

"Don't take less than ten gold pieces for this one."

The innkeeper would set off again and ask for ten gold pieces, receiving a counteroffer of five. He'd return to the inn and find that Nicholas had left and not come back, as though he were angry.

Nicholas spent the rest of his life in this way, traveling with a sack on his shoulder and his dog trotting behind him. His paintings and drawings continue to fetch high prices even today. So ends this summary of his story.

9.53   Let's return to our account of the admirable public works of Paris. First, there are eight hundred churches in this city, not counting the monasteries and convents. Each church contains several collection chests, some reserved for the poor people of the quarter, and some for those who'd come down in the world, having once led a life of ease before sinking into poverty and need. These last are too proud to beg, or to admit to being indigent, so each church keeps a collection chest just for them. Two priests are assigned to disburse the collected funds in a discreet manner, so that no one knows who the recipients are.

The other collection chests are reserved for the poor people of the quarter, including the blind, the housebound, the elderly, the senile, and widows with children. Two upstanding residents of the quarter are put in charge of disbursing the funds from the collection chests according to the needs of each recipient. The names of the recipients are registered in a ledger.

9.54   I never saw a single person begging for alms in Paris. In fact, I once saw a one-legged soldier being beaten violently and mercilessly by some of the governor's men, and when I asked an onlooker why they were beating him, he replied that they'd seen him begging. I was astonished.

"In your country, would they really beat up someone just for begging?" I asked him. "Even a man like that, without a leg, who can't work? How is that allowed?"

"That man deserves it," he replied. "After all, the king—may God save him—takes care of war invalids and pays them a pension. Anything they need, they get free of charge, so they have no excuse to beg. It's a slap in the king's face!"

9.55   I asked to hear more.

"There's a big hospital," I was told, "for invalids and crippled soldiers, built by the king. They have physicians, surgeons, a chapel, and priests to receive confessions. Lunch and dinner are prepared every day, and there's a bed for every man to sleep in, and other comforts of that sort. So, what excuse would an invalid have to go out begging? The only reason is greed! That's why anyone caught begging is punished on the spot. And at the hospital, they make an example of beggars by stretching them out on a wooden plank and flogging them on the buttocks with a bull-pizzle whip."

Each church also has a collection chest dedicated to the hospital in its quarter. In addition to the aforementioned churches in the city of Paris, there is the Church of Notre-Dame. It is a very imposing church with a large bell, about the size of a small dome. The bell is situated at the top of a tall minaret and supported by four pillars, and is nearly a handspan thick. In the center of the bell is an iron ringer, which is attached to pulleys and ropes that dangle down to the church's lower level. To ring the bell with any force, it takes a team of twelve men to pull on the ropes. It takes some effort to make the ringer strike the side of the bell, but when it does, it clangs loudly enough to frighten the citizens, and you can hear it from seven miles away. They only ring it on rare occasions, such as when a king, prince, cardinal, or other important figure dies. 9.56

Inside Notre-Dame are eighty chapels, each the size of a small church. In the center of the church is a grand altar that can be approached from two sides. Each of the church's seven doors opens onto a different quarter of Paris—every one of the quarters as large as the walled city of Aleppo. Be assured that this is no exaggeration. Travelers have reported that Paris is seven times as large as Istanbul; it has some streets that would take a vigorous walker a whole hour to travel from beginning to end. The head of this church is a cardinal sent by His Holiness the pope, vested with powers similar to those of a second pope over the region of France. 9.57

Among the cardinal's men was one named Christofalo, who was the brother of Paulo Çelebi in Aleppo. He was one of the cardinal's senior officers, occupying a rank higher than the others and serving as his chief steward.

9.58   When I was there, it happened to be the Feast of Corpus Christi. The custom of the Parisians is to hold three processions of the Blessed Sacrament. The first takes place on the day of the feast itself, which is a Thursday. The second is on the Sunday, and the third is on the following Thursday. On the day of the procession, people decorate their walls, doors, and shops with their finest fabrics and adornments, and scatter flowers in the streets. At each intersection, a platform is set up in the shape of an altar. When the procession reaches the altar, they expose the Blessed Sacrament and recite some litanies, hymns, and other supplications.

9.59   On the day of the grand procession from the Church of Notre-Dame, which passed through the quarter in which I was living, I stood at the window, watching it go by. There were more than five hundred priests and deacons, all wearing vestments of gold brocade, and carrying camphor candles and gold crucifixes. Following the priests and deacons came the cardinal himself, who stood beneath a large canopy supported by twelve poles carried by twelve men. Under the canopy, the cardinal held the ostensorium, the vessel that holds the Blessed Sacrament.

9.60   As I stared at the ostensorium, I felt as though I were looking at the sun! The sheer number of diamonds, rubies, emeralds, and other precious jewels covering it made it so dazzling that you could hardly train your gaze upon it. And yet you couldn't look away either. As I stood there gaping in astonishment at this spectacle, my master came over to my side.[142]

"Read me what's written on that canopy," he said.

I looked closer and made out some white baize letters appliquéd on dark-red cloth. They read: "There is no God but God . . ." and the rest of it.[143] I was shocked to see such an inscription upon the canopy.

9.61   "What does it say?" my master asked.

I told him, and he was appalled. Refusing to believe it, he ordered me to go over to the neighbors' house to get a better look at the inscription from their window. I did as he asked and scrutinized the inscription again, and found that I'd read it correctly the first time. I returned to my master to confirm my observation.

"I can't be mistaken, because the cloth is red and the letters are in white baize," I said. "How could I be wrong?"

Convinced, my master ordered me to go visit the cardinal and relate to him what I'd seen.

"The cardinal is certain to treat you most honorably for this service," my master said, "and will also reward you with some money."

I waited until two o'clock in the afternoon and went to the cardinal's palace.

9.62

"What is your business?" the gatekeepers asked me. I explained that I had a message for His Holiness the cardinal.

"What is your message?" they asked.

"I've been ordered to convey it to His Holiness alone."

A gatekeeper was delegated to accompany me into the palace to the cardinal's quarters. There, a servant boy invited me to follow him. We climbed to a higher floor and entered a room, where I saw an imposing man sitting on a chair.

9.63

"Who are you, and what country are you from?" he asked, scrutinizing me.

"I'm from Syria," I replied. "The city of Aleppo."

"To which community do you belong?" he asked me—in refined Arabic!

"I'm from the Maronite community," I replied.

"Greetings, countryman!" he proclaimed, welcoming me with great warmth. "Do you know who I am?"

"No, sir."

"I belong to the Zamāriyā family.[144] My older brother's name is Paulo Çelebi, and I have another brother named Yūsuf. The head of the family is Zamāriyā, the procurator of Jerusalem in Istanbul, where he lives with the ambassador."

"I know *khawājah* Paulo Çelebi and his brother Yūsuf of Aleppo!" I said. "Everyone does. They have a fine reputation."

"What brings you here?" he asked. "I spotted you from my window as you were coming in with one of the chamberlains to see His Holiness the cardinal. Do you have any business with him? If you tell me what it is, I'll take care of it for you."

"God save you, sir! There's nothing I need myself, but I have a message for His Holiness."

"And what's the message? I'm his steward, and no one may see him without my permission."

9.64 I felt compelled to tell him about the inscription I'd seen. When I did, he was astonished.

"Is this really true?" he demanded, repeating the question over and again.

"Yes sir! Your Excellency can see it for yourself," I replied.

"There's no need for you to see the cardinal," he replied. "Let me look into the matter myself. Come back and see me tomorrow, and I'll let you know if you were right about what you saw. Then we can go see the cardinal."

9.65 The rest of the day passed without incident. The next day, I went back.

"What you told me was true!" he said. "I went to tell His Holiness about your message. Right away he called for the sacristan and ordered him to bring the cloths that were draped over the canopy of the Blessed Sacrament."

Now, when the sacristan brought the cloths and they saw the inscription written upon them, the cardinal demanded that the sacristan explain where the cloths had come from.

"Your Holiness, these are antique banners taken from our enemies in the Maghreb," said the sacristan. "They were deposited in the storeroom of the sacristy. I used them to cover the top of the canopy to keep it from being smudged by the dirt falling from the rooftops."

The cardinal ordered them to burn the cloths right away. But why were the banners in the Church of Notre-Dame in the first place?

The reason was that when the French kings would win a war against the Maghrebis, they would take their banners and display them in the church as a memorial, offering prayers of thanksgiving.

"There's no longer any need for you to see the cardinal," the steward said after he finished recounting what had happened. He insisted that I come back to visit him regularly, and sent me on my way.

In the quarter of the Church of Notre-Dame, there is a large hospital named Hôtel de Dieu, which means "Altar of God."[145] It was so called because it admitted all who came to it, no matter what community they belonged to, no questions asked, whether they were poor or rich or just a simple laborer. In other words, it accepted all people on an equal basis. I shall now describe the excellent organization of this hospital and the wonderful care it provided. 9.66

First, when an invalid arrives at the hospital, he encounters a man of dignified bearing seated at the door, surrounded by servants at his beck and call. He asks the invalid if he is a foreigner or a native of the city, how old he is, and whether he has a baptismal certificate with him.

Next, he asks whether the invalid is a Christian or belongs to a different religion. Once he has answered all the questions, the man registers his name and the date on a ledger hanging on the wall, which contains a list of all 1,500 patients in the hospital at the time, a figure that fluctuates. He then admits the invalid, accompanied by one of his servants, into the building. There, the patient comes upon a chapel with priests taking confession. One of the priests receives him, brings him into his cell, and prepares him for confession. After hearing his general confession, the priest absolves him of his sins and sends him to see the chief doctor to be diagnosed.

Following the examination, the patient is handed off to one of the apprentice doctors supervised by the chief doctor, with an order to move the patient into the ward reserved for people with the same illness. There are many wards in the building, by which I mean halls, each one dedicated to a specific illness. On either side of a given gallery, there are beds covered with red broadcloth. A 9.67

unique number—which they call *numéro*—is appliquéd in white cloth at the foot of every bed. There are about two hundred beds on the two sides of the ward, and at the back is an altar dedicated to a saint. Each day, a morning mass is held for the ward's patients.

9.68 As I was saying, when the doctor takes charge of his new patient, he brings him into a large room containing many cubbyholes, or lockers. Each contains a hospital gown. They have the patient change out of his clothes, which he places in a locker, and into a gown. The patient's name is written on the locker so he can find his clothes again once he has recovered from his illness and is about to leave the hospital. And whenever someone wishes to visit a relative or friend in the hospital, he first has to check the chief doctor's ledger.

"Go to the third or fourth or fifth hall," they tell him. "Search for bed number such and such, and you'll find your patient there."

In the absence of such a system, one could spend three days searching the hospital for a person without finding them!

9.69 In each hall, a doctor is designated to distribute medicines to the patients every morning and evening. Following mass each morning, the patients are served soup, and again at lunch and dinner. I witnessed a soup service. A man pulls a cart that has a large pot sitting on it. A second cart carries a long, narrow case containing tin bowls. The servants ladle soup into the bowls and hand them to the patients, proceeding down to the end of the ward. I also saw many noblewomen sitting beside the patients, serving them and keeping their spirits up. If a patient needs anything, the women send a servant to fetch it.

9.70 When a patient needs to answer the call of nature, the woman tending him seats him on the chamber pot and, afterward, goes and empties it. Even though she has four or five servants at her disposal, she doesn't allow a single one to tend to her patient. She sees to his every need, enduring every filthy service and foul odor. I also witnessed that when an invalid is on the verge of death and fighting for his life, they quickly summon a priest to administer the extreme unction. All who pass by his bed stop to offer prayers and supplications on behalf of the patient. If he dies, they hold a funeral service right there, then transport his body to the cemetery nearby.

Right next door to the hospital is a second hospital reserved for 9.71 women. The only men permitted to enter are priests and doctors. It matches exactly the hospital I just described. On the lower level is a convent of about two or three hundred nuns, devoted to serving the sick. They clean, sew, and patch their clothes, and knead and bake their own bread. A great river runs by the hospital—the one that runs through the middle of Paris—and I saw them there, laundering the patients' clothes.

I was told that there is a hidden area inside the women's hospital 9.72 devoted to girls who fall into disgrace. Before the signs of their pregnancy become visible, their families send them there without anyone's knowledge. As soon as a girl delivers her baby, it is taken from her and given to the wet nurses. The girl is released, and they raise the newborn. Once grown, it is apprenticed to an artisan to learn a craft. Many of these children have become skilled master artisans themselves. Some have risen to lofty positions and others have become officials. Still others have entered monasteries, becoming monks, and in some cases abbots and even saints.

The blessed hospital is responsible for all of these many works of 9.73 charity. I've recorded just a small portion of what I witnessed and heard about this place called Hôtel de Dieu in French, or "Altar of God."

The hospital is supported by the income from various charitable trusts and properties, which include a vast number of villages, plots of land, houses, and shops. It also receives funds from donation chests in all the churches, supplied by everyone who leaves cash in the offering boxes. Many merchants and city nobles leave sums of money to the hospital in their wills. All this is to say that its sources of funding surpass its expenses by a considerable margin.

In Paris, there is also a hospital devoted to delinquent chil- 9.74 dren.[146] It is located in a monastery just outside the city. I visited the monastery, and they brought me in to see the place where the children were held. It was a long room, with a wooden beam traversing the entire length of it. Iron stakes had been pounded into the beam, and the children were tied to the stakes with a chain. They were separated from each other in such a way that none could quite reach his neighbor, and they sat on straw mats, at work on one thing or another for the monastery. They received bread and water by way of nourishment, and twice a day they were stretched out on a whipping frame made of planks and flogged across the buttocks. Each remains at the hospital until the father or mother consents to let them leave. Otherwise, they stay for good.

In Paris, there are schools for every science and branch of knowledge found anywhere in the world. This is because the king, when a particular science was unknown, would send to distant climes for experts to come and teach that subject in France.

9.75   During my time there, a curious incident befell the king. One night, as he was lying in bed, he was seized by an uncanny foreboding, making him profoundly anxious. Terrified, he was unable to remain in bed, and he got up and left his bedchamber. Outside, his sentries stood guard as usual. The king always had a personal guard of forty strapping men to watch over his sacred person day and night, as was the ancient custom. The king scrutinized his guards to see if there were any interlopers among them, but didn't see one.

"Did a stranger enter my quarters?" he asked.

"How could anyone have, sire?" they replied.

He ordered them to light some candles and search the palace. They did as he instructed, searching everywhere, accompanied by the king, but found no one. They returned together, and the king went back to his pavilion and lay down in his bed.

9.76   But his anxiety-filled delusions returned, twice as vivid. He got up again and went outside.

"Is there an enemy here?" he cried out to the guards. "Tell me the truth!"

"Sire, we just searched every room and found no one," they said, throwing themselves at his feet. "The palace gates are shut and guards are standing watch. How could a stranger or an enemy get in?"

The king was at a loss. Guided by a divine inspiration, he ordered them to accompany him into the palace gardens. They relit the candles and followed the king into the palace again. They opened the gate that led into the gardens, and toured them with their candles blazing, searching among the trees and in every nook and cranny. Once again they found no one, and turned to head back to the palace.

Then one of the king's guards, candle in hand, spotted a shadow in a cypress tree. He stopped, raised the candle, and saw a man hiding in the tree. He told the king, who ordered them to bring the man down. It turned out to be a young man, heavily armed. The king ordered them to take his weapons away. 9.77

"What are you doing here?" he asked the young man. "What is your purpose? Speak truthfully, and as God is my witness I will do you no harm."

"I'm your mortal enemy, king of the age!" the young man replied. "I snuck in and hid here to kill you in your bed!"

"What has driven you to try to murder me?" the king asked. "What did I ever do to harm you?" 9.78

"My religion compels me to kill you—you are the enemy of our faith," the young man replied.

"Yours may be a vile faith that compels you to murder me for no fault at all, but mine is a holy faith that compels me to forgive you," the king said. "Go, and tell your people so."

The king ordered them to let the man go, and they set him free outside the palace. Then the king went back to his private chambers and lay in bed. He no longer felt that sense of foreboding, for God had saved him from death through a manifest miracle.

Once this news had spread throughout Paris, the nobles and state officials all came before the king to congratulate him on his deliverance from the danger he had faced. They requested that he convene 9.79

a general council, including all the bishops and the abbots of the monasteries. Once all had gathered for the council and assumed their appropriate places, the Duke of Orléans came forward and informed the king that there were many Huguenots in the kingdom of France, heretics who were enemies of the Catholic faith. They'd managed to corrupt many guileless people of the flock, and were working to corrupt more.

"Sire, we fear they'll spread their heresy throughout all of France," he said.

9.80 When the king heard the duke's words and had his report confirmed, he ordered a royal edict drawn up then and there, to be proclaimed throughout France.

"Six months from today, any Huguenots found in my kingdom will be killed, and their property seized by the monarchy," the edict announced. "Let them all settle their loans and debts, and freely sell their homes, plots of land, orchards, and other properties. Once this period has elapsed, those who remain do so at their own risk."

The king further ordered the bishops, priests, and abbots to send letters throughout France proclaiming the edict of the cardinal of Paris, which stated that anyone who was aware of the presence of a Huguenot should report this to the local authority, on pain of excommunication. And so they wrote to all the bishoprics so that each bishop could inform his flock about the edict.[147]

9.81 The king also ordered that a royal gatekeeper be stationed at every point of entry to French lands, to prevent any heretics from entering the kingdom. Anyone without a certificate of baptism would be turned away. For the next six months, the Huguenots began to leave France, one group after another. Some went to English lands, others to Flemish lands, and still others dispersed throughout Italy. Some went to Germany and cities elsewhere, until France was entirely cleansed of them.

9.82 Some time later, a shoemaker in Paris was returning home after an evening out when he saw two strangely dressed people entering a doorway. He thought they might be thieves, so he went into his own house and repaired to a window to spy on the place they'd entered. Three more people entered as he watched. Then another three or four. People kept arriving until midnight. This sight surprised the shoemaker, particularly since the building they'd entered had been abandoned for a long time.

"I'm going to keep an eye on this place to find out who these people are," he said to himself.

He stayed by the window until three o'clock in the morning. Suddenly, he saw some people leave the building, followed by some others. This went on until the last people to leave shut the door behind them.

When morning came, the shoemaker went to see the governor 9.83 and told him about the people he'd seen coming and going during the night. After hearing his story, the governor ordered the shoemaker to come back that evening, and not to tell a soul about what he'd witnessed in the meantime. When the shoemaker returned, the governor ordered two of his men to accompany him and hide in his house to find out if he was telling the truth. They weren't to breathe a word to anyone.

As they hid in the shoemaker's home later that night, groups of people began arriving at the abandoned house once again. The governor's men waited to see them emerge, and sure enough, the people eventually came out of the house and closed the door behind them, just as the shoemaker had told the governor.

They returned to the governor and reported what they'd seen. 9.84 Immediately, the governor sent spies to make peepholes in the walls. After a while, they figured out what the place was and who was meeting there. When the Huguenots had lived in Paris, they would gather once or twice a month at that place and hold council. When the governor realized that this was still going on, he carried out a thorough investigation and reported his findings to the king. The king gave an order to have the Huguenots followed, up to the moment they entered the house. Then they were to be locked inside. Meanwhile, the king's men were to climb to the roof and . . . bring the building down on their heads. If anyone survived, they were to be killed on the spot. The house was to be razed to the ground and the lot was to be left unpaved as a reminder to future generations. In the end, five hundred men were killed, and their property was seized by the monarchy.

9.85   I once passed by that place, accompanied by a Parisian. When I saw the unpaved lot, I was surprised, and asked my companion why every street in Paris was paved with black stones except that one. He told me this story, explaining that the lot was left unpaved as a memorial.

9.86   While I was in Paris, an ambassador arrived from Istanbul. He had been dispatched by His Majesty Sultan Aḥmad to request eight anchors from His Majesty the sultan of France, as he had recently constructed five ships for the sultan's fleet. The ambassador was received most honorably and welcomed into Paris with a great procession. One of the king's palaces was prepared as a residence for him, furnished with a staff of cooks and an ample pantry. He had forty officials in his retinue, as well as many servants. The king appointed one of his own interpreters to serve him, and after a few days granted the ambassador an audience in the company of Pontchartrain, minister for the Orient. The king showered the ambassador with honors and prepared a sumptuous banquet for him.

9.87   After they'd dined, the king had the ambassador shown around the beautiful grounds of Versailles. He was shown the royal gardens and the water spouting from the trees, the pools, the fountains, and especially that arching vault made of water, which I described previously. After taking in all these sights, the ambassador returned to the palace that had been prepared for him in Paris. The nobles of the city began to pay him visits, congratulating him on his safe arrival. The wives of nobles and princes also came along for curiosity's sake.

9.88   Each day, I'd go to the ambassador's palace and sit with his officials. Often, the interpreter wasn't present, so I would interpret for the ambassador and some of the nobles' wives. The ambassador was astounded by the gracious modesty of these women, their refined and pleasant conversation, and their sparkling repartee. He mused that the women of Frankish lands had far better manners and were more respectable than the women of his own country.

Once the city's nobles were done calling on the ambassador, he began to repay their visits. He gazed upon their homes, with their orderliness and good management, and their comfortable way of life. It struck him that there was a notable difference between the law and order in Frankish countries and law and order in his own land, which was beset with tumult, trouble, oppression, and tyrannical leaders who lorded over their subjects.[148] He would privately confess all this to his officials, who would tell me what he'd said, as they were in agreement with him.

After a few days, the minister told the interpreter and some 9.89 senior government officials to take the ambassador to l'Opéra. This was a place where extraordinary and wondrous plays took place during the wintertime. People would go there twice a week. The interpreter, acting on behalf of the minister, invited the ambassador to go that very evening, and he accepted the invitation.

I happened to be at the ambassador's palace at the time. When I heard the news, I was overjoyed. I went to tell my master about it, and begged his permission to let me join the ambassador's retinue and witness the spectacle. I received his permission and headed back to the ambassador's palace to wait until the appointed hour.

The representatives of His Excellency the minister arrived and 9.90 invited the ambassador to accompany them. He left the palace with his entourage, and I joined them. The ambassador and the minister's men climbed into a royal carriage and headed off to the opera. We all entered together. It was a vast space with tall columns and two long galleries—one on each side. The galleries were divided into small sections, each of which could accommodate no more than eight people. The sections were like boxes, and each had its own door. Inside each box were a balustrade and benches made of ornately carved walnut.

9.91   Each box had a price. For example, a seat in the first set of boxes, which was at the very end of the gallery, cost a piaster.[149] The second set of boxes was higher up and closer to the stage; a seat in one of those boxes cost two piasters. The third set of boxes, which directly faced the stage, had a price of one gold piece per seat. Whoever wished to attend a play—either alone or in a group of eight or five or three people—had to visit the opera the day before to see the agent, who would sell him a ticket for the number of people attending and the category of box in which they wished to sit. Once he'd received the money, the agent would write out a ticket in his own hand, certifying that he had received payment for a specific number of people, and indicating which box they were permitted to enter. The people, upon arriving at the opera, would hand their ticket to the usher, who would lead them to the seats indicated on the ticket. Then the door to their box would be locked so no one could go in.

9.92   They brought the ambassador into the first box, the place of honor, and the closest to the stage. His retinue were given the second box, and the doors were kept open for the sake of space. When we sat down, all I could see was a curtain hanging across the width of the stage. After a few moments, a great white light began to glow behind the curtain. It was so bright it seemed to me the sun itself was shining on it. A moment later, the curtain rose, revealing an astonishing scene. First, there was what appeared to be a mountain in the very center of the stage. It was covered with trees, among which peasants walked with their donkeys. And at the foot of the mountain was a village, where peasants, men and women alike, bustled in and out of their houses. A group of cows, goats, and other animals stood nearby, together with some shepherds. I had to look twice to confirm that everything I saw—people and beasts alike—were real, and not specters or phantoms. It was unmistakable: They were creatures of flesh and blood!

9.93   A few moments later, the stage was plunged into darkness. A large cloud floated down out of thin air and settled on the ground. Inside the cloud was a tall man with a white beard. He wore a royal crown and carried a crooked cane, and was so striking in appearance that you couldn't take your eyes off him. He intoned some obscure and incomprehensible words, and suddenly twelve young girls and twelve young boys emerged from the cloud. Not one could have been older than fourteen. They wore golden royal robes and were as luminous as moons, and they lined up on the right and left sides of the stage. Then the musical instruments began to play, and the boys and girls joined in with voices as pure as gold filament. The harmony of voices and instruments was so mesmerizing that I utterly lost track of time.

The orchestra played for half an hour. Then it fell silent, and the 9.94 old man began to chant some verses in a melodious voice. As he did, the boys and girls walked forward to him in pairs, responding with their own verses, set to melodies so beautiful they would charm a king. Once they finished singing, the orchestra began to play again and continued for the rest of the hour. Then the old man climbed into the cloud once again, and it rose into the air and disappeared. Meanwhile, everything else that had been onstage flew up too, and vanished in the blink of an eye! In its place appeared a palace as splendid as the palace of the king of France, complete with towering columns, pavilions, salons, crystal windows, and other beautiful features.

The palace had an arched entryway made of black and white 9.95 marble. From it emerged a king in purple robes, a crown upon his head, and emanating a royal aura. He held a scepter in his hand and was surrounded by a retinue of ministers and grandees. The king strode forward to a designated spot, and the boys and girls came out to greet him, kissing the ground before him, then returning to stand in line once more. The instruments began to play again, and the boys and girls sang along in sweet, angelic voices until the orchestra fell silent and the stage went dark. A moment later, a large cloud floated down from the sky, and a beautiful young maiden emerged from it along with a pair of small children. They looked like angels, as each had wings and carried a bow and arrows.

9.96   The maiden began to converse with the king while the children shot blunt arrows at him. When he spurned her attempts to win him over, they quarreled and turned away from each other. Looking furiously at the king, the maiden climbed into the cloud with the two children, and it rose up and disappeared. Suddenly, the ground split open and a demon appeared! He had a long tail and contorted skin, and as he emerged from the earth he spat fire and smoke in the face of the king. Then he vanished into thin air, leaving the king ranting and raving and foaming at the mouth like a madman.

9.97   At the sight of the demon and the mad king, the retinue of ministers and nobles fled in terror, fearing they might suffer the same fate. The king was left alone, reciting verses about what had befallen him and asking himself if he was dreaming or awake, all the while in a state of delirium. Suddenly, four bedposts emerged from the ground, followed by a freshly made bed with a pillow set upon it. Seeing it, the king settled into the bed and fell asleep. After he drifted off, four trees sprang up out of the ground at the four corners of the bed. As the trees grew taller, they sprouted branches thick with foliage and soon towered over the bed, sheltering it like a canopy. The king appeared to be sleeping in a garden.

9.98   Then some beautiful maidens with reed flutes emerged from beneath the king's bed. They began to dance around it, playing soft, sweet lullabies on their flutes as they spoke to the sleeping king in their own languages. A few moments later, he woke up, and everything around him disappeared. He returned to reciting verses as he had before he'd fallen asleep; then the cloud with the maiden descended to the stage once again. She fawned over him, trying to seduce him, but the queen appeared and caught the sorceress weaving her spells upon the king. The angry queen lashed out at the maiden, who climbed into her cloud and escaped into the air.

9.99   The queen then turned to the king and began to reproach him bitterly. How could he debase himself with such a woman, a sorceress who had driven him to madness? At this rebuke, the king flew into a rage, drew his weapon, and plunged it into the queen's waist!

The weapon passed through the queen's body, its point emerging from the other side, and she fell to the ground, dead. At the sight of the dead queen, her servant girls fled in horror and told the nobles what had happened. Rallying together, the nobles summoned some soldiers and climbed onto the throne to depose the king. Then a great cry went up in the palace, and everything on stage disappeared except for a white marble basin, with a marble fountain in the shape of a lion. Water spouted from the lion's mouth into the basin, and overflowed into a second basin, which overflowed into a third.

At last the musical instruments began to play, and the young 9.100 boys and girls emerged on stage again, dancing together in pairs in a respectable manner, without a hint of wantonness. When they finished dancing, they bowed to the ambassador and the rest of the audience, and exited. The marble basin then rose into the air, disappearing without a trace! I was beside myself with wonder. From the moment the curtain had gone up, that basin had remained on stage without moving, while everything else changed. I'd concluded that the basin must have received its water through a pipe or a spring. But that was before it rose into the air! Then the stage went completely dark, and I couldn't see a thing. The play was over.

What I've recounted about the opera house and the play is nothing compared to the experience of seeing and hearing it for oneself. It was simply indescribable!

The ambassador got up from his seat along with the interpreter 9.101 and the minister's men, and they all made their way toward the exit. On either side stood all the women who'd been present at the play, most of them princesses, wives of the city's nobles, and other royals. As we walked by, I heard one of the princesses make fun of the ambassador. I understood French, of course, so I turned to her and replied in the same language.

"My lady, why would you speak ill of my master?"

Realizing that I had understood what she'd said, the princess quickly disappeared into the crowd of women, deeply embarrassed and ashamed of her rudeness. In the meantime, we made our way through the crowd and left the opera. Each climbed into his own carriage and went on his way, the ambassador returning to his palace and I to my master's house.

9.102   I found several of my master's friends waiting for me. They were there to hear my account of the evening, and to have a laugh at my expense. When I presented myself before them, they asked me about what I'd seen and heard. They wanted to know—was I impressed?

"Everything I saw and heard was astounding," I replied. "But the most amazing thing was the basin with the water spouting out of the lion's mouth from the beginning of the play to the end, when it just rose up into the air, together with the water! Of all the illusions I saw, that was what impressed me most."

9.103   They all burst into laughter.

"That was the simplest effect of them all!" one of my master's friends replied.

"Then, for goodness' sake, clear up my confusion, kind sir!" I said.

"The basin is made of wood, painted to look like marble," he explained. "There's a tank full of water sitting behind it, its interior coated with pitch. A bucket wheel feeds the water from the tank into a pipe, which flows into the lion's mouth. When the water reaches the last basin, it goes back into the tank."

The bucket wheel was turned by a young boy, and the entire quantity of water that circulated through the fountain amounted to no more than a wineskin's worth, with scarcely a drop going astray. The basin was attached to some pulleys and had black cords that were invisible in the darkness. When they were pulled, the basin would rise easily. All the other theatrical effects made use of the same mechanism.

"What about the old man in the cloud?" I asked.

"That's the Sultan of the Air, and the king's name is Bacchus," he replied. "The title of the play is *The Slumber of King Bacchus*, and everything you saw was related to episodes from that king's life."[150]

He went on to tell me that the opera had cost a great deal of 9.104
money to build. All the young girls and boys I'd seen, along with
everyone else on stage, had been trained there. He explained how
each of the set changes took place, astounding me even more.
It would take far too long to explain all of this, as the changes are
operated by an ingenious system of pulleys and wheels that allows
the entire scene to be transformed in the blink of an eye. The area
behind the stage is vast and quite distant from the spectators, which
is what permits one to see the shapes of things but not the mecha-
nisms behind them.

There's another place called the Comédie, which puts on won- 9.105
derful farces and comedic plays similar to the shadow plays we have
at home, except they are played by real people. These plays have a
main character named Harlequin, just as ours have the characters
of Iwaẓ and Karagöz.[151] Every one of their plays makes reference to
contemporary events, and features miserable drunkards, down-on-
their-luck loafers, cowardly and panic-stricken soldiers, and other
similar characters, especially foolish and uncouth women. The dialogue is convincing and to the point, making an example of these
detestable and blameworthy characters so that the audience might
learn from their ways.

In some churches, on specific days, a lesson is given on how to 9.106
distinguish truth from falsehood. This lesson benefited all sorts of
people—women and men, educated and ignorant, young and old,
wed and unwed, priest and monk. The best example of a lesson that
I encountered proceeded as follows. A wise priest—a philosopher,
in fact—would come to the pulpit. Facing him, below the pulpit,
was another philosopher who was well versed in all the frivolous
chatter of the masses and their superstitions. The priest on the
pulpit would begin to preach the truth, and the second would contradict him with falsehoods, reproducing the claims of those people
deceived by Satan, enemy of the good.

Then the priest on the pulpit would refute these words with evi- 9.107
dence from the Holy Bible, showing him how he'd been deceived

into holding these corrupt views. The priest down below would then begin to confess his sins, recounting only those most common among people. The priest of the truth would reply by invalidating his confession, which was full of tricks and justifications as tangled as a spiderweb, which only added another sin to his record. He'd then teach him how to confess truthfully, without fabrication or ambiguities. This lesson was especially relevant to garrulous women, who were prone to spinning tales to their confessors, and to other similar types.

9.108 In all the other churches, catechism classes were held for children on Sundays and holidays, beginning at one o'clock in the afternoon and continuing until the evening. The children would gather in their neighborhood church along with a learned teacher. The student who had memorized the previous week's lesson would stand in the middle of the assembled group and recite what he'd learned. If he did so faithfully, the teacher would give him a medallion or a picture, setting him apart from those students who hadn't learned their lessons. This would make the others more zealous about doing their work the following week.

Similarly, the schools would hold debates on Sundays and holidays for all the students who studied philosophy. Teachers and pupils would sit together and hold debates on philosophical matters, and whoever articulated the finest argument would receive a silver medallion from his teacher and be named head boy. The same went for those who studied logic, theology, astronomy, and similar sciences.

9.109 I once visited an art school in the company of an artist who was teaching me how to draw. It was Holy Thursday, the eve of Good Friday. As I arrived at the school, I saw four masters of drawing, standing apart from everyone else. They were famous for their skill in illustration, and I accompanied them as they entered the school, as I was there by invitation of my teacher. Once inside, we came to an enormous room furnished with benches on all sides.

A tall wooden cross stood in the center of the room, with three steps at its base. At that moment, a young man appeared. He must have been about thirty years old, and had a perfect physique. He was stark naked except for a white loincloth.

The masters told the young man to go up onto the cross, which 9.110 he did. There were ropes hanging from the two ends of the crossbar, where the nails would have been. Taking a rope in each hand, he placed his feet on a ledge that was nailed to the wooden plank. Once he was settled, the masters began discussing among themselves how to proceed, and soon reached a consensus.

"Lean forward and hang, as though you were dead," they told him.

He slackened his body, bending his knees while leaving his feet planted on the ledge so he was hanging by his hands. Then they told him to loll his head to the side, which he did, looking for all the world like a dead man. He was the very image of Our Lord the Messiah, dead upon the cross.

When everything was prepared and the four masters were satis- 9.111 fied with the scene being represented, they instructed all the pupils to enter the room and to draw the crucifix as it was composed before them. All came in, took their places, and spent an hour drawing with pencils on paper. The young man came down off the cross to take a short break before assuming the same pose he had before. After another hour, the pupils had finished their drawings and presented them to their masters, who scrutinized them carefully and chose one as the finest. They gave the pupil who had produced the drawing a gold medallion on a chain to wear around his neck, and declared him to be top of his class.

Other places were devoted to teaching fencing, which is similar 9.112 to the sport of stick and shield we have here at home. Other places offered instruction in riflery, shooting, cannon firing, and horsemanship. In sum, there were schools dedicated to every art and discipline in the world, even ones that taught dance and how to play musical instruments.

There are many ladies of light virtue in Paris. Their homes are 9.113 each marked by a sign hanging on their doors of a large heart made of thorns. There are also plenty of scoundrels among the citizens, including one woman in particular who played a trick so dastardly that it deserves to be recorded for all posterity. This is how it went: She rented a beautiful ball gown, fit for a wealthy lady, and a carriage, drawn by four horses, with some footmen to ride on the back of it, and drove off to the monastery devoted to the reform of delinquent children.

Upon arrival, she summoned the abbot and begged him to help her with her dissolute son, who had squandered the family's money by gambling at cards and other debaucheries. His father was dead, she explained, and she planned to bring the young man to the monastery under false pretenses. Would the abbot help her by seizing him when they arrived, binding his feet, and flogging him each day? She handed the abbot some money to cover a month's expenses and told him not to feed her son anything but the usual bread and water until he was reformed and she returned to pick him up.

9.114 "Don't be fooled by anything he tells you, because it's all trickery and lies," she added. "He'll say, 'I'm the son of the merchant so-and-so, and my father has no idea where I am. Let me go home to him! That woman isn't my mother!' But don't believe him. Keep him here until I return at the end of the month to see if he's straightened out or not. I'll decide then whether to free him or keep him here."

"Don't you worry," the abbot said. "I know a thing or two about delinquent children. Go right ahead with your plan."

9.115 She climbed into her carriage and told her driver to take her to a place called Le Palais, which means "the palace." This was a place reserved for the wealthy merchants of India, who sold expensive Indian merchandise such as *barjādāt*, fine and costly *khāṣṣāt*, and other types of fabric. Arriving at the palace, she headed directly to see the chief merchant, a wealthy man, stopping her carriage outside his shop. The merchant ordered his servants to place a footstool at the door to help the lady step down from the carriage. Hoisting her by the upper arms,[152] they whisked her into the shop to meet the merchant, who welcomed her most graciously. The lady sat down and took out a letter.

"My brother sent me this letter from Spain, requesting that I forward him some things," she said. "Perhaps you'll have some of what he's looking for." 9.116

"Such as?" asked the merchant, and the woman rattled off a list of products.

"I have what you're looking for," the merchant said, as she'd requested the most luxurious and valuable of Indian fabrics. He began to bring out one piece after another, and for every ten things he showed her, she would choose five or six and refuse the rest. She continued in this way until the order was complete.

Then she set about negotiating with him like a seasoned merchant, making a note of all the discounted prices she'd bargained for. They concluded the negotiation, added it all up, and arrived at a total of over five thousand ecus. They bundled up the fabrics for her and stowed them in the carriage. Then the lady rose to leave. 9.117

"Have one of your servant boys come along with me to collect your money," she said.

The merchant turned to his only son.

"Son, go along with the good lady and pick up the money," he said. The merchant began to prepare a carriage for him, but she refused, insisting that the young man ride in her own carriage. Then she told her driver to take them to an address in a certain quarter of the city.

They set off, and soon passed by the monastery that reformed juvenile delinquents. As the carriage drew up alongside the gate of the monastery, the woman pulled the cord attached to the horses' bridles, and they came to a stop. She stepped out of the carriage. 9.118

"I wish to speak to the abbot of this monastery about an urgent matter," she told the merchant's son. "Why don't you come along, and have a look at the monastery and all the disobedient children in shackles?"

The boy got out of the carriage and went into the monastery with the lady. As they entered the courtyard, she summoned the abbot.

"This is the boy I was telling you about," she said. They began to chat, and the boy wandered off into the monastery to look at all the children in chains. As soon as he disappeared, the woman bid the abbot farewell. She left the monastery, climbed into her carriage, and set off to the address she'd previously given her driver. When they arrived, she had the horses stop at the street corner, and told the men to unload the bundles from the carriage and leave them where they'd stopped. She paid them for the hire of the carriage and their services and sent them on their way. Then she brought all the bundles into her house, and no one was the wiser.

9.119 As for the boy, when he was done touring the monastery and tried to leave, they grabbed him and chained him up like the other children.

"Why are you tying me up? I'm just visiting, along with that lady. Go ask her!"

"Sit down, you miserable wretch," they replied. "Been squandering your father's money at cards, have you?"

The boy was flabbergasted.

"I'm the son of so-and-so, the merchant," he protested. "That woman purchased some Indian fabrics from my father, and I was just going to collect payment for them."

At this, one of the men went off to tell the abbot what the boy had said. But the abbot refused to believe it, having been forewarned by the boy's "mother" that he was a scoundrel and a liar.

"Don't believe him," the abbot replied. "And let's give him a few extra floggings too."

The boy spent three days at the monastery, surviving on bread and water, and receiving a merciless flogging twice a day at the hands of his jailors, who paid no mind to his protestations.

9.120 In the meantime, the merchant had spent the morning awaiting his son's return.

"The lady must have invited him over for lunch," he thought to himself when the boy hadn't appeared by midday. By late afternoon, there was still no sign of him and the merchant was baffled by his son's tardiness. At nightfall, the boy still hadn't turned up, so his father ordered the servants to go to the homes of all the nobles and chief merchants to inquire as to the whereabouts of their young master. Perhaps they'd find him, or at least discover where he'd gone.

The servants spread out. Each headed to a different quarter of the city and began to snoop around. But the whole night passed without them locating even the ghost of a trace of him. They returned to their master with the bad news that they'd turned Paris upside down but hadn't uncovered a single clue. Distraught over the disappearance of his son and the loss of his property, the merchant went to see the governor of Paris and told him what had happened.

The governor immediately issued an order to have posters printed and placed at every street corner stating the facts of the case, adding: "An ample reward awaits anyone who knows this woman or has heard of her. And anyone with information who does not come forward will be hanged!" The governor's order was carried out, and the posters were plastered at every street corner. Two days passed with no incident. On the third day, it so happened that one of the servants of the monastery had come into town to purchase some things for the monastery. As he walked by a poster, he paused to read it. As soon as he did, it dawned on him that the boy had been telling the truth. He hurried back to the monastery. 9.121

"The city's on fire with the news of a lost boy!" the servant told the abbot. "And the governor has vowed to hang anyone who knows something about him and doesn't come forward." The abbot immediately went off to see the boy. He asked him for his story, and the boy recounted the very same facts the posters did. It was only then that the abbot believed him. He set the boy free, and took him back to his father, explaining the entire affair to him from start to finish. As for the goods, the damnable woman absconded with them all, 9.122

and no one was ever able to figure out who she was. And so it was that the she-devil swindled the merchant.

9.123   One day, as I was walking down the street, I saw someone running by, shouting, "*La Sentence!*" He was carrying some printed papers, which he was selling for two silver coins.

"What are those papers?" I asked a friend. "And what's *la sentence*?"

"They're broadsides that report why a criminal is being hanged," he said, going on to explain why broadsides were issued. When the courts condemned a man to death, the execution would always be held at ten o'clock in the morning. The man's crime would be recorded on a piece of paper along with the punishment necessitated by the crime, be it hanging, decapitation, drawing and quartering, or whatever capital punishment is typically handed out to criminals. After the judge issues the sentence, it's printed on sheets of paper and sold throughout the city for two silver coins apiece.

9.124   As for the criminal condemned to death, he is taken to a chapel inside the courthouse to meet the chief confessor, who hears his full confession. This lasts two hours, ending at noon. After leading the condemned man in the act of contrition, the confessor grants him absolution. Lunch is then served, and the priest and the criminal dine together. After lunch, the priest withdraws, and is replaced by a monk from the order of Saint Augustine, who admonishes the condemned man, reconciling him to his fate and giving him courage to face it. The priest returns and remains at the condemned man's side until the evening.

9.125   At this point, the executioner arrives. He knocks at the door, enters, and places a noose around the condemned man's neck. The three men leave the chapel, descend the steps of the courthouse, and climb into the wagon together, making their way to the place designated by the authorities for the hanging. The executioner ascends the ladder propped against the gallows, followed by the criminal, who stands a step behind him. The monk comes next, with a crucifix in his hand. He holds it up in front of the criminal's eyes, urging contrition and courage in the face of death.

The monk then turns to face the assembled crowd, leading them 9.126 in the prayer of eternal rest. It's a prayer that is practically shouted, and is followed by a second prayer. All the while, the priest continues to urge the condemned man to contrition for all his sins. When the second prayer is complete, the priest turns to the crowd again and exhorts them to ask the Virgin Mary to intercede on behalf of this soul, which will soon be departing from our midst. The crowd begins to pray and weep, begging the Virgin to intervene for the sake of the man's soul. At the end of the prayer, the priest makes the sign of the cross over the criminal and descends the ladder.

At that moment, the executioner pushes the condemned man off the ladder, the noose tight around his neck, and climbs onto his shoulders, the man's head between his legs. He swings him back and forth three times to snap his neck, then jumps off. Then he takes the body down off the gallows, puts it into the cart, and sells it to the doctors, who take it to their medical school so they can dissect it for the instruction of their students.

After my friend finished explaining all of this, I asked him what this particular man had done to deserve to be hanged.

"The story of this poor man is strange and remarkable indeed," 9.127 he replied, launching into it.

There was once a very rich merchant who had no sons. One day, he visited an orphanage for bastard children, and saw a perfectly beautiful child among them. He was precocious, well-spoken, and intelligent, and exceeded all the other children in beauty, manners, and modesty. The merchant was drawn to the boy, and asked the director of the orphanage if he could take him home and raise him as a son.

In France, children are fostered by master artisans of differ- 9.128 ent trades. Anyone who advances in his trade and is recognized as a master artisan is required to take on one of these children as an apprentice. He treats him like a son, and teaches him the trade.

Once the child has grown up and learned the trade well, he's free to do what he wishes. He may remain with his master, for example, or find another. He might even become recognized as a master artisan himself, working on his own. This practice is one of the many virtues of that country.

9.129 So the merchant adopted the child, received a document to this effect, and took him home. When the man's wife saw the boy, she too fell deeply in love with him. They were both so enamored that they amended their will, stipulating that the boy should inherit from them when they died.

The merchant then attended to the boy's education, arranging to have an instructor teach him how to read and write. Once the boy had completed his studies, the merchant involved him in his business and gave him a thorough education in the methods of bookkeeping and accounting. The boy began to assist his father in all of his commercial dealings, from purchases and sales to bargaining and negotiation, and eventually surpassed his father in his trade.

9.130 When the young man was about twenty years old, his mother suggested to his father that they marry him off while they were still alive. The father agreed, and arranged an engagement to a fine young lady, the daughter of a fellow merchant. He set aside some of his wealth for his son, the girl's father did the same for her, and they drew up a marriage contract at the courthouse. Recorded on the contract was the sum of money gifted to the betrothed couple by their parents. After a period of time, the wedding was held and they were married.

The young man left his father's business and set up his own shop. He began to operate on his own with the blessing of his father, who could see that his son was a shrewd merchant and had already begun to earn a living from his commerce.

9.131 Everything was going well until one day, when the young man went to see his father to ask his advice about a particular matter. His father didn't seem to be home when the young man arrived, so he went by his office to search for him. He wasn't there either.

The young man was about to turn around and go home when he noticed something. There were a pair of bond certificates sitting in a cubbyhole at his father's desk. The certificates had been issued by the king, one for five hundred piasters and the other for three hundred. It was customary for the king, when his expenditures had grown onerous, to issue bonds in order to be able to pay the salaries of the military. His generals would take these bonds, sell them to the merchants at a modest discount, and use the money to pay their soldiers.

This was a wartime practice, and once the treasury was flush again, the merchants would present their bonds and receive money in exchange, as was guaranteed by the royal seal. When the treasury was delayed in repaying its debts, the merchants would buy and sell these bonds among themselves, treating them like currency. For example, if a merchant were to buy some goods for 1,500 piasters, he might say to the seller, "I'll give you a bond for five hundred piasters, plus a thousand in cash." The negotiation would proceed along these lines.

Now, when the young man saw the bond certificates, he was overcome with greed. 9.132

"My father isn't in business anymore, and has no need for these bonds," he thought. "In fact, he might even have forgotten all about them!"

The young man pocketed them and returned to his shop without anyone knowing he'd set foot in his father's office. A few days later, while purchasing some merchandise from another merchant, he introduced the two bonds into the negotiation, as was customary. The transaction was completed smoothly, and each man went his way.

Time passed; then one day a broker came to see the father. 9.133

"I've got some cheap merchandise for you, a real steal!" the broker said. "Believe me, I can get it for you at a good price."

Confronted with the prospect of a good deal, the merchant agreed.

"I have some bonds worth eight hundred piasters, and I'll pay the rest in cash," he said.

The broker was satisfied. They drafted an offer, which the broker took to the seller, who accepted it, and sent the goods to the merchant through the broker. Once he'd received delivery, the merchant opened his cashbox and counted out the amount he owed minus the value of the bonds. Then he went into his office to get the bonds, but to his surprise he couldn't find them.

9.134   The merchant hunted through his papers and account books, to no avail. Bewildered, he turned to his wife and servants, asking them who had entered the office.

"No one ever goes in there besides you," they replied.

As his astonishment grew, he was forced to pay in cash the remainder meant to be covered by the bonds. This rankled him. Meanwhile, he continued to turn his whole office upside down, searching for the bonds, but eventually gave up hope. He did, however, mention the lost certificates to his fellow merchants.

"Don't worry, they'll turn up soon enough," one of them said. "Tell us the date they were issued, and we'll be able to recognize them when, inevitably, they fall into the hands of one of us."

9.135   The merchant gave them all the issue dates of the two bond certificates. A month later, they turned up in the course of a transaction. When the trader involved studied them, he realized right away that they were the bonds his fellow merchant had lost. He took them to their owner, who immediately recognized them.

"But how does this get me anywhere?" he wondered to himself. "How can I be sure that it wasn't this fellow who pilfered them from my office? On the other hand, I can't believe that an honorable and upstanding merchant would sneak into my office and take my property."

"Why don't you go tell the governor about your situation?" the other merchant suggested. "He'll be able to find the person who stole them."

9.136   So the merchant went to see the governor and informed him about the matter, telling him how the bonds had been recovered by his colleague. The governor ordered two of his men to retrace the course of events and take the merchant with them. They went to see his colleague and demanded, by authority of the governor, that he tell them where he'd gotten the bonds. He named a certain trader, and they went off to interrogate him in the same way. He in turn pointed them to yet another trader, and the trail continued in this way until they finally arrived at the merchant's son.

When they asked him where he'd gotten the bonds, he was struck dumb. That was when they knew they'd found the thief. They escorted him to the governor, to whom the terrified young man presented himself. 9.137

"Where did you get these bonds?" the governor asked him.

He was unable to utter a word, and the governor ordered him to be jailed and tortured until he told the truth. Finally, the young man confessed that it was he who had stolen the bonds from his father's office. The governor sent him to court, where he was sentenced to hang in front of his own house, to symbolize his violation of the trust placed in him, and to serve as an example to others who were also invested with people's trust.

When his father heard this news, he regretted what he'd done, but it was too late for such regrets. He immediately went to see the governor, begging him to intercede. 9.138

"That young man is my adopted son and my heir," he pleaded. "I have no quarrel with him, and all my property belongs to him!"

"Didn't he steal the bonds, taking advantage of your trust by absconding with them without your knowledge?" the governor asked. "That is why he has been sentenced to hang."

Without hope of swaying the judge, the merchant sought out the nobles of the city, begging them to save his son from death, but they could hardly contravene the law. So the merchant made his way to the king's court, throwing himself before the state's high officials and showering them with gifts. They too were powerless to reduce the sentence. Finally, the case reached the king himself by way of some princes, but they too were unable to change the judgment handed down by the court. Having lost all hope, the merchant returned home to weep and wail with his wife. No one was able to console them for a very long time.

9.139 And that was that. I went to the courthouse in the evening and saw an empty cart sitting uncovered, parked by the steps. A few soldiers waited on their horses, along with their commander. After a few moments, the executioner emerged from the courthouse holding the noose of the condemned man, who had his hands bound in front of him. The priest followed behind, and they all descended the steps and climbed into the cart. The priest kept one hand on the young man's shoulders and with the other held a crucifix in front of his face. All the way to the gallows, the priest never stopped admonishing the young man and preparing him to face death.

When they finally arrived, I saw a wooden plank mounted on a tripod, with one end protruding. A ladder was propped up against it. The executioner climbed the ladder, followed by the young man, who ascended a step behind him, the noose around his neck and the other end of the rope in the executioner's hand.

9.140 The priest then mounted the ladder, holding the crucifix, and placed it before the face of the young man, who could only stare up at the window of his house as he wept. As the prayers came to an end, everyone in the crowd was crying for this handsome man in the bloom of youth, who stood there in the fine suit he had worn to his wedding. I heard he was only twenty-two years old. This was what really stung the hearts of the assembled crowd, who wept and wailed as though each of them were losing a beloved only son.

After the preliminaries were complete, the executioner pushed the young man off the ladder. They then brought his body down to the cart, which was driven away by the doctors. As for the executioner, he wasn't able to come down the ladder until the soldiers surrounded it, out of fear that the mob would lynch him. Executioners are loathed by the French.

9.141 Another day, when I was at Pont Saint-Michel, near our house, some people walked by selling *La Sentence* papers again—that is, the broadsheet. Two people had been sentenced for highway robbery and for killing the victims they'd robbed. As the evening drew near, I went to the courthouse to watch the proceedings. I saw two carts by the waiting soldiers, as I recounted earlier. The two men were brought out under guard, their hands tied behind their backs. With them were two priests and an executioner. Each of the prisoners was put in a cart and joined by a priest holding a holy crucifix.

They took them to a public square, and when we all arrived, I saw that a platform had been set up. It was about waist high, and lying across it was a thick wooden cross, skewed like the cross of Saint Peter.[153] The soldiers took firm hold of the first man, brought him up onto the platform, freed his hands, and stretched him out naked upon the cross. Each of his forearms was tied with stout bindings to a separate arm of the cross, as were each of his legs, leaving his head to hang free between the two planks. 9.142

Once the man was tied down, the executioner read his sentence to the assembled crowd: He was to have his four limbs broken. Then another man came forward with a long, stout metal truncheon. The priest led the crowd in prayer. When the three prayers were complete, the executioner turned to the robber bound upon the cross and struck one of his forearms with the truncheon three times. With each blow, I could hear the bones shatter. Then he moved to his second forearm and his legs, striking them each three times. The man was left without a single unbroken limb. 9.143

The executioner then struck the man across the belly, telling him that this was an act of mercy by the king, so that he would die more quickly. They then untied him from the cross and placed him in a wagon wheel, stuffing his body through it as though it were so much ground-up flesh.[154] They then lifted the wagon wheel up and hung it on a wooden axle by the platform. There the man was left, with his head dangling out of the wheel, whimpering.

Next, they brought the second man forward to the platform. When he saw the state his friend was in, he fell to his knees, begging the priest not to let them execute him in that grisly way, and to 9.144

let him be strangled before his limbs were broken. The priest felt a pang of sympathy for him, so he turned to the soldier who had been appointed by the judge to carry out the sentence, and interceded on the man's behalf. It was only after a considerable amount of persuasion on the part of the priest that the soldier granted his request and ordered the man to be strangled. They spread him out on the cross like his friend, strapping him down in the same way, and wrapped a rope around his neck. The end of the rope was then pulled through a hole in the platform and tightened by twisting it round and round. He was immediately strangled.

The executioner then set about breaking his bones and putting him in a wagon wheel like his friend. They left the two of them there until the first one died, a sight that horrified and distressed all the onlookers. The crowd then dispersed, and everyone went on their way feeling utterly shattered and dejected by what they'd just witnessed.

9.145   Another day, I saw some people running by, and I joined them. We arrived at a crossroads, where I saw a woman with her forearms tied to the back of one of the carts used to collect garbage. She was naked to the waist. The cart had stopped at the crossroads and the executioner read out the record of her crime. She was guilty of leading young men astray by procuring for them women who were not registered as prostitutes. For this crime, she was sentenced to be paraded in disgrace through the streets of Paris. After reading the sentence, the executioner flogged her twelve times with a bull-pizzle whip, shredding her flesh. Then the cart lurched forward, pulling her as she stumbled barefoot behind it. The cart continued to drag her along, exhausted, until she nearly died. What a hideous spectacle and humiliating affront to all women!

9.146   On another day, I went to the courthouse to observe the proceedings after a sentence had been published. There, I saw an old woman in her seventies being escorted down the steps by the executioner and the priest. They all climbed into the cart, which was surrounded by soldiers sent by the authorities. The carriage set off, and soon came to the gallows, where the three of them ascended the ladder.

The executioner read aloud the sentence, which began by 9.147 recounting the story of how this woman had worked for many years as a servant in the home of a particular noble. The husband and wife who employed the old woman loved her dearly, as she had served them and raised their children. Now, the father of that nobleman had once lost some silver vessels. They were never found, and neither was the thief who'd stolen them. Years passed, and the nobleman's father died. Then one day, the nobleman happened to be visiting Toulouse when he was invited to the home of one of his dear friends. As they sat at the table to eat, he spotted one of his own plates among the others, which he recognized by its mark.

"Who'd you buy that plate from?" the man asked his friend after the meal was over.

"One of my friends," he replied. "I'd asked him to have some plates made for me in Paris, and he sent this one, along with some others."

He gave the nobleman the name of his friend, a merchant in 9.148 Paris. After some time in Toulouse, the nobleman returned to Paris, bringing the plate with him, along with some other silver plates that had been taken from his house. When he got back to his mansion, he waited a few days before inviting the merchant over and asking him where he'd purchased the silver plates. The man mentioned a certain silversmith, whom the nobleman then summoned. The silversmith, in turn, told him he'd received the plates from yet another person, a man wearing foreign clothes.

Armed with this information, the nobleman went and reported the incident to the governor, who dispatched two investigators to find and bring in the man who had sold the plates to begin with.

The governor's men set off, following the trail of clues, and even- 9.149 tually arrived at that old servant woman. When it became apparent that she couldn't name anyone else as the source of the plates, they arrested her and brought her before the governor. She was made to confess that she'd stolen the plates, and was sentenced by the courts to hang.

Now, the executioner didn't read out this whole story. He merely said that she'd betrayed her master. And given that she'd been entrusted with his confidence, she was condemned to hang. As the old woman stood upon the ladder, she begged the assembled crowd to pray and offer supplications on her behalf. In the end, she was made to hang like all the other criminals, as an example to every entrusted servant.

9.150   Around that same time, Paris was seized by an epidemic, leading to an untold number of deaths. Anyone who caught this particular disease would succumb within twenty-four hours. The city's inhabitants prayed to God to spare them from His wrath, and sought the intercession of Saint Geneviève, the city's patron saint. It was then decided that the body of the saint should be carried through the city in a procession while the people prayed to her for mediation. Perhaps, if they did that, the heavy blows of God's wrath would abate. The people went to consult the bishop of the Church of Saint Geneviève and ask his permission to let them hold the procession, but he refused to let the body of the saint leave the church for fear that this blessed treasure might be harmed. The other bishops of Paris urged him to reconsider, along with the abbots of the monasteries and even the cardinal himself, but he wouldn't budge.

9.151   So the nobles and judges of Paris gathered and together went to see the bishop of the Church of Saint Geneviève, imploring him to grant their request. To allay his fears that the treasure might not be returned by the cardinal or anyone else, they drafted an edict promising to bring the saint's body to its resting place, to which each affixed his signature. The body was kept in a silver coffin, set upon three marble pillars, which had produced many miracles in the past. It was customary for people to hang the shirt of a sick person on a reed and suspend it over the coffin, allowing the shirt to brush it. The saint would then relieve the invalid's distress in proportion to the extent of his faith.

As a result of these efforts, the bishop finally relented and let   9.152
them bring the body of the saint down from its resting place. Then
the cardinal, who is a kind of second pope for the kingdom of
France, ordered all the clergy to march in procession. This included
pastors, priests, monks, and higher clerical authorities from all the
churches and monasteries in each of the seven quarters of the city,
a total of eight hundred churches and monasteries. The clergy were
to don their finest vestments and carry candles as they marched.
He also decreed that it was to be a general holiday and the masses
would not be permitted to work.

On the appointed day, the procession set off with its priests,   9.153
monks, and deacons all decked out in their most magnificent robes,
and with candles ablaze. Four bishops carried the saint's coffin on
their shoulders. They passed through the streets of Paris as wave
after wave of priests, monks, and deacons chanted angelic hymns
with stirring voices and beautiful melodies. The procession lasted
for two hours, and the number of participants was estimated at
ten thousand. Meanwhile, the laypeople remained in their shops,
offering supplications to God Most High to accept the intercession
of the saint and to make His anger subside. And this our Lord did,
bringing an end to the epidemic. I was in Paris at the time, and I
witnessed the procession and the ensuing miracle that God worked
through the intercession of the saint.

I also learned something about Saint Geneviève's story. She had   9.154
once worked for a rich nobleman of Paris, in whose home she lived
as piously as a nun. She displayed a great love for the poor, offering
them charity from her own wages and handiwork, as well as the
food discarded by the household. But her master, who was a hard-
hearted, uncharitable man, learned of her good works, and threatened her.

"The day I catch you giving anything to the poor will be the day I
beat you and toss you out of my house," he snarled. "Be certain of that."

He ordered the other servants to remain vigilant and keep an eye
on Geneviève. If they caught her doing it again, they were to inform

him so he could punish her. Poor Geneviève was deeply saddened, and had to cease her charitable work, fearing her master's wrath. She did, however, sometimes save a scrap of bread from the food she received for herself, hiding it until she had a chance to give it to the destitute.

9.155   One day, after her master had left the house, she collected some scraps of bread, bundled them in the gathered folds of her robe, and left the house to distribute these among the poor. As she walked out the door, her master happened to be returning home. He saw that she was carrying something in her robe.

"What do you have there?"

Trembling in fright, she was at a loss for words. But then our merciful Lord caused her to speak, casting words into her mouth!

"Roses," she replied.

As it was winter at the time and there were no roses available, her master was astonished.

"Show me these roses!"

She unwrapped the folds of her robes and uncovered the contents to reveal some double-flowered roses, long out of season. Her master was amazed.

"Tell me the truth," he said. "Wherever did you find these roses?"

Geneviève felt compelled to speak the truth, confessing that her robes had previously been full of scraps of bread.

"I spoke the word 'roses' without being aware of what I was saying," she explained.

9.156   It was then that her master realized a miracle had just occurred for the sake of his servant. He informed the bishop, who after some investigation was able to confirm that the miracle was indeed genuine. The wealthy nobleman then had a convent built, to which he sent his servant Geneviève. Alongside the convent he built a church, which he endowed with a trust. Geneviève lived in the convent and was eventually elected Mother Superior on account of her piety and the saintliness of her angelic conduct. After she died, her body would work several miracles, whose stories are too long to recount here. It was because of these miracles that her body was placed in a silver coffin and set upon three columns, with the aim of allowing invalids from different countries to visit the saint and to be healed of their maladies. Ever since, she has been known as Geneviève, the patron saint of Paris.[155]

Chapter Ten

The Last Days of 1708

10.1　On the fifteenth of December, Paris experienced a bout of cold weather so extreme that the trees froze stiff. So did the Seine—the river that flows through the city. The sheet of ice covering the river was as thick as a handspan and carriages could drive across it as if they were upon dry, rocky ground. The icy weather lasted fifteen days, killing people across the seven quarters of Paris, each as large as the city of Aleppo. In all, eighty thousand people perished, not counting the young children, the poor, and the foreign inhabitants of the city, and the church bells tolled for them all.[156] Women were found huddled in bed with their children, and husbands embracing their wives, frozen to death because their homes were on the higher stories. The buildings of Paris have five stories: The higher up one lives, the cheaper the rent.

10.2　The children of peasants who had come from their villages to the city looking for work were found dead on the roads, covered in manure. Paris was a ghost town. Everyone stayed home, confined to a single room, sitting by the fire, as I myself did. I spent fifteen days shut up in my room, warming myself by the fire.

The priests of the city were forced to set up braziers on the altars of their churches to prevent the sacramental wine from freezing. Many people even died while relieving themselves, because the urine froze in their urethras as it left their bodies, and killed them. Indoors, it was so cold that copper casks cracked, and people had to break their bread with adzes and moisten the pieces with hot water in order to eat them.

As for the orchards and trees, what can I say? They withered away completely. The same went for the vineyards and olive groves, as well as the crops, which froze after having yielded two or three harvests for the year. This bout of God's wrath struck the entire region of France.

After the fifteen days of cold had passed, I left my room and went to get a shave. The freezing walk home from the barbershop left me stiff as a statue. It was so cold that the hairs of my mustache began to fall out, and I was certain I was going to die. When I finally arrived at my room and they saw me in my condition, they ran to tell my master. He came to see me and immediately ordered the servants to strip off my clothes. They were unable to pull off my outer robes because my forearms were frozen stiff, so he told them to slit the sleeves open. 10.3

Once my clothes were off and I was naked as the day I was born, they lit the fire. We had purchased a flask of eagle fat in the city of Tunis during our travels, and they slathered me with it from top to bottom, moving me close to the fire so the fat would melt all over my body. Then they warmed up a white sheet and wrapped me in it. Two young men picked me up and carried me to my bed. I lay there like a statue, unable to move arm or leg. They covered me with three or four blankets and wrapped me up tightly. I was so hot that it felt as if I were lying in the innermost depths of a bathhouse. 10.4

They kept me in bed for twenty-four hours. I then returned to my normal self, able to move my arms and legs without pain. I rose from my bed, once again in very good health, put on my clothes, and 10.5

walked around the house. Two days later, my master commanded one of the servant boys to take me out for a two-hour run through the streets of Paris, and not to let me stop until I was dripping with sweat. That did me good, and I was right as rain again.

10.6   A short while later, Paris was struck by a famine, which led to a great rise in the cost of food. The city's administrators were compelled to take a count of the number of people in each home, and, by order of the governor, to issue each person a small ration of bread to keep them from starving. The bakers all had lists of the members of each family, and someone representing the city authorities sat at every bakery, armed with a register of all the families and everyone's name. The result of this system was that no one could obtain an ounce more food than that allotted to them. After a few days, peasants began leaving their towns and villages, and streamed into Paris to beg for food so they wouldn't die of hunger. I saw many of them lying in the street, starving to death, for no one could afford to share their own meager ration with them. Many people died of hunger.

10.7   Confronted with this catastrophe, the city's nobles, together with its bishops and officials, puzzled over what to do. Thanks to God's mercy, an inspired solution presented itself: They would put the peasants to work building houses outside Paris, paying them with funds from the city's charitable endowments. There was a hill on the outskirts of Paris that they planned to clear away. Once that was complete, they would level the earth and build upon it.

In the meantime, wheat had begun to arrive from other countries, but the price remained high. They built a bakery in the area to make bread for the workers, giving every man and his wife and children—those of them able to work, that is—a loaf of bread weighing two *ūqiyyah*s, along with a wage of two *jarq*s, which is to say eight *'uthmānī*s, or four soldi. The peasants began to work there, relieving the burden on the city. This was the state of affairs until the crisis finally ended, with shipments of wheat arriving from the lands of the East, the Maghreb, and other places. Demand attracts supply, after all.

Later, when I went to Marseille, I witnessed the arrival of four 10.8
galleys sent by His Holiness the pope. They were accompanied by
barges loaded with wheat, as Marseille had experienced a famine
even more severe than the one in Paris. It was so extreme that people
were breaking into homes and stealing all the food they could find.
The governor was forced to erect a gallows in every neighborhood,
and station soldiers to put an end to breaking and entering. Finally,
the ships that had been sent to the East to purchase wheat from the
Province of the Islands and various lands arrived in Marseille. There
were about three hundred ships and boats in all. Wheat was suddenly plentiful in all the regions of France. Bread became available
again, but a *ratl* of bread now cost a *zolota*, which is to say three
quarters of its previous price. That was how it remained until prices
rose again and everything returned to normal. This is what I witnessed with regard to the rise of prices in France in the year 1709.

During that time, I became discouraged and discontent with life 10.9
in those parts. An old man, who was assigned to oversee the Arabic
Library and could read Arabic well and translate texts into French,
would visit us often. At the time, he was translating into French,
among other works, the Arabic book *The Story of the Thousand and
One Nights*.[157] He would ask me to help him with things he didn't
understand, and I'd explain them to him.

The book was missing some "Nights," so I told him a few stories
I knew and he used them to round out his work.[158] He was very
appreciative, and promised that if I ever needed anything, he would
do his utmost to grant it.

One day, while I was sitting chatting with the old man, he said, 10.10
"I'd like to do something special for you, a favor of sorts. But only if
you can keep it a secret."

"What?" I asked.

"You'll find out tomorrow," he said.

After we'd finished chatting, he left.

He returned the next day. "Good news!" he said. "If my plan succeeds, you'll be very happy."

"Tell me," I said, "what is this favor you have in mind?" And he began to tell me about a certain nobleman who was an important figure in the government.[159]

"He asked me if I knew of someone who could be sent on a voyage like the one undertaken by Paul Lucas," the old man explained, referring to my master. "It occurred to me to tell him about you, since you've traveled before and you know what's involved. So he ordered me to bring you to him so that you two could speak. I'll wait for you in such and such a place tomorrow and we can go see him together. But take care not to tell your master or he won't let you go."

10.11 We agreed and he left. The next day, I went to the meeting place and found him waiting for me. I accompanied him to the nobleman's palace. He went in, and after a little while the servants invited me to enter. I presented myself before the nobleman. He welcomed me courteously and invited me to sit down. Then he began to ask me about the lands we'd toured and the things we'd found: the old coins and carved idols, the books of history about ancient kings, and other such antiquities my master had brought with him.

"Yes, my lord," I replied, "I did buy all these things, and I know a great deal about them. I learned about them all from my master."

10.12 "Then go, see to your affairs, and leave your master," the nobleman told me. "Afterward, come back to me and I'll send you on a mission. I'll arrange for a royal decree just like your master's mandate, and commission you to all the ambassadors and consuls in the Orient. I will also give you letters of recommendation so that whatever you request from the consuls during your tour will be granted, and whatever you purchase will be conveyed to them for dispatch to the chamber of commerce in Marseille. You will have a daily salary in ecus, and all your expenses paid. And when you return to me safely, I will elevate your standing and establish you in a position with a substantial income." When we were finished talking, he said, "Go now, do as I ask, and come right back."

I left in a state of confusion. What was I to do? On the one hand, I was fed up with all of the nerve-racking frights I'd encountered on this journey. On the other hand, I was worried that this new opportunity wouldn't end in success. So I remained hesitant, somewhere between fear and hope.

I'd been in this sort of frightful situation before. One day, I 10.13 bumped into an Armenian from Persia named Yūsuf the Jeweler, who worked in Paris as a merchant of valuable jewels such as diamonds, rubies, emeralds, pearls, and other expensive stones. Without even knowing who I was, he greeted me in Turkish. I returned the greeting, and he asked me which country I was from.

"Syria," I said. "From the city of Aleppo."

At this, he greeted me again very warmly and asked me about some of his acquaintances and how they were doing, and whether or not they were still alive. I answered all his questions, telling him that so-and-so was alive and that so-and-so had died, while so-and-so had traveled abroad, and that sort of thing. After a while, we set off on a stroll and eventually arrived at our house. I bid him farewell and started up the stairs, but he followed me, asking, "On which floor do you live?"

"The third," I told him, and he went on his way.

I told my master about this man I'd bumped into, and how he'd 10.14 greeted me warmly and showed great affection and friendship. I also told him that Yūsuf was well known in Paris and that he was in the good graces of the city nobles.

"So why didn't you invite him in?" my master asked. "If you see him again, you must insist that he come to our house. I'd like to discuss jewels and precious stones with him so I can determine whether he knows all there is to know about them."

My master was a foremost expert on the science of precious jewels, including their unique properties and values. That was why he wanted to meet Yūsuf and test his knowledge.

One morning several days later, while my master and I were 10.15 sitting warming ourselves in front of the fireplace, having had our coffee, there was a knock at the door. I jumped up to open the door, and it was Yūsuf the Jeweler. I welcomed him and begged him to come in and have coffee with us.

"I can't come in right at this moment," Yūsuf replied. "I have some urgent business to attend to, and I'd like you to come along and act as an interpreter between me and a certain gentleman. You see, I just don't know how to make him understand my particular situation. I don't speak French very well; I do speak some Italian, but this gentleman doesn't understand Italian. So I'm wondering if you'd be willing to translate for us."

"Wait a moment," I said, "so I can get my master's permission. Then I'll go with you."

10.16   I went in to my master and told him what had happened. He stood up and insisted that Yūsuf come in, and the man was unable to refuse. He came in and my master welcomed him with great ceremony. We brought him some breakfast and coffee, and were attentive to his needs. Then the two of them sat down and talked about precious stones for about an hour. Afterward, my master agreed to send me along to translate for Yūsuf in his urgent business.

"What is this matter, exactly?" my master asked him. "If you tell me, I can tell you what to do about it."

"It's a secret," Yusuf replied. "If you wish me to tell you what it is, sir, give me your oath that you'll keep the secret."

"Go ahead," my master said. "Don't be afraid. Your secret is forever safe with me."

10.17   Yūsuf told him the story from beginning to end. It so happened that he'd gotten engaged to a girl and had signed a contract of engagement in court.

"Then some people came to me," said Yusuf, "saying they wanted me to marry the daughter of a rich merchant in India. He'd been there for many years, doing business, and had no desire to return to Paris. These people said to me, 'The girl's uncles want to marry her off to you and send you to her father in India, because they're afraid that he might die and his money be lost, since he's very old.'"

"The trouble is," Yūsuf continued, "these people don't know that I'm already engaged. So I'm at a loss! Can I abandon one girl and marry another?"

"I can think of a solution," my master replied, "but you mustn't pursue it. It isn't advisable."

Yūsuf insisted, begging that he tell him what it was, and my master said, "Promise me that you will not do it," and Yūsuf promised.

"Seeing that you're a foreigner, you could pretend that you received a letter from your family asking you to return home for an urgent matter like the death of your father or one of your business partners—that sort of thing," my master began. "You'd then tell your fiancée's family that you're absolutely bound to return to your country because of this terribly urgent matter and that you want to break off the engagement. The girl would be free to marry someone else, but you could tell them that if you returned unmarried, you'd marry her." 10.18

My master continued: "In that case, they wouldn't be able to prevent you from leaving, or from breaking the contract and dissolving the engagement. Now, when they broke the contract, you'd go to the family of the second girl and say that you have some money owed to you in such and such a city and you'd tell them, 'I'll just go collect it and come back after a few days and marry your daughter.' When you eventually returned after some time and married the second girl, no one would have a claim against you, nor would anyone be able to prevent you from getting engaged."

When Yūsuf heard this, he thanked my master profusely and went on his way. But his greed got the best of him, and he went and did just what my master had told him. He disappeared for a while, then came back to marry the merchant's daughter. 10.19

It was Lent at the time, and because the girl's family wanted them to get married quickly and send Yūsuf off to India, they received permission from the cardinal to do so during Lent, when there are usually no weddings held. The cardinal gave permission and they announced the marriage.

Now, in this country, when a foreigner wants to get married, the impending nuptials are announced in the cathedral on the three preceding Sundays. The priest says, "A person from such and such a country intends to marry. If anyone knows him to be already married, he must inform the bishop." And anyone who knows but doesn't speak up risks being excommunicated by the church.

10.20 So they read out the banns on the first Sunday and the second Sunday, and nothing turned up. But on the third Sunday, there happened to be a Chaldean priest in the congregation. He went to the bishop and said, "I know that this man is married in Syria, in the city of Aleppo."

In fact, it was true that Yūsuf was married to a woman named Maryam, daughter of Jabbār. He'd fathered a son with her, then traveled abroad. This must have been him, because when I returned to Aleppo myself I asked this woman what her husband looked like, and her description resembled the man I saw in Paris: tall, dark-skinned, and thin. But only God knows whether he really was the same man or not.

10.21 When the Chaldean priest testified to this and his claim was confirmed, the governor of the city was informed about the situation. He demanded that Yūsuf be arrested, his money be seized, and that he be hanged. The priest who had informed the governor was telling the truth, so Yūsuf disappeared without a trace. They launched a search for him but there was no sign of him. After three days, they went to his house to seize his property but couldn't find a thing. Apparently he'd taken valuable stones from various nobles' homes with a plan to sell them all, but the governor's men didn't find any of them; he'd simply stolen them and fled. As the search resumed, they arrested some of Yūsuf's neighbors and friends, and threatened to torture them if they didn't reveal where he was hiding. One of those people was me.

10.22 While I was out and about on an errand at that time, two of the governor's men suddenly seized me and ordered me to go with them. I was terrified and asked them what they wanted.

"Come see the governor, and he'll tell you what we want!"

I went with them, terrified out of my wits.

We passed by the coffee shop of my dear friend Iṣṭifān the Damascene, a man who was very fond of me.[160] When I first arrived in Paris, my master told me to seek him out because he was my countryman. We had become friends, and he had told me his story.

When Iṣṭifān first came to Paris, he was a beggar, but no one   10.23
would give him any alms. He decided to go to Monsieur Christofalo Zamāriyā to ask for a letter from the cardinal granting permission to beg for alms at the door of the Church of the Virgin. Christofalo's heart went out to him, and since he was the steward of the cardinal and very close to him, he gave Iṣṭifān what he wanted. That way people would give him charity, because he was a stranger and because he was confirmed to be truly poor and in real need.

Iṣṭifān stood by the door of the church, pleading for assistance. When the people saw that he had an edict from the cardinal, they began lavishing alms on him. He eventually amassed almost two hundred piasters.

Then the feast of Saint Michael came around. The city of Paris has   10.24
seven quarters, each named after a saint. When a saint's day arrives, a festival is held in some open space for seven days, full of goods for sale and spectacles to see. People come from other towns to trade because there are no customs duties levied on goods bought and sold at that time, unlike the rest of the year.

On the feast of Saint Michael, I went to the square to see the   10.25
sights. I saw a black monkey in a steel cage who looked as ugly as a devil, and also a two-headed snake! Eventually I came to a certain building. A man was outside, beating a drum.

"What's this?" I asked some people. They responded that inside was a wondrous spectacle. I wanted to look at it, and the proprietor asked for a quarter. His price was more expensive than the other entertainments and I didn't want to give him more money. But some people interceded and convinced the owner to accept four sovereigns, and he invited me in.

When I went inside, I saw a single little camel. I regretted my decision and told the owner, "We have plenty of those where I come from, and they're all bigger than that!"

"That's your problem," he replied, as he had already taken the quarter from me.

10.26   But let's get back to the story. It was suggested to this Iṣṭifān fellow by some charitable people that he buy two kettles and some cups and whatever else he'd need to make coffee, and go to the festival—that is, the feast of Saint Michael. The man did as they suggested and opened a café there. And since he was a foreign man from the East—and because there weren't any other coffee sellers— he had a lot of customers.

Paris didn't have many cafés in those days, and anything novel was a source of delight. Soon, Iṣṭifān couldn't keep up with the demand, so he hired assistants to help serve the crowds that descended on him. All in all, he made another two hundred piasters over seven days, so he'd earned four hundred piasters in total.

10.27   When the festival ended, Iṣṭifān went back to the city and opened a coffee shop. The customers arrived in such numbers that, in the space of a single year, he had earned a tidy sum and became known throughout Paris as Iṣṭifān the Coffee Man. People would come to his café from all seven quarters, including nobles, merchants, and many others. When his fame reached the palace of the king, in Versailles, the king's minister ordered him to open a café there so that the princes wouldn't have to go all the way to his café in Paris. Iṣṭifān did as the minister asked and opened a café in Versailles. He then stayed on, serving coffee at the royal palace. He rubbed shoulders with the grandees of the state, and became quite the celebrity.

10.28   It came to pass that a very wealthy widow with many properties set her sights on Iṣṭifān. She sent some people to propose the marriage and he agreed. They were married and she bore a girl who later was afflicted by an illness that crippled her. Her father sent me a message saying that since he had no choice but to remain in Versailles, where he'd opened his café, I should marry his daughter and take over the café in Paris. "You're from the East, so you'll be more popular with the customers than a Frenchman."

When I heard these words—and had seen the girl, who was beautiful, even if crippled—I responded to his request by asking for some time to discuss it with my master before giving him my answer. The messenger agreed and left, on the condition that I respond within two or three days. I consulted my master, but he didn't consent to me marrying the girl because she was a cripple. When the messenger returned for my answer, I didn't give him a definitive response. 10.29

"Leave me alone for a while so that I have some more time to think about it," I told him.

This was where things stood on the day when the governor's people arrested me, as I recounted earlier. When we passed in front of Isṭifān's coffee shop, he saw me and ran out quickly to ask the governor's people, "Why are you holding this young man, and what is his crime?" 10.30

"The governor's been told that he's an associate of Yūsuf the Jeweler," they replied, "and he might know where Yūsuf is hiding. If he doesn't talk, he'll be tortured."

Isṭifān couldn't persuade the governor's men to let me go. But then my master appeared, for news had reached him of my arrest. When he saw me in custody and scared out of my wits, he rebuked the men who were holding me prisoner and ordered me to go home.

"Don't you know that this young man works for me and that I brought him from the Orient to work in the king's Arabic Library? What do you want from him?"

They told him the story of how the governor was hot on Yūsuf's trail and that they'd seen me chatting with him. 10.31

"That's why we arrested him," they told my master. "We didn't know he worked for you."

"He's with me," my master replied. "I'll stand surety for him, and if there's anything the governor needs to know, I'll tell him."

So the governor's men released me and left. But I was still terrified, and I was suddenly sick and tired of the country. So I resolved to leave Paris and carry out the nobleman's commission I mentioned earlier, so I could travel abroad like my master. My mind made up, I asked him for permission to go back to my country. This request took him quite by surprise.

10.32   "Is there anything I haven't given you? Aren't you happy living here with me?" he asked. "I've gone to a lot of trouble for your sake, you know. I brought you to this country as an act of goodwill, so that you could have an honorable position in the king's service and live a happy and comfortable life. Do you want to throw that chance away and go back to being a captive of the Muslims the way you were before?"[161]

Hearing him, I changed my mind about leaving. My master was always telling me, "The minister is busy with what's going on at the moment, but when peace comes, I'll keep my promise and get you into the Royal Library."

10.33   Reassured, I decided not to go to the nobleman. After three days, he sent for me and I went, along with the old man I mentioned earlier. He greeted me and said, "Why have you delayed in coming to see me? I've been waiting for you!"

"Alas, my master was unable to give me permission to leave him, my lord," I said. "He's done so much for me, bringing me to this country for my own good and saving me from captivity amongst the barbarians. I don't want to offend him."

"But I too want to help you, and give you a place with me," the nobleman said. "You will always be under the king's protection and mine. Give word to your master that you received a letter from your family requiring you to go back to your country. Do what I tell you, and come back to me so I can prepare you and send you off."

10.34   Upon hearing this. I was dumbstruck and could only nod in assent. I left in a state of complete bewilderment, but divine intervention was at work. I returned home to my master.

"My lord," I said, "I have received a letter from my brothers. I can't stay here any longer."

When my master heard these words, he became more furious than he'd ever been.

"You Orientals are a disloyal lot!" he raged. "If you want to leave, go ahead!" Then he handed me a hundred thirds and cried, "Godspeed. You'll regret this one day, but it'll be too late!"

He stormed off, leaving me alone to pack up my things. I left   10.35
them with one of our neighbors and went to the diligence station, which was where the stagecoaches departed for Lyon. There were two stagecoaches, which left on specific days. As soon as one arrived at Lyon, the second would depart Paris. Each stagecoach was pulled by a team of eight horses and had room for eight passengers inside. An exterior platform between the two rear wheels of the coach was reserved for the servants accompanying their masters. The price for a seat inside was two piasters per day, and for a seat outside one piaster.

Why is the fare so high? you might ask. Because the carriages are   10.36
like little palaces, with four crystal windows and leather upholstery. Inside, there are four benches covered in scarlet,[162] which seat no more than eight people. The coach is pulled by eight strong horses, which are relieved every two hours by a fresh team waiting by the side of the road. That way, the length of the journey is halved.

At noon, it would stop at an inn reserved for the two stage-   10.37
coaches, and the passengers would disembark and go inside. There, they'd find a table waiting for them, set with all the necessary accoutrements. A sumptuous lunch would be served, including delicacies that wouldn't even appear in nobles' households, along with soft bread and splendid wine. Four or five servant girls carrying goblets served anyone who called for more wine.

With lunch complete, the passengers and their servants—who ate the same food, but at a separate table—would climb aboard the stagecoach again, now accompanied by a bottle of wine, a glass, and a jug of water for those sitting inside, in case they wanted a drink on the road. At sunset, the coach would pull into another reserved inn, where the passengers would have another splendid dinner. They'd spend the evening together, chatting until it was time to go to sleep.

10.38 The beds were covered with blankets during the winter months, and thin white cotton felt in the summer. A prie-dieu sat by the bed with an icon and crucifix before it, for prayer. Each bed had three mattresses, and everyone received two fresh, clean quilts and a clean nightgown. In the morning, all would go to a church located by the inn and attend mass. By the time they returned, a breakfast of soft bread, cheese, and sweet wine would have been prepared for them. Following breakfast, they'd climb into the coach and set off again. They'd stop for lunch, dinner, and an overnight stay as previously described; this routine would continue until they arrived at Lyon. The journey, which ordinarily took twenty days, passed in ten.

10.39 When I arrived at the way station, I registered my name on the passenger list and paid for a fare. It happened to be a Tuesday, and the usual departure day was Thursday. I was advised to spend Wednesday night there, as the coach would depart before dawn the next morning. Having written my name on the list of passengers traveling on the exterior of the carriage, I then went to visit His Excellency the nobleman, and told him I'd left my master and purchased a fare on the diligence.

"Why were you in such a hurry? You should have come to see me first," the nobleman said. "Ah well, that's quite all right."

10.40 He summoned his clerk and ordered him to compose a letter to a duke at the king's palace in Versailles, asking him to have an edict drawn up according to the stipulations in the letter. He folded the letter, sealed it, and ordered me to go to Versailles and deliver it to the duke. I took the letter and left, but decided to wait until the evening to set off for Versailles, as I didn't want my master to learn of my visit. When evening came, I took a coach to Versailles and was duly admitted to the royal palace. The guards recognized me from the time I'd spent eight days there, when we were displaying the animals I mentioned previously, so no one prevented me from entering.

Once inside, I inquired as to the whereabouts of the duke and was taken to a room within the palace, where I found him pacing. I bowed before him and handed him the letter. The duke read it by candlelight, then turned to greet me cordially. 10.41

"Follow me!" he said.

We went to the place where the king's edicts and orders are drawn up. It was a large room full of scribes. Summoning the chief scribe over, the duke read him the letter and ordered him to draw up a corresponding edict, and took his leave.

I remained there, waiting for the completion of the edict. Time passed. Finally, the chief scribe came back to see me. 10.42

"Can I help you?"

"I'm waiting for the edict," I replied.

"And what use is the edict to you before it is presented to the king for authorization?" the man said, smiling.

"When will that happen?" I asked him.

"Monday," he said. "That's when the council meets and edicts are presented to the king. Those he approves receive the royal seal, and the rest are shredded."

Upon hearing these words, I felt the world crowding in on my miserable self! I regretted my decision to reserve a stagecoach ticket, for I now had no choice but to depart Paris on Thursday. Leaving the palace, I checked in to an inn, where I had dinner and spent the night. The next morning, I returned to Paris to see His Excellency the nobleman.

"Did you go to Versailles?" he asked when he saw me. 10.43

"I did, and I delivered the letter to the duke," I said, recounting what had happened at the palace, and how the edict would not be issued until next Monday even though I was due to depart on Thursday.

"Not to worry," the nobleman said. "Go to Marseille, and I'll send you the edict and your letters of recommendation in a few days."

He summoned his clerk and told him to draw up a letter to the chief merchant of Marseille who oversaw the affairs of those merchants involved in trade with the lands of the East.

10.44 "Lodge this young man with you until such time as you receive an edict via express courier," the letter read. "In addition, provide him with a letter in your own hand, introducing him to all of the consuls residing in Oriental lands and asking them to grant him any sum of money he requests, in exchange for receipts. Furthermore, whatever goods he entrusts to them should be forwarded to the chief merchant of Marseille."

The nobleman then ordered the clerk to compose a letter of introduction to His Excellency the French ambassador in Istanbul, requesting that he secure an edict for me from the vizier recommending me to all the local governors.[163]

10.45 He bid me farewell and I left with the letters, returning home to pick up my things from the neighbors' house. I dropped them off with the proprietor of the way station, then went to say goodbye to all my friends and acquaintances. Among them was *khawājah* Christofalo, the second-in-command to His Holiness the cardinal, who gave me a letter to take to his brother, *khawājah* Zamāriyā, who lived in Istanbul. He was the syndic of Jerusalem, appointed by the sultan himself, and was a man of very high rank. *Khawājah* Christofalo asked his brother to keep an eye out for me.

10.46 That was how I spent my remaining hours in Paris before setting off for the city of Lyon. After a ten-day journey, we arrived safe and sound. I then booked passage on one of the cheap coaches that travel between Lyon and Marseille. They were long carriages with bales of goods piled on top of them, pulled by six cart horses. I stretched out on the bales in utmost comfort, happily spared from the aches and pains of travel!

We'd stop at noon for lunch at one inn, and at another for dinner and the overnight stay. I complimented my fellow travelers on this way of life of theirs—effortless journeys that didn't require carrying a heavy load or suffering any fatigue, during which they ate good food and slept in soft beds. The servants at the inn took care of looking after and feeding the horses, even bringing them out of the stables in the morning and hitching them up to the carriage. A single coachman was responsible for driving the carriage, and nobody had any fear of danger on the roads. I dined with the passengers each night, and no one charged me for my supper. We made our way to Marseille in this fashion, traveling in the greatest of ease.

After our safe arrival, I checked in to the same inn where my 10.47 master and I had stayed on our way to Paris. The proprietress of the inn welcomed me and gave me a place to sleep, and after an hour I went to the chamber of commerce and asked to see the chief merchant. I presented myself to him and gave him the nobleman's letter, which he opened and read. Then he jumped to his feet and greeted me most cordially.

"His Highness the nobleman has asked me to have you stay at my home until he sends you the edict," the merchant said. "I'll also provide you with a letter of introduction to the consuls, as he requests in this letter."

Now, I'd assumed that the edict would have reached Marseille 10.48 before me, because the postal horses arrived in the city once a week. It was then that I began to suspect that my plan was falling apart, so I decided not to stay with the chief merchant.

"I'm staying at an inn called Petit Paris," I told him. "When the edict arrives, let me know and I'll return."

"As you wish."

I stumbled out the door as though I were drunk, though I hadn't had a sip of wine! I regretted what I'd done, but it was too late now. At that moment, I remembered my master telling me, "You'll be sorry!"

I waited until the following week, afraid yet hopeful that my 10.49 luck would change. When the post arrived, I went to see the chief merchant.

"Have you received any news from the nobleman?"

"No news, and no letters either," he replied.

It occurred to me then to send the nobleman a letter myself, asking him if he was going to send me the edict or not. This I did, and he soon responded with a letter in his own hand.

"I'm surprised that you never received the edict," it read. "I sent it to Marseille with one of my friends," and gave the name of the individual.

I set about looking for the man, hoping to find a trace of him somewhere in Marseille, but my search turned up nothing. A third week passed with no sign of him, then a fourth. Finally, I came to the conclusion that my arrangement with the nobleman had fallen apart.

10.50 My hopes dashed, I wrote a reproachful letter in response, heaping shame on such a man—some nobleman!—who conspired to separate me from my master, dooming us both to failure. And yet, as it would turn out, this was all for my own good, and part of God's plan. I sent the letter and put the whole affair out of my mind.

10.51 It was around that time that a traveler arrived from Paris and checked in to the inn where I was staying. One day, while we were chatting, he asked me where I was from and how I'd come to this country. So I explained how I'd come to France with a man named Paul Lucas, who was one of the king's explorers. I told him how I'd gone to Paris with him, and recounted my story from beginning to end, including my encounter with the nobleman who deceived me and led me to leave my master, and eventually broke the promise he'd made.

"What you've said is all true, brother," the man said, "but His Excellency the nobleman isn't to blame. The fault rests with your master. Let me tell you how this story came to an end.

10.52 "The old man who used to visit you was the one who tricked the nobleman into sending you off on a journey," he continued. "He'd learned that your master was trying to secure a position for you in the Arabic Library. So, fearing that the position in the library would slip from his grasp, he played this little trick and convinced the nobleman to send you away.

"Now, on the night when the nobleman sent you to Versailles to get an edict from the king, one of your master's friends happened to see you there. He went and informed your master about how you'd given a letter to a certain duke, who then took you to meet with the head of the chancery, who in turn drew up a royal edict recognizing you as a traveler on behalf of the crown.

"When your master learned about all this, he went straight to 10.53 Versailles to see the duke, and extracted the complete story from him. He was furious, for the position of a traveler appointed by the king was his own! So he went immediately to see His Excellency the nobleman, and defamed you to him.

"'Be careful with these types, my lord!' he said. 'Orientals are a traitorous lot, and it's quite possible that this fellow will take advantage of your authority to steal from the consuls then vanish to his homeland. And if that happens, you'll have no power to make him do anything. Permit me instead, as a token of my esteem for Your Excellency, to replace that man as your servant! In return, I promise to send you everything I collect during my travels.'

"When he heard that, the nobleman changed his mind and decided to finance your master's travels instead," the man concluded.

And this was, in fact, how things came to pass. Some time after I 10.54 returned home to Aleppo, my master turned up in the city as well. I went to meet him, and invited him to pay a visit to my family's home, where I received him most honorably and put myself at his service. He spent the night at our house, and I prepared a bed for him in my loft. After my brothers left, my master and I were left alone. As we sat chatting, he began to reproach me.

"Why didn't you tell me about your agreement with the nobleman to go on a voyage? That was the lowest thing you could have done to me! I never expected you'd treat me that way, because I meant to do right by you. But you threw away your best chance!"

After much discussion and quarreling, we finally fell asleep. The following day, we had breakfast and went into town together. At the time, I'd opened a textile shop, and he would visit me each day.

We'd go off together to hunt for old coins, medallions, and precious stones, just like old times.

10.55 One day, we went to the jewelry souk, and he saw a pierced stone, the color of carnelian, in a case. He bought it for two *miṣriyyah*s and handed it to me.

"Hang this around your mother's neck, and she'll be cured of her illness."

When he'd stayed at our house, it had occurred to me to let him see my mother, who had suffered from a chronic illness for the previous twenty years. No doctor had been able to cure her, so we took her to my master and explained her symptoms: She couldn't sleep or speak, and never wanted to leave the house on a walk or to attend mass, and she hardly ate anything. It was only with great effort that we managed to feed her; as a result, her body had shriveled to a thin stalk.

10.56 We hung the stone around her neck, and that night she slept soundly, as she used to do before! The next day, she changed her clothes and asked to be taken to the bathhouse. When she returned, she was the picture of health. All of us were astounded by the power of that stone, which seemed to have worked a miracle! I asked my master to tell me what it was called, and to explain its powers.

"It's called *cheramide* in Italian," he said. "It has the special property of instantly drawing out the black humor. Your mother was suffering from melancholy, that's all."

10.57 Anyway, the man I met at the inn in Marseille told me that the nobleman had sent my edict to my master, allowing him to set off on a voyage at the nobleman's expense.

"The nobleman isn't interested in you anymore, so you may as well give up on this whole affair," the man said.

My suspicion is that this man was sent by the nobleman to convey this information to me. In any case, that's the end of the story of why I left Paris.

10.58 Now, back to what I was saying. I remained at the inn in Marseille, waiting to catch a ship bound for Alexandretta. Every day, I went to the chamber of commerce where the merchants gathered from ten in the morning until noon, and again from two in the afternoon until the early evening. That was where all of the commercial activity took place. The merchants who had business in the Eastern lands could be found there, along with those who traded with the New World, Spain, the Maghreb, and other lands. Whenever these merchants were planning to dispatch a ship, they'd post a notice with the name of the ship and its destination.

One day, I went down to the chamber of commerce and saw a notice posted with the name of a ship headed for the port of Alexandretta. I happily went to see *khawājah* Samatan, who was my very best friend. He had been a merchant in Aleppo, and my oldest brother had worked as his warehouseman. *Khawājah* Samatan was very fond of me, and would often invite me to his house and treat me as a cherished guest. So I told him that a ship was preparing to sail for Alexandretta, and that I planned to be on it.   10.59

"I know about the ship," he said. "I'll put in a good word for you with the captain, and have him take you aboard for free."

I thanked him and wished him well, and went home to pack my things. As I was intent on sailing with that ship, I said goodbye to all the foreign gentlemen of Aleppo I knew. A few days later, however, the owners of the ship changed their mind and decided not to sail, fearing the threat of pirates. I was devastated when I heard this, as I'd been anxious to leave and was starting to feel at my wits' end. I went to the chamber of commerce to see if there might be a ship headed to the Levantine coast.   10.60

There were only two: one bound for Istanbul and the other for Izmir. I made some inquiries about the captain of the Izmir-bound ship, sought him out, and asked if he would take me aboard. He agreed, but demanded that I pay my fare of forty piasters—not including food and drink—in advance. All I had was ten piasters! What was I to do?

I returned to my friend *khawājah* Samatan and told him what had happened. He wasn't pleased with my plan to go to Izmir.   10.61

"Be patient, and perhaps a ship will be dispatched to Alexandretta soon enough," he said. "I'll get you on board for free."

"But I can't bear to stay in this country any longer!" I said, pleading with him. "I'm fed up, and my patience has run out! I absolutely must leave!"

"Let me give you some advice," he replied. "Go upstairs to the consul's residence, which is above the chamber of commerce. Ask the consul to order the captain of the ship to take you with him. Tell him, 'I'm a penniless foreigner in this country, and don't have a job to earn a living.' I guarantee you that he'll order the captain to take you with him."

10.62   I did as he advised and went to see the consul early the next morning. As luck would have it, I arrived as a priest was preparing to lead a mass at the consul's residence, so I quickly went inside and began to help the priest. After the mass, the consul left with several merchants for a walk in the courtyard. I followed them, and presented myself before the consul, bowing deeply as custom required. Speaking in French, I told him what *khawājah* Samatan had instructed me to say.

"Where are you from?" he asked when I was done speaking.

"Syria," I replied.

"What brought you to this land?"

"I came with a Frenchman, and traveled with him to Paris," I explained. "When he left me, I came back here to find a way to return to my country. I spent all my money getting back to Marseille, and don't even have a coin to spend on food."

10.63   After hearing me out, the consul ordered one of his servants to summon the captain.

"Wait here," he said, turning to me. "Don't go anywhere."

A few minutes later, the captain appeared, and the consul ordered him to take me with him.

"In keeping with our custom, this man ought to be sent back to his land, as he's a stranger here and has no money," the consul explained.

"Yes sir," the captain replied, and turned to me and said, "Get into a rowboat with your bags this evening and come out to the ship. We sail early tomorrow morning."

I thanked the consul and the captain from the bottom of my heart, and went to tell *khawājah* Samatan what had transpired, and to thank him.

"All that's left for me to do now is to go see the owner of the ship," 10.64 he said. "We'll need to get a letter from him vouching for you to give the captain, so no one causes any trouble for you on the journey. You were put on the ship against his wishes, after all."

So he took me to see the shipowner, a friend of his, who greeted us warmly when we arrived.

"I'd like to have this young man travel aboard your ship," *khawājah* Samatan explained. "As a favor to me, would you be willing to write a letter to the ship's captain vouching for the boy and entrusting him to his care?"

"It would be my pleasure," the man replied, and immediately drafted a letter to the captain commending me to his charge. He encouraged the captain to watch over me and not to accept any payment for my expenses. In fact, if I needed anything at all, the captain was to provide me with it. The shipowner sealed the letter and handed it to me, then we bid him farewell and left.

With the letter in hand, I returned to the inn where I was staying. 10.65 No sooner had I arrived when a delivery appeared for me. It was a sack full of provisions for the road: hardtack, some cheese, a sack of little dried fish, a jar of olives, and a small barrel of wine. Then the *khawājah* himself came to wish me farewell. I thanked him dearly for the gift, heaping praise and gratitude upon him.

"The captain might not invite you to dine at his table," the *khawājah* said. "Take these provisions with you, so you don't have to depend on him."

I gave him a letter to send to my brother in Aleppo via the over- 10.66 land postal service to Istanbul. The letter, which informed my brother of the date of my departure by ship from Marseille to Izmir, arrived safely in my brother's hands some time later. Not long after that, however, my family received news that a vessel bound from Izmir to Alexandretta had been wrecked, and all aboard had perished. My brothers and my relatives were overwhelmed with grief, as they knew I'd traveled from Marseille to Izmir, and felt certain I had been on the stricken ship. Not receiving word from me—as I'd stopped sending letters after leaving France—they lost all hope and mourned me, praying for my soul's eternal rest.

10.67   Back to the story. After I said goodbye to the *khawājah*, I had my bags brought to the harbor and loaded them into a rowboat. I got in, and off we went to the ship, which was anchored beyond the harbor channel. I climbed aboard the ship. It was a large vessel named *La Galatane*,[164] and had twenty-four cannons. There were eighty soldiers on board, not counting the crew. As a precaution against pirates, the ship held only a half load, so it was really half warship, half merchant ship.

We spent the night there. Early the next morning, we raised the anchors, unfurled the sails, and set off. It was only once we were out on the open sea that I handed the letter to the captain. He read it and smiled.

"Rest easy," he said, then left me to my own devices, and didn't invite me to dine with him.

10.68   We sailed all day without incident. The following morning, I noticed that the officers had gathered together and were preparing the ship for combat, readying the cannons and muskets. Each cannon had a notice hung upon it with the names of the crew members responsible for firing it; there was also a list of soldiers tasked with firing the muskets. Finally, they came to me.

"Name?" they said.

"What do you want my name for?" I asked.

"When the enemy shows up, you'll have to pick up a musket and fight like everyone else!"

"Leave me be," I said. "I'm a foreigner, and I don't know anything about war, or how to fire a musket for that matter."

"I suppose you could go hide in the hold when you see us fighting the enemy," the captain said, turning to me. "But if I were you, I wouldn't disappear in the middle of a battle, because the soldiers won't think twice about killing you!"

So I was forced to put my name down and enlist like everyone 10.69 else. The day passed without event. Then, on our third day at sea, we spotted a large pirate ship in the distance. When it caught sight of us, the ship headed in our direction, dead set on attacking us and seizing our ship. We turned to face them, opening the gunports as the soldiers lined up with their muskets, with poor little me among them!

We drew near the pirate ship, and were followed by a second ship, which had left Marseille with us. It was bound for Istanbul, and it too had prepared for a battle. When the pirates saw two large ships bearing down on them, they turned tail and we gave chase. Realizing that our vessels were French, the pirates raised a French flag once they started taking fire, and hailed us over their bullhorn, announcing that they too were French. Once we determined this to be the case, we left them alone and went on our way. It was only then that my fear dissipated, and I thanked God Almighty that the pirates didn't belong to an enemy nation! For a moment, I'd lost all hope and had been certain I was going to die.

One day, when I went down into the hold of the ship to have 10.70 lunch, I noticed a handsome young man by my side. He bore all the signs of a well-to-do person, yet he scarcely had any clothes on, wearing only a decrepit, ripped old tunic that revealed the flesh beneath, and no shirt. My heart went out to this abject, melancholy young man and I invited him to join me for lunch, which he did. I gave him a jar of wine to drink, and chatted amiably with him. When we'd finished our lunch, I took a shirt, vest, and tunic out of my basket and gave them to him to wear. He refused at first, but finally accepted and put them on, thanking me profusely. We sat down and struck up a conversation, and I asked him what his story was.

"If you'd like to know, I suppose I'll tell you," the young man 10.71 began. "I'm one of the secretaries of the French ambassador in

Istanbul.[165] The ambassador sent me to Paris with some letters for the minister about a very urgent matter, which had to do with an audience with Sultan Aḥmad. After having presented gifts from the king of France, the ambassador prepared to meet the sultan in the company of the grand vizier and the dragoman. They passed through the third gate of the palace.[166] Now, the Ottomans have a very old custom. When an ambassador enters the third gate of the palace, the chief eunuch comes forward to relieve the ambassador of the rapier he wears at his side, out of respect for His Majesty the king. But when the gatekeeper tried to do so, the ambassador pushed him away and refused to let them take his rapier!

10.72   "The grand vizier was flabbergasted and the dragoman just about lost his senses, pleading with the ambassador to let them take his rapier in accordance with their ancient custom. But he refused to let them lay a hand on it.

"'I've been ordered to greet His Majesty the king wearing my rapier,' he told the grand vizier.

"'Impossible!' the grand vizier replied. 'I cannot allow you to appear before His Majesty with a rapier.'

"So the ambassador left without an audience and returned to his palace. In the meantime, the grand vizier wrote a letter to the French king's minister, apprising him of the ambassador's insolence. As for the ambassador, he wrote his own account of the incident, and handed it to me to deliver personally to the minister. He also warned me not to let anyone know that I was traveling on his behalf.

10.73   "I took the letter and boarded a French ship, along with two companions. No sooner had we set sail than we were attacked by a pirate ship. They seized our vessel and robbed us of all our possessions! They even stole our clothes, leaving us naked. One of the sailors took pity on me and offered me this ripped tunic. Eventually, they dumped us in the harbor of Livorno and we were reduced to begging for food to stay alive. And yet, I still had the letter.

"I was determined to complete my mission, so I gradually made my way from Livorno to Marseille. But after several days in Marseille with no clothes and no food, I realized that it was all but impossible for me to reach Paris, for no one had taken pity on me as you did. I was compelled to send the letter with the postal service and return home to my superior, so I wouldn't die there."

When I heard this sad story, I consoled the young man and tried to distract him from his troubles. In this way, an affectionate bond developed between us and we became close friends. I told him my own story from start to finish.

One night during our voyage, we drew near the island of Sicily. It was governed by Austria, which was at war with France.[167] The ship was on guard, fearing the possibility of pirates attacking us from the island. The sky was luminous that evening, as the moon was in the fourteenth night of its cycle. Suddenly, the night watch spotted what seemed to be a vessel sailing away from the island, so they woke the captain and the rest of the crew.

When the captain spied the vessel, he ordered our ship to pursue it. Meanwhile, the other ship that had departed Marseille with us also spotted the vessel and likewise set off in pursuit. We soon caught up to the vessel, drawing up on either side of it. All that was left to do was to send a longboat full of soldiers to seize it. When our quarry realized they were caught between two ships and had no way to escape without being fired upon—which could only lead to the sinking of their ship—they lowered their sails and came to a standstill. We put our longboat in the water with the soldiers so we could seize the enemy ship and hitch it to our own, but as soon as the longboat approached them, they swung their cannons up, barring it from coming any closer. Then they hoisted their sails and took off again with the help of a wind gusting over their poop deck, which is to say their stern.

At this sight, we set off in hot pursuit together with the other ship, and closed in on it once again. But they pulled the same maneuver as before and escaped a second time! On the third chase, our two ships began to spray the enemy vessel with shot, hoping to prevent it from slipping away again. As soon as the fusillade began,

10.74

10.75

10.76

the captain of the enemy ship could be heard telling his crew to go down into the hold so they wouldn't be struck by the shot raining down on them. His voice was recognizably French, so our ships ceased fire.

"Identify yourself!" we called out over our bullhorn.

"I'm Captain So-and-So!" he replied.

It was the same captain who had left Marseille with us in order to benefit from our protection.[168] As soon as our crew confirmed that it was indeed that captain, they regretted their action and offered their apologies to the man.

10.77 The next day, we sent the ship some new sails, as the old ones had been shredded by our shot, and advised its captain not to stray far from us. Then we set off again, and sailed without incident until we drew near to the port of Izmir.

A heavy gale then rose up from the land, blowing us back into the vicinity of the Morea. We fought our way back, but the wind and waves tossed us in the direction of Istanbul, where we found ourselves stranded among the reefs. We spent all day and night between the rocks, certain our ship would be wrecked and we'd all perish. But the next day, our Lord sent us a wind from the coast and we were able to sail away from the reef, thankful to the Almighty Creator for His beneficence and grace!

CHAPTER ELEVEN

In the Lands of the East

We arrived safely in the port of Izmir, and once the ship had dropped   11.1
anchor I disembarked along with the young man I mentioned earlier. As soon as I got out of the rowboat and set foot on dry land, I
saw the Muslim customs inspectors, and my heart skipped a beat. I
was overcome with an awful sense of foreboding, as though I'd been
taken prisoner, and instantly regretted what I'd done. How could I
have left the lands of the Christians to return to being a prisoner of
the Muslims?

My friend turned to me and told me to follow him, and we soon   11.2
arrived at the residence of the French consul. It was a stately house
with janissaries guarding the door, and was full of dragomans, servants, and other attendants. We went upstairs and the young man
asked to be admitted to meet with the consul. With permission
granted, we presented ourselves before him and the young man
set about recounting the story of how he had been dispatched to
France by His Excellency the French ambassador in Istanbul.

"We were robbed by pirates," he explained, "and are now on our
way back to Istanbul to see His Excellency."

Having learned who the young man was, the consul immediately summoned one of his dragomans and ordered him to take us to an inn. The consul recommended us to the innkeeper, entrusting us to his care until such time as a ship was ready to depart for Istanbul.

11.3   The dragoman brought us to a very fine inn frequented by ship captains and traveling merchants, and we were given a place to sleep with clean beds and fresh white sheets. It was just as orderly as the inns in French lands, if not more so. We spent the rest of the day there, savoring delicious food and drink for lunch and dinner, and enjoying the wonderful service.

"As long as you're with me, you won't need to worry about your next meal," said the young man the next day. "Come on, follow me."

So I did, gazing upon the sights of Izmir as we went on our way. By the harbor was a large quarter inhabited entirely by Frankish merchants and other Franks involved in commercial dealings. Their women sat in the shops just as they did in Frankish lands. It was called the Frankish quarter. The main city of Izmir was about a mile away, and that was where the Muslim merchants and the governors lived, just like any other city. The only other people who would enter the Frankish quarter were Muslim merchants or other subjects who had a reason to be there.

11.4   The young man brought me to a Jesuit monastery. When we went inside and the abbot saw us, he was stupefied because he recognized the young man, whom he'd known from Istanbul. They greeted each other, and the abbot ushered us into the dining hall, offering us refreshments and treating us most cordially. He asked the young man about the state he was in and his threadbare clothes, and the latter told him the story. The abbot then offered his consolations and sympathy, for he knew how much His Excellency the ambassador loved this young man. After all, he'd been the chief of all the embassy officials.

When it was time to leave, the young man asked the abbot if he could borrow a few piasters from him, which he would repay to the abbot of the Jesuit monastery in Istanbul, as if he were using a promissory note.

"Of course," said the abbot, opening the monastery's cashbox and inviting the young man to take as much money as he needed.

He took fifteen piasters and wrote a receipt for the abbot. Then we bid him farewell and set off. As soon as we left the monastery, the young man handed me the money.   11.5

"Keep this with you," he said. "Travel expenses."

Then we went to the Capuchin monastery, where the abbot similarly invited us in for refreshments. The young man borrowed ten piasters from him, which he also gave me after we left.

"Just in case the money we took from the Jesuit abbot wasn't enough, I thought I'd pick up another ten piasters," he explained. "That way, we'll have plenty and won't have to worry about running out."

Now I had twenty-five piasters, all in *zolota* coins. So off we went,   11.6 touring the city and seeing the sights, buying treats, and having a great time. We spent fifteen days in this fashion, eating and drinking and strolling about. Finally, a large ship arrived from Egypt. It was carrying coffee, rice, and fabric, and was headed for Istanbul. The dragoman came by and encouraged us to leave on that vessel.

"Come on, brother," said the young man, rising to his feet. "Let's get on that ship and get out of here!"

I told him I was taking the next caravan to Aleppo.

"Come now, brother," he replied. "If you think I'm going to part with you before we get to Istanbul, you can forget it!"

In the end, he got his way, and we went off with the dragoman.   11.7 When we arrived at the harbor's customs office, I saw the customs officer waiting, the captain of the ship seated beside him. The dragoman strode up to the customs officer and instructed him, on behalf of the consul, to allow us to embark upon the ship and to place us in the care of the captain. Then the dragoman handed us off to the customs officer, who in turn handed us off to the captain, telling him to take care of us, as instructed. The dragoman paid our *nawlūn*, which is to say our travel fare; then the captain summoned some sailors over from a dinghy, ordering them to take us to the ship and give us a private cabin, and to take good care of us.

We went with the sailors to the dinghy, and saw that the dragoman had sent over fifty *uqqah*s of hardtack, a wheel of cheese weighing five *uqqah*s, some fried fish, and a demijohn of wine. He'd also given us each five piasters of travel money. Once on board, we brought our baggage into our cabin and spent the rest of the day there.

11.8   Early the next morning, we raised the sails and set off. Soon enough, we arrived at the straits of Istanbul, which are long and broad. The journey from the entrance of the straits to the port of Istanbul was to take four or five days. But as we approached the straits, a wind blew out from the coast, preventing us from entering. The captain was compelled to drop anchor in the port of Gelibolu, a little town outside the straits.[169] Each day, we'd leave the ship and tour the town, returning by night to sleep on board. After five days, a favorable wind blew from the sea, so we raised our sails once again and entered the straits.

11.9   Two days later, another wind blew out from the coast, preventing us from going any farther. So we anchored in a small harbor for a couple of days until the wind changed and we could set off again. We soon arrived at the port of Küçükçekmece, where we dropped anchor.[170] That night, two ships appeared, heading in our direction. The captain suspected that they might be Maltese pirates, so he immediately sent word to the citadel, which began to fire its cannons at the two ships. Our ship joined the barrage, aiming to prevent the ships from entering the port. But the ships dropped anchor far from the citadel and lowered their sails, a sign that they had no hostile intent. But this wasn't enough to stop the cannons.

11.10   After a while, the two ships raised a banner indicating that they came in peace, but this too didn't stop the assault. All the passengers on our ship soon retreated to the citadel, while the port's inhabitants fled to the mountains in fear of the pirates. Finally, when the people on the two ships realized that their signals of peace had not convinced the citadel, they sent out a dinghy with the ship's clerk and three officers. As soon as it arrived in the harbor, the men were seized and brought up to the citadel, where they were asked to identify themselves and explain their reason for entering the straits.

"We're two Flemish ships, and we've been sailing around, trying to purchase wheat from the Province of the Islands," they explained. "But no one will sell us anything unless we have an edict from the vizier. So we decided to go to Istanbul to secure one but ran into some French pirates along the way. We fled and came here to seek refuge in the citadel. What's the matter with you, anyway? Why have you been firing your cannons at us as if we were your enemies?"

But the people in the citadel weren't convinced. They seized the men, and the sailors who had been with them in the dinghy, and threw them in jail.

Then the chief of the citadel came down to our ship along with some of his men, and consulted with our captain about how to proceed.

"Why don't you and I go out to their ship?" he suggested. "I have two Frankish men from France on board whom we can bring along to act as interpreters. One of them speaks Turkish."

They agreed, and immediately prepared a dinghy to take us out. We all jumped in and headed toward the larger of the two ships. We climbed aboard, entered the captain's cabin, and found him sitting with his crew. They had before them some lighted candles, bottles of wine, and goblets, and all were in a very merry mood.

The captain and his men rose to their feet and greeted us. Then they served us some sweets, fruit preserves, and delicious refreshments, and we spent the next couple of hours having a wonderful time together. Finally, we bid them farewell and prepared to return, resolving to have their men sent back from the citadel. That was when the Flemish captain asked our captain if he would be so kind as to let the Flemish ship's clerk travel to Istanbul with us so that he could request the edict granting permission to trade in wheat. Our captain agreed, and brought the clerk back to our ship.

11.11

11.12

11.13

11.14   After a few days, the winds became favorable again, blowing from the sea, and we set sail with the Flemish clerk aboard. We soon arrived in Büyükçekmece,[171] where we dropped anchor and went to tour the town. Wouldn't you know it, the Flemish fellow covered all of our expenses! The longer we remained in the harbor, though, the more anxious he became about getting to Istanbul, because the two ships were awaiting his return. So he began to make inquiries about whether it was possible to travel to Istanbul from there by land, and was told it was a journey of three days or less. He then asked to have some people rounded up who could take him to Istanbul, and a mount was brought over right away.

11.15   The Flemish man then turned to me and my friend, and invited us to go with him, but we refused, explaining that we'd already paid our fare, and that the captain wouldn't let us go off on our own. After all, he'd been tasked with delivering us directly to the ambassador's residence in Istanbul. But the man continued to insist.

"I'll pay your fare," he said. "I can't travel by myself! I don't speak the language!"

We felt sorry for the fellow and went back to the ship to lock up our things inside our cabin and ask the captain's permission to travel the rest of the way to Istanbul by land, for the sake of the Flemish man.

"But I guaranteed the customs officer that I'd be responsible for you," the captain said. "And he insisted that I deliver you to the French ambassador's house."

"Look, we've left our bags on board the ship," we said. "Once they arrive, we'll come to the ship and give you a document from the dragoman certifying that we arrived at the ambassador's house. Then we'll take our things."

11.16   The captain was satisfied, so we bid him farewell and rejoined the Flemish fellow. He had already procured a couple of mounts for us and prepared ample provisions for the road. We climbed onto our mounts and set off. Soon thereafter, we arrived in Istanbul, coming first to a place called Kum Kapı, the entrance to the city. There was a place there called Yedi Kule, where I saw some deep holes dug into the earth.

"What are these holes for?" I asked.

"Excavating marble," our muleteer explained. "You find it in these parts."

We continued for about an hour until we arrived at the large port where the customs authorities were located. We got off our mounts and rented a dinghy to take us out to Galata. When we arrived, the Flemish man went to the home of the Flemish ambassador in Beyoğlu, while I remained where I was, uncertain what to do and where to go. I was a stranger, after all.

Turning to my friend, I asked him to point me in the direction of a place where I could stay, but he shook his head.

"Follow me to the residence of my master, His Excellency the ambassador," he said. "That's where you'll be staying."

I tried to refuse, but he grabbed me and pulled me along, and together we went up to Beyoğlu, where all the ambassadors lived. It was a spacious quarter, occupying an elevated position. We visited Kız Kulesi, the "Maiden's Tower," named for the young woman who resisted the siege of Istanbul in that fortress. She held out there for a long time, and it was only with considerable difficulty that the fortress was conquered. Hers is a long story.

We made our way higher up into the quarter until we arrived at its central square, where the palaces of the ambassadors were located. The French ambassador's palace was the grandest and most beautiful of them all, and encompassed a delightful garden. A company of armed janissaries stood at the outer gate.

As we passed through, everyone rose to greet my friend. We entered the inner pavilion where the ambassador's residence was located. When the embassy staff saw the state my friend was in, they were astonished. Some went to inform the ambassador, who summoned the young man in.

11.17

11.18

11.19

"Follow me," he said. I obeyed, and we presented ourselves before His Excellency, who was surprised to see the young man in such a condition.

"Whatever happened to you?" he asked, incredulous.

"My lord, allow me to tell you my story," the young man said, bowing so deeply that he swept the ground.

The ambassador gave him permission to speak, and the young man bowed again and launched into an account of his journey, from the time he left until the moment he arrived, as I described earlier. Upon hearing it, the ambassador commiserated with the young man and did what he could to console him.

11.20   Then he inquired about me: "And who might this young man be?"

"My lord, my life was in this man's hands, as it was in God's," he said. "He found me and diverted my thoughts from my misfortune. He gave me some of his own clothes to wear, and brought me all the way home."

He told the ambassador my story. Luckily I happened to have, tucked away in a pouch, the letter of recommendation to the ambassador that the nobleman in Paris had given me. I pulled it out and handed it to him. Upon reading it, the ambassador welcomed me cordially.

11.21   "How might I be of service to you?" he asked.

"My lord, if it pleases you, perhaps you would accept me as one of your servants."

"Alas, I've received word from the king of France, summoning me back to Paris," he explained. "But you are welcome to remain here in my palace until the new ambassador arrives. I'll arrange to have you employed in his service, and I'll recommend you to him."

The ambassador turned to the young man I'd accompanied and ordered him to take care of me and give me a bedroom, and to have me dine with the embassy officials at the second table. I thanked the ambassador for his benevolence and we departed.

11.22   The young man summoned the embassy's steward and conveyed to him the order of His Excellency that I should have a bedroom prepared. Then the young man got dressed in a magnificent suit and reassumed his former aspect. At lunchtime, they invited me to join the embassy officials at the second table, which was next to the ambassador's table. My friend seated me at his side and began to praise me to all of his companions.

"If you love me, then honor this young man!"

Everyone at the table then began to serve me, slicing pieces of those wonderful delicacies and grilled fowl, and setting them before me. Meanwhile, the ambassador's orchestra had struck up as soon as the ambassador was seated and played throughout lunch, just as it would at dinner. This was in accordance with embassy protocol, and the musicians played fine instruments, similar to those I'd seen in Paris.

I spent a period of time at the ambassador's residence, eating and 11.23 drinking and amusing myself. Then one day, I asked my friend if we could go out to see the sights of Istanbul.

"Of course," he replied, and the next day we went down to Galata after lunch. Along the way, he left me for a moment to go relieve himself. As I waited, a drunken janissary walked up and began to accost me coarsely in his inebriated state. My friend returned to the scene, where he found the janissary clutching me and demanding money for arak. Scolding the janissary, the young man kicked him in the leg, knocking him to the ground. I was suddenly afraid that this would lead to trouble, but my friend left the man lying on the ground and walked off without giving him a second glance.

"Come along," he said to me. "There's nothing to fear."

We went down to Galata and toured the neighborhood before 11.24 boarding a dinghy to Istanbul. Our first stop was the Valideh Caravansary, a luxurious caravansary built of stone. Inside it was another caravansary, and inside that one yet another! The whole complex was full of rooms populated by merchants, boat skippers, and money changers, and its storehouses held an uncountable amount of money, due to the fact that the caravansary was impervious to fire. That was why all of the merchants and money changers lived there.

We toured the caravansary, admiring the sights. I spotted some Aleppans I knew, but who didn't seem to recognize me. That suited me, as I didn't want to be noticed. Among them were Ibn al-Qārī, Shukrī ibn Shāhīn Çelebi, and many others. One of them, a certain *khawājah* Azāt who lived near my brother's house, did recognize me. He strolled up to say hello and introduce himself, then invited me and my friend to his room, where he served us coffee and treated us most cordially.

11.25 From there, we headed to the grand bazaar, which contained just about every sort of merchandise one could imagine. We then visited the Bālistān souk, which was also constructed of stone, as it included many storehouses. The souk had everything you could want, from furnishings and weapons to precious fabrics and expensive furs such as sable and ermine. There were special cashboxes in the souk meant to protect money from a fire, which many people took advantage of to safeguard their wealth. No one ever bothered to lock up their shop because, when evening came, the two gates of the souk were closed and secured with strong locks. Guards were stationed outside the entrances all night long. As a result, the souk was as secure as the sultan's own treasury.

11.26 The next stop was Hümayun Gate—that is, the gate to the king's palace.

"Come in with me," the young man said. "I'd like to show you the imperial mint."

We passed through the gate into an immense courtyard, traversed by three paths. The first, which was to the right, led to the women's palace, where the king's harem was located. Anyone who entered it without warning would be flogged with a cane. The second path, which lay in the middle, led to the king's inner palace. It was accessible only to the vizier and the other nobles of the realm. The third path, on the left, led to the mint. All were welcome to visit it without fear or trepidation.

11.27 We walked over to the mint and went inside. It was spacious. There were two glowing furnaces, which received the rods of silver and gold. On one side of the furnaces was a large heap of silver rods, and on the other a pile of gold ones. In another spot, some people sat hammering the rods to make them even, while others cut the rods into perfect piasters, half piasters, and quarter piasters with the help of presses. One person would lay the rod across the anvil while another turned the press, cutting the piaster, which fell to the ground. Some other people would then stamp the freshly cut coins with the aid of another press, marking them on both sides with the sultan's name and seal, and the date. All of this without a single hammer blow!

We left the mint and headed over to the church of Hagia Sophia. 11.28 Today, it has become a royal mosque, as it is situated near the royal palace. Every Friday, the king comes to the mosque to pray. We admired the mosque from the exterior, as Christians were not allowed to enter. But even from the outside, I could see that the church, which had been built by ancient Christian kings, was indescribably marvelous. We continued on to the Valide mosque, which had no equal in all of Istanbul.[172] It was open to all, except for the section beneath the qibla dome.

From there, we passed by the palace of the Keeper of the Seal, by whom I mean the grand vizier. The street was full of people going in and out of the palace with complaints and petitions and other such things. I saw a pasha walk by with two royal footmen and no one gave him a second glance, just as though he were an ordinary person! We spent the day regarding such remarkable spectacles, returning home in the evening.

A few days later, His Excellency the ambassador received word 11.29 that the Venetian ambassador had recently arrived in Istanbul and was to have an audience with the king in three days. Upon his arrival, he'd sent gifts to the king and would meet with him three days later, per the usual protocol. The French ambassador told his steward to prepare the costumes and notify the embassy officials to get ready for the parade. Whenever an ambassador was to be received by the king, it was customary for all the other ambassadors to send their officials to parade before him. The French ambassador would usually send forty of his own officials, all decked out in ceremonial costumes sent by the monarchy. They were made of scarlet fabric with gold embroidery on their sleeves and breasts. They wore rapiers damascened in gold and hats hemmed with gold thread, as well as curly blond wigs. According to what I heard, each outfit cost more than five hundred piasters.

11.30   Once the steward had finished making his preparations, it transpired that the company of forty officials was short three men. So he sent for three more, and I was one of them. On the appointed day, everyone got suited up as described, including me, and we headed off to the Venetian ambassador's residence. The procession lined up, stretching from the ambassador's house all the way down to Galata. By the time the ambassador reached the harbor of Galata, the king's boats had arrived. The ambassador got into the lead boat, while his entourage rode in the other ones, and they set off for Sirkeci, the port of Istanbul. From there, various ranks of janissaries, sent by their chief, along with other figures from the grand vizier's staff, paraded before the ambassador in the direction of the king's inner palace.

11.31   The vizier, the ambassador, and the chief dragoman would enter alone and make their way to the king's private pavilion, which was accessed via three steps. They would climb the first step and the second, but before climbing up to the third, the king would pass, on his way to the second chamber. At that point, the vizier, the ambassador, and the dragoman would still be on the second step. Then the king would stop, and the dragoman would present a brief request to address the king on behalf of the ambassador. When he was finished, the king would ask the ambassador for the news of his peers, and the dragoman would respond on his behalf. Finally, the king would enter the second pavilion, followed by the ambassador, who now wore a caftan on his shoulders, given to him by the king. His entourage also received caftans, a sign of the king's acceptance of their presence.

From there, they would continue on to the council hall, where   11.32
the ambassador would be seated in a chair reserved for him, and
served drinks, sweets, coffee, and incense. Finally, he would leave
the palace, preceded by the king's retinue—harem guards, confec-
tioners, gardeners, cooks, and many others—who accompanied
him all the way to the harbor. The ambassador would board the
king's boat with a few members of each company, and they'd deliver
him to his own palace along with the king's footmen and janissaries,
and all the embassy officials.

As I was saying, the procession of officials extended from Galata
all the way up to the ambassador's residence in Beyoğlu. When we
returned, I saw that a banquet table had been set up for the janissaries and other guests. It was a hundred arm spans long, and laden
with sweets and compotes served upon plates of braided rattan. But
as soon as the janissaries arrived, they pillaged the table, snatching
up all the sweets and other plates in an instant, leaving it devoid of
anything that could be called food!

However, a second banquet table reserved for the embassy offi-   11.33
cials had been set up inside the ambassador's palace. There one
found a wealth of fine dishes, such as tarts and dumplings, grilled
chicken thighs, and many others besides. At each corner of the table
was a barrel of wine along with several crystal glasses. We were
invited to eat and drink, so we dug in to the food and downed the
good wine. We drank to the health of the ambassador, crying out
"*Che viva!*" and the clamor of our merrymaking resounded outside
the walls of the palace.[173] Then we left and each returned home.

This is what I witnessed of the ambassador's audience. Of course,
I wasn't able to observe what happened between his entrance to
the king's palace and his departure. I heard about it from those who
were present, but God knows best!

A few days later, a high-ranking emissary arrived in Istanbul. He'd   11.34
been sent by the king of France specifically to remove the French
ambassador. He took control of the embassy, and assumed the role
of caretaker. The former ambassador's tenure was terminated, and

everything began to change in anticipation of the arrival of a new ambassador.

So I began to feel a sense of despair once again. I couldn't remain in the ambassador's mansion any longer because the emissary had dismissed most of the embassy officials and curtailed their wages. Those lovely banquets accompanied by music would be no more. Unsure of what to do, I decided to move my things to an inn in Beyoğlu. But just as I was preparing to leave the embassy, the abbot of the Jesuit monastery in Galata, with whom I'd become friends, passed by. He greeted me when he saw me.

11.35   "Where are you going?"

"To the inn."

He didn't look pleased about this.

"I don't want you to go live at the inn," he said.

"Where am I supposed to go, Father?"

He thought for a moment, then looked up at me.

"Are you willing to work, my son?"

"Yes, Father," I said. "But where can you find me a job?"

"There's a Venetian merchant near our monastery in Galata. He's a good man, and a wealthy one too. If you like, I can mention you to him."

"Whatever you think is best, Father," I replied. "I'm in your hands."

"Spend another day here at the embassy, and I'll take you to meet him tomorrow," the abbot instructed, before bidding me farewell and departing.

11.36   The next day, the abbot sent for me.

"I spoke with the *khawājah*, and he has agreed to take you on as a cellarman," the abbot said. "Let's go see him."

We went to the *khawājah*'s house, and when we presented ourselves before him, he rose to his feet and greeted the abbot.

"This is the boy I told you about," the abbot said. "You can be confident that he'll be trustworthy and hardworking."

The *khawājah* agreed to hire me, and gave me a wage of fifty piasters per year. I'd also receive half the sum of the door fee, which was earned on the basis of merchandise sold. The other half would go to the cook and another employee. Then the priest went on his way, and the *khawājah* put me in charge of all the kitchenware, silver, dinnerware, and so forth. He also gave me a key to the cellar.

I brought my things from the ambassador's house to the *khawājah*'s, placing them in my own room, to which he'd given me a key. Then I set about tidying up the house, which I discovered was quite filthy. I began by doing some sweeping and putting everything in its place. I made the beds of the *khawājah* and his clerk, and arranged the table in the dining room. Then I went down to the cellar and brought up some cheese, olives, and other necessities.

This work was familiar to me from my time in Aleppo, when I'd spent twelve years working for *khawājah* Rimbaud the elder and *khawājah* Rémuzat after him, just before I left Aleppo to join the monastic order. When the *khawājah* arrived for lunch in the company of his clerk, he saw how clean and neat everything was, and was overjoyed.

After I'd spent a month working for the *khawājah*, he asked me one day if the demijohn of wine was empty.

"It's not even half empty," I replied.

The *khawājah* turned to his clerk, remarking, "When the last fellow was in charge, a single demijohn of wine wouldn't last the month!"

Now, the cook happened to hear what the *khawājah* said, and so did the other servant. They weren't pleased about it, and from that day forth they harbored a bitter resentment toward me, because I'd inadvertently exposed their pilferage. However, I was unaware of the grudge they bore.

After a while, I began to notice the treacherous glances they cast at me, but I paid them no mind. It was the cook, in particular, who was dead set against me. So I told the *khawājah* about him, and he dismissed the fellow on the spot!

The *khawājah* set about searching for a new cook, but when he had trouble finding a suitable replacement, he became frustrated.

11.37

11.38

11.39

"Don't worry," I said. "I'll cook for you until you find someone."

"Do you know how to cook?" he asked.

"Yes."

"Praise the Lord!"

I'd learned how to cook from the man who used to cook for my master, *khawājah* Rimbaud. When he was fired, I took his place. All the *khawājah*s used to love my cooking, marveling at the fact that I was just a boy. So, anyway, I started cooking for the Venetian merchant, and consequently the other servant fell under my authority. He was very upset about this, since the *khawājah* was overjoyed with my cooking and stopped looking for another cook.

11.40   The house was now my domain; I gave the orders and did as I pleased. One night, a traveler passed by for dinner, and the *khawājah* ordered me to prepare more food than usual. But when I told the other servant to go and get something for me, or to perform some task or other, he refused. That was how much he resented me!

Angrily, I began to scold the man and ridicule him, and wouldn't you know it, he pulled out a knife and strode toward me, seething like a devil. He wanted to kill me! Appealing to my guardian angel for help, I threw myself at him and pried the knife out of his hand! Tossing it aside, I began hitting him as hard as I could.

11.41   The *khawājah* heard us shouting at each other, and rushed into the kitchen, where he found us locked in combat. Shouting at both of us, he pulled us apart, then turned to face me.

"Is this any time to fight, while we have a guest in the house?" he demanded. "Go back to work!"

With no opportunity to tell him what had happened, I said a quick prayer and went back to preparing dinner and serving it. Afterward, once the guest had left, I told the *khawājah* the whole story, and he reassured me that it wasn't my fault.

"I'll throw him out tomorrow morning, you can be certain of that," he said. "I know all about these Greeks. A wicked, spiteful lot. They can't be trusted, you know."

He wouldn't let me leave him until my spirits had risen. Then I wished him good night and went up to my bedroom. I bolted the door from the inside, afraid of what treachery might come my way while I slept. But instead, I spent the night lost in thought.

"Even if the *khawājah* dismisses that troublemaker, what if I bump into him in the street and he pulls out a knife and kills me?" I thought to myself. "The Greeks in these lands wouldn't think twice about murdering someone. When they do, they turn themselves in and enlist with the janissaries, simple as that."

At this thought, my imagination ran wild, and my anxieties kept me up all night long. What was I to do?

Then a thought crossed my mind. I'd run into a friend of mine from Aleppo at the Jesuit church, a Maronite named Ḥannā ibn al-Zughbī. After we'd greeted each other, I'd invited him over to the Venetian *khawājah*'s house, where I was living, and served him some refreshments and welcomed him as my guest. Then I asked him why he'd come to Istanbul.

"I came to this country to learn the craft of calendering textiles, a trade that doesn't exist in Aleppo," he explained.[174] "Fortunately, God led me to a master artisan, who's agreed to come with me to Aleppo, and he's bringing along his calendering machine, which is made of tempered steel. This was exactly what I'd hoped for, and I'm just waiting for the next caravan to Aleppo. We plan to be on it."

After I told him the story of how I'd ended up there, he encour- aged me to return home with them.

"Stop wandering," he'd said. "Better to be safe than sorry."

He'd gone on in that vein, but I declined to follow his advice. From time to time, he'd bring up the subject again, urging me to travel home with them, but I always said no. On that sleepless night following my fight with the Greek servant, however, I remembered his words and made up my mind to go to Aleppo with them.

The next day, I went in to see the *khawājah* and asked permission to leave his service. He did his best to make me change my mind.

"Don't you worry, I'm going to throw that fellow out of my house," he promised. "I want you to be happy."

Unconvinced by his entreaty, I remained resolved to go through with my plan and repeated my request. When he saw that I'd really made up my mind, he paid me the remainder of what I was owed in wages, and half the door fee, as we'd agreed. Then I bid him farewell and gathered all my things, after handing over the silver, dining utensils, and other household implements I'd been safeguarding. I left the house and went straight to the Jesuit monastery next door.

11.46   I went to the abbot, told him the story of what had happened, and asked his permission to stay in the monastery until the caravan was ready to depart for Aleppo.

"My son, we can't admit laypeople and such into the monastery," he explained. "But I can give you a key to the community guesthouse, where the French ship captains and other travelers stay. There's a priest staying there at the moment, waiting for a bishop to arrive from Christian lands so they can travel together to Persia."

I thanked the abbot and took the key. He sent the monastery's workhand along to show me the way to the place, which was near the harbor.

11.47   When I entered the house, I saw that it had two floors filled with small rooms. Each room had a bed with two mattresses, a quilt, and clean blankets. I put my things in one of the rooms on the lower floor, then went to the souk to buy an earthenware pot and two dishes, which I used to cook for myself. The priest would come by to see me after sunset, then go up to his room, which was directly over mine. Sometimes I'd chat with him upstairs for a while before going down to my own room.

On the first night, I awoke at midnight to the sounds of pacing overhead. These sounds filled me with fright the first night and the second, but on the third I got out of bed and went upstairs to see where the sound was coming from. Peering through the cracks in the door to the priest's room, I saw him kneeling on the floor. He had a crucifix in his hand, which he thumped against his chest as he prayed. Then he'd lean forward and put his head against the floor. After witnessing this scene, I was able to go back down to my bed and sleep without fear.

"Father, don't you ever sleep?" I asked the priest on the fourth day. "What are you doing up there anyway?"

11.48

He let out a mournful sigh.

"My son, as I look around at all the Muslims of this city, whose souls are damned, I feel sorry for them," he said. "Satan has led them astray from the path to the Kingdom of Heaven, so I pray to Our Lord Jesus Christ to enlighten the mind of the Grand Muslim himself, the Ottoman king. Perhaps the flock will follow him. As it stands, they have no shepherd besides the Devil himself."

"Pray with me," the priest continued, turning to me. "Perhaps God will accept your prayer."

"But that doesn't make sense," I replied, flabbergasted. "Who would believe such a thing could happen?"

"What is impossible for man is possible for God," he replied.

Amazed by the fervor of this priest, I went back down to my room, leaving him to pray and beseech God all night long.

Now, this priest taught me how to make a certain type of eye-drop medicine suitable for every type of eye-related ailment and pain.

11.49

"Don't be afraid to use it for any sort of eye pain," he said as he made it in front of me. "This medicine will put bread on the table for the rest of your life."

He also taught me other useful things related to bodily health. In those days, I wasn't aware of the importance of learning new things. I was a vagabond, under the sway of youthful and foolish passions.

I used to spend my time going out and touring the city of Istanbul, admiring its buildings and souks and avenues. It so happened that Sultan Aḥmad had, at that time, ordered the construction of five large imperial ships, each with four holds and seventy or eighty cannons. I heard that the ships had been completed and that the king had ordered them to be placed in the water on the next Thursday.

11.50

This was to be a grand spectacle! I joined a group of Aleppans who planned to rent a dinghy and go watch.

11.51 When the day came, all of Istanbul went down to the sea. The harbor was crammed so full of boats you could practically walk across them. I'd heard that there were twelve thousand boats in Istanbul harbor that paid taxes to the state, which didn't include the boats of the officials, each of whom had two or three vessels for personal travel and recreation.

They lowered the first ship into the water, and a great din rose from the crowd. All were shouting, "Allah! Allah!" as they slaughtered animals as ritual offerings. The other ships followed one at a time, as the king himself looked on, along with his ministers and all the grandees of the state. What a marvelous day it was! This was what I saw when those ships were launched in Istanbul. It's one thing to hear about it, but quite something else to witness such a rare event.

11.52 A few days later, eight royal galleons sent by the sultan of France arrived in Istanbul. One by one, they entered the harbor, and as they passed before the king's palace—which is positioned toward the left side of the harbor when you're entering it from the sea—the galleons fired their cannons in salute. The smallest ship had seventy cannons and more than seven hundred soldiers on board, not including the sailors. After the first ship fired its cannons, the second one entered the harbor and fired its cannons from both sides, followed by the third, which did the same.

The neighborhoods on the outskirts of Istanbul trembled at these sounds, and the people thought the Franks had captured the city. Many people fled into the wilderness. The smoke hanging over the harbor was so thick you could scarcely see the person standing next to you—or hear them, for that matter.

11.53 The minister then sent one of his chief officers to the French admiral with a request that they cease firing their cannons, because His Majesty had developed a headache. So the remaining galleons entered the harbor without firing their cannons, anchoring in the usual way. The dragomans of the ambassador came down to receive the admiral in most honorable fashion. They then went to see the grand vizier, informing him of the arrival of eight galleons dispatched by His Majesty the king of France, who had sent eighty anchors to His Majesty Sultan Aḥmad, for his new ships, which he hoped the sultan would accept as a gift. Furthermore, the king of France had dismissed his ambassador for not fulfilling his duties appropriately.

The vizier arranged to have the admiral brought to him the following day, and ordered that the French ships be reprovisioned with victuals. He presented the admiral with expensive gifts, showering him with honors on behalf of the king.   11.54

"Is there anything you are in need of that we might provide?" the vizier asked the admiral.

"Perhaps you might inform His Majesty the king that our lands are experiencing a rise in prices because of the shortage of wheat," the admiral said. "We ask that His Majesty the king might issue an edict authorizing us to tour around the Province of the Islands and purchase your crops without encumbrance."

"Request granted," the vizier replied immediately, and sent him on his way.

When the vizier brought the admiral's request to the king, the latter issued an imperial edict in his own hand ordering that the eight galleons be loaded up with good wheat, for which they would not pay a cent. The galleons remained in port for twenty days, until the vizier sent a group of galleys off to the Province of the Islands to gather the requested wheat. In the meantime, two hundred prisoners were given their freedom, which they gained by diving into the sea and climbing aboard the galleons, because, from the moment a prisoner grasped the side of a galleon, he was officially saved, and no one had the authority to take him back once he was safely aboard. They were pardoned as a gesture of goodwill toward the king of France.   11.55

Around that time, one of the princes of the kingdom of Sweden arrived in Istanbul. His intent was to tour the region, and his coterie   11.56

were searching for local guides who spoke Italian and Turkish. One of my friends—the embassy official who'd traveled with me from Marseille—came to see me, proposing to get me a job as a dragoman for the Swedish prince. I agreed to his proposal and gave him my word that I'd travel with him. I'd heard that the prince planned to return to Sweden overland following his tour of the region, so I made up my mind to leave Istanbul with him.

11.57   The very same day, as I was about to go meet the prince, who should pass by but Ḥannā ibn al-Zughbī. When he learned of my impending departure with the prince, he wasn't happy. He began to admonish me and did all he could to prevent me from leaving.

"The caravan is leaving for Aleppo in two days," he said. "I've already rented a mule for you from Aḥmad the Aleppan muleteer, and I gave him a deposit."

11.58   In the end, I succumbed to his protestations and decided against traveling with the prince, giving Ḥannā my word that I would return to Aleppo with him.

"In that case, we must prepare ourselves for the journey," he said. "We'll need to bring along a few things that will serve us well on the road, like an *uqqah* of pepper; a few dirhams' worth of cloves, ginger, and other spices; some pack needles; and some soap. These things will be worth more than money once we leave Istanbul, and the people of the villages will give us whatever we need in exchange for them. This way, we'll save a lot of money."

11.59   What he said made good sense. I took out a gold piece, handed it to him, and told him to buy whatever he deemed necessary, and off he went. In the meantime, I put my affairs in order, and went to say goodbye to the abbot and to my friend the embassy official. Then I waited for Ḥannā to return. He appeared two days later.

"Let's go," he said.

11.60   I departed Istanbul in the middle of June 1710. I grabbed my bags and we went down to the harbor together, where he'd rented a dinghy to take us to Üsküdar. An old man, the master calenderer, was waiting there with their baggage. I loaded my bags into the dinghy and we crossed over to the harbor of Üsküdar, where we unloaded, and then went to the caravansary and rented a room. We waited there for the muleteer and the caravan.

The concubines of the pasha of Afyonkarahisar then arrived at the caravansary, along with our muleteer and various others. We asked our man why he was late. 11.61

"I was forced by the pasha's men to let them load up my beasts, whether I liked it or not," he explained. "We had no choice—the other muleteers and I—but to drop our other loads and carry the pasha's goods. I did manage to set aside three mounts for you by pretending that I only had seven, but I must travel to Afyonkarahisar with the pasha. If you're willing to come with me, you're welcome to. Otherwise, you should feel free to find another muleteer."

At this news, we became despondent and didn't know what to do. We made the rounds of the other muleteers, looking for someone else to hire, to no avail. So we were resigned to traveling with our original muleteer to Afyonkarahisar. 11.62

We spent the day there. The following day, the pasha arrived in Üsküdar and the concubines immediately loaded up and set off, with us close behind. When we arrived at a gulf of water blocking our path,[175] we crossed it in a dinghy together with our beasts, then pressed on with the concubines until we arrived at Gavur Köy.

The convoy halted in a desolate spot, a mile from the village. Meanwhile, my companions and I made camp just below the village, in a field as lovely as a garden, with trees and a freshwater spring. Shortly after we arrived, our muleteer made his way over from the other spot and told us to make camp with the rest of the convoy. 11.63

"The people of this village are a pack of thieves," he said. "They'll rob you in the night."

I didn't want to budge, and neither did my companions. 11.64

"We don't have anything," we said. "What are they going to take from us?"

The muleteer wasn't able to change our minds, so we spent the night in that spot, and he sent his brother to sleep in our camp with us. He told his brother that when it came time for the convoy to leave, he'd shout out to him to have us load up and set off as well. Meanwhile, we tied our bags to our bodies, in fear that the village people might indeed come for us in the night, and then went to sleep.

In the middle of the night, the convoy loaded up and the muleteer called out to his brother to have us load up as well. The brother responded, but he did so while half asleep, and he then turned over and went back to sleep! Meanwhile, the rest of us slept on, oblivious to what was happening. An hour later, the young man woke up and listened for the sounds of the convoy, but he didn't hear any bells. That was when he knew it had left, and he began to shout and curse us.

"We're going to get robbed!" he yelled. "They're going to take our things, and our animals too!"

11.65   We scrambled to our feet, loaded our bags on our mounts, and galloped away, soon arriving at the spot where the convoy had been camped. There wasn't a soul to be seen, only the remains of a campfire. And two roads.

"Which road should we take?" we asked the young man.

He didn't know. We stood there, confused and afraid. What if the villagers came after us while we were so vulnerable and robbed us? Suddenly, I was struck by divine inspiration. My horse had frequently traveled this road, and surely knew which way to go!

11.66   I got off the horse and loosened its halter. It walked forward toward the upper road, and we followed behind, each mounting his horse and galloping on. We soon arrived at a peak. A deep valley stretched out ahead of us, and the jingling of bells could be heard far below. It dawned on us that we'd taken the wrong road, and our spirits sank. As we turned around and prepared to return the way we'd come, the young muleteer shouted out to his brother. He lay down and pressed his ear to the ground, hoping to hear a response.

"Didn't we tell you that we should have taken the upper road?" is what he heard them saying, so we felt profoundly relieved. It was they who had chosen the wrong road, not us!

We waited for the convoy to arrive at our spot, and then we all 11.67 followed the correct road until morning came. Two hours later, the pasha caught up with us and passed by, and we followed behind him. It rained heavily that day, and our bags were soaked in the downpour, which lasted until the evening, leaving us in a sorry, sodden state. The pasha, faced with the incessant rain, decided to veer off into a village just off the road. He and his coterie rode into the village, kicking the people out of their houses and settling in.

Meanwhile, the troops set up camp outside, pitching their tents and huddling beneath them, while we were left standing in the center of the village, the rain pouring down on us. When we begged the peasants to give us a place to stay, even a lowly stable, to protect us from the torrent, they swore to us that their own women and children had already taken refuge there among the livestock. What were we to do?

We stood there, trying to think of a solution to our troubles, and 11.68 Almighty God provided one. A handsome young man suddenly appeared before us, and asked my companions who I was. He'd noticed that I was dressed differently, like a Frank in fact. My hair tumbled loosely from my head, and I wore a calpac made of marten fur.

"Tell him I'm doctor," I said to them.

At this news, the young man implored my companions to let me go with him to visit an invalid he had at home.

"If you shelter us at your house tonight, I'll come see your 11.69 invalid," I replied to him, speaking in Turkish.

"It would be a blessing to have you," the young man replied, "but I fear that one of the pasha's men might discover where I live. Then my wife and I will be forced to leave the house so they might commandeer it. Why don't you follow me at a distance?"

I agreed to his plan, and the young man set off. We followed him through the thickets behind the village until we came to a cave. The young man disappeared inside. We approached the mouth of the cave and found him waiting for us. Then we descended together into the cave and came to a door, which he rapped upon with a particular knock. It swung open, revealing three young men inside.

11.70 My companions and I were suddenly seized by the panicked thought that we'd fallen into a den of thieves! As we stood there dumbstruck and fretting helplessly over this prospect, the young men came out and took hold of our horses, brought them inside, and invited us in as well. We went in: The cave had rugs on the ground and a stove in the center. When they handed our bags to us, the men discovered that they were all wet, so they fired up the stove to dry our clothes as the young man who'd led us to his home welcomed us warmly.

11.71 Night had fallen in the meantime, and we rested a little as our clothes dried. Then the young man ordered the others standing before us to bring in some dinner. One of them went to set the table, place some bread upon it, and lay cloth napkins across our laps. He brought in a jug full of water and an earthenware cup for us to drink from as we sat there, stunned at this wondrous turn of events. It was nothing less than the work of God Almighty, who had sent us this young man to give us shelter and treat us so generously!

Dinner was served. A large platter of rice with lamb appeared, followed by a second platter of stewed vegetables and a plate of chicken cooked in the *kazan kebabı* style. It was a sumptuous meal indeed, and we dug in together with the young man.

11.72 After dinner, they brought a basin and a pitcher for us to wash our hands, followed by a large pot of coffee. We all had a round of delicious coffee, followed by a second, then filled our pipes and sat back to chat with the young man for a while.

"Where's that sick person you mentioned?" I asked. "It's time I had a look at him, now that you've treated us so generously."

"Please finish your pipe," the young man said. "I'll trouble you to come see him when you're done."

We finished smoking, and the young man rose to his feet and invited me to follow him inside. We walked down a corridor and arrived at the door of the women's quarters. He knocked and told them to make themselves scarce, as we were coming in.

The door opened onto a splendid interior courtyard. He led me 11.73 to a luxuriously furnished room, where an old man lay upon a bed. It was the young man's father, the village elder. I sat at his side and felt his pulse. He panted weakly, unable to catch his breath. It turned out that he was suffering from an excess of humors trapped in the stomach.

"Don't worry, you're not in danger," I said, consoling the old man. "You've got some humors acting up inside, but I'll take care of them early tomorrow morning, and that'll give you some relief. You'll be out of your bed soon enough, just you wait."

I turned to his son and instructed him to have two chickens boiled overnight to make a purgative that would be ready by dawn.

"No salt," I specified, and I told him to wake me up early so that I could administer the purgative myself. Then I said good night, and returned to my companions.

Now, I happened to have some special tablets with me, which my 11.74 master had acquired for his travels. He used to administer them to people, and I'd witnessed their effects. They were quite unlike other purgatives, as they were composed specifically to address the four bodily humors—namely, black bile, phlegm, yellow bile, and blood. Within two hours after swallowing a tablet, a person would be cleansed of the humors that had accumulated inside him. Relieved of his ailment, he'd return to work as usual, feeling as though he'd never taken a purgative! I experienced this firsthand, and also witnessed its effects in others, and I had ten or twelve of these tablets left over. My master had given them to me to put aside for safekeeping, then forgotten about them.

After leaving the sick man, I opened up my traveling sack and 11.75 took out one of the tablets. I ground it up and put it in a paper envelope, ready for the next day. Then I went to sleep along with my companions. Early the next morning, the young man came to wake me, and I got up hurriedly, taking the envelope with the purgative in it. We went to see the sick man, who was asleep. I asked for a cup of chicken broth, stirred the purgative into it, and handed it to the old man, telling him to drink it to the very last drop.

He swallowed the broth. A quarter of an hour later, he suddenly became very agitated and grew so dizzy that he seemed about to faint. I ordered that he be given a bowl of broth.

11.76 A moment after drinking the broth, he demanded a basin and began to vomit, filling half of it with yellow bile, phlegm, and other odious fluids. When he finished vomiting, I ordered them to give him another bowl of broth to drink, and once he'd consumed it, he asked to be taken outside. Upon his return, I gave him another bowl of broth, and we alternated in this way—with him vomiting his guts out and me giving him broth to drink—until his insides had been purged of all those foul fluids and humors. Two hours later, he sat back, relaxed, and asked for his pipe.

11.77 I asked them to add a little bit of rice to the broth and to boil some soup to feed the old man, along with a little bit of chicken. In that way, he would regain enough strength to get out of bed and go where he pleased. I said goodbye to the old man and began to head back to see my companions.

"Wait a moment, doctor," the sick man said, pulling a pouch from beneath his pillow and extracting some coins to give me.

"God forbid I accept any payment from you, as it was you who did a great favor for us," I protested. "You accepted us into your home and fed us at your table, and your son treated us most honorably. I have no way to repay you for such kindness!"

11.78 The old man gave the coins to his son to pay me, but I refused and went back to find my companions, only to discover that our hosts were serving us breakfast and coffee! Then they brought out four boiled chickens, forty boiled eggs, some cheese, and bread, laying them out on the camp table we had with us. Suddenly, we heard the first bugle call of the pasha's convoy. They brought our horses out of the stable, having provided each with a bag of boiled barley, and loaded them up with our bags as we pulled on our shoes and prepared to leave.

The second bugle sounded. We mounted our horses and bid farewell to the young man, thanking him profusely for his generosity. Finally, the third bugle sounded as the pasha climbed onto his mount and set off, with us following behind. As we left the village, we spotted our muleteer, who was searching frantically for us like a madman. He was dumbstruck when he saw us.

"Where have you been? Where did you pass the night? I've spent all night looking for you!" 11.79

We told him the whole story, and reassured him that his mounts had been properly cared for and given their fodder in the morning.

"If only you'd taken me with you!" he said cheerfully. "Then I wouldn't have had to suffer all night in the rain!"

I told my companions that, from that moment on, they were to inform anyone who asked about me that I was a doctor. In that way, the rest of our journey would pass most gloriously! And sure enough, the news began to spread after that day, and many of the pasha's men started calling upon me to treat them. I'd prescribe remedies and sometimes give them some of my purgative tablets. Soon enough, we were traveling with the pasha's entourage, basking in the glow of their esteem. They sought out my company and treated me very generously, and invited me to stay in their tents.

The convoy arrived in Eskişehir, a small yet prosperous city. It contained a *qablūjah*, one of those springs that spouted intensely hot sulfurous water. A sort of bathhouse was built around it, where the city's inhabitants would bathe. The pasha pitched his tents about three miles outside the city, and word spread that he would remain encamped there three days. We were forced to wait in town until the pasha's convoy set off again, so we rented a room in a caravansary and spent the night there. 11.80

Staying in the same caravansary was a Christian man from Afyonkarahisar, who came by to visit us. When he asked my companions about me and they told him that I was a doctor, he came over to 11.81

show me one of his eyes. It was festering and covered with a white film, and he begged me to treat it with collyrium. My heart went out to the man, and I took out the little pot of ointment I mentioned earlier. I put a few drops in his eye and told him to come back in the morning so I could give him another dose.

On the third day, we left the city and went out to the camp, arriving in the afternoon. My companions and I knew that the pasha was to travel the next day, so we sat near the camp, chatting and passing the time. Suddenly, something occurred to me.

11.82 "The pasha's men all think I'm a doctor," I said to my Aleppan friend, Ḥannā ibn al-Zughbī. "What do I do if the pasha gets ill? I know only a little about medicine!"

"Don't worry," he said. "God will guide you when the time comes."

While we were in the midst of this conversation, two of the pasha's attendants suddenly appeared, asking for the doctor. Someone pointed in our direction. They strode over to us.

"Which of you is the doctor?" they asked.

"I am," I said.

"The steward of the pasha's harem would like to speak with you," one replied. "Come with us."

11.83 Heart pounding, I stood up and went with the two men. It seemed that when the pasha had become feverish, he'd left his camp and moved, along with his harem, into the house of the village chief. He had ordered the two men to go into the city and find a surgeon to bleed him.

"But sire, we have a very skilled Frankish doctor with us in the convoy," they replied.

"Bring him to me!" he said.

And that was how I ended up standing before the house where the pasha was staying. There was an old man at the door. It was the steward of the pasha's harem.

"Greetings," he said when I presented myself to him. "Please come in, and have a look at His Excellency the effendi, who is ill and feeling indisposed."

I told the steward I was sorry, but I didn't have my doctor's kit   11.84
as I had sent it ahead to Aleppo by ship while I traveled by land to
see the sights.

"Our pasha isn't really ill; he's just under the weather," the steward explained. "Yesterday evening, he went to take a bath at the hot
springs. When he came outside, covered in sweat, he caught a draft.
As a result, his face became swollen and he developed a fever."

The steward ushered me inside. I found the pasha in a room,
asleep in bed. I crouched down beside him and felt his wrist. He
was very hot, apparently in the throes of a high fever. He looked terrible: His face was swollen and he was snorting like a bull.

"I need a little rose oil," I said to the harem steward.   11.85

"I'll send someone to the city to bring some right away," he
replied.

When the pasha heard my request for rose oil, he ordered the
harem steward to go find the quartermaster and ask him for a vial
of Frankish rose oil, which the pasha had received from a Frankish
doctor.

"There are two vials in all," the pasha said. "Bring one."

Soon enough, the steward returned with the vial of oil, and I had   11.86
the idea of adding some other ingredients, just to make it seem like
I'd done something to the oil. I went to find my companions and
consulted with Ḥannā.

"The best thing for treating swelling is *jādhbūn* ointment," he
assured me.[176]

I happened to have some, so I broke off a little piece and returned
to the pasha. I ordered the harem steward to bring me a copper
plate, emptied part of the vial of rose oil into it, and placed it over
a flame. I dropped the piece of ointment in and let it melt entirely.
Then, resting the pasha's head on my knee, I began to spread the
salve all over his cheeks, chin, and neck.

"Warm up two muslin cloths for me," I ordered the old man,   11.87
and after I finished anointing the pasha with the oil, I wrapped one
around his head like a scarf and tied the other around his forehead.

Then I propped his head up on a pillow. The pasha turned to me and complained that he had a terrible headache.

"Let me bring you something to relieve it," I said.

I happened to have in my possession a certain herb from Egypt, similar to anise, which was a tried and true remedy against headaches. I dashed off to get it, put it in the pasha's palm, and urged him to swallow it. Then I asked the old man to bring His Excellency the pasha a cup of coffee. He drank it down, and they brought him his pipe, which he smoked until his headache dissipated and he sat back, relaxed and happy. I kissed the skirt of the pasha's robe and instructed the harem steward not to feed him a single morsel until I came back to check on him. Then I went to find my companions. Barely an hour had passed when someone came to fetch me again. The harem steward was waiting for me when I arrived.

11.88   "The pasha wants to eat!" he said. "But you told me not to feed him anything. What am I supposed to do?"

"Prepare some soup for him, with a lemon on the side," I instructed. "I'll go check on him now, and come back and tell you if you can feed him or not."

I went in to see the pasha and took his pulse. He still had a fever, but it had subsided somewhat.

"Sire, I can't permit you to eat anything as long as you still have a fever," I explained. "Wait a little longer, if you will, until it subsides completely. Then you may have some soup, but nothing else."

The pasha accepted my recommendation to refrain from eating, and I rejoined my companions. In the meantime, they had prepared dinner, so we dined together and drank some coffee. The sun had set by then, and the pasha was hungry and demanded some food. The old man summoned me again and told me that the pasha couldn't wait any longer, and felt he had to eat. I went in to see him, and found him irritated about the delay in bringing him some food. I knelt down before him and felt his pulse again. The fever was gone.

11.89   "Bring the soup and lemon," I said to the old man.

Immediately, a large porcelain bowl of chicken soup appeared, along with a porcelain platter with a chicken. I squeezed a few drops of lemon into the soup and invited the pasha to eat. He finished the entire bowl, then asked for the chicken to be sliced so he could eat it.

"Easy there, my lord," I said. "We don't want the fever to return, now do we?"

The pasha consented, but I could see that he was still ravenous. So I cut off a wing from the chicken and presented it to him as a lone concession. He turned to his harem steward.

"See how these Frankish doctors take care of the sick?" he remarked.   11.90

After he finished eating the wing, they washed his hands and brought him a cup of coffee and his pipe. He declared that he was feeling better and that his fever had broken. This was all thanks to Divine Providence—may God be praised! It had nothing to do with my own knowledge but rather with the inspiration I received from God, who in His goodness guided me through this crisis.

I untied the muslin cloths enveloping the pasha's face and saw that the swelling had subsided, with only a little remaining. So I warmed up the ointments again and applied them to his cheeks and throat, and tied on the cloths as before. Then I kissed the skirt of his robe and asked his permission to take my leave.

"What do you say? Am I able to travel tomorrow?" the pasha asked.

"I'll come check on you early tomorrow morning, my lord, and will give you an answer then," I said, then left him and returned to my companions.

The next morning at dawn, I was summoned to the pasha. I went   11.91 to see the harem steward and asked him how the pasha was feeling.

"He's doing fine, and he slept well during the night," the steward replied, ushering me in to see the pasha, who was sitting up, smoking a pipe, and looking right as rain.

"Well, what do you think? Am I cleared to travel?" he asked.

"The choice is yours, my lord," I said. "However, if you do decide to travel today, let this leg be a short one. I wouldn't want the sun to dissolve your humors."

"Good idea," he replied, and ordered the harem steward to send word to the chief baggage officer to set up the next camp a two-hour journey from where we were. He also gave the order to sound the first bugle call, which was the signal for departure.

11.92 I stepped forward, kissed the skirt of the pasha's robe, and set off to see my companions, to whom I excitedly brought the news that His Excellency had made a full recovery. We all thanked God, loaded our baggage on our horses, and prepared to travel as soon as the third bugle sounded. The pasha set off, accompanied by the sounds of a marching band. We traveled for two hours, and arrived at the next encampment. The pasha went into his large, sumptuous tent, and the soldiers entered theirs. My companions and I were given a tent near the quartermaster's, as we were now recognized as part of His Excellency's coterie.

11.93 No sooner had I dismounted from my horse than the pasha's chief valet approached.

"His Excellency the pasha summons you."

I followed the valet to the pasha's tent, where I found the harem steward waiting for me and we entered. The pasha was reclining against a couple of cushions. I came forward and kissed the skirt of his robe, then stood at attention. He invited me to sit beside him and held out his hand. I took his pulse and congratulated him on his recovery.

"I'd like you to give me a little of whatever you put in that rose oil," he said. "The salves you made me were very helpful; they eased the swelling right away."

"It would be my pleasure," I replied, and went to get what he'd requested, bringing back a large piece nestled within a clean piece of paper. Then I kissed his robe once again and presented it to him, to his delight. I asked his permission to leave, and left the tent. But before I'd taken a couple of steps, one of the other valets called me back in to see the harem steward.

"His Excellency, our effendi, has ordered that you be provided with proper lodgings," he said, and summoned the convoy captain.

"See to it that the pasha's chief physician is afforded lodgings and fodder for his horses," he told him.

The convoy captain asked me how many people were traveling in my party. I told him there were three of us. From that moment on, whenever we arrived in a village, the convoy captain would hand me a document affixed with an official seal to give the local shaykh. The shaykh would then arrange for us to be lodged in a house whose owners would wait on us, prepare our dinner, and provide fodder for our horses.

A few days later, we arrived in the vicinity of Afyonkarahisar, which fell under the pasha's jurisdiction. The pasha set up camp in a spot that was a day's journey from the city, and we learned that he intended to remain there five or six days to collect money from the peasants and the landowners subject to his authority. The pasha paid the muleteers who had traveled with him from Üsküdar, and discharged them.

Our own muleteer then appeared, giving us notice that we would be leaving for Afyonkarahisar that very night. Upon receiving this news, I decided to ask the pasha's permission to depart. But my companion, Ḥannā, dissuaded me.

"What if the pasha doesn't want you to go?" he said. "You're under his authority now, so if he tells you to stay here, what are you supposed to say? Let's just leave now, before we get stuck here."

I saw the wisdom of his words and decided not to go to the pasha, fearing that he might prevent me from traveling. We waited until midnight and set off, traveling until we arrived in Afyonkarahisar at noon the next day. As we entered the city, I happened to bump into the fellow whom I'd treated for eye pain in Eskişehir. When he saw me, he showered me with embraces and kisses, welcoming me with great affection, and invited me to stay at his house!

"I'm sorry, I can't, as there are three of us," I said. "Instead, could you perhaps recommend a good place for us to stay, and we'll invite you over?"

11.97 The man took us to a caravansary, and told its proprietor to give us a good room. We went upstairs with him, where he opened a room for us, and the man who'd taken us to the caravansary had some furnishings brought over from his own house: a straw mat, a carpet, and a mattress. Making us promise not to prepare any dinner, he went on his way. When evening came, our dinner was delivered to us on a platter, and was followed by the man himself, who strode in with jug of arak and a jug of wine too. He sat down and we dined together as night fell.

"I'll never be able to repay the great favor you did me," he said. "You cured my eye of that squint, when I couldn't see anything out of it!"

"Don't thank me, brother, thank God—curing your eye was His work," I said. "In fact, I didn't think the medicine would work."

11.98 The man returned home after thanking me profusely, and we spent a most comfortable night at the caravansary, not waking up until the sun rose the next morning. After breakfast and coffee, we were sitting and chatting when a young man appeared. He was a Christian lad, a tall, strapping fellow. He asked me to visit his house to examine someone's eyes.

"Sorry, brother, I'm not going to anyone's house," I said. "Bring this person to me, and I'll examine his eye here."

The young man had, it seemed, heard about me from the squint-eyed fellow I'd cured, who'd sent him my way. Even after he begged me, I continued to refuse to go with him. The man became despondent, and took me aside.

"The person I told you about is my wife!" he confided. "She's a young bride—we've only been married for a year, and she can't very well enter a caravansary."

The young man pressed his face to my hands.

"For the love of God, please come with me! What are you afraid of? We're Christians!"

11.99 At this, I felt compelled to go with him, though my friend Ḥannā didn't like it one bit. What if the news got out that there was a doctor in town? If that happened, I'd never escape, especially if the authorities found out. There were no doctors in these parts, Ḥannā reminded me, which was why he didn't want me to go with the young man.

In the end, though, I took my little flask of ointment and went to the man's house. As soon as we arrived, he led me to the dining table and invited me to have lunch with him. After we ate and had our coffee, they brought the young woman before me. She was a beauty. I peered into her eyes, and they seemed to be perfectly fine, with no indication otherwise.

"What's the problem exactly?" I asked the young man. "As far as   11.100
I can tell, her vision is fine."

"She can't see anything," he replied.

I turned to the young woman and asked her what she was able to make out of the world around her.

"I see blackness," she replied. "I can't tell the difference between black and white, or a man and a woman."

That was when I realized she had cataracts, a condition that was untreatable according to just about every doctor. I felt sorry for her, and even though I knew it would do no good, I put some drops in her eye, as a way of comforting her husband, and gave him some of the medicine to administer later. I bid them farewell, feeling terrible for the young woman, and returned to my companions.

When I arrived, a group of people was waiting for me. There were   11.101
sick people, some experiencing eye pain themselves, and others who wanted to take me home to examine their invalids. What was I supposed to do? I had no idea! I began going around, putting drops in some people's eyes and prescribing remedies to others, before sending them away. Soon, word got around town that there was a very skilled Frankish doctor staying at a certain caravansary. People came in droves, flowing in and out of the place as I struggled to stave them off as best I could.

Three days after our arrival, the proprietor of the caravansary   11.102
suddenly appeared in the company of two officials who served the

local governor. They invited me to come with them to see the governor, for the following reason: It seemed that an imperial chamberlain was passing through town, at the head of a company of forty cavalrymen. He'd been sent by the grand vizier to deliver a certain young man to his maternal uncle, Nāṣīf Pasha, the pasha of the hajj pilgrimage. Nāṣīf Pasha was a famous and powerful man in the empire at that time. For years, he'd led the pilgrimage to Mecca and brought it back safely to Damascus. He'd brought the Bedouins to heel and kept the roads open. On account of this achievement, he'd acquired a great deal of power and fame.

11.103   Now, Nāṣīf Pasha had become enraged with his nephew—his sister's son—and vowed to kill him. It seemed that the nephew had embezzled some funds that he was responsible for collecting from the territories under his uncle's jurisdiction. When he learned that his uncle wanted him dead, the nephew fled in the middle of the night and vanished. He traveled in secret all the way to Istanbul and sought the protection of the vizier, to whom he explained his predicament. The vizier felt sorry for him and took him in, but Nāṣīf Pasha soon learned that his nephew had found refuge at the palace, and was furious that he'd managed to escape.

11.104   Out of revenge for this injustice, the pasha seized the treasury of Egypt for two years. He sent word to the vizier that no monies would flow to Istanbul until the nephew was released to him, as he had a score to settle. The vizier was compelled to send the nephew in the company of a chief chamberlain, who was given instructions to let the young man meet with his uncle and then to bring him back safe and sound to Istanbul. He was also told to complete the journey without delay, spending no more than a specific number of days, on the authority of an edict signed by the king himself.

The young man was terrified that he'd be put to death as soon as he arrived. He knew his uncle wouldn't be intimidated by the vizier, or even the sultanate itself. As they traveled, his anxieties grew so severe that he became sick with fright and could no longer ride. Faced with this predicament, the chamberlain was uncertain what to do. He dispatched one of his men to visit the governor of Afyon-karahisar, asking him to send a surgeon to bleed the invalid.

The imperial guard arrived and explained the situation to the governor, who immediately called for a skilled surgeon to be dispatched to treat the young man. Now, by sheer coincidence, the imam of the pasha with whom we'd traveled to Afyonkarahisar happened to have come to town and was staying in his quarters in the pasha's palace. When this fellow heard about the governor's order, he weighed in. 11.105

"There was a Frankish doctor who traveled with us from Istanbul," he said. "He was the one who treated the pasha when he fell ill en route, and brought him back to health."

"I'll ask His Excellency the pasha if we might make use of him," the imperial guard replied.

At that moment, some people in the governor's coterie who were present informed the governor that the Frankish doctor who accompanied the pasha happened to be staying at a certain caravansary. Upon learning this, the governor ordered them to bring him in.

This, then, was the reason for the appearance of those two individuals, who ordered me to come with them to see His Excellency the governor. I was stricken with terror upon hearing these words, for I assumed that the pasha must have ordered the governor to arrest me when he found that I'd taken off without his permission. I got up from my seat and went with the two men, overcome with terror and fright. My thoughts turned darkly morose and my fear mounted as I imagined being flogged with a cane or shackled in irons. 11.106

By the time we arrived at the palace, I was scared out of my wits. I presented myself before the governor and noticed that the pasha's imam was standing beside him, just as I feared. On the other side of the governor sat an imperial guard. 11.107

"Is this the doctor?" the governor asked the imam.

"Yes."

"The chief chamberlain is going to be passing close to town," the governor said as he turned to address me. "There's someone important traveling with him, and he's ill. They've sent this imperial guard to us to ask for a doctor. Since you're here anyway, would you be so kind as to go examine the sick man?"

11.108   At these words, I felt my spirit and senses come back to life, and I quickly apologized to His Excellency the governor, explaining that I didn't have my doctor's kit with me.

"What good would it do for me to go out and see him in the middle of nowhere, a place without any of the things I'd need to treat him?"

"Go as a matter of respect for the chamberlain," the governor urged me. "Do whatever you can, under the circumstances, and there will be something in it for you."

The imperial guard also tried to talk me into it, promising I'd make a pretty penny, but I dug in my heels. That was when the pasha's imam turned to the governor and told him not to force me, since I was under the protection of the pasha.

11.109   So the governor had a surgeon summoned to be dispatched with the imperial guard, and allowed me to depart. I returned to my companions, feeling overjoyed that I'd somehow managed to get out of that jam, and told them the whole story. My friend Ḥannā went to tell our muleteer that if he wasn't planning to travel soon, we'd be finding someone else to take us.

"There's a caravan ready to depart for Konya, and every one of my beasts has a rider, so we can go," the muleteer replied. "We'll be setting off the day after tomorrow, without fail. Get your affairs in order."

We bided our time anxiously over the next two days, fearing that the pasha would summon me. But they passed without incident, and we left with the caravan as planned, arriving in due course near the city of Konya.

11.110   While we were on the road, we happened to see the chamberlain pass by us with his forty cavalrymen. One of their company peeled off and galloped over to our caravan.

"Who's the caravan chief here?" he asked when he rode up, and was directed to our muleteer.

"The chamberlain asks that once you arrive in Konya you send him the Frankish doctor who is traveling with you," he said. "Don't let him out of your sight, no matter what! If he disappears, you'll have to answer to His Excellency."

"It's as good as done, sire," the muleteer replied.

The guard then set off to see his master. They entered the city before us, as they were riding postal horses. The reason for all of this was that the guard who had gone to the governor to request a surgeon had seen me at the palace, and had in fact spoken to me there. When the chamberlain's party passed us, the guard recognized me and told the chamberlain I was the one who had refused to return with him. That was when the chamberlain ordered him to warn the caravan chief to keep his eye on me and prevent me from disappearing till they summoned me. When our muleteer told me all this, I was seized with fright again. It seemed I'd fallen out of the frying pan and into the fire! All I could do was put my trust in God and my fate in His hands.
11.111

We arrived in Konya, and the muleteer demanded that I accompany him to the place where he would be staying.
11.112

"That's how it has to be," he said. "I'm under strict orders from His Excellency the chamberlain."

We went into a stable with him, where he tied up his beasts. No sooner had we arrived than a constable appeared, representing the city's governor. One of the chamberlain's imperial guards was with him, and they ordered me to come with them to see His Excellency the chamberlain. We went to the chamberlain's lodgings, and I was escorted up some stairs and brought before the man himself.

"Why didn't you want to come with my attendant when you were in Afyonkarahisar?" he asked, regarding me with a baleful eye.
11.113

"Please forgive me, my lord!" I cried, throwing myself before the chamberlain and kissing the skirt of his robes. "It would surely have been a great honor to oblige Your Excellency's wishes, but I was unable to do so for lack of a doctor's kit! Without it, I'm unable to treat anyone. This was the reason for my response, I swear it!"

Hearing this, the chamberlain's temper eased, and he invited me to sit down. After I was served some coffee, he told me the tale of the sick young man who was with him, as recounted earlier. He said a few things to butter me up then urged me to examine the patient and treat him, and do all I could to help him recover swiftly.

"I've been granted only so many days by the sultanate to deliver him," he explained.

"I'll go if you insist, God help me!" I replied, consenting to his request.

11.114 The chamberlain ordered one of his servants to take me to the sick young man, whom I found lying on a mattress, huffing and puffing like a dragon. When I examined him, I found he had a burning fever, as hot to the touch as though he'd been thrown into a furnace. I was at a loss. How was I supposed to treat a man in his condition? Then, quite out of the blue, Almighty God—His name be praised!—inspired me with an idea I wouldn't otherwise have had. I turned to the servant assigned to attend the young man and asked him to bring me a bezoar stone and some rosewater.[177]

"I don't have any," he replied, taking out a pouch full of coins. "Go into town and buy whatever you need."

11.115 I wouldn't accept the pouch and told him instead to give it to one of his men, who should then accompany me to the souk to buy what we needed. He chose two footmen to accompany me, and we went to the souk. I asked the shopkeepers for bezoar stones, but nobody had any. What could I give the young man to drink instead of bezoar stones? I bought a bunch of seeds, tamarind, pears, and rosewater, then headed back to the chamberlain's lodgings. As I was leaving the souk, a local man approached me.

"Are you looking for bezoar stones?"

"Yes."

"I know someone who's got them," he said. "But he won't put them out for sale because he's afraid that the people you're with won't pay a fair price."

When I heard this, I handed the seeds to one of the footmen and ordered him to return to the chamberlain's lodgings and have the seeds pounded, while the tamarind and pears were to be macerated to soften them. Meanwhile, I told the footman who was carrying the pouch of money to stand at a distance and wait for me. The two did as I asked, and I turned to the man from the souk, asking him to lead me to the bezoar stones. 11.116

"Come with me," he said.

He took me to see an old man sitting in a shop. 11.117

"This is the fellow who has what you want," he said, and left.

I approached the old man and asked if he had any bezoar stones.

"I do. Will you pay a fair price?"

"Yes."

He opened a case and took out a box with five stones in it. I selected the finest among them, an olive-colored one. He demanded fifteen piasters for it, and I managed to bargain him down to twelve. Then I went to find the footman and ordered him to pay the man.

The stone in hand, we headed back to the chamberlain's lodging, where I immediately grated it into a large cup and gave it to the sick young man to drink. Then I squeezed the juice from the seeds into another large cup and gave him that to drink as well. I mixed some vinegar and rosewater in a vase and told the attendants to daub his extremities with it, while I macerated some more tamarind and Mardin pears. I alternated between giving the young man the juice of those seeds to drink, and the water from the tamarind and bezoar stones, and did not stop until the evening. Finally, the fever broke and the young man recovered. He opened his eyes and sat up in bed. He requested his pipe and a cup of coffee, and I asked him how he was feeling. 11.118

"I'm feeling better, thank goodness," he replied, and I bid him farewell and instructed his attendants not to let him consume 11.119

anything besides the fluids I'd prepared. As I headed out to rejoin my companions, one of the chamberlain's men met me at the door and ordered me to come and see his master. I accompanied him to the chamberlain's residence, and went upstairs to find him waiting for news of the invalid.

"He has recovered, thank goodness," I informed the chamberlain, to his great pleasure.

"Can we travel tomorrow?"

"I'll let you know tomorrow morning," I said. "If he remains in the condition he's in now, then you can travel."

I then asked permission to return to my house, but he refused, invited me to sit down, and ordered his servants to bring me some coffee and a pipe of tobacco.

11.120 "Where are you from?" he asked, after I'd had some coffee.

"I'm from Aleppo," I said. "My father was a doctor named Bidaut; he died when I was a young boy. I was sent to the land of the French to stay with my uncle in the city of Marseille. After studying medicine I wanted to return to my homeland, so I boarded a ship to Izmir, and continued on to Istanbul. From there, I decided to travel by land to Aleppo so as to take in the sights, and had my doctor's chest forwarded to Aleppo by sea. I'm on my way back to Aleppo as we speak."

11.121 "I used to be a customs officer in Aleppo!" the chamberlain said. "Many of the French merchants were friends of mine. Let's see, there was *khawājah* Sauron, *khawājah* Bazan, Bonifay, Rousseau, and Simon. My best friend of all was a fellow named *khawājah* Rimbaud, who used to speak Turkish. I used to visit him often, and sample some of his flavored liqueur. As I recall, he had a warehouseman named Anṭūn who'd fetch it for me."

At this, my blood ran cold. For I thought he'd recognized me and seen through my lie, as *khawājah* Rimbaud had been my master and that of my brother Anṭūn. And it was I who used to bring him the aromatic liqueur and put myself at his service! It seemed, however, that he didn't recognize me after all, as I was a twelve-year-old boy at the time. I thanked God that the chamberlain had not recognized me, then asked his permission to let me return to where I was staying.

"Off you go," he said. "But be sure to rise before dawn, and return to check up on your patient. Then we absolutely must be on our way." 11.122

"Yes sir," I said, and went to rejoin my companions. They'd been waiting anxiously for me. I told them the whole story from start to finish and we all thanked God Most High for His loving-kindness, before falling into a restful sleep.

Sometime past midnight, two of the sick man's attendants came to wake me, looking stricken. 11.123

"Hurry! The boy is dying!"

I shot up, tore out of the room, and dashed off with them, frantic with worry. As we made our way back, I peppered them with questions, urging them to explain why the fever had returned. Neither would respond truthfully. Finally, one of them took me aside.

"After you left, the agha ordered some ice to be brought," the attendant confided. "He chewed an *uqqah*'s worth, and put the rest on his chest and stomach."

Now I understood why he'd relapsed, and I had a worthwhile excuse to give the chamberlain to save my own skin!

When we arrived at the residence, I went in to see the patient and found him in a pitiable state. His fever had returned—but now it was twice as severe as before—and he looked ready to succumb at any minute. Feigning shock, I turned to interrogate his servants. 11.124

"What have you given him to eat?" I demanded. "And what did he do? Tell me the truth!"

"We didn't give him anything!" they replied, denying any wrongdoing, so I turned to the servant who was responsible for the young man.

"I'm no prophet, so I don't know if you're telling me the truth," I said. "But if you're lying to me, this man is going to die and you're all going to pay the price."

11.125   At this, the attendant took me aside and quietly explained what happened. The sick young man had begged them not to tell me the truth.

"He chewed some ice and put the rest on his chest, and that's why he got sick again," the attendant said. "But please, for the love of God, don't tell the chamberlain, because he'll take revenge on us! What's done is done."

Then I ordered them to extract some more juice from the seeds, and I gave the young man a large cup of bezoar water to drink. I treated him as I had the previous day, until morning came and the chamberlain received word that the illness had returned. He was furious, and summoned me before him.

"Did you lie to my face yesterday when you said that he had recovered?" he demanded, fixing me with a wrathful eye. "Now I hear that his illness is worse than before! Do you take me for a fool?"

11.126   Finding him so angry, and seeing that he was likely to take his anger out on me, I was forced to tell him what had transpired during the night—how the young man had eaten the ice and put it on his chest, as they'd told me. He erupted again, this time at the boy.

"I'm going to make him travel anyway, and if he dies along the way I'll tie a rope to his feet and let them drag his corpse like a dog," he said. "I won't risk my own neck on account of him!"

I threw myself before him, clutching his hands and begging him to wait another day in the hope that the young man would recover slightly before traveling. I then returned to treat him with the emulsions and other medications until that evening, when he began to recover.

11.127   In the meantime, the chamberlain had ordered that a litter be prepared for the young man to ride in when they set off the next day. He summoned me and asked me to travel with them as far as Damascus, so as to treat the patient along the way.

"My pleasure," I said, and he said, "Go pack so you're ready to leave with us tomorrow morning."

And off I went to tell my companions that I'd be accompanying the chamberlain to Damascus.

My friend Ḥannā wasn't happy about this, and warned me not to go.

"What if something happens to the sick man on the road, and he dies?" Ḥannā said. "His uncle is Nāṣif Pasha. If they say that the doctor caused his death, who's going to save you from Nāṣif Pasha? He'll kill you, without a doubt! And even if the young man arrives safely, aren't you afraid that the doctors over there will put you to the test? You don't know a thing about medicine! What do you suppose will happen to you then? You'll be in an even bigger pickle!"

As Ḥannā continued to caution me against going, my anxiety mounted. What was I to do? I'd given the chamberlain my word that I would go with him. I spent that night in a panic, wondering what I could possibly say to an official who occupied the rank of a vizier.

When morning came, the muleteer we'd hired received word that the chamberlain was about to depart, together with the sick man's litter. My companions decided to join the chamberlain's convoy and break off once we arrived at Antioch, where we'd continue on to Aleppo. They loaded up their horses and gathered their provisions, preparing to leave. Then I was summoned to see the chamberlain, and when I arrived I saw the litter and the horses saddled up, and everyone ready to depart.

"Where's your bag?" he asked. "I had a fast horse saddled up for you. Go get your things, and come back at once! I'm waiting."

I returned to grab my bag and set off with the chamberlain, only to find that the people who were preparing to travel with us had changed their minds about going. I asked what the reason was.

"We'd originally planned to go along with the litter," one of them explained. "But then an old man advised us not to. He said, 'The chamberlain swaps horses every two hours. Wherever they stop, there's a new mount waiting for him, so they travel the distance of two days in a single day. Can your horses keep up with him?' This is why we decided not to go."

CHAPTER ELEVEN | 299

11.131 Hearing this, I changed my mind about leaving with the convoy. I'd been willing to take the risk of leaving the chamberlain once we got to Antioch and vanishing from sight. Then, when I learned I would be the only one traveling with him, I had given up hope. But now I had an excuse that just might satisfy him. I went to his camp. They'd put the sick man in the litter and his attendants were milling about, waiting for me. I went upstairs to see the chamberlain, knelt to kiss the hem of his robes, apologized, and begged his forgiveness. I explained that I didn't have the strength to ride without stopping, swapping horses as we went—I would die on the road. I begged him to release me from my obligation, for I didn't have the ability to make the journey.

11.132 At this, the chamberlain took pity on me, thank goodness.

"You're free to go now," he said, then mounted and rode off. But the sick man and his attendants tried to talk me into going.

"Don't worry, we'll take care of you on the road," they said.

Their master, the sick man, also promised he would give me a horse once they arrived in Damascus and would send me to Jerusalem, all expenses paid, and pay me a hefty fee besides. But I was afraid that Ḥannā's prediction would come true and some mishap would occur on the road, so I declined to join them. The master lost hope of convincing me, but was not at all pleased. As he ordered the litter driver to set off, one of his footmen suggested he give me a tip of some kind. So he reached into his pouch, grabbed some coins, and threw them to the ground in a fit of pique. His attendants picked them up and handed them to me: There were twelve *abū kalb* thirds in all. Then they set off.

11.133 I returned to my companions, and we spent five days in Konya following the chamberlain's departure. Then a caravan set off for Aleppo, which we traveled with until we drew close to Adana. There was a narrow mountain pass, only wide enough to allow one person through at a time.[178] A toll officer sat there, collecting the *isbanj* tax—a piaster and two thirds—from anyone traveling in that direction. All the Christian travelers, that is; no one else had to pay. When we reached the pass, the collector's men stopped us and demanded the toll.

After he'd collected some money from my companions and the others, the officer turned to me and demanded that I pay in exchange for a ticket, as the others had done. 11.134

"If I paid your sultan the poll tax, I'd pay this too, but I don't, so I won't," I fired back.[179]

He studied me for a moment, then turned to my companions.

"And who might this fellow be?" he asked them.

"A Frankish doctor."

The officer believed them, as he'd seen that I looked different in my clothing and wig, so he greeted me and invited me to sit with him.

"Pardon me, sir, but I didn't realize who you were!"

Once he received payment from everyone else, he let us go. We mounted and set off, riding until we arrived at the bridge of Misis.[180] I was riding ahead of the caravan, and when I approached the bridge, I found myself face-to-face with a pair of officials, who blocked my way and asked me to come along to their superior, the master of Misis. In my terror, I assumed that someone must have double-crossed me and let slip that I wasn't a Frank. I told them that I didn't want to go with them until my companions arrived and I could give them my horse for safekeeping. 11.135

They waited patiently, not forcing me to accede. The reason they'd come was that their master was suffering from some aches and pains, and he'd received word that a Frankish doctor was traveling with this particular caravan. So he had sent these two to wait for me to arrive and bring me to his house, which was next to the bridge.

Once my companions arrived, I handed my horse over to them and went with the two officers to see their master, who was the governor of the town. When I presented myself before him, he welcomed me and told his servants to remove my shoes. Then he invited me to sit at his side, and ordered some coffee and a pipe for me to smoke. I was surprised at this treatment, and wondered why 11.136

a man who held the high rank of local governor was being so warm and friendly. As I was mulling this over, the governor spoke.

"Come a little closer," he said, and when I obliged, he wailed, "Oh doctor, put an end to this pain of mine and I'll give you anything you ask!"

"What sort of pain is it?" I asked, and he showed me his forearm, the flesh of which was decayed. He was suffering from snail fever, which had eaten away at his body, his innards, and his skin. At this sight, I set about remonstrating that I recognized the disease but didn't have the medicine with me to treat it. This only made him plead all the more.

11.137   "Never fear," I said. "I'll prescribe an ointment for you to apply topically, which will dry up your lesions. As for your insides, I'll have to put together a paste specifically meant to treat this illness. I don't have any with me at the moment, but I can put some together for you in Aleppo. It's composed of a group of drugs that can't be found nearby. Perhaps you have someone you could send to Aleppo. I'll give him a jar of the paste, and once you start using it, you'll be healed before the jar is finished. It's a tried and true remedy."

11.138   "Where can I find you in Aleppo?" he asked.

"My shop is in the Abrak market. Ask anyone and you'll find me."

"And what's the prescription you mentioned?"

"Take fifty dirhams' worth of blue vitriol—which they call *göztaşı* in Turkish. Soak it in a glass container full of water for twenty-four hours. Once it's dissolved, pour the water into a cup and moisten a cloth with it, then use it to wipe your ulcers. That should dry them up," I said.

"Send one of your men over to the caravan tonight and I'll give him some pills for you to take for three nights, before you go to sleep," I continued. "I'll also give him some powder for you to press on your ulcers."

11.139   Then I got up and asked his permission to depart, whereupon I returned to my companions who were with the caravan, encamped across the bridge by the water's edge. When evening came, we were wondering what we should have for dinner when suddenly a sumptuous feast, with three different dishes, appeared on a platter. The master of Misis had sent it, and his servants encouraged us to come right up and dig in. So we all sat down in that field overlooking the river, and enjoyed an ample supper. When we were done, we got up, washed our hands, and thanked God Most High for the grace He had shown us.

A pot of coffee, also sent by the master, then appeared, and we all had some. The attendant who had brought the coffee came over to me. 11.140

"The master sends his greetings," he said. "And he asks that you give me what you'd promised him."

"With pleasure," I said.

I opened my bag and took out fifteen purgative pills. I happened to also have some burnt alum powder, for ulcers. I put a little in a piece of paper, gave it to the attendant, and explained how to administer it. After daubing the ulcers with the blue vitriol water, the master was to sprinkle some of the powder over them and apply some pressure until they dried up. As for the pills, he was to swallow five of them before going to sleep. I said all this to the attendant before sending him on his way.

We spent the evening in that spot, then got on the road at midnight. I don't know what became of the master of Misis. We kept on until we arrived at the province of Adana, which was known as Ramazan Province. It is situated on a mountain plateau covered with trees and freshwater springs, a veritable paradise on earth. Before reaching the mountain, we'd passed a village called Ereğli, which was as verdant as an orchard, full of trees and plentiful water.[181] 11.141

Once in the province, we set up camp. The countryside was full of so many people that it looked like a fully inhabited city! Every man with a family had put up screens between the trees, creating a place for his wives and children to sit. During the summer, all the residents of Adana would flee the city because of the intense heat and stifling conditions, and come to this province. They'd spend 11.142

the summer there, people of every profession: merchants, tailors, carpenters, and other artisans. There was even a market, furnished with all the same things one would find in the city.

11.143   We passed the evening in that place then took to the road again at midnight, headed for the city of Adana. Along the road, we came upon some men, women, and children making their way to the countryside at night, carrying torches as though they were parasols. By morning, we'd arrived in Adana, and set up camp beneath the bridge there, under one of the dry arches.[182] This bridge has forty arches, and I've never seen such an edifice in all my travels. The smallest stones used to construct it were the size of Frankish tombstones. The whole structure is simply indescribable. It was built by Empress Helena, the mother of Emperor Constantine. She also built other bridges, as well as a paved road from the outskirts of Istanbul to the city of Jerusalem, and towers in various ports. Her story is too long for me to recount here.

11.144   Shortly after we halted beneath those arches, a Christian man came over to us accompanied by a person wearing the uniform of an official. He wanted to confirm that we'd all paid the toll at the mountain pass I mentioned earlier.

"Show me your papers," he demanded.

After all had shown their papers, he came over to me. I crouched, pretending to fumble around for my papers, and the other people in the caravan told him to leave me alone.

"He's a Frankish doctor," they explained. "He doesn't need to pay the toll. Even the master of Misis wouldn't take anything from him. In fact, he treated him as a guest."

11.145   At this, the official pulled away and left me alone. We spent the rest of the day there, and when the sun went down, the muleteers elected to start moving again.

"Why do you want to leave early?" we asked them.

"We're heading for a pass called Karanlık Kapı, or the Gate of Darkness," they said. "It's full of bandits; if we don't want to run into them, we need to cross at night."

We did as they asked: All of us mounted and we set off into the night. We soon arrived at the pass. Constructed of black stone, its interior was plunged in profound darkness, terrifying anyone who entered. With God's help, we emerged safely, and as we continued the road began to descend. To our right was a lofty mountain, thick with trees. To our left was a vast thicket, beyond which lay the sea.

We pressed on apprehensively. As midnight approached, the humid sea air became cool and we could see the dew settling on us, heavy as molasses. The fog was so thick we could scarcely keep our eyes open, and men were falling off their horses left and right. As for me, I was feeling too drowsy to continue at that pace, so I galloped ahead of the caravan and stopped about a mile down the road. I dismounted and went to the side of the road, into the thicket. I wrapped the horse's reins around my wrist and lay down as if I didn't have a care in the world, such was the extent of my fatigue. 11.146

I fell asleep instantly, and when the caravan passed I was still sleeping. When my horse saw all his fellow horses passing by, he began to whinny. But I remained sound asleep, dreaming that a horse was whinnying! The caravan passed, making a din, then rumbled away. In his eagerness to join his fellows, my horse tugged on his reins. That woke me up, and I immediately pricked up an ear, listening for the caravan's bells, but didn't hear a thing. Meanwhile, the horse was pulling on the reins with all his might, trying to drag me along after his harness-mates. 11.147

I held fast to the reins, but had no way to mount him while he was pulling me forward! I ran along in terror, remembering what I'd heard about the brigands in these parts who robbed people and killed them. As I prayed to the Virgin Mary and the saints for help, my strength began to flag. How much longer could I keep running alongside the horse?

It then occurred to me to wedge my foot into the horse's surcingle and hoist myself up. I stood in front of him and tried to calm him down but he wouldn't let me climb up. Instead, he ran off again, dragging me along! At that point I gave up and decided to let go 11.148

of the reins so I could slow down and walk. Whatever happened would happen: I didn't care anymore. Wouldn't you know it, when I did that, the horse calmed down and began to walk slowly as well! This was nothing short of a miracle worked by the Virgin Mary, to whom I'd appealed for aid, along with my guardian angel. Once the horse slowed down, I put my foot in his forward surcingle, heaved myself up, and mounted him. As soon as I was on his back, he immediately set off at a gallop of his own accord, bringing me back to the caravan without anyone suspecting a thing. After being scared wide awake, I felt revived again and thanked God Most High for His beneficence.

11.149   We pressed on to[183] an area full of rocks. I spotted a smooth trail through and steered my horse toward it. Then I proceeded down the trail, knowing I'd be leaving the caravan behind, along with the rocky terrain. I continued to follow the trail until I arrived at a mountain cave . . . I urged my horse on but it wouldn't take another step, halting in its place . . . some violent lashings to make it walk, and so the animal was compelled . . . that cave. Meanwhile, I wasn't paying attention . . . and so we found ourselves stuck in that place. Below it was . . . a great river. And on its right side, there was another . . . only . . .[184] Payas, and arrived in the morning and entered through the gate to the souk, which opened onto the space outside the walls. Lo and behold, as soon as we made our way into the middle of the souk, a man emerged from his shop and came over to embrace me, showering me with affectionate greetings. I didn't think I knew the man, so I was taken aback by his warmth.

"Don't you recognize me, brother Ḥannā?" he asked. "It's me, Ḥannā ibn Mikhāyīl Mīro, your dear friend from Aleppo!"

As soon as I heard these words, I suddenly realized exactly who he was. I gave him a hug and apologized for not recognizing him right away. This fellow used to visit Aleppo with his father and stay at Khān al-ʿUlabiyyah where we lived. His father had established a partnership with my brother Anṭūn, and they would correspond.

We invited father and son over to our house on many occasions, and became very good friends. That was why he recognized me.

Ḥannā had someone take my horse to my companions in the caravan, which was headed for lodgings outside the souk, then took me by the hand and led me to his house. He ushered me upstairs to a belvedere overlooking a vast orchard, extending as far as the eye could see. The orchard was planted entirely with citron, lemon, and orange trees; what an exquisite sight it was! We sat down and Ḥannā ordered his servant to prepare lunch for us, but I begged him not to let them cook anything greasy, as I'd made a vow not to eat any fat from the time of my arrival in Adana until I reached Aleppo, fearing I'd have indigestion. At this, he gave an order for them to prepare a plate of *mujaddarah* with rice, some saltwater fish, bottarga, and other tasty dishes. 11.150

Then he had a bottle of fine aged arak brought over, and poured me a glass. I had a drink and was bowled over by how strong it was. At length, when I had gathered my wits again, I turned to my friend. 11.151

"Brother, what kind of arak is this?"

"It's the sort that prevents indigestion," he explained. "If not for this drink, we'd all be suffering from bad vapors in the gut."

A little while later, they set the table and brought the delicious foods. He then tried to give me another drink of arak, but I wouldn't accept. Instead, we drank some good wine with our lunch. When we were finished, we had coffee and went for a stroll through that magnificent orchard, fit for a king. As we passed, the gardeners plucked citrons and sweet lemons for us, and other fruits too, such as pomegranates and cucumbers.

I stayed at his house until the late afternoon then returned to my companions. We spent the night on the seashore, and at midnight set off for Alexandretta. When we arrived, we pitched camp by the spring and spent the day there. After gathering some fodder for the horses, we set off again, passing Belen during the night, and continuing to Khān al-Jadīd. From there, we journeyed to Qurṭ Qulāq 11.152

and Jisr al-Jadīd, and from there to Antioch. We camped on the banks of the Orontes River and spent the night there.

11.153   The next day, we set off again, passing through the souk of Antioch. I got off my horse and made a stop at the bakery of an Armenian from the region of Sassoun, to buy some bread. After the baker weighed the bread, I took out some Ottoman coins to pay for it. But he wouldn't accept them, demanding *jarq* coins instead, which I didn't have. Annoyed, I grabbed him by the collar and forced him down.

"You'd better accept the sultan's coin or I'll drag you to a judge!" I scolded. "To think that you'd ask for Frankish coins instead!"

A crowd of people gathered around us and struggled to pry my hands from his collar. They took my money, gave me the bread, and bid me farewell.

11.154   I mounted and set out through Saint Paul's Gate in pursuit of the caravan. Somehow I lost my way and took the wrong road. Before I knew it, I found myself on a path that ended in the middle of some orchards. I wandered for a good long while among the mulberry trees and waterwheels, with the caravan moving farther away with every passing minute, and I felt increasingly panicked. But my distress was followed by divine deliverance! It took the shape of a passing peasant, whom I begged to guide me to the road.

"Follow me," he said kindly, and led me out of the orchards and back to Saint Paul's Gate, where I'd started. He showed me the road the caravan had taken, then left me to find my way.

11.155   "What if I run into thieves on the road," I thought, "and they strip me of my clothes and take my horse?" So I stayed put for a while, hoping to catch a glimpse of someone I knew, but to no avail. Torn between fear and hope, I finally forced myself to set off on my own, entrusting my fate to God. I rode that horse as hard as I could, until I spied someone down the road coming in my direction. It was the brother of our muleteer! When they'd realized I wasn't with them, the muleteer had halted the caravan and sent his brother back to Antioch to find out what had happened to me. He was very happy to see me, and asked why I'd left the caravan. I explained the whole story to him, and my heart finally stopped racing. Relieved that I'd been saved, I returned to the caravan with him, and told everyone why I'd been delayed.

Traveling onward, we arrived at a place known as the Valley of the Jinn. It was aptly named,[185] because we found it very challenging to traverse, full of dangers and perilous stretches of road. We spent a whole day crossing that valley, finally arriving in Harim, where we spent the night. The next morning, we set off again, passing many villages and farmlands, and arrived two days later in Khān al-'Asal, where we stayed the night.

11.156

The next day we entered Aleppo. Just before we arrived, there was a great earthquake, bigger than any that anyone had ever heard of. It's said it lasted more than five minutes, but we didn't sense it at all, because we were riding at the time. As soon as we entered the city, I went straight to my brother's house in Zuqāq al-Khall—this was the end of the month of July, in the year 1710—so as to avoid making a public spectacle of my homecoming.

When my brothers and sisters heard about my arrival, they all came over to congratulate me on my safe return, and brought me fresh clothes to wear. From Anṭūn's house, I went to the home of my brother 'Abdallāh, where I was visited by family members and relatives, who all came by to pay their respects. It seems they'd heard I'd drowned at sea, as I'd last written a letter to my brother Anṭūn from Marseille, telling him I was boarding a ship to Izmir, and planned to continue from there to Aleppo. Well, they received the news that a ship bound from Izmir to Alexandretta had been lost at sea and all aboard had perished. They were convinced that I was one of the drowned, given that they hadn't received any more news from me, and prayed for my soul's eternal rest. Of course, that was because when I traveled from Izmir to Istanbul in the company of the aforementioned embassy official, I didn't send a letter to my brother informing him of my plans. This was why my family were so overjoyed to see me safe and sound in Aleppo.

11.157

11.158　　I spent three or four days at my brother's home, until fresh clothes had been prepared for me. Then I got dressed, shaved my head, and donned a turban. They had a certificate of safe conduct drawn up for me, and once I had that in hand, I left the house and went to repay the visits to my family, loved ones, and relatives.[186] I then returned to the city and to my brother's warehouse. A few days later, my brother ʿAbdallāh opened a cloth shop for me. He put me under the supervision of my uncle Shāhīn Ghazzālah till I had learned the cloth-selling trade. I would spend twenty-two years working as a cloth merchant.

11.159　　My brother was afraid that I would go on another journey. But God's plan for me was different. During this period, I was engaged, got married, and had children. It's perfectly evident to me now that God Most High—may He be praised—had called me to a life of marriage, for when I had left Aleppo in secret, my plan was to become a monk. It was a matter of good fortune that I encountered that traveler in the village of Kaftīn who dissuaded me from my plan, and, as fate would have it, I traveled with him to all of those lands I've described. But let me go back to what I was saying.

11.160　　A year after I began working in the cloth trade, my former master, *khawājah* Paul Lucas, the one I had traveled with, arrived in Aleppo. He stayed at the home of the French consul. When I heard he had come to town, I went to pay my respects. As soon as he saw me, he embraced me, then scolded me severely for having left him without explaining my reasons. At that moment, some other *khawājah*s came by to see him so we had to cut short our reunion, saving it for another day.

Some time later, I figured out why he was back on the road. It seemed that when he'd learned that the nobleman I mentioned earlier had sent me on a voyage of exploration in his stead, he managed to change the nobleman's mind, promising to take my place and travel on his behalf. This was why he had come to Aleppo again: to carry out his mission for the nobleman.

A few days later, I invited him to visit and have dinner at our house. He accepted, and I invited my brothers to join us for dinner. I was still a bachelor in those days, and I had furnished a room on the second floor for my own use. I prepared a sumptuous meal, then went to fetch him from the city and brought him back to the house and my waiting brothers. They greeted him most cordially, and when it was time for dinner, we sat at the table. Following the meal, we sat and chatted with *khawājah* Lucas.

I then remembered that I'd once told him about my mother's illness, and how the doctors had been unable to cure her. When I reminded him of that, he told me to bring my mother out so he could determine what her ailment was. We brought her out, and as soon as he looked at her, he knew what sort of illness she was suffering from.

"Be sure to remind me to give you something for her," he said to me after letting my mother go. "It will rid her of this illness."

We spent the rest of the evening in his company, until ten o'clock. I'd prepared a bed for him, as comfortable as could be, and he slept soundly until the morning. After some coffee, we went off together to the city.

He would often pass by my shop, and sometimes I'd join him for his customary tours around town, looking for antiques like coins, books, and rare and valuable gems—that sort of thing. The day after our dinner, he came by my shop.

"Take me to the jewelry market," he said.

When we arrived, he set about scrutinizing the contents of the jewelers' cases. In one of them, he found a stone resembling a carnelian, with a hole bored through it. To my surprise, he purchased it from the jeweler for two *miṣriyyah*s.

"What do you want with that worthless stone?" I asked him after we'd left the shop.

"I bought it as a treatment for your mother," he replied, and told me to thread the stone and hang it around my mother's neck so it rested against her skin. "She'll recover," he said.

11.161

11.162

11.163

"We've had so many doctors try and fail to cure her," I thought, chuckling to myself. "How's this stone going to be any different?"

11.164 But I didn't contradict him. I simply took the stone and did as he instructed, and didn't give it a second thought until later that week, when I came home from the old city and was told that my mother had announced that she wanted to go to the public baths that day, after she changed her clothes. She hadn't been to the baths in three years! Nor had she joined us at the table for meals. She hadn't been able to sleep and never spoke to anyone. But on that day, she sat at the table and had a good lunch, chatting with us all like she used to do, then went off to the baths. Everyone was astounded. How had she made a full recovery?

When my mother returned from the baths, she joined us for dinner and showed a good appetite—as though she'd never been ill. We were all baffled.

"There's really nothing to it," I told them. "It's because of the special properties of that stone I hung around her neck."

11.165 They wouldn't believe me until I asked my master about it. When I told him that my mother had made a recovery, he gave me further instructions.

"Tell her to take care not to remove the stone from her neck, or else the black vapor will return and she'll suffer a relapse," he said. "The stone has the special property of drawing out the black vapor."

He was right. A year later, the stone fell off her neck while she was in the baths, and her melancholy returned. I went in search of a similar stone, to no avail. She remained melancholic until she died.

11.166 Another day, he came over and started to scold me.

"How is it you've never told me there's a place here called 'the Kanakia'?"[187] he demanded. I had no idea what he was talking about.

"What is this place, and who told you about it?" I asked.

"It's an underground passage that leads to the city of Antep."

Now I understood. He was talking about al-Khannāqiyyah; it's also known as the Cave of the Slave.

"Why would you be interested in such a dangerous and frightful place?" I asked. "No one who has gone in has ever come out! It's a vast, dark cavern, full of crooked passages that send people in circles and prevent them from escaping. Many have entered; none have come out alive."

"Have you ever been?" my master asked. "To investigate whether all this is true?"

"This is how *everyone* describes it," I insisted. "Are they telling the truth or lying? I don't know."

"I want to see it for myself, to find out the truth," he said. "And I'd like you to find me an old man who knows the place and who can guide us there. I'll pay him well. I plan to head out on Thursday, so be sure to bring him with you then, without fail!" 11.167

"Consider it done," I replied, and he went on his way.

I didn't think much of his plan, and told myself that when Thursday came, I'd go see him and put the whole affair out of his mind.

On Thursday morning, I was on my way to the city as usual when I happened upon an old Christian man named Abū Zayt. Now, this fellow was very old, and had spent his whole life in the countryside. For a time, he would bring grapes to the Christians for their presses. When the season was over, he'd become a wood peddler. He would meet up with the camel drivers transporting wood, bring the drivers to Aleppo, and sell the wood. When I came upon him, he was standing at the top of a hill, waiting for the camel drivers to arrive with the wood. It occurred to me that this fellow might know how to find the cave. 11.168

I went up and greeted him, and asked him if he knew anything about the Cave of the Slave, in al-Khannāqiyyah. 11.169

"I've gone inside plenty of times," he replied at once. "I know where it is, but I've never reached its very end."

I was delighted to hear this, and told him about my master's plan.

"There's a Frankish fellow who would like to explore the cave," I explained. "Come see him with me, and he'll give you a handsome tip if you guide him to the cave."

"It would be a pleasure and an honor," he said. "Let's go!"

11.170   Off I went with the old man, who brought a companion along with him. We arrived at al-Khannāqiyyah, and the *khawājah* turned up shortly thereafter with a company of Franks and their servants. They were armed and had brought along some ammunition and a sack of straw.

"Did you find someone who knows where the place is?" my master asked me as soon as they arrived.

"Yes," I said, and pointed to the old man. My master was overjoyed, heaping praise on me. We told the old man to take us to the spot.

"Follow me," he said.

We did as he asked, and soon arrived at a vast cave, hollowed out of the limestone, whose entrance was at a considerable elevation. It was known as the Castle of al-Tamātīn, and was the hideout of a certain rebellious slave, for whom it was named.

11.171   We entered, and made our way to the bottom of the cave. There we found a small door, hollowed out of that mountain of chalk. Beyond it was the Cave of the Slave, according to the old man. None of us, in our fear, was willing to proceed any farther, but the *khawājah* tried to embolden us. He ordered the servants to take out their candles—he had had six candles made of beeswax. We sat down, they took out some food and drink for us, and we ate and drank. Then he ordered the servants to light two candles and fill a bag with straw. He strode over to the door and fired at it a pistol full of lead powder, emitting a powerful din that echoed for three minutes.

11.172   Now we swore we'd never go in! When the *khawājah* saw our trepidation, he forged ahead, followed by two servants, one carrying a candlestick and the other the bag of straw, sprinkling straw as he walked so they wouldn't lose their way. When we saw the *khawājah* going ahead on his own, we found the courage to follow him, leaving two servants behind to guard our supplies, and also the door, so no one could block our way out again.

We descended into the cave, terrified. Two men walked ahead with candles, while one sprinkled straw behind us so we would not lose our way. It was plain to us that everything we'd heard about the cave was a lie. The path did not have a single twist or turn; it was straight, easy to walk along, with plenty of headroom, and two hundred feet wide. There was nothing to see but the bones of dead animals. The passage was carved out of limestone. We had walked along it for about fifteen minutes, when suddenly the candles flickered out and it became difficult to breathe. No one seemed to be able to catch their breath, and the whole place felt suffocating. It had no source of air, after all! Fearing for our lives, we started to turn back.

"Don't be afraid," the *khawājah* said in encouragement. "This is a large space, and there's no chance of suffocation. Let's press on a bit longer, then we can head back."

We did as he asked. About a hundred feet farther along, we came to a dead end. But above our heads was a sort of stone shelf hewn out of the mountain rock.

"Why do you people say that this underground passage opens onto Antep?" the *khawājah* asked the old man. "We've just reached the end of it!"

"The entrance to the passageway is past that perch up there," the old man replied. "But they filled it in to prevent people from entering and losing their lives."

On hearing this, the *khawājah* mounted the shoulders of one of the servants and climbed up to that very spot. Using his poniard, he dug around in the earth and found that it was blocked with gravel. That was when he realized we had reached the end of the cave, and that what had been said about it was a lie. He climbed down. The old man was embarrassed, because those who had pretended that the passageway led to Antep turned out to be liars.

We made our way back, emerging from the entrance to the cave. Then we explored the rest of al-Khannāqiyyah, investigating one spot after another. Some people cutting limestone asked us what we were looking for. When we told them, they referred us to an old man who could help us. He was nearly ninety years old.

"He'll show you the entrance to the underground passageway that emerges in Antep," they said. "He's been in these parts for a long time, and knows them well."

We asked them to bring the old man to us. When he appeared, the *khawājah* handed him a third of a piaster.

"Show me the passageway that leads to Antep," he said.

"Follow me," the old man replied.

11.176 We followed him to one of the many caves in the area, whose steep, sloping entrance had been entirely filled in with earth.

"When I was a boy, I used to come here with my father," the old man said. "The entrance to the passageway was open then, but some time later the governor ordered that it be filled in, to prevent people from going in and getting killed." He continued as follows: "Now, they say that a group of young men were once celebrating a wedding with the groom and came here to take a look at the passageway. Well, they started goading each other to go inside, and eventually they all did. Not a single one returned. They all died, lost underground. None of them thought to bring a good, long rope with them to tie to the entrance of the passageway. They could have held on to it and used it to get out again."

After he finished telling this story, the *khawājah* asked him about the passageway we'd explored earlier. What was it?

11.177 "Oh, that one," the old man said. "When Aleppo was first built, they used to cut limestone out of it, for construction. The proof is that it has a pit every hundred feet. That was where they'd dig out the limestone."

It was true: When we were in the passageway, we saw pits like that, blocked up. The *khawājah* commended the old man. Then he pointed out that this whole area seemed to be a mountain of limestone. Why then would they put themselves to the trouble of excavating it from a cramped cave?

"For two reasons," the old man replied. "First of all, the limestone there is more solid. For construction purposes, it's as durable as granite. The second reason—and this is the truer one—is that the kings of times past used those passageways to march their soldiers underground, so no one would know they were coming. They pretended they were excavating the limestone for construction, but the secret purpose was to be able to move their troops underground."

The old man's words fascinated the *khawājah*, who found them believable. He also accepted the old man's claim that the filled-in passageway emerged in Antep. We left him then, and returned the way we'd come. Climbing up to the vineyard known as al-Qulayʿah, we had lunch and spent the rest of the day there. When evening came, each went on his way. 11.178

This is the end of my story, and of my wanderings. I ask God's forgiveness for any undue additions or omissions.

Completed on the third of March in the
year 1764 of the Christian era.

Afterword: Ḥannā Diyāb and the *Thousand and One Nights*

PAULO LEMOS HORTA

Scholars of the *Thousand and One Nights* have long known that a Syrian Maronite named Ḥannā Diyāb played a role in the genesis of some of the most famous stories added to Antoine Galland's early-eighteenth-century French translation of the story collection. However, before the identification of Diyāb's *Book of Travels*, evidence for the Aleppan traveler's distinctive contribution was frustratingly slim. Galland's diary offers a brief glimpse of his first meeting with Diyāb in the Paris apartment of Paul Lucas, a French collector of curiosities, in 1709. There, Galland discovered that the young traveler "[knew] some very beautiful Arabic tales."[188] The French translator also took notes on a series of sessions from May 5 to June 6, during which Diyāb told him fifteen fantastical stories. Although Galland requested manuscripts of these stories from Diyāb, references in his journal suggest that he received only one: "Aladdin and the Wonderful Lamp." Such were the meager resources available to researchers of the *Nights*, and for decades they seemed content to relegate Diyāb to a footnote in their analyses of a story collection whose impact on Western literature has been extensive.

The publication of Diyāb's *Book of Travels* at last offers the opportunity to rescue the author from the margins of *Nights* scholarship and to revise our understanding of the origins of Galland's most popular tales, including "Aladdin and the Wonderful Lamp," "'Alī Bābā and the Forty Thieves," and "The Ebony Horse." A mixture of memoir and travelogue, *The Book of Travels* is dominated by the author's journey from Aleppo to Paris in the service of Paul Lucas, a shady procurer of curiosities for the court of Louis XIV. Looking back on that journey fifty years later, Diyāb notes that while in Paris he met with an unnamed translator, recognizably Galland, who was working on the *Thousand and One Nights*, and that he supplied the man with enough new stories to allow him to finish the collection. There is no evidence that Diyāb offered stories he thought belonged to the *Thousand and One Nights*. Like the storytellers who plied their trade in the coffee shops of Aleppo, he may have retold old tales or created new ones from familiar elements. Although his stories were soon to become popular, Diyāb does not seem to have learned of the impact of his intervention in literary history.

The Book of Travels offers an opportunity to explore the resonances that emerge when Diyāb's narrative is examined alongside the tales that passed into Galland's *Nights* through his agency. Diyāb's memoir reveals his ability to weave anecdotes and story motifs into a compelling tale of a life shaped by ambition and curiosity. Its pages offer clear evidence of his attraction to religion, magic, and mystery; his thirst for adventure; and his willingness to break from what was conventionally expected of a junior member of an Aleppan merchant family. His lasting contribution to the Western storytelling corpus known as the *Arabian Nights* can now be viewed through his fascination with difference, strangeness, and wonder. As Diyāb comes to the fore as a personality and as a narrator, his encounter with Galland in Paris can no longer be dismissed as a mere footnote to the history of the *Nights*. The so-called orphan tales—that is, the tales with no extant Arabic original—can no longer be seen as authorless.[189] Their origins lie not only in the French literary practice of Galland but in the imagination and narrative skills of the Syrian traveler who first told them in 1709.

The opportunity for Diyāb to insert his tales into the extensive corpus of stories of the *Thousand and One Nights* arose from the fundamental mutability of the original Arabic collection, which had always invited storytellers to continue the sequence of tales in a potentially infinite demonstration of the possibilities of invention and recombination. In the early Arabic manuscripts of the *Nights*, only the frame tale and a few early story cycles remain constant. These are nocturnal stories told by the brave Shahrazad to save her own life and the lives of the other women of the kingdom—an attempt to use the lure of "what happened next" to prevent her husband, Shahriyar, from having her killed the next morning. As the frame story explains, King Shahriyar has been cuckolded by his queen and, having dispatched her and her lover, has resolved to marry a virgin each evening and to promptly execute her the next day. When Shahrazad volunteers to be his next victim, the string of stories begins, each more marvelous and astounding than the one before. No authentic Arabic collection of *Thousand and One Nights* tales offers the mythical number of 1,001 nights of storytelling, but each offers new additions and variations that build on the central core of the tales' oldest components. As the stories entered Western literature through French, this pattern continued. When Galland's Arabic manuscript ran out of stories, his publisher, and then Galland himself, added new tales intended to continue the pattern of ever more wondrous stories to meet French readers' insatiable appetite for Shahrazad's tales.[190]

Diyāb's arrival in Paris with Paul Lucas in 1709 was therefore providential for Galland. Of the sixteen stories Diyāb offered him during their meetings, the French translator inserted ten into his version of *Les mille et une nuits*.[191] These ten tales have proven to be among the most influential *Thousand and One Nights* tales and have been repeatedly translated, adapted, and republished in various formats. It is not just that Diyāb's tales were the most widely read: As French scholars have argued, their impact on European languages was so great that they ultimately influenced how the story collection as a whole was received and interpreted.[192] Despite having many affinities with tales contained in Arabic manuscripts of the *Thousand and One Nights*, the tales added by Galland and Diyāb seem more consistently otherworldly and marvelous. Their emphasis on supernatural elements—embodied in the powerful jinni of the lamp in "Aladdin" and the flying carpet in "Prince Aḥmad and the Fairy Perī Bānū"—has colored perceptions of the *Nights* as a whole. So too has the greater attention in their tales to precious jewels, luxurious materials, and elaborate ceremonies. In literary scholarship, these elements have been attributed, in too facile a manner, to the particular assumptions of the European Orientalist, as epitomized by Galland. Given the absence of information on Diyāb, it was Galland who was seen as adding elements he thought representative of Islamic culture, such as superstition and love of luxury, to inform and entertain his readers. It was also Galland who was credited with the literary skill needed to elevate "mere folklore" into a text deserving of a place on European bookshelves.[193]

While neglecting Diyāb's distinctive contribution to Western versions of the *Nights*, several literary critics have lauded Galland as the de facto author or creator of the *Thousand and One Nights* as a work of world literature.[194] In evaluating his achievement as a translator of one Arabic manuscript of the *Nights*, critics often stress that he reworked the original tales instead of merely translating them. This emphasis implies that the Arabic text from which he worked was merely raw material requiring the literary intervention of a French master to become worthy of European attention. When critics turn their attention to Galland's versions of Diyāb's tales, the achievement of the French Orientalist appears even more impressive, and the Syrian storyteller is confined to obscurity. In this reading of the "orphan tales," Galland, taking only the bare outlines of plot from his Syrian informant, drew on his own travels in the Orient and his research as an Orientalist to fill in the fabulous details of voyages, palaces, and magical objects. The French translator is placed within the long line of creative storytellers who have contributed to the making and remaking of the stories attached to the *Thousand and One Nights*. The credit for stitching and weaving—even when this involved plot elements that Galland's notes indicate came from

Diyāb—and for making tales sing on the page has gone to Galland.[195] Diyāb, meanwhile, is either forgotten completely or credited only with providing the material that Galland's sophistication transformed into a literary product worthy of being consumed in Enlightenment Paris.

Galland has been credited not only with making the *Nights* more marvelous, but also more modern. In adapting the tales to the conventions of prose writing in vogue in eighteenth-century France, Galland, it is claimed, gave greater psychological richness and depth to the characters. The French translator was able to transform sparse notes from Diyāb's oral performances into compelling tales of ordinary characters caught up in extraordinary predicaments, according to Sermain, editor of the most recent edition of Galland's *Les mille et une nuits*. Drawing on French literary conventions, Galland invented dialogues and inner monologues, and gave narrative coherence to the rudimentary story elements offered by Diyāb. Characters were developed with more sympathy, and the hero of humble origin was developed as a moral example to French readers.[196] Galland is understood to have done more than feed the appetite for fairy tales in and beyond the French salons of the early eighteenth century. He is also said to have opened up the tales in terms of character and technique so they could resonate with mainstream literary trends in French prose throughout the eighteenth century, which coincided with the greatest penetration of the *Nights* in cultural consciousness. To this day, it is axiomatic in French scholarship that the modernity of the *Nights* tales is a result of their handling by Galland, and subsequently Diderot and Voltaire, and their circulation in both overt and subterranean currents of European modernity.[197] If the stories appealed in Europe, it was because they had become more modern, and Galland and Paris were the agents of their modernity.

A careful consideration of Diyāb's *Book of Travels* should disrupt this narrative of Galland's authorship and allow us to recognize Diyāb's distinctive contributions to the tales added in French to the corpus of the *Nights*. These contributions include his creative agency as a storyteller and the modernity of his narration of the eighteenth-century world. The narrative skill he reveals in *The Book of Travels* lends credence to the argument that the "beautiful" tales he related to Galland in 1709 contained more than mere fragments that had to be stitched together by the European translator to achieve their effect. If Diyāb's account of his journey is made up of some forty embedded anecdotes and stories, as Johannes Stephan has suggested,[198] then the author demonstrates considerable facility in weaving them together to form his own narrative. Like other travel accounts from the period, the text can be seen as a particular mixture of fact and fiction that partakes of both Arabic and European storytelling traditions. Throughout the manuscript, descriptions of foreign lands mingle with entertaining anecdotes that Diyāb has heard or read to create an engaging account of a life composed of stories. Diyāb's effort to integrate elements familiar from other contexts can be recognized in the presence of motifs from the tales of Nizami and Boccaccio. Examples include the tale of the woman buried alive and the story of the jilted painter who is promised and then denied the hand of a beautiful young woman in marriage. The memoir thus confirms Galland's journal notes, which reveal Diyāb's ability to combine existing story elements into new tales.[199]

Diyāb's *Book of Travels* shares motifs and themes with the added French *Nights* tales, as well as a manner of telling. In his memoir, the Syrian author mixes elements from different sources or embeds stories to build suspense. This skill is equally evident in the tales Diyāb offered to Galland for the *Nights*. When Diyāb tells the story of his arrest in Paris, for instance, he builds suspense by frequently interrupting the narrative, as he interpolates tales about unusual characters and their struggles with the backdrop of Enlightenment Paris.[200] The use of such embedded stories is central to the construction of tales in the Arabic corpus of the *Nights*. Some of the stories Diyāb told Galland—most importantly the three stories interlinked in "The Caliph's Night Adventure"—adopt this structure as well. Other Diyāb stories demonstrate the creative possibilities that result from linking or mixing elements from the rich storytelling culture of his homeland. The tale of "ʿAlī Bābā and the Forty Thieves," which began its life as the "Tale of Hogia Baba" in Diyāb's first narration to Galland, demonstrates the power of linking existing motifs to create a tale of intrigue and suspense. Diyāb's version combines three popular story elements—the magical cave, the gang of thieves, and the clever slave girl. All of these elements existed in some form prior to his intervention, but it was his telling of the tale to Galland that first brought them together into a new tale. Galland's rewriting alters the name of the main character and drops the food motif from the story of the magical cave.[201] Even so, it preserves the balance between the elements contributed by Diyāb, and it is these elements that are central to the story's appeal.

Creating tales by combining motifs is central to Diyāb's narrative practice, as it was for the many storytellers who contributed to the constantly mutating *Nights*. The author of *The Book of Travels* proved to have precisely the skills and talent necessary to give him a place among the many storytellers, compilers, and editors of the *Nights* tales over the centuries. There is no doubt that Galland made some additions to the stories he received from Diyāb and incorporated into *Les mille et une nuits*. The additions to "Prince Aḥmad and the Fairy Perī Bānū" are obvious, and add to the exotic quality of the three princes' travels in search of a marvelous artifact to win the hand of the beloved princess.[202] However, these interpolations drawn from Galland's academic work fail to demonstrate the kind of literary inventiveness that critics would like to attribute to him. More than these opportunistic insertions, Diyāb's mixing of story elements to create a compelling narrative deserves pride of place. Within the modern history of storytelling, the impact of Diyāb's tales is remarkable, as their plots and motifs have been codified two hundred years later as tale types by researchers. The folk-narrative historian Ulrich Marzolph has argued that Ḥannā Diyāb introduced more tale types to the narrative repertoire of the Western world than any other storyteller. Marzolph has found no fewer than four international tale types whose first appearance can be traced to the stories Diyāb told Galland.[203] If these tale types now strike us as some of the most basic plots in world literature, then it is time to acknowledge that this is a result of Diyāb's creative abilities.

Diyāb's imprint on the tales transmitted to Galland may transcend the deployment of techniques already in evidence in the core tales of the original collection. Some of the distinctly "modern" qualities attributed to the Diyāb stories appear to have echoes in *The Book of Travels*, raising the question of whether it was Diyāb who imparted this particular sensibility to the *Nights*. If the Diyāb-Galland stories indeed display more self-reflection and psychological depth than other *Nights* stories, *The Book of Travels* may explain why, as Diyāb's approach to narration in that work involves a great interiority. *The Book of Travels* is written in the first person and the narrator asserts his individuality as an observer, even hoping to spare his readers the disappointments he experienced in his life.[204] The narrator seeks to impose his authority on the work as an author rather than relying on the collective authority of a chain of guarantors, or expressing his subjectivity by quoting poetry as other travelers had.[205] The work is remarkable in capturing the emotional qualities of Diyāb's younger, more naive self, and comments in a thoughtful way on the choices that determined his path through life.[206] His description of the sense of alienation he experienced as a novice monk is striking. He writes about himself freely, confessing his difficulties and self-doubt, and when he is laid low, he feels that the world has shrunk before his eyes.[207]

In the journey that takes Diyāb from Aleppo to Paris and back, his conscious self-fashioning is evident in moments of disguise and deception. Diyāb admits to the lies and deceits that play a critical role in facilitating his journeys, as the text's French translator has noted. When on his return voyage he confidently claims to be a doctor like his father before him, and that he studied in Marseille, he is admitting to deliberate deceit. For the French translator, these are the moments where Diyāb most clearly reveals his modernity—when he demonstrates his understanding of social expectations but refuses to be bound by those constraints.[208] This distinctive stance is signaled at beginning of the memoir in an episode in which he ignores his family's order to return to Aleppo, clearly asserting his right to choose his own path in this narrative.

Life on the road with Paul Lucas offered Diyāb the opportunity to reinvent himself and provided an apprenticeship in the life of the merchant-traveler, including an immersion in a barter system defined by ruses. Paul Lucas was the consummate self-made man, who registers in the courtly correspondence of more erudite rivals and patrons as a "marvelous" autodidact.[209] What earned him this moniker was an almost preternatural ability to gauge the value of ancient coins and medallions by a combination of touch and experience, which left them baffled by his ability to bring back hundreds of coins for the cabinets of the court without a forgery among them. Doubtless, the unacknowledged labor of servants such as Diyāb helped him secure his hoard of treasures, among them manuscripts in languages he did not claim to know. But one should not discount the possibility that the self-taught Lucas accumulated a substantial store of practical knowledge that had long allowed him to survive as a jewel merchant and thrive within trading routes and markets of the Levant, the experience that recommended him to his patrons at court.

Lucas adopts the guise of a medical doctor to facilitate their passage through the lands along their Mediterranean route, and Diyāb describes the ruses of his mentor without censure. His own efforts to mirror these subterfuges later in the journey show Diyāb acting as the agent of his own destiny. Though the young Diyāb was complicit in the subterfuges Lucas deployed to swindle locals out of precious objects, his admiration for Lucas's practice of medicine was genuine, and he regrets not having learnt more when he presents himself as a physician on his return journey. Pontchartrain's instructions governing the commission given Lucas during this journey explicitly prescribed his adoption of the guise of a physician to deflect attention from his real aim of collecting items for the French court's cabinets of curiosities. To this end, a passport was drawn up in Lucas's name that identified him as a doctor, and Lucas was advised not to reveal he traveled to acquire coins, medallions, and manuscripts for the French monarch (for fear this knowledge might drive up prices and invite hostility).[210] Lucas himself describes adopting the title of physician in his previous voyage for the purpose of avoiding suspicion.[211] Diyāb had cause to take the Frenchman for a doctor. The Richelieu collection at the National Library in France preserves Lucas's commission from a naturalist at court to procure herbs and learn about medicine not native to France.[212] As part of his guise, Lucas may have traveled with common remedies to pass for a doctor in his travels.[213] Some success in this regard must have been evident (as Diyāb attests), for in this, as in his other voyages, Lucas traveled on a tight budget and relied greatly on bartering his cures for information, hospitality, and goods.

Diyāb's memoir is also notable for its interest in the testing of social boundaries, displaying an increased awareness, relative to previous Arabic travelogues, of social distinctions between Christians and Muslims, and between Maronites and other Christians.[214] These issues emerge at several points on his journey to Paris with Lucas, and again when he attempts to gauge where he fits into a social hierarchy with regard to other Maronites and Eastern Christians in Paris. At one point, he must weigh an offer of marriage into the family of a café owner that would offer him a foothold in the French capital against Lucas's elusive promise of an appointment as the king's Arabic librarian. In some cases, this attentiveness to social distinction involves navigating gendered assumptions, as in an early episode in which Diyāb is enlisted in an effort by a Maronite husband to convince his wife to cease veiling. Diyāb's comments attributing differences in women's behavior to the state of girls' education indicate a willingness to include consideration of social practices within a narrative marked by dramatic and marvelous events.

Diyāb's writing self-consciously explores efforts at shaping his identity, attentive to the roles and constraints that shaped the lives around him. In light of this evidence, literary critics should be cautious about ascribing any modern qualities in the *Nights* tales to Galland as translator, or indeed "author." Judged only from the rough notes on his meetings with Galland, the stories Diyāb told in 1709 offer moments in which the characters seem to possess a complex inner life. In "The Ebony Horse," characters are plagued by internal conflicts at several critical moments in the story, as when the king of Persia wonders whether he really ought to trade the princess for the wondrous flying horse. In "The City of Gold," a Diyāb story that Galland chose not to insert into the collection, the third prince is described in the diary notes as having "a more open, more lively, and more penetrating mind than those of his two elder brothers." Understanding that his father would never permit him to journey beyond the kingdom to satisfy his desire for adventure, he is careful to dissimulate and keep his travel preparations a secret. Even some elements of interiority in "ʿAlī Bābā and the Forty Thieves" attributed by at least one scholar to Galland himself, including the moment when Cassim forgets the words he needs to speak in order to escape the cave, are part of Diyāb's original telling of the story, as the notes from Galland's journal prove.[215]

Diyāb's interest in the lives of ordinary characters caught up in dangerous events that they are helpless to control resonates with the greater stress on characterization in the added *Nights* stories, when compared to the scholarly preoccupations that dominate Galland's work outside the *Thousand and One Nights*. Looking back on his time in Paris in *The Book of Travels*, Diyāb is attentive to the predicament of the economically marginal as the capital experienced the effects of economic crisis and harvest failure in the winter of 1708–9. While Galland makes no comment on the bread riots that occurred in his neighborhood on the day Diyāb delivered the conclusion of "Aladdin," Diyāb's record of his time in the city mentions beggars at cathedral doors and former soldiers forbidden to ask for alms. In *The Book of Travels*, Diyāb is particularly sympathetic to the plight of the condemned he finds in the broadsides advertising their executions. In one episode, a young man takes debt titles from his father's shop to his own through a misunderstanding and ends up on the scaffold despite the protestations of his family. Diyāb lingers over this public and private tragedy, detailing the execution and the lamentations of the assembled crowd. This story of an everyday tragedy played out on the streets of Paris offers an obvious thematic link to the plight of a young protagonist like Aladdin.[216] There is nothing like it in Galland's journals.[217]

If greater attention to social life and material culture are indeed a distinguishing feature of the Diyāb-Galland tales,[218] then *The Book of Travels* suggests that Diyāb was more likely than Galland to have nurtured those concerns. Diyāb's dreams of advancement in Paris as a servant of the royal court share a certain affinity with the fantastic journey of Aladdin, while other stories told to Galland offer a darker perspective on the possibilities of social ascent. In "Khawājah Ḥasan al-Ḥabbāl," two friends try to change the fortune of a poor rope maker by giving him money but are unable to alter his circumstances (though he does find fortune via other means). Diyāb's oral telling of the tale included details about how valuable coins might be hidden in the head garments of the rope maker at the center of the experiment ("[he] hid it in his turban as all the poor people do").[219] The particular social circumstances of women also serve as a significant element in the Diyāb stories described in Galland's notes. In "The Two Sisters Who Envied Their Cadette," the princess is given the same education as her elder brothers, with instruction in reading and writing, the sciences, riding, spear throwing, and playing musical instruments, and proves herself superior when the characters are tested. In "Qamar al-Dīn and and Badr al-Budūr," which Galland left out of the *Nights*, there is comparable stress on the significance of a woman receiving the same education as a man, and the female protagonist succeeds in rescuing her beloved cousin by outsmarting the servants of the sultan's court and beating his favorite at chess. Despite the long interval that separates them, the Diyāb who narrates *The Book of Travels* shows significant affinities in interests and approach with the storyteller who offered tales of wonder to a French translator in Paris.

When these examples are considered against the evidence regarding Galland's own literary efforts, the case for seeing Diyāb as a significant contributor to the distinctiveness of the added *Nights* stories appears even stronger. Galland did indeed spend time in the Ottoman world and achieve success as an Orientalist scholar, but his other writings include little evidence that he was adept at the kinds of literary flourishes French critics have attributed to him. If Diyāb broke with the convention of the Arab travelogue by embracing the first-person pronoun in *The Book of Travels*,[220] Galland's journal of his time in Constantinople in 1672–73 seems determined to erase his own voice and perspective.[221] Although Galland had a French tradition of journal writing to draw upon, his own journal of this formative period in his life barely registers events in his life, or interest in the lives of others. It does little to construct a narrative,[222] and shows no interest in the kinds of interiority deemed new to the added *Nights* tales. Instead, it is given over to the cataloging of the manuscripts and books that were his main scholarly interest at the time. Scholars have fixated on the journal's rare and vivid description of an army heading out for battle in May 1672 as a sign of how Galland's personal experience of the Orient would have informed his retellings of the stories offered by Diyāb.[223] Yet Galland's journal generally eschews the kind of elaborate descriptions of the settings and customs of Constantinople that are assumed to be a part of the translator's literary repertoire. The same is true of his *Nights* translation as a whole. Despite Galland's gesture toward the ethnographic goal of explaining the Orient to his readers through his translation of the *Thousand and One Nights*, he did little to follow through with this program in the text (and he supplies very few notes). The translation reveals a literary approach to anthropology, rather than an anthropological approach to literature, as Madeleine Dobie aptly puts it.[224]

If Galland's diaries are any guide, the intellectual interests he pursued while translating the *Nights* and meeting with Diyāb are the same as those he pursued during his time abroad. In Paris, Galland devoted the bulk of his day to the Greco-Roman interests and numismatic projects that were his primary passion. He spent his most intense hours of study on lectures and writing projects related to the Greco-Roman classics, while his evenings were spent on translating the *Nights*, a task that required less energy and attention.[225] His diary reflects a clear preference for translation from a text rather than the exercises in expansion and development that he is presumed to have undertaken with Diyāb's outlined stories. Galland notes in his journal that he asked Diyāb to write out the stories he had told him. He records that he did indeed receive a text of "Aladdin," which is the one he presumably used in the creation of the published version of the story. While it has not yet been proven, there remains the intriguing possibility that Galland was not attempting to replicate the stories he heard from Diyāb using the shorthand notes from his journal, but was working, rather, from fuller manuscripts that contained some of the distinctive elements identified by scholars of the *Nights*.[226]

Little in Diyāb's Paris diaries reveals Galland to be capable of the kind of literary creativity and empathy necessary to create the depth of character or the "modern" interiority that some scholars perceive in the Diyāb-Galland tales. Immersed in the Greco-Roman classics, Galland evinces no curiosity about the world around him, not even in the tragic events that still held Diyāb's interest fifty years after they occurred. In many ways, the critical edition of Galland's diaries only deepens the mystery surrounding the personality at their center. The editor's notes, but not the entries themselves, point to the workings of history just outside Galland's door as war, famine, and bread riots brought suffering to many Parisians.[227] But the Orientalist preferred the world of fixed texts to the infinite stories beyond his doorstep. In his editorial work on travelogues or the *Bibliothèque orientale*, or his translations from the Qur'an and of a history of coffee, Galland preferred to let the work speak for itself. His writings over the decades do not suggest the voice of an emerging storyteller capable of providing psychological depth to the protagonists of the *Nights*.

Viewed against the labors of the French Orientalist, Diyāb's *Book of Travels* offers more convincing evidence of a narrator immersed in the lore of storytelling and attuned to the power of a carefully constructed fiction. Despite the fifty-year gap between Diyāb's journey to Paris and the production of the travelogue, the figure of Paul Lucas casts a long shadow over the tale it contains. Lucas was himself the author of popular French travelogues.[228] His quest for treasures and curiosities for the French court determined the itinerary of Diyāb's travels from Aleppo to Paris,[229] and his penchant for the marvelous resonates with both *The Book of Travels* and the stories Diyāb would contribute to the *Nights* in Paris. Lucas's journeys through the Mediterranean to Egypt, Constantinople, and Persia were not connected to any practice of scientific inquiry. He was neither a geographer nor an archaeologist, and he had no training in ancient or foreign languages. In essence, he was an old-fashioned treasure hunter with an insatiable appetite for precious objects and fantastic stories. The son of a merchant from Rouen, he had made his reputation traveling through the Mediterranean and Ottoman world to procure precious stones, medals, and manuscripts for his patrons at the court of Louis XIV. Drawing on the conventions of the French picaresque novel, Lucas styled himself in the mode of a fictional character. In his third travelogue, he declares, "Nothing resembles more the life of errant knights than the life of travelers, and the situation I found myself this night, and where I have found myself a hundred times, reminds me of the pleasant notions of Don Quixote de la Mancha." The travelogues he produced from these journeys were full of exotic landscapes, marvelous objects, and fantastic adventures, and could include sketches of entire cities that Lucas had never visited, including Mecca and Medina.[230]

When in 1707 Diyāb met Lucas in a caravan departing from Aleppo, he attached himself to a master who believed that fantastical tales were no less valuable than precious artifacts. For Lucas, travelers who sought to know the essence of a foreign culture needed to seek out the folktales and legends that circulated among the common people. Having lost his last interpreter, and unable to communicate with the leader of the caravan out of Aleppo, Lucas was in need of Diyāb's linguistic skills. Traveling with Lucas through the Mediterranean and on to Paris, Diyāb would have played a critical role in the gathering of marvelous tales and the objects with which they were associated. In his account of their time together, Diyāb captures the power of personality that Lucas brought to his pursuit of the treasures and curiosities he gathered on commission from the French crown. Aware of the lies and ruses Lucas used to navigate these uncertain territories and to acquire items with little concern for the destruction this caused, Diyāb is still willing to trust the Frenchmen enough to follow him to Paris in the hope of securing a position for himself at the royal court.

Beyond the interest in precious objects that drove Lucas's and Diyāb's travels together, the two men shared an abiding interest in tales of miracles and magic. In the Levant and throughout the journey to Paris, Diyāb's experiences were shaped by Lucas's preference for traveling with priests and relying on a network of religious sanctuaries.[231] Lucas possessed a genuine interest in the material remains of the Christian past in Cairo. He and Diyāb together visited the site where the Holy Family was said to have taken refuge, and both describe it in their respective travelogues. In Greece, Lucas was fascinated by the Christian marvels of the Orthodox Church, and he shared Diyāb's interest in the material culture of Marian devotion.[232] Diyāb's *Book of Travels* parallels these interests in recounting an intense religious experience in Tunis and in recording the many miracles associated with the Blessed Virgin of the Black Mountains.

Diyāb also incorporates episodes of miraculous healing into his travelogue—healing effected by the marvelous power of amulets and secret potions or the intercession of the Virgin herself. Similar motifs appear in the tales Diyāb told Galland, most notably in "Prince Aḥmad and the Fairy Perī Bānū," where the princess is healed by a magic apple that can cure any illness. The supernatural power of the elixir of life contained in the philosopher's stone, and wielded by Lucas himself, is dramatized in stories included in the travelogues of both men. Lucas spins a wild tale of finding the secret of the philosopher's stone by meeting with an Uzbek dervish in Anatolia and retracing the steps of Nicolas Flamel in Paris. Diyāb recounts the use of the elixir to save the life of a desperately ill Lucas during a stop on their journey in Tunis. Such fantastical tales were part of the storytelling repertoire of magic, medicine, and miracle that were shared by Diyāb and his French master for the critical months during which they journeyed to Paris.[233]

One might justly ask how much this common enthusiasm for marvels both natural and material would have informed Diyāb's storytelling preferences after he arrived in Paris and found an avid listener in Antoine Galland. After a journey of many months, Diyāb would certainly have gained a sense of the kinds of stories that would attract a French collector of curiosities. In his *Book of Travels*, he recalls paying meticulous attention to Lucas's note-taking as he accumulated the observations and anecdotes that would go into his own popular travelogues. Even if his personal preferences had not run parallel to those of Lucas and the growing reading public clamoring for more stories in the mode of the *Nights*, Diyāb would have been well prepared to deliver tales of marvels to the French translator who asked him for stories.

An examination of Diyāb's narrative of his experiences during the year and a half of his journey with Lucas before his encounter with Galland in Paris allows us to speculate about how they might have shaped specific elements within the stories that were later circulated through versions of the *Nights*. The resemblance of the magician from "Aladdin and the Wonderful Lamp" to Lucas, also noted by Bernard Heyberger,[234] leads me to further specify ways in which this story parallels elements of Diyāb's putative memoir.[235] Both "Aladdin" and *The Book of Travels* relate a tale of youthful adventure and feature a young man bred in the streets of a mercantile center. If Aladdin is too lazy to learn his father's trade as a tailor, Diyāb makes a more conscious decision to depart from the path of his brothers. Both young men are shaped by an absent father (dead in the case of Aladdin and presumed dead in the case of Diyāb) and a melancholic mother. In both stories, the youth falls under the sway of a mysterious father figure, a man in possession of magical objects or abilities. And Lucas, I would add, was taken in his travels in the Levant for a magician. Just as the Maghrebi magician enlists Aladdin in his quest for riches, Diyāb is drawn in to Lucas's quest for marvelous objects and stories with the promise that he would secure him a royal appointment to the library of Arabic manuscripts. Just as Aladdin wields the power of the magician's ring and discovers the jinni of the lamp, Diyāb relates tales of Lucas's amulets that can heal and speaks of the miraculous power of his philosopher's stone. Though Diyāb's tale of his younger self offers the doubled vision of an older narrator and a stronger note of skepticism, he has constructed it using a classic narrative pattern visible also in the tales he told Galland.

The self-fashioning that speaks to the "modernity" of the Diyāb-Galland tales is evident in Diyāb's portrait of Lucas. *The Book of Travels* is filled with moments that highlight the performative aspect of the French traveler's authority on the journey. At their first meeting, Lucas is traveling in his favored disguise of a physician. After one of the caravan's first stops on the road to Tripoli, his declaration that two skulls near the ruins of an old church and convent must belong to ancient kings has no grounding in any archaeological procedure. When he recruits a young goatherd to lower himself into a small cave to retrieve a ring and a lamp, Lucas resembles a tomb raider rather than a scholar. Such masquerades are as much a part of the story of Aladdin as the pursuit of fabulous riches and the use of magical objects. Diyāb, like Aladdin, would follow his roguish father figure in spite of his skepticism about his credentials and intentions. While it may be too much to imagine that Diyāb saw himself in the figure of Aladdin, the story of his travels with Lucas contains thematic parallels that may be the work of a shared creator. Both stories contain the marvelous motifs of supernatural and precious objects associated with the tales added to the *Nights*, and issues of identity that have been perceived as modern. In *The Book of Travels*, Diyāb explores the possibilities of cultivating a new identity on the model of Lucas, and himself assumes the guise of a physician on his return journey to Aleppo. For his part, Aladdin will slowly grow into the new persona created artificially through the power of the jinni of the lamp—a young man at last worthy of the trappings of wealth and power.

As *The Book of Travels* moves on to chronicle Diyāb's experiences in Paris and his visit to the Palace of Versailles, it offers an even more powerful riposte to those who seek to attribute the marvels of the added *Nights* stories solely to Galland.[236] In the travelogue, Diyāb evokes the grand spectacle of elaborate ritual and excessive luxury that accompanied his presentation to King Louis XIV. His descriptions of the radiant beauty and luxurious attire of the ladies of Versailles are reminiscent of the descriptions of the princesses in the tales of "Aladdin" and "Prince Aḥmad." An encounter in the palace with a lovely woman wearing a diadem studded with diamonds, rubies, emeralds, and other precious stones leaves Diyāb convinced he has encountered the king's daughter. Such details will recur in the tale of Prince Aḥmad when the titular character meets the fairy princess Perī Bānū emerging from her palace, adorned with jewels.[237] In describing her throne, Diyāb will use the same list of precious stones that appears in *The Book of Travels* decades later.[238] The women of Louis XIV's court may have appeared marvelous enough to inspire the description of a fairy princess in a tale later spun for Galland. Yet it is just as likely that these are stock phrases that signal Diyāb's attempt in both instances to capture the splendor and wealth of a marvelous realm. Diyāb's fascination with the rapid construction and excessive luxury of the Palace of Versailles is another clear link to the stress on magnificent material settings in the stories he related to Galland. Given the elaborate description of Versailles's gardens and glittering dome, it is unlikely that a French Orientalist scholar was needed to make Diyāb's tales more appealing to readers hungry for the wonders of the *Nights*.

The notes Galland jotted down during Diyāb's 1709 performance of his "beautiful" tales provide evidence of the Syrian storyteller's gift for combining old elements to form new tales half a century before he displayed the same skill in *The Book of Travels*. Three centuries later, literary historians are finally beginning to understand that the tales Diyāb gave Galland are not "orphan tales," as defined by the absence of an Arabic manuscript source, but rather "Diyāb's tales,"[239] the work of a gifted and curious young man who continued to exercise his narrative skills throughout his life. We also need to reevaluate how our underlying assumptions about the "modern" and the "marvelous" have been shaped. In seeking to identify what differentiates the Diyāb-Galland tales from the rest of the stories in the *Nights*, critics have failed to disentangle the marvelous from associations with the fabulous luxuries of the Arab world, or to decouple modernity from images of a literary Paris.

Beyond Galland's presumed modern sensibility, Diyāb's own fascinating journey through the Mediterranean in Lucas's service and his explorations of the spectacular facades and social mores of Paris and Versailles demonstrate a sophisticated narrative command. At the level of storytelling and technique, we cannot limit our understanding of Diyāb's contribution to new tales included in Galland's *Nights* to the conveying of a repository of marvels or recombining of folktales. Nor should we limit it to the possible imprint of autobiographical experiences. In light of *The Book of Travels*, Diyāb is equally likely to have contributed to the inner monologues and self-reflection that mark out the new added tales from those of the original story collection. The added tales have been seen as essentially French, but as we reflect upon the author that emerges from *The Book of Travels*, we may learn to read them as the product of a more complex Syrian-French genesis—shaped as much by Ḥannā Diyāb as by Antoine Galland.

Notes

1   The first five folios of the manuscript are lost. The extant text begins in the middle of an account of the monastery of Saint Elishaʿ, in the Kadisha Valley of northern Lebanon, to which Diyāb and some friends have traveled from Aleppo to join the Maronite monastic order. The first folios may have contained a table of contents, like the one in Ilyās al-Mawṣilī's *Kitāb al-Siyāḥah*, of which Ḥannā Diyāb owned a copy.

2   Fahmé-Thiéry et al. suggest that the steward is Tūmā al-Labbūdī, a member of Diyāb's family who is known to have been at the monastery at the same time and who in 1711 succeeded Jirmānūs Farḥāt as the monastery's superior (Diyāb, *D'Alep à Paris*, 54n1). However, that Tūmā dates his first monastic experience to August 1706 (al-Labbūdī, "Sīrat Al-Ḥibr aṭ-Ṭayyib al-dhikr ʿAbdallāh Qarāʿalī al-Marūnī al-Ḥalabī," 82). Since he became a novice around the same time as Ḥannā Diyāb, he cannot be the steward referred to here.

3   This curious expression may allude to the baggy outer garment that lemon sellers use to hold their wares.

4   This is likely Yūsuf ibn Shāhīn Çelebi, who is listed among the three Aleppans who leave the monastery with Diyāb (see folio 6v). A certain Ilyās ibn Abū Yūsuf Shāhīn from Aleppo (who might be the brother of the abovementioned) is to be found among the students of the Maronite college in Rome in 1711 (Gemayel, *Les échanges culturels entre les Maronites et l'Europe*, 121).

5   *Labneh*, a cheese made of strained yogurt. This word is obscured by a stamp in the manuscript; it may have read *jibneh* (cheese).

6 At this point in the narrative, there is a shift of tense from perfect to imperfect, as Diyāb begins to recount the day-to-day routine of monastic life, rather than the events of a specific day.

7 *Dīwānkhāna* is a term used throughout the Islamicate world, variously denoting an audience hall, sitting room, or guest quarters. Diyāb uses it mostly to refer to outdoor seating areas meant for social gatherings and recreation.

8 The evening and night prayers, respectively.

9 The midday prayer.

10 Jirmānūs Jibrīl Farḥāt (d. 1732) was the abbot during Diyāb's stay at the monastery of Saint Elishaʿ.

11 A reference to the biblical Parable of the Workers in the Vineyard (Matthew 20:1–16).

12 Maronite monks were forbidden to consume animal fat, as they were in general not allowed to eat meat. They were also permitted to travel only in pairs and with the abbot's permission. See "Qawanīn al-Ruhbāniyyah al-Lubnāniyya," 195 and 198. The following sentence is struck out in the manuscript: "I've ordered Brother Mūsā to put you on the mule when you get to Bsharrī, so do so and obey his commands along the route."

13 The term *rās al-nahr* (riverhead) may refer to the source of the Kadisha River, where the monastery of Saint Sergius (Dayr Mār Sarkīs, also known as Dayr Rās al-Nahr) is located. It is a six-mile walk from the monastery where Diyāb was staying.

14 Jirmānūs Farḥāt mentions the harm done to the monastery by the Ḥamādah, a tribe that gained authority under Ottoman rule over the northern area of Lebanon as tax collectors, during their tenure as governors of the Bsharrī district ("Tārīkh Taʾsīs al-Rahbāniyyah al-Lubnāniyyah," 129). Maronite families cooperated with them, but later portrayed them as oppressors as part of an effort to foster ties with the French as a new protecting force (see Winter, "Shiite Emirs and Ottoman Authorities: The Campaign against the Hamadas of Mt Lebanon, 1693–1694," 216ff.).

15 Jirmānūs Farḥāt, in his "Tarīkh Taʾsīs" (128–29), interprets the crowding of Saint Elishaʿ as a trial for the young order, but in Diyāb's account he appears concerned about the opposite problem: the loss of novices from the monastery.

16 ʿAbdallāh Qarāʿalī (1672–1742), one of the three founders of the Lebanese Maronite order in 1695, was indeed the superior general of the Lebanese Maronite order, but happened to be absent during Diyāb's stay, as he was involved in opening the monastery of Yuḥannā Rashīma. His biographer mentions the superior's return in late 1706, which may be the moment Diyāb is referring to here.

17 Aforementioned in the lost opening folios of the manuscript.

18 Given Rémuzat's hostile reaction to Diyāb's return, it may be that he had advised him not to leave Aleppo to join the monastery in Lebanon. This encounter is likely also described in the lost folios.

19 The prayer to which Diyāb refers is not the Christian morning prayer that he observed at the monastery but rather the Muslim call to prayer at dawn (ṣalāt al-fajr), which was preceded by a recitation (salām). See Barthélemy, Dictionnaire, 354.

20 Diyāb variously refers to Louis XIV as *sulṭān Frānsā* and *malik Frānsā*, which we have rendered as "sultan of France" and "king of France," respectively. While it may be argued that Diyāb uses the words *sulṭān* and *malik* interchangeably, *sulṭān Frānsā* nicely conjures a juxtaposition with the Ottoman sultan. Whether this was consciously intended by Diyāb is impossible to say; nonetheless, we have elected to preserve the distinction between the two words.

21 A monument located to the west of the al-Fayḍ neighborhood, in the western suburbs of Aleppo.

22 A reference to the Royal Library in Paris, which began collecting Arabic, Persian, and Turkish manuscripts in the seventeenth century.

23 This must be one of the many Byzantine "dead cities" of northwestern Syria. Around the village of Sarmadā on Mount Barīshā, about a day's ride north of Kaftīn, are the remains of a Roman temple, several tombs, and a Byzantine monastery, among other sites. See Mattern,

A travers les villes mortes de Haute Syrie. Promenades archéologiques en 1928, 1929, 1931, 118–19.

24   *Abū kalb* or *ebu kalb* was the name given to a type of Dutch coin (Pamuk, *A Monetary History of the Ottoman Empire*, 99).

25   Bernard Heyberger (introduction to Dyab, *D'Alep à Paris*) points out several intriguing similarities between Ḥannā Diyāb's account of this episode and the tale of Aladdin, which Diyāb would later tell Antoine Galland. The sequence of events is significant: A young person sets off on a voyage with a stranger, someone climbs down into a cave, and a ring and a lamp are discovered in a subterranean setting. Paul Lucas includes a report of these same events in his account of his later travels through Syria (Lucas, *Troisième Voyage*, 109–10). In his *Deuxième Voyage* (164), he describes the trip from Aleppo to Tripoli as having taken place between March 24 and April 6, 1707.

26   According to Lucas's *Deuxième Voyage* (164–85), the stage recounted in this chapter took place between the beginning of April and June 9, 1707. Lucas records that they left Tripoli for Beirut on April 6.

27   Fahmé-Thiéry et al. suggest that this is Gio Battista del Giudice, called Shidyāq Ḥannā al-Muḥāsib in Arabic (Diyāb, *D'Alep à Paris*, 75). He belonged to the well-known Khāzin family. He bore the title of *cavaliere/chevalier* ("knight") by 1701.

28   Christians under Ottoman rule typically wore blue turbans, but certain semiautonomous cities, including Beirut, which at the time was controlled by Maronite notables from the Khāzin clans, had less severe sartorial restrictions. The white turban was usually reserved for Muslims, and the green was the exclusive preserve of those who claimed descent from the Prophet Muḥammad.

29   An *īwān* is a near-universal feature of Islamicate architecture, a three-walled room whose fourth wall opens onto the exterior.

30   The *mīrī* was a tax to be paid on all land owned by the Ottoman sovereign (see Inalcik, *An Economic and Social History of the Ottoman Empire, 1300–1914*, 103–18) which in the seventeenth century the Khāzin family collected in Kisrawān.

31 A *ma'ṣarānī* is an artisan who extracts the oil from sesame seeds (Barthélemy, *Dictionnaire*, 533).

32 In this instance, the *thulth* ("third") is probably equivalent to an *akçe*, a silver coin.

33 A *miṣriyyah* ("Egyptian") was a coin of Egyptian origin normally worth one-fortieth of a piaster, or half a piece of silver.

34 The signet ring of the biblical King Solomon is known as the Seal of Solomon. In the legends about Solomon that developed in later Jewish, Christian, and Muslim cultures, the ring was associated with magical powers that allowed Solomon to control demons and speak to animals. In the Arabic-speaking world, the Seal of Solomon is typically represented by a six-pointed star and commonly used as an amulet.

35 Lucas (*Deuxième Voyage*, 180) recounts his wanderings through this area later, after his return from Jerusalem. He mentions visiting a cedar forest planted by the famous prince Fakhr al-Dīn al-Ma'nī, as well as the Druze princes' residence (evidently Dayr al-Qamar), and the village of 'Abāy (spelled "Abeie"), which he situates in the region of Kisrawān. As used by Diyāb and Lucas, the expression "Druze mountains" means the region between Beirut and Sidon inhabited by Druze clans. It was thus more extensive than the Chouf district of present-day Lebanon.

36 Diyāb refers to these friars as *al-Sakalant*, a reference to the Zoccolanti ("sandal wearers"), a branch of the Franciscan Order of Friars Minor.

37 Lucas recounts that his trip to Jerusalem took place between April 12 and May 6, 1707 (*Deuxième Voyage*, 165–79).

38 According to Lucas, both travelers stayed together in Sidon between June 3 and 9, 1707, before finally embarking on a ship to Cyprus (*Deuxième Voyage*, 179–85).

39 According to Paul Lucas (*Deuxième Voyage*, 185–86), the events recounted in this chapter took place between June 9 and July 9, 1707.

40 This individual was probably Antonio Callimeri, who belonged to a well-known Cypriot family (Diyāb, *D'Alep à Paris*, 87n2). There is no mention of him in Paul Lucas's travelogues.

41   İnalcik, "A Note on the Population of Cyprus," explains that after the Ottoman conquest of the island many Anatolians married Christian women in Cyprus. The Ottomans, for reasons of taxation, did not encourage conversion to Islam.

42   This building is very likely the former Hagia Sophia church of Nicosia, which the Ottomans had turned into the Selimiye Mosque in 1571. Thomas S. R. Boase ("Ecclesiastical Art," 170) mentions a 1948 renovation of the porch that uncovered an undamaged voussoir sculpture under the plaster.

43   This is Diyāb's first encounter during his travels with unveiled women in public, an experience he will have several times, and will continue to remark upon.

44   Jennings, *Christians and Muslims in Ottoman Cyprus and the Mediterranean World, 1571–1640*, 160–61, notes that trading wine in Cyprus was usually permitted.

45   According to Paul Lucas, *Deuxième Voyage*, 186–207, the events recounted in this chapter took place between July 10 and October 27, 1707. The French translation (Diyāb, *D'Alep à Paris*, 95n1), with reference to Martin, "Souvenirs," 472, suggests that Ḥannā Diyāb's dating may be more accurate, as he or Lucas would by then have noticed, as they traveled southward, the rise in the levels of the Nile that took place in Cairo as early as mid-July.

46   Diyāb opposes the notion of *maḥabbah* ("charity") with the *ẓulm* ("oppressive conditions") he encountered in Cyprus and for which he blames the Greek population. After centuries of Venetian rule over the island, the Greeks reestablished dominance over the Latin denominations by confiscating Maronite churches and forcing Maronites to obey the Orthodox authorities.

47   In seventeenth- through nineteenth-century Aleppo, a *qinṭār* might have weighed between 487 and 564 kilograms.

48   Maurice Martin mentions this monument, the Cleopatra obelisk, in his "Souvenirs," 472. Lucas refers to it as *l'aiguille de Cléopâtre* (Cleopatra's needle). Lucas has a drawing of it in his *Troisième Voyage*, 137.

49 Note that there is another place called the Cave of the Slave, encountered later in the travelogue, when Diyāb returns to Aleppo.

50 Until the early nineteenth century, hundreds of these deep underground water reservoirs still existed in Alexandria. They were probably built during the Ptolemaic or early Roman period, and partially rebuilt and restored during the Islamic period (McKenzie, *The Architecture of Alexandria and Egypt, 300 B.C. to A.D. 700*, 220). Lucas mentions them in his *Premier Voyage du Sieur Paul Lucas dans le Levant*, 52.

51 It is unclear where Diyāb may have encountered this kind of astrological lore.

52 According to Lucas, *Premier Voyage*, 53, who calls it a *germe*, this was a small, flat boat that was uncovered and had a single large sail.

53 Rosetta and Damietta, at the western and eastern ends of the Nile Delta, respectively, are each about one hundred miles away from Cairo.

54 This merchant is also mentioned in Lucas, *Deuxième Voyage*, 207.

55 Whereas Diyāb recounts a longer stay in Cairo before the visit south to Fayoum, Lucas reports that they spent a longer time in Cairo on their return north to the Mediterranean (*Deuxième Voyage*, 198–207).

56 The Church of the Virgin of the Pot of Basil (*Qaṣriyyat al-Rīḥān*), as deduced by Fahmé-Thiéry et al. in Diyāb, *D'Alep à Paris*, 106n2, is one of the oldest church foundations in the old city.

57 Matthew 2:13–23. Diyāb must be referring to the crypt below the Abu Serga church (the Church of Saints Sergius and Bacchus), parts of which are dated to the tenth century (Davidson and Gitlitz, *Pilgrimage*, 3). It is situated beside the Church of the Virgin of the Pot of Basil.

58 According to one explanation current in the Middle Ages, the famous pyramids of Giza, which stand some seven miles away from Old Cairo, were the granaries built by the patriarch Joseph to save Egypt from famine. Here, though, Diyāb is apparently describing a ruined structure in Old Cairo; cf. the account by the French traveler Antoine Morison, who visited in 1704 (*Relation*, 154).

59 Estrangelo is the oldest form of the Syriac alphabet.

60 The *ʿashrāwī* is a dromedary that can survive for ten days at a time without drinking water.

61 Fahmé-Thiéry et al. have identified this figure as Giovanni Battista della Fratta, a controversial healer and missionary who had been living in Fayoum since 1688 (Diyāb, *D'Alep à Paris*, 115n3 and 127nn1–2).

62 While he does not specify their religion, the distinction that Diyāb makes between the peasants and the Copts suggests that the former were either Muslims or practiced a form of religion unfamiliar to Diyāb.

63 A type of reed used in the manufacture of mats.

64 Diyāb may be drawing a distinction here between the areas of Lucas's expertise, such as medicine, that he believed rubbed off on him, and those that did not.

65 Diyāb repeatedly mentions his mother's melancholy and Lucas's successful attempt to treat it.

66 Today, *kazan kebabı* designates a meat dish prepared in a sort of cauldron.

67 This is the ancient obelisk of Begig, which the seventeenth-century British traveler E. W. Pococke describes in detail, noting that it was forty feet tall (*A Description of the East and Some Other Countries*, 59–60).

68 Lucas recounts this adventure differently. See *Deuxième Voyage*, 193.

69 Diyāb calls the vermin *qamal*, usually "lice." His description, however, suggests a different insect.

70 "Tripoli of the West" is the city of Tripoli in present-day Libya, as opposed to the city of the same name in Lebanon.

71 A reference to the War of the Spanish Succession (1701–14), which pitted the Bourbons of France and Spain against the Grand Alliance of the Holy Roman Empire, Great Britain, the Dutch Republic, and the Spanish Habsburgs.

72 According to Lucas's *Deuxième Voyage*, 207–20, this part of the trip took place between October 27, 1707, and June 4, 1708.

73 The Gulf of Sidra is formed by the contours of the northern coast of Libya. It extends over 100 miles inland and is over 250 miles wide.

74 Diyāb appears to be describing a waterspout.

75 *Qaṣb* (usually *qasb*) is a type of dried date.

76 Paul Lucas does not seem to be part of this excursion in Diyāb's account (cf. *Deuxième Voyage*, 208).

77 In his *Deuxième Voyage*, 208, Lucas writes that the passengers ate dates until their arrival in Tripoli on December 10, 1707, after thirty-four days of sea travel.

78 Diyāb uses the cryptic term *al-aḍāt* (elsewhere *al-aḍāwāt*) to refer to an administrative district of the Ottoman Empire known as the Province of the Islands, which comprised most of the islands of the Ottoman-controlled Mediterranean.

79 The spahis (from Turk. *sipāhī*), in the Ottoman Empire, were feudal cavalrymen paid with land grants.

80 The literal meaning of the phrase Diyāb uses here (*twaḍḍayt bi-l-ḥalīb*) is "I performed my ablutions with milk," a colorful expression suggesting that he had to use milk to hide his flushed appearance.

81 The "Tower of Skulls" (*Burj al-ru'ūs*) was built in the mid-sixteenth century. It stood until 1848, when it was torn down by the ruler of Tunis, Aḥmad Bey, and replaced with a memorial.

82 The French translators suggest that Diyāb uses the word "Ismāʿīlīs" to refer to Muslims in general, not just to members of the Ismāʿīlī sect (see Diyāb, *D'Alep à Paris*, 161n2). This seems doubtful, as the term does not appear elsewhere in the travelogue.

83 Diyāb here refers to the catastrophic defeat of the naval forces of the Holy League, led by Philip II of Spain, by the Ottoman fleet at Djerba in May of 1560. Philip's forces had seized and fortified Djerba earlier that year, as part of a strategy to wrest control of the southern Mediterranean coast from the Ottoman navy.

84 The term for "heretics" here (*arfāḍ*, sing. *rāfiḍī*; literally "rejectionists") is a derogatory label used by some Sunnis to designate various Shiite sects.

85 This thermal bath is located in present-day Ḥammām al-Anf, on the way from Tunis to al-Ḥammāmāt, which the two travelers passed through as well. Lucas transliterates the town's name as "Mamelif" and, like Diyāb, describes the healing power of the water (see his

Deuxième Voyage, 219–20). Contrary to what Diyāb says, however, Lucas claims to have actually taken a bath, albeit with difficulty.

86　According to Lucas, the travelers arrived in Tunis after February 21, 1708 (*Deuxième Voyage*, 219–20).

87　The Bardo was the palace of the Ḥafsid dynasty (1229–1574), which was restored as a royal court by the Murādī beys in the middle of the seventeenth century.

88　The four major monastic orders at this time were the Benedictines, the Carthusians, the Cistercians, and the Cluniacs, but not all of these had a significant presence in North Africa or the Near East. Diyāb may have had in mind, instead, mendicant orders such as the Dominicans or Franciscans.

89　In spite of the hour and a half it took for Diyāb and Lucas to travel to the palace, the distance between Bardo and the city is only a little over a mile as the crow flies.

90　The animals are jerboas, a desert rodent found across Asia and northern Africa. These animals would come to play an important role in Diyāb's story.

91　In other words, the hunter catches the jerboa by plugging up its burrow so the animal cannot retreat into it any farther than the length of the hunter's arm.

92　On Jesuit devotional practices, see the helpful note in Diyāb, *D'Alep à Paris*, 179n2; see also Heyberger, *Les chrétiens*, 358–70.

93　Paul Lucas was actually only forty-three years old at this time, not sixty, as Diyāb supposed.

94　The harbor to which Diyāb refers here was probably not Carthage but La Goulette, the port of Tunis at the time (see Diyāb, *D'Alep à Paris*, 186n3).

95　As argued by Fahmé-Thiéry et al. (Diyāb, *D'Alep à Paris*, 190n), the word *mīnā* must be Diyāb's transliteration of the Lingua Franca *maina* ("lower away!"), the imperative of *mainar* ("to lower a sail"; cf. the obsolete English "amain"). "The word is Pan-Mediterranean . . . the filiation of meanings is 'to lower'; 'to surrender' (from 'to lower flag or sails in sign of surrender'), as an exclamation of 'mercy!'" (Kahane et al., *Lingua Franca*, 279–82).

96 For Lucas's account of this episode, see *Deuxième Voyage*, 222–24.

97 A lazaretto is another term for a quarantine station.

98 In addition to Seals of Solomon, certain gemstones, including a few varieties of agate, are referred to by the name *sulaymānī*.

99 Swollen lymph nodes in the groin and armpits were a well-known symptom of the bubonic plague.

100 Livorno was the principal port through which coffee was introduced to Europe, beginning in 1632 (Diyāb, *D'Alep à Paris*, 203n2).

101 The term *ghaṭā* refers to a wrap made of silk, cotton, or satin, attaching at the waist with a corded belt, and used by Syrian women to cover their head and back (see Barthélemy, *Dictionnaire*, 578.) A *sitār* is a general term for a veil, screen, or covering.

102 Diyāb uses two different terms (*ḥijāb* and *sitār*) to refer to the veil. The former may designate a specific item of clothing while the latter indicates the more general practice of veiling.

103 A *khimār* is a veil that covers the bottom half of the face but not the eyes.

104 The buried-alive motif was both popular and a source of anxiety in eighteenth-century Europe (Brendnich, "Frau," 200). Diyāb recounts it in the stolen-ring version known from fifteenth-century Cologne (Bolte, "Die Sage von der erweckten Scheintoten," 356–57), adding a semi-scientific explanation for it.

105 When a cannon was not in use, its touchhole—which provided access to the powder charge—was protected from seawater, debris, and accidental ignition with a lead apron.

106 The term *kīs* may refer, generically, to a sack or purse. In this instance, however, it also designates a specific amount of money, equivalent to five hundred piasters (see Barthélemy, *Dictionnaire*, 735).

107 Addobbati draws parallels between Diyāb's tale and, among others, the novella of the *Three Rings* (*Tre anelli*) from Boccaccio's *Decameron*, which begins with a similar confrontation between a Jewish merchant and a sovereign (*Il mercante*, 834–36).

108 A reference to the Santuario della Madonna di Montenero, in the hills outside Livorno.

109   Diyāb recounts here the well-known foundational story of the Santuario, involving a lowly shepherd finding an icon of Mary between
the rocks of the Montenero (see Gagliardi, "'Ave maris Stella': Il santuario mariano di Montenero presso Livorno," 196), to which he adds
the popular motif of the returning icon. Ilyās al-Mawṣilī invokes the
same motif when describing the founding the Church of the Virgin
Mary of Quinche in Ecuador (Matar, *Lands of the Christians*, 65–66);
instead of a shepherd, it is a Native American who finds the icon three
times in the same place. Diyāb's contemporary, the Aleppan bishop
Arsāniyūs ibn Shukrī (ms Gotha arab. 1549, 193r) mentions a reap-
pearing cross in the northern Spanish town of Burgos.

110   Note that Diyāb says that this area (the poop deck) was located at the
front of the ship, but in all likelihood it would have been at the rear.

111   The legendary association of Mary Magdalene with the city of Marseille, established as early as the thirteenth century, appears as part
of the story of Mary Magdalene (Maryam al-Majdaliyyah as in Diyāb's
book, or "al-Majdalāniyyah") in the hagiographic collection that
Ḥannā Diyāb owned (*Akhbār*, vol. 3, fol. 51v).

112   The cave is the Grotte de Sainte-Baume, some twenty-five miles outside of Marseille. Merling is a type of fish.

113   Diyāb is describing a "Way of the Cross" (*via crucis*), a series of depic-
tions of the suffering of Jesus Christ on the day of his crucifixion.
Worshippers follow the path from one station to the next, contem-
plating the trials of Jesus as a form of spiritual pilgrimage.

114   A reference to the Garden of Gethsemane, at the base of the Mount of
Olives, where Jesus went to pray following the Last Supper.

115   Bonifay, Roux, Samatan, Rémuzat, and Rimbaud were sons of rich and
influential merchant families in Marseille, and most were French deputies in Aleppo between 1698 and 1724. For details about them and the
others, see Teissier, ed., *Inventaire des archives historiques de la Chambre de Commerce de Marseille*, 182–83, and Diyāb, *D'Alep à Paris*, 248n2.

116   The region of Provence was incorporated into the French realm
in 1486, but its cities remained resistant to the Bourbon monarchy
through much of the seventeenth century. Diyāb's assumption that

Provence was a region separate from France suggests that the process of incorporation remained, to an extent, incomplete.

117 Diyāb makes an error in dating here, recording the year as 1709 rather than 1708. Various events described much later in the text (such as the Great Frost) took place well before March 1709. Lucas gives June 29 as the date of their departure from Genoa and July 1708 as the date of their arrival (*Deuxième Voyage*, 224).

118 Diyāb appears to be conflating two French cities: Aix-en-Provence, a city of jurists; and Avignon, with historic ties to the papacy. The Provençal name of Aix is very similar to Diyāb's "Āzāy." See further Diyāb, *D'Alep à Paris*, 251n1.

119 This is the Astronomical Clock of Lyon, which remains in the Cathédrale Saint-Jean to this day. The presence of an astronomical clock there was documented in the fourteenth century.

120 The sentence beginning "Below the dome . . ." is in the margin of the text. The final word is unreadable.

121 Apparently the Pont Saint-Esprit, which connects Provence with Languedoc, hence "the interior of France." It is, however, approximately 125 miles south of Lyon. It must have been after leaving Avignon, not Lyon, that the travelers crossed the Rhône.

122 Evidently a porcelain *verrière* or *refraichissoire*, a receptacle used to keep bottles and glasses cool.

123 Diyāb's dating implies that the travelers left Provence some time before they stayed at this particular inn. This is another indication that he has confused the order of events.

124 This section is not numbered in the manuscript, nor is it called a chapter. There is, however, an indentation in the text block, which suggests a break in the narrative.

125 Correcting Diyāb's February 1709, which is inaccurate, just as it was at the beginning of Chapter 8. Based on the report Lucas made upon his return (Omont, *Missions archéologiques*, 347), it seems the pair arrived in Paris on October 25, 1708.

126 Diyāb refers here to several jerboas that Paul Lucas acquired during the North African leg of their voyage. See §5.109–10.

127 That is, slate.

128 This word is illegible, but is likely *al-ṣayd* ("the hunt").

129 In *Deuxième Voyage*, 198, Lucas claims he had brought seven of these animals from the town of Fayoum.

130 It was through Diyāb's mediation that *jarbū*ʿ, the Arabic word for *jerboa*, entered the French lexicon (Elie Kallas, "Gerboise: L'entrée du terme arabe ğerbūʿ à la cour de Louis XIV").

131 This view on the history of the sect gained currency among renowned Maronite clerics and historians beginning in the fifteenth century. This does not mean that Lucas did not say what is attributed to him: He may have simply been repeating something that Diyāb (or other Maronites) had told him.

132 In fact, she was the wife of Louis XIV's grandson, Louis le Petit Dauphin.

133 The word shouted by the princess may have been *turc*, as this was the common French designation for Muslims at the time.

134 The princess referred to here is Françoise Marie de Bourbon, one of Louis XIV's illegitimate children. Her governess, the future Madame de Maintenon, would become Louis's second wife.

135 Following this point, the narrative appears to shift to Diyāb's voice rather than Lucas's.

136 Diyāb here describes the Machine de Marly, a hydraulic system built between 1681 and 1685 to supply water to the Palace of Versailles from the River Seine. The engineer, Arnold de Ville, in reality obtained the task by competition (Thompson, *The Sun King's Garden: Louis XIV, André le Nôtre and the Creation of the Garden of Versailles*, 247ff.).

137 The Bosquet du Marais, commissioned in 1688, contained a fountain shaped like "a bronze tree with tin leaves that sent forth water from the tips of its branches" (Thompson, *The Sun King's Garden*, 157–58). The bosquet was destroyed in 1705, a few years before Diyāb arrived in Versailles, but similar tinworks may have existed elsewhere on the grounds.

138 By the 1680s, Louis XIV had indeed completed the transfer of his chief residence to Versailles, though the reason was not his illicit marriage to Françoise d'Aubigné, marquise de Maintenon.

139   The marriage was a secret one, as the marquise was the king's second wife.

140   We were not able to identify this trompe l'oeil painting.

141   The motif of drawing a fly on the portrait to dupe other artists is a legend known from the life of Giotto di Bondone, who tricked his master Cimabue as recounted in Vasari, *Lives*, 35. It appears as international tale type H.504.1.1 in the Aarne-Thompson Index.

142   On this episode see Nicholas Dew, *Orientalism in Louis XIV's France*, 1–3. His source is Antoine Galland, who records the incident in his journals.

143   The inscription is the *shahādah*, the Muslim profession of faith: "There is no god but God, Muhammad is the Messenger of God."

144   This is Christofalo (Christophe) Maunier, who was one of Antoine Galland's competitors for the position of professor of Arabic at the Collège royal; see Galland, *Journal*, vol. 1, 256n256 and 266n282.

145   Diyāb mistakes the word *hôtel* (hotel, hostel) for *autel* (altar).

146   Louis XIV established juvenile detention centers (*maisons de correction*) in the late seventeenth century at the hospitals of Bicêtre and La Salpêtrière. See Gossard, "Breaking a Child's Will: Eighteenth-Century Parisian Juvenile Detention Centers."

147   This is the Edict of Fontainebleau, signed by Louis XIV in 1685, which ordered that the Huguenots be expelled from French territory on pain of death.

148   This sentence twice uses the word *niẓām*, which Diyāb uses to refer to various forms of propriety, good order, and good management. This passage suggests that he (or at least the Ottoman ambassador whose views he is communicating) saw the domains of city planning, household management, and political leadership to be linked.

149   The piaster was a silver coin used in the Ottoman Empire. Diyāb may have been referring to the French silver ecu, which weighed only slightly more than the piaster.

150   The identity of the theatrical production attended by Diyāb is uncertain. The translators of the French edition believe it to have been the opera *Atys*, by composer Jean-Baptiste Lully and librettist Philippe

Quinault, which premiered in 1676 (Diyāb, *D'Alep à Paris*, 299–306). However, the description provided by Diyāb does not match the plot summary of that opera, nor is the title he supplies that of any French opera known to us. There are similarities between his account and the plot of *Sémélé*, an opera by composer Marin Marais and librettist Antoine Houdar de la Motte, which premiered at the Théâtre du Palais-Royal on April 9, 1709. It was performed twenty-five times between its premiere and its final performance on May 21, 1709, and was never revived (Pitou, *The Paris Opéra*, vol. 1, 310–11).

151   The principal characters in the well-known shadow puppet plays once performed throughout Ottoman lands.

152   Presumably, they carried her in this way so her feet would not have to touch the ground.

153   As noted by Fahmé-Thiéry et al., Diyāb probably had in mind the cross of Saint Andrew, which is shaped like an X (Diyāb, *D'Alep à Paris*, 322n).

154   This grisly torture method involves weaving the body through the spokes of a wagon wheel once the bones have been broken, while the person is still alive.

155   This story combines elements drawn from different sources. Geneviève, according to her hagiographers, distributed bread among the poor but did not work as a maid for a rich man. Diyāb's retelling features the famous "miracle of the roses," probably taken from the hagiography of Elisabeth, queen of Portugal. The hagiographic collection, of which he probably possessed a copy, contains both stories (*Kitāb Akhbār al-qiddīsīn*, vol. 3, fol. 20r, on the roses; and vol. 1, fol. 40r–42v, the vita of Geneviève).

156   The winter of 1709, known in England as "The Great Frost" and in France as *le grand hiver*, was the coldest European winter in five hundred years (Luterbacher et al., "European Seasonal and Annual Temperature Variability, Trends, and Extremes since 1500").

157   This is Antoine Galland, the first European translator of the *Thousand and One Nights*.

158 Diyāb makes several appearances in Antoine Galland's journal; see *Le journal d'Antoine Galland*, vol. 1, 286, 290, 320–34, 346–63, 373–76, 378, 483, 504. The stories he told Galland include "Aladdin and the Enchanted Lamp" (May 5, 1709), "The Blind Man Bābā ʿAbdallāh" and "Sīdī Nuʿmān"(May 10), "The Ebony Horse" (May 13), "Prince Aḥmad and the Fairy Perī Bānū" (May 22), "The Two Sisters Who Envied Their Cadette" (May 25), "ʿAlī Bābā and the Forty Thieves" (May 27), "Khawājah Ḥasan al-Ḥabbāl" (May 29), and "ʿAlī Khawājah and the Merchant of Baghdad" (May 30).

159 This was very likely François de Camps, abbot of Signy (Galland, *Le journal d'Antoine Galland*, 1:483n938).

160 This individual is identified by Antoine Galland in his *De l'origine et du progrès du café*, 51–52, as one Étienne of Aleppo, who opened a café in the Rue Saint André des Arts facing the Pont Saint-Michel, close to Lucas's apartment in Paris. In his account of a fair at which Étienne sold his wares, Diyāb presumably conflates the story of Pascal, which he had also heard in Paris, with that of his neighbor and Aleppan friend in Paris.

161 Here, Lucas expresses the view that the Christian communities of the Ottoman Empire were oppressed by their Muslim rulers, a feeling that Diyāb admits to sharing later in the journey.

162 An expensive woolen broadcloth.

163 Diyāb is referring here to an Ottoman minister, perhaps the grand vizier himself.

164 For other possible readings of the ship's name, see Diyāb, *D'Alep à Paris*, 359n1.

165 The Comte de Ferriol served as ambassador in Istanbul from 1699 to 1711. His refusal to present his rapier is recorded by other historical sources, which call it *l'affaire de l'épée* (*D'Alep à Paris*, 362n1; Bóka and Vargyas, 'Le marquis Charles de Ferriol ambassadeur de France à Constantinople (1699–1703),' 93ff.). Since the incident took place in January 1700, it is unlikely that Diyāb met the messenger in 1709.

166 Ambassadors were received by the sultan just inside the Gate of Felicity (*Bab-üs Saadet*) of Topkapı Palace, which opened onto the Third Courtyard of the palace, the sultan's private domain.

167 At the time of Diyāb's travels, Sicily was in fact under the rule of Savoy. The Austrians were given the island in 1720 in exchange for Sardinia.

168 It appears that Diyāb neglected to mention a third ship that had left Marseille at the same time as his and the other vessel.

169 Gelibolu (Gallipoli) is not at the entrance of the Dardanelles Strait but at the end. Diyāb appears to have misremembered its location.

170 All Ottoman place names are given here in their modern Turkish form.

171 Diyāb has mixed up these stages of the journey, as Küçükçekmece would have come after Büyükçekmece, not before (Diyāb, *D'Alep à Paris*, 369n2).

172 This mosque, known today as Yeni Cami (New Mosque), was completed in 1665, and so would have been relatively new at the time of Diyāb's visit.

173 The toast to the ambassador's health was deciphered by Fahmé-Thiéry et al. (*D'Alep à Paris*, 381n1).

174 Calendering is a process used to thin, coat, or smooth a material such as paper or fabric, in order to produce different sorts of finishes. Calendering machines achieved their effects by passing material through sets of pressurized rollers.

175 This is the Gulf of Izmit, an arm of the Sea of Marmara.

176 Fahmé-Thiéry et al. (*D'Alep à Paris*, 402) suggest this is saffron.

177 Bezoars are undigested masses produced in an animal's gastrointestinal system. They were once thought to have medicinal properties, for example as an antidote against various poisons.

178 These are the Cilician Gates.

179 As Diyāb is pretending to be a Frankish doctor, his argument is that he is not a subject of the Ottoman Empire and therefore should not have to pay the toll that Ottoman Christians pay.

180 Here again it would seem that Diyāb has mixed up the stages of his journey, as he would have arrived at this bridge after passing Adana (see Diyāb, *D'Alep à Paris*, 422n3).

181   Diyāb has probably mixed up the stages of his journey again, as this town comes before the Cilician Gates (Diyāb, *D'Alep à Paris*, 425n2).

182   Diyāb is referring here to the ancient Roman bridge spanning the Seyhan River in Adana, known today by the name Taşköprü.

183   The manuscript here reads: "We pressed on to Payas . . ." However, a symbol before the word "Payas" indicates the insertion of a marginal note. The note is partly illegible, which accounts for the lacunae in the translation.

184   This marks the end of the marginal note.

185   *Jinn* (genies, demons) were thought to inhabit desolate and treacherous territories.

186   Christians living under Muslim rule frequently required "safe-conduct" documents.

187   Paul Lucas appears to have struggled with the sounds *kh* and *q* in Arabic: Diyāb hears his attempt to pronounce Khannāqiyyah as "Kanakia," which he does not recognize. Lucas himself describes his visit to the grottos and refers to this location as "Connaquie," (*Troisième Voyage*, 101).

188   Galland, "M. Diyab quelques contes Arabes fort beaux," in *Le journal d'Antoine Galland*, 1:290.

189   Mia Gerhardt's term in *The Art of Story-Telling: A Literary Study of the Thousand and One Nights*, 14.

190   Galland sought out other sources and manuscripts even before he had finished the tales in his manuscript of the *Thousand and One Nights*.

191   "Aladdin," "The Caliph's Night Adventure," "The Blind Man Bābā ʿAbdallāh," "Sīdī Nuʿmān," "The Ebony Horse," "Prince Aḥmad and the Fairy Perī Bānū," "The Two Sisters Who Envied Their Cadette," "ʿAlī Bābā and the Forty Thieves," "Khawājah Ḥasan al-Ḥabbāl," and "ʿAlī Khawājah and the Merchant of Baghdad."

192   For Jean-Paul Sermain, Galland's revision and elaboration of the added tales served to alter European interpretations of the entire corpus of the *Nights*. Through these added stories, Sermain argues, Galland taught the reader how to read the *Nights* as a whole. Sermain, "Notice," in Galland, *Les mille et une nuits*, i–xiv.

193 Mohamed Abdel-Halim (*Antoine Galland: Sa vie et son oeuvre*, 283) argues that Diyāb contributed "primitive" elements acculturated through their expression in Galland's hand.

194 See May, *Les "Mille et une nuits" d'Antoine Galland, ou, Le chef-d'oeuvre invisible*; Schwab, *L'auteur des "Mille et une nuits": Vie d'Antoine Galland*; and above all, Larzul, "Les Mille et une nuits de Galland," *Les traductions françaises des "Mille et une nuits,"* and "Further Considerations on Galland's *Mille et une Nuits*: A Study of the Tales Told by Hannâ."

195 "If Galland pieced and patched together from other stories," Marina Warner ventures, "he was only doing what storytellers have always done, before and since" (*Stranger Magic: Charmed States and the Arabian Nights*, 77).

196 Sermain, "Présentation," in Galland, *Les mille et une nuits*, 1:xvii–xxxii.

197 A view also expressed in Warner, *Stranger Magic*.

198 See introduction to *The Book of Travels*, p. xxiii.

199 See Stephan on the possible influence of Nizami's retelling of *Majnūn Laylā*, vol. 2, note 225 to the main text, on Boccaccio in note 168; and Heyberger on Boccaccio in the introduction to Dyâb, *D'Alep à Paris*.

200 Horta, *Marvellous Thieves: Secret Authors of the Arabian Nights*.

201 As first noted in Chraïbi, "Galland's 'Ali Baba' and Other Arabic Versions."

202 In the first prince's journey, for instance, Galland inserts a description of Indian temples from the work of a Persian historian he has translated, and in the journey of the third prince he inserts a short description of the Sodge Valley taken from the *Bibliothèque orientale d'Herbelot*. Abdel-Halim, *Antoine Galland*, 235, 280–82. Larzul, "Further Considerations," 261.

203 Ulrich Marzolph, "The Man Who Made the Nights Immortal." See Marzolph's discussion of Diyāb's contribution to international folk narrative in *101 Middle Eastern Tales and Their Impact on Western Oral Tradition*.

204 See Stephan, Introduction, p. xxvi ff; Fahmé-Thiéry, "Ecriture et conscience de soi."

205 *Interpreting the Self: Autobiography in the Arabic Literary Tradition,* ed. Reynolds, 72ff.

206 Fahmé-Thiéry, "Ecriture et conscience de soi."

207 Such moments of introspection and sadness are not unprecedented in the premodern Arabic travelogue, as Michael Cooperson has reminded me—one need only think of Ibn Battuta's arrival in Tunis, when he despairs that he alone knows no one there to greet him. Gibb, *The Travels of Ibn Battuta in Asia and Africa, AD 1325–1354,* 1:12.

208 Fahmé-Thiéry, "Ecriture et conscience de soi."

209 Henri Duranton, editor of modern scholarly editions of all three of Lucas's published travelogues, provides the most precise portrait of Lucas in his introduction to the first volume. He cautions against the bias of accounts by some of the traveler's more erudite but less popular contemporary and near-contemporary authors. A good primer on some primary sources on Lucas is provided in Omont, *Missions archéologiques françaises en Orient aux XVIIè et XVIIIè siècles.* Omont corrected the misperception that Lucas was a purported archaeologist or scholar. Note that Omont only reproduces a small fragment of the sources on Lucas in French archives.

210 Comte de Pontchartrain (Louis Phélypeaux) to Marquis de Ferriol, French ambassador to Constantinople, letter dated April 1, 1704, Bibliothèque Nationale de France, ms. franc. new acq. 801, fol. 3–6, reproduced in Omont, *Missions archéologiques,* 330. These instructions were likely written up for the minister by the court numismatist Jean-Foy Vaillant, since in the draft manuscript they refer in the first person to Vaillant's own experience of collecting ancient coins in Italy in the guise of a doctor in the 1670s.

211 *Voyage du Sieur Paul Lucas dans le Levant: Juin 1699–juillet 1703,* ed. Duranton, 64.

212 Undated memorandum to Lucas from Mr. Juillien, professor of botany at the Royal Garden, *Correspondance et papiers de Paul Lucas, voyageur et antiquaire français,* Richelieu Collection, Bibliothèque Nationale de France, Monnaies et Médailles, carton 1, dossier 27. (Not reproduced in Omont.) Among other natural marvels, the

memorandum details medicines to be sought, notably opium. Lucas is admonished to "examine above all the familiar remedies which they use to recover from illnesses; what ingredients they employ and with what preparations," and to remark "on the effects produced by the drugs they take, and the drinks they use, whether by necessity or for amusement." My translation.

213   When, in the voyage related in his first travelogue, Lucas's dragoman cautions him that he will be asked to produce remedies if he is introduced as a doctor, Lucas reassures him that he has some. *Voyage du Sieur Paul Lucas dans le Levant: Juin 1699–juillet 1703*, 64.

214   Here I follow Fahmé-Thiéry, "Ecriture et conscience de soi."

215   Sermain, in Galland, *Les mille et une nuits*, 1:xxix–xxx. The suggestion that Cassim is too dazzled to recall the password is already in Diyāb's performance of the tale as recorded by Galland in his diary: "he no longer remembers the words, so much was he occupied by what he had just seen." Marzolph and Duggan, "Ḥannā Diyāb's Tales, Part II," 442.

216   Recall that after the disappearance of his palace the crowds do not want to see him summarily executed.

217   Horta, *Marvellous Thieves*, 43–44.

218   Dobie, "Translation in the Contact Zone: Antoine Galland's *Mille et une nuits: Contes arabes*," 35.

219   In the translation by Marzolph and Duggan, "Ḥannā Diyāb's Tales, Part II," 445.

220   Fahmé-Thiéry, "Ecriture et conscience de soi."

221   Galland, *Voyage à Constantinople (1672–1673)*.

222   "You will not find any of these adventures that engage the attention of readers," Galland wrote of his Constantinople journal to a correspondent. "I was no doubt not born for these unusual things, and my personality inclines me even less to fictions." Quoted in Horta, *Marvellous Thieves*, 32.

223   Madsen, "'Auf, Auf, ihr Christen': Representing the Clash of Empires, Vienna 1683," 83–84.

224 Dobie, "Translation in the Contact Zone," 32.

225 In their edition of *Le journal d'Antoine Galland*, Bauden and Waller detail the lectures on Homer and other classical authors Galland would attend, and sometimes reference, in their notes to his diary.

226 For more on the topic of Diyāb's manuscript of "Aladdin," see the forthcoming book by Ibrahim Akel, who has recently verified the authenticity of such a manuscript. Akel writes that at this point it is too early to confirm the same with regard to "'Alī Bābā." (Personal communication, email dated May 5, 2020). One should recall further the ambiguity of Galland's diary entry (January 10, 1711) that affirms he finished his tenth volume rendering an Arabic text given to him by Diyāb—this could refer to "Aladdin," which ends in that volume, or possibly to "The Caliph's Night Adventure."

227 *Le journal d'Antoine Galland*, ed. Bauden and Waller.

228 Available in Henri Duranton's modern editions from l'Université de Saint-Étienne: *Voyage du Sieur Paul Lucas dans le Levant: Juin 1699–juillet 1703* (1998), *Deuxième Voyage du Sieur Paul Lucas dans le Levant: Octobre 1704–septembre 1708* (2002), and *Troisième Voyage du Sieur Paul Lucas dans le Levant: Mai 1714– novembre 1717* (2004). Duranton cautions against accepting the dismissal of Lucas by more erudite contemporaries jealous of his commissions and the success of his travelogues, which ran to several editions and were translated into German.

229 Lucas was not on this journey strictly in charge of his own itinerary; Pontchartrain's instructions advised him where to go, and even the order of the stops to be made. Lucas's first travelogue made evident his love of Persia, yet on this journey it was to be avoided because it would not yield Greco-Roman antiquities.

230 The above quote is in my translation. The three travelogues were edited for length by members of the French Academy, who also inserted references to Greek and Latin classics. What was picaresque, marvelous, and fanciful in the texts—including the portraits of the never-visited holy cities of Islam—originated with Lucas, as can be

corroborated with reference to a partial manuscript that survives, *Voyages de Paul Lucas*, MS 3820, Bibliothèque nationale de France. Bibliothèque de l'Arsenal (consulted March 2019).

231 In addition to the consular network his commissions urged him to rely on. Lucas's interest in the historical and material culture of Marian devotion exceeds the terms of the many court commissions he traveled with. In his first travelogue, he recounts gifting a chalice to the chapel of the Virgin in Old Cairo.

232 Lucas shared with Galland as one of his most prized personal possessions brought back from the Levant—in his journey with Diyāb—a sculpture of the Virgin, as Galland recorded in his diary shortly after first meeting Diyāb at Lucas's apartment (Monday March 18, 1709): "a portrait of the Virgin in sculpture of around six inches in height and five in width in which the face, the throat, and the hand are of chrysolite, and the coat that serves her as a veil is of jasper. The material clothing is of amethysts and the background of a dark oriental agate, all exquisitely worked." My translation. *Le journal d'Antoine Galland*, ed. Bauden and Waller, 287.

233 Horta, *Marvellous Thieves*, 70–71.

234 In relation to their first excursion, where Lucas and Diyāb retrieve from an underground vault two skulls, a ring, and a lamp. Heyberger, introduction to Diyāb, *D'Alep à Paris*, 29.

235 See "The Storyteller and the Sultan of France," in Horta, *Marvellous Thieves*, 44–54, and "Tales of Aladdin and Their Tellers, from Aleppo to Paris."

236 Larzul sees as new to and characteristic of Galland's prose in the added tales the use of superlatives for the "creation of his marvelous environment," citing the example of "Aladdin" ("Further Considerations," 267). But she did not know Diyāb's *Book of Travels*. Invited into a princess's private residence, Diyāb sees "the wives of the princes, as radiant as moons, wearing dresses that glittered so luminously from all of the jewels set into them. The sight was just indescribable." Aladdin observes of the jewels in the vault, in Yasmine

Seale's translation: "their size was unimaginable and their beauty without description" (*Aladdin: A New Translation*, 18).

237 Horta, *Marvellous Thieves*, 47. Larzul ("Further Considerations," 268), in contrast, assumes only Galland could have specified the jewels in this portrait of Perī Bānū.

238 Johannes Stephan notes the parallel: see Chapter 1 of his dissertation, "Spuren fiktionaler Vergegenwärtigung im osmanischen Aleppo," 31–33.

239 As I suggested at the concluding session of the second international workshop on Ḥannā Diyāb, "New Perspectives on the 'Orphan Stories' in the *One Thousand and One Nights*," convened by Christina Vogel and Johannes Thomann at the University of Zurich, February 28–29, 2020.

GLOSSARY OF NAMES AND TERMS

Names and terms appear as they do in the translation.

abū kalb   name given to the Dutch lion dollar, a coin that circulated in the Ottoman Empire.

Adana   a large city in southeastern Anatolia, home to some thirty-five thousand people in the late seventeenth century.

Afyonkarahisar   a city in central-west Anatolia, named for a nearby citadel (Turk. *kara hisar*, "dark fortress") and for its cultivation of opium (Turk. *afyon*).

agha   "chief" or "master," a title given to Ottoman government officials, mostly those associated with the military.

alājah   a luxury fabric made of a mixture of silk and cotton.

Aleppo   a city in northern Syria, home to a large community of European merchants during the seventeenth and eighteenth centuries.

Alexandria   a major port city on Egypt's Mediterranean coast and home to a large European trading community in Diyāb's time.

Antep   modern-day Gaziantep, an important town in southeastern Anatolia.

Antioch   a city in what is now Turkey, about fifty-five miles west of Aleppo.

Arabic Library   the collection of Arabic manuscripts in the French Royal Library (the *Bibliothèque du Roi*).

Asyūṭ   an Egyptian town that was a center for cotton and linen weaving. Linen from Asyūṭ was exported to Europe.

Bālistān souk likely a reference to the oldest section of the Grand Bazaar, known as the Bedesten, built by the Ottoman emperor Mehmed II in 1455.

Barbary a common Western European name for Northwest Africa, designating Morocco and some western Ottoman provinces, including Tripoli and Tunis (see Maghreb).

barjādāt a type of clothing or fabric.

Bey of Tripoli Khalīl Pasha, ruler of the Ottoman province of Tripolitania from 1702 to 1709; deposed and executed by Qaramānlī Aḥmad Bey in 1711.

Bey of Tunis al-Ḥusayn ibn ʿAlī (r. 1705–35), the bey of Tunis and the founder of the Husaynid Dynasty.

bey a Turkish title bestowed on dignitaries of the Ottoman Empire, especially rulers of provinces.

Beyoğlu a quarter in Istanbul, on the European side, north of the Golden Horn; during the period of Diyāb's visit mostly inhabited by Christians and foreign diplomats.

Bsharrī a village in the province of Tripoli adjoining the Qadisha valley, in present-day northern Lebanon.

Būlāq Ottoman Cairo's principal port on the Nile.

Cairo the largest city in the Arabic-speaking lands of the Ottoman Empire, today the capital of Egypt.

Callimeri, Antonio a Cypriot interpreter, protégé of France, and graduate from the Greek college in Rome.

calpac (Ottoman Turkish) a form of headgear covered in sheepskin or fur, in Diyāb's time worn mostly by non-Muslims and Europeans.

çelebi an honorary Ottoman Turkish title given to persons of high status or good education.

cheramide a brick-colored precious stone.

chevalier knight; a French title of nobility conferred during the seventeenth and eighteenth centuries upon members of influential families such as the Khāzin clan of Kisrawān (Lebanon).

Christofalo see *Zamāriyā*.

Cilician Gates   a pass through the Taurus Mountains, which has been used for millennia to travel between the lowlands of Cilicia and the Anatolian plateau.

Damietta   a port city at the eastern end of the Nile Delta, about one hundred miles from Cairo. Along with Rosetta, it is one of the two principal Nile ports on the Mediterranean Sea.

de Camps, François   (1643–1723) French historian, theologian, antiquarian, numismatist, and abbot of Signy.

diligence   a large, public, long-distance stagecoach that could carry up to sixteen people. They were common in France and England during the eighteenth and nineteenth centuries.

dirham   an Ottoman silver coin and a unit of weight, equivalent to one-tenth of an ounce during the seventeenth century.

dīwānkhāna   an audience hall, sitting room, or guest quarters. In Diyāb's use, mostly an outdoor seating area meant for social gatherings and recreation.

Djerba   an island off the coast of Tunisia, captured by the Ottomans from the Spaniards in 1560. The island's main town is Houmt Souk, which was called Djerba in Diyāb's time.

ecu   a French silver coin.

effendi   Ottoman title of respect for a member of the civil administration.

Fagon, Guy-Crescent   (1638–1718) botanist, physician to Louis XIV, and director of the Royal Gardens at Versailles.

Farḥāt, Jirmānūs   (1670–1732) Aleppan Maronite cleric, poet, grammarian, lexicographer, and traveler active in spreading knowledge of Arabic among Christians; he was made bishop of Aleppo in 1725.

Fayoum   an Egyptian town located southwest of Cairo in the Fayoum Oasis and linked to the Nile by a canal.

fils   a coin whose value varied between eight and eighteen for one *pāra*; known in Ottoman Egypt as a *jadīd*.

Frank   (Ar. *franjī*, pl. *franj*) a European (distinct from *fransāwī*, pl. *fransāwiyyah*, "French").

Frankish   (Ar. *franjī*) the Mediterranean lingua franca, a hybrid idiom used among seamen, traders, and other travelers. When used as an adjective, equivalent to "European" (e.g., "Frankish lands").

Galata   a quarter of Istanbul on the northern shore of the Golden Horn, south of Beyoğlu; today called Karaköy.

Galland, Antoine   (1646–1717) a French Orientalist and scholar of classical languages, an expert in numismatics, and a traveler to the Ottoman lands. He contributed to the encyclopedia *Bibliothèque orientale d'Herbelot* and was the first translator of the *Arabian Nights* into a European language.

Gate of the Janissaries and the al-ʿAzab Gate   two of the three main gates to the Cairo Citadel, one of the city's main monuments, dating to the Ayyūbid period.

ghuzzī   an Ottoman functionary of Egypt; the term derives from *ghuz*, "the Oguz," the Turks claimed as ancestors by the Ottomans.

Grand Vizier of the Ottoman Empire   the chief minister of the empire and the second most powerful figure in the political hierarchy.

Greek (Ar. rūmī, pl. rūm)   a speaker of Greek, usually of Greek Orthodox (*krīkī*) denomination; sometimes also a Latin Christian; distinct from *yūnānī*, "Ancient Greek."

Ibn al-Zughbī, Ḥannā   an Aleppan Maronite, and a friend of Diyāb's who accompanies him during his Anatolian journey.

Ifrīqiyah   a region of North Africa with indistinct borders. Diyāb's usage suggests that he took it to encompass present-day Tunisia and western Libya.

isbanj   (Turk. *ispenç*, "a fifth") a tax paid by non-Muslims for pasturage, e.g., of swine.

Iṣṭifān the Damascene   an Armenian who at the end of the seventeenth century opened one of the first coffeehouses in Paris.

jadīd   see *fils*.

jakhjūr   (Turk. *chāqshīr*) a type of trousers fastened around the waist with a band, and sewed to light leather boots around the ankle hems.

janissary   an elite Ottoman infantryman.

jarq   (Turk. *charkhī*, a five-piaster piece) a coin worth four ʿ*uthmānī*s, or two soldi.

jūkhadār   (Turk. *chohadar*) originally a lackey, footman, or valet; for Diyāb, an attendant, bureaucrat, or high-ranking embassy official.

Kaftīn a village in northern Syria, close to Aleppo and to several ruined Byzantine cities.

Karanlık Kapı (Gate of Darkness) a pass in the Nur Mountains of south-eastern Anatolia (the Amanus range in Ancient Greek), along the Cilician highway to Syria.

kazan kebabı a type of meat dish, cooked in a large pot.

khan a caravansary, i.e., a roadside staging post with lodging for travelers and their mounts; also, a warehouse and hostel, often built in the outskirts of cities; for Diyāb, also a market or marketplace, and, in one case, a dormitory for prisoners.

Khan Abrak a marketplace in Aleppo, found in the Sūq al-Qaṣābiyyah.

Khan al-ʿAsal a town on the western outskirts of Aleppo.

Khan al-ʿUlabiyyah a monumental sixteenth-century caravansary near Bizzeh Square in southern Aleppo.

khāṣṣāt (sing. khāṣṣah) a type of fine, tightly woven cotton.

khawājah an informal honorary title given to foreign or Christian merchants during the Ottoman period; Diyāb's first designation for Paul Lucas, later replaced by *muʿallimī* ("[my] master," "boss").

Khāzin family a Maronite landowning family of Mount Lebanon whose members wielded considerable economic and political power between the sixteenth and nineteenth centuries. Beginning in the seventeenth century, they gained political privileges through close economic collaboration with French authorities, for which some members were awarded the title of chevalier.

Kız Kulesi (Maiden's Tower) a small tower that stands on an island in the Bosphorus, near the coast of Üsküdar. The tower dates to the twelfth century.

Konya a city in central Anatolia.

Larnaca (Ar. Milāḥah) a coastal city in southeastern Cyprus.

Lemaire a family of diplomats originally from Joinville in the province of Champagne; one member, Claude, was French consul in Tripoli and later in Aleppo.

Livorno (Ar. Līkūrnā, from Genoese Ligorna) a coastal town in the Italian province of Tuscany and a commercial center in the early modern period.

londrin   a type of lightweight, fulled woolen cloth, made in France and
   England and exported to the Levant.

Lucas, Paul   (1646–1734) traveler, adventurer, and antiquarian in the service of Louis XIV; the son of a Rouen goldsmith and the author of three
   travelogues covering the period between 1699 and 1717; known during
   the European Enlightenment for his fanciful reports of distant places.

Madame d'Orléans   (1677–1749) Françoise Marie de Bourbon, the young-
   est daughter of Louis XIV with his mistress the Marquise de Montes-
   pan; wife of Philippe II, the Duke of Orléans and Regent of France
   during the minority of Louis XV.

Madame de Bourgogne   (1685–1712) Marie Adélaïde of Savoy, wife of
   Louis XIV's grandson, Louis le Petit Dauphin, Duke of Burgundy, and
   mother of Louis XV.

Madame de Maintenon   (1635–1719) Françoise d'Aubigné, second wife of
   Louis XIV.

Maghreb   the "West," i.e., the western territories of North Africa, including present-day Morocco, Algeria, Libya, and Tunisia.

miṣriyyah   a coin of Egyptian origin normally worth one-fortieth of a piaster, or half a piece of silver.

Messina   a city on the northeastern tip of Sicily, just across the narrow
   strait separating the island from the south of Italy.

mīrī   a tax on land owned by the Ottoman sovereign.

Misis   a town in southeastern Anatolia, about seventeen miles east of
   Adana. Also called Mopsuestia.

mithqāl   a measurement of weight equivalent to one and a half dirhams; in
   Diyāb's time, around four and a half grams.

Monseigneur the Dauphin   (1661–1711) Louis le Grand Dauphin, son of
   Louis XIV and heir to the French throne, father of Philip V of Spain,
   and grandfather of Louis XV of France.

Morea   the region now referred to as the Peloponnese.

Mouski quarter   a district in central Cairo, in the seventeenth and eighteenth centuries home to many European consuls and merchants
   (and thus also called the Frankish quarter), as well as several Jewish
   families.

mujaddarah   an ancient Near Eastern dish composed of lentils, rice or bulgur, spices, and onions. It remains a staple of many local cuisines, especially in the Levant.

L'Opéra   the Paris Opera (known at this time as the Académie Royale de Musique) was housed in the Théâtre du Palais-Royal on the rue Saint-Honoré from 1673 to 1763.

pāra   a silver Ottoman coin first issued in the early eighteenth century.

Paulo Çelebi   see *Zamāriyā.*

Peloponnese   see *Morea.*

piaster   see *qirsh.*

Pontchartrain   Jérôme Phélypeaux (1674–1747), a French politician who served as secretary of state for the Maison du Roi and for the navy under Louis XIV.

Province of the Islands   a province comprising all the major islands of the Ottoman Mediterranean, with the exception of Crete; also known as the Eyalet of the Archipelago.

qabiji   (Turk. *qapuči*) originally a gatekeeper or porter, then a palace guard or chamberlain, later a senior palace official or eunuch who guarded the sultan's harem; for Diyāb, also a French royal border guard, or a cavalry commander.

qinṭār   a measurement of weight equivalent to one hundred *raṭl*s, variable according to time and place; in seventeenth- through nineteenth-century Aleppo, probably between 487 and 564 pounds.

qirsh   (piaster) a heavy silver coin worth forty *pāra*s.

raṭl   a measurement of weight whose value varied according to time and place; in seventeenth- through nineteenth-century Aleppo, probably between 4.87 and 5.64 pounds.

rayyis   chief, captain, boss, superior.

Rémuzat   (or Rémusat) a famous merchant family of Marseille with long-lasting ties to cities in the Ottoman Empire. One member, Auguste Rémuzat, was France's deputy consul in Aleppo, and apparently also the young Diyāb's second patron and employer.

Rimbaud   a merchant family from Marseille that supplied many deputies or principal merchants of the French nation in Aleppo during Diyāb's lifetime.

riyāl   an originally Spanish silver coin (*real*) of considerable value, widely used in Ottoman lands until 1714, when the Ottomans in Tunis banned its use and began to mint their own. Also called *riyāl qurūsh* (*riyal quruş*).

Rosetta   a port city at the western end of the Nile Delta, about one hundred miles from Cairo. Along with Damietta, it is one of the two principal Nile ports on the Mediterranean Sea.

Rūm, Rūmī   see *Greek*.

Saint Elishaʿ   a monastery on the hillside below the village of Bsharrī, and the main residence of the Maronite Lebanese order during the time of Diyāb's stay.

Saint Geneviève   the patron saint of Paris, according to the Roman Catholic and Eastern Orthodox rites.

Samatan   a French merchant originally from Marseille, prominent in Aleppo between 1698 and 1708.

sanjaq   an administrative subdivision of an Ottoman province (Turk. *eyalet* or *beylic*), administered by a *sanjaq bey*.

Sauron   a prominent French merchant in Aleppo during the first two decades of the eighteenth century.

Sfax   a commercial city on the coast of what is now Tunisia.

shāhbandar   an Ottoman term meaning "harbormaster" (literally "king of the port"); in Diyāb's use the main representative of a group of merchants or the manager of a trading port.

shāhiyyāt   (Ar., sing. *shāhī*) An Ottoman silver coin.

shāsh   a long strip of cloth used to wind a turban.

soldi   (It., sing. *soldo*) An Italian silver coin worth half a *jarq* or two ʿ*uthmānī*s.

Sousse   a coastal town in what is now Tunisia.

Sultan Aḥmad   (1673–1736) the twenty-third Ottoman sultan, known as Aḥmad III.

thulth   in Diyāb's use, a coin worth a third of a piaster; also a third of a dinar, or a third of a *pāra*.

Tripoli   a city in northern Lebanon, situated on the Mediterranean coast.

Tripoli (of the West)   the capital of present-day Libya, situated on the Mediterranean coast.

Tunis   the capital of present-day Tunisia, situated on the Mediterranean coast.

ūqiyyah   a measurement of weight whose value varied according to time and place. In Diyāb's Aleppo, it was equivalent to one-twelfth of a *raṭl* or one-sixth of an *uqqah* (around seven and a half ounces; see Barthélemy, 905).

uqqah   a measurement of weight whose value varied according to time and place; in Diyāb's Aleppo, it was equivalent to four hundred dirhams, half a *raṭl*, or six *ūqiyyah* (about 2.8 pounds).

Üsküdar   an ancient city on the Asian side of the Bosphorus, today a district of Istanbul.

'uthmānī   another word for *akče*, a silver coin worth a third or a quarter *pāra*.

Yūsuf Çelebi   see *Zamāriyā*.

zolota   a coin worth thirty *pāra*s, or three-quarters of a piaster (*qirsh*). The name comes from the Polish *złoty*, a currency exported to Ottoman lands during the seventeenth century.

Zamāriyā   a French family residing in Aleppo, some of whose members held important diplomatic posts. The head was Pierre Maunier. Diyāb met Maunier's son Christofalo (Christophe) in Paris, where he served as the steward of Cardinal de Noailles. Diyāb knew Christophe's brothers, Paulo Çelebi (Paul) and Yūsuf Çelebi (Joseph), in Aleppo. The oldest brother, known as Zamāriyā, served as syndic of the Holy Land in Istanbul.

Zūq Mīkāyīl / Zouq Mkayel   a village in Kisrawān, between Jounieh and Beirut in what is now Lebanon, in Diyāb's time administered by the Khāzin family and inhabited, perhaps exclusively, by Maronites.

Zuqāq al-Khall   (Vinegar Alley) a predominantly Christian quarter on the northern edge of Aleppo. In Diyāb's time, it served as a point of entry to the Christian suburbs.

Bibliography

Manuscripts

Bibliothèque nationale de France
Voyages de Paul Lucas, MS 3820. Bibliothèque de l'Arsenal.
"Comte de Pontchartrain (Louis Phélypeaux) to Marquis de Ferriol,
French Ambassador to Constantinople," MS franc. Nouv. acq. 801.

Gotha, Forschungsbibliothek
Arab. 1548: *Riḥlat Saʿīd Bāshā*
Arab. 1549: *Riḥlat al-Ab Arsāniyūs Shukrī*
Arab. 1550: *Riḥlat al-shammās Ḥannā al-Ṭabīb*

Syrian Catholic Archdiocese of Aleppo
Ar 7/25: *Kitāb Mufīd fī ʿilm al-niyyah*

Université Saint Joseph (USJ), Bibliothèque Orientale
BO 29: *Kitāb Siyāḥat al-ḫūrī Ilyās al-Mawṣilī*
BO 594–597: *Kitāb Akhbār al-qiddīsīn*
BO 645: *al-Durr al-nafīs fī sīrat al-qiddīs Fransīs*

Vatican Apostolic Library
Sbath 108: *Kitāb Siyāḥat al-ḫūrī Ilyās al-Mawṣilī* and *Riḥlat Saʿīd Bāshā*
Sbath 254: [*Kitāb Siyāḥat Ḥannā Diyāb*]

Abdel-Halim, Mohamed. *Antoine Galland: Sa vie et son oeuvre*. Thèse en
lettres, Paris: A. G. Nizet, 1964.

Addobbati, Andrea. "Hanna Dyab, il mercante di storie." *Quaderni Storico*
3 (2016): 830–42.

Al-Asadī, Khayr al-Dīn. *Mawsūʿat Ḥalab al-muqāranah*. Ḥalab: Jāmiʿat
Ḥalab, 1981–88.

Barthélemy, Adrien. *Dictionnaire arabe-français: Dialectes de Syrie: Alep,
Damas, Liban, Jérusalem*. Paris: Geuthner, 1935.

Bauden, Frédéric and Richard Waller, eds. *Le journal d'Antoine Galland
(1646–1715): La Période Parisienne*. Vol. I. Leuven, Belgium: Peeters, 2011.

Blau, Joshua. *On Pseudo-Corrections in Some Semitic Languages*.
Jerusalem: The Israel Academy of Sciences and Humanities, 1970.

Boase, Thomas S. R. "Ecclesiastical Art." In *A History of the Crusades*,
edited by Kenneth M. Setton, 165–95. Madison, WI: The University
of Wisconsin Press, 1977.

Bóka, Éva, and Katalin Vargyas. "Le marquis Charles de Ferriol
ambassadeur de France à Constantinople (1699–1703)." *Acta Historica
Academiae Scientiarum Hungaricae* 31, nos. 1–2 (1985): 87–112.

Bolte, Johannes. "Die Sage von der erweckten Scheintoten." *Zeitschrift des
Vereins für Volkskunde* 20 (1910): 353–81.

Bottigheimer, Ruth B. "East Meets West: Hannā Diyāb and *The Thousand
and One Nights*." *Marvels and Tales* 28, no. 2 (2014): 302–24.

Brednich, Rolf Wilhelm. "Frau: Die tote F. kehrt zurück." In *Enzyklopädie
des Märchens: Handwörterbuch zur historischen und vergleichenden
Erzählforschung*, Vol. 5, edited by Rolf Wilhelm Brednich and
Hermann Bausinger, 199–203. Berlin: de Gruyter, 1987.

Chraïbi, Aboubakr. "Galland's 'Ali Baba' and Other Arabic Versions."
Marvels and Tales 18, no. 2 (2004): 159–69.

Commission des Antiquités. "Note sur Paul Lucas." *Bulletin de la Commission
des Antiquités de la Seine-Inférieure* 10, no. 3 (1897): 338–40.

Davidson, Linda Kay, and David M. Gitlitz. *Pilgrimage: From the Ganges to
Graceland; An Encyclopedia*. Santa Barbara, CA: ABC-Clio, 2002.

Dew, Nicholas. *Orientalism in Louis XIV's France*. Oxford, UK: Oxford University Press, 2009.

Diyāb, Ḥannā [Hanna Dyâb]. *D'Alep à Paris: Les pérégrinations d'un jeune syrien au temps de Louis XIV; Récit traduit de l'arabe (Syrie) et annoté par Paule Fahmé-Thiéry, Bernard Heyberger et Jérôme Lentin*. Paris: Actes Sud, 2015.

———. *The Man Who Wrote Aladin*. Translated by Paul Lunde. Edinburgh: Harding Simpole, 2020.

———. *Von Aleppo nach Paris: Die Reise eines jungen Syrers bis an den Hof Ludwigs XIV*. Translated by Gennaro Ghirardelli. Berlin: Die Andere Bibliothek, 2016.

Dobie, Madeleine. "Translation in the Contact Zone: Antoine Galland's *Mille et une nuits: Contes arabes*." In *The Arabian Nights in Historical Context: Between East and West*, edited by Saree Makdisi and Felicity Nussbaum, 25–49. Oxford, UK: Oxford University Press, 2008.

Dozy, Reinhart P. A. *Supplément aux dictionnaires arabes*. Beirut: Librairie du Liban, 1968.

Duranton, Henri. "Paul Lucas." In *Christian-Muslim Relations: A Bibliographical History*. Vol. 13 (1700–1800), edited by David Thomas and John Chesworth, 548–55. Leiden, Netherlands: Brill, 2019.

Fahd, Buṭrus. *Tārīkh al-rahbāniyyah al-lubnānīyah bi-farʿayhā l-ḥalabī wa-l-lubnānī, 1743–1770*. Vol. 4. Jūniyah, Lebanon: Maṭbaʿat Kuraym, 1966.

EI2 = Bearman, P., Th. Bianquis, C. E. Bosworth, E. van Donzel, and W. P. Heinrichs, eds. *Encyclopaedia of Islam*. 2nd ed. 13 vols. Leiden, Netherlands: Brill, 1960–2009.

EI3 = Gaborieau, Marc, Roger Allen, Gudrun Krämer, Kate Fleet, Denis Matringe, John Abdallah Nawas, and Everett K. Rowson, eds. *Encyclopaedia of Islam, Three*. Leiden, Netherlands: Brill, 2007–.

Fahmé-Thiéry, Paule. "L'arabe dialectal aleppin dans le récit de voyage de Hanna Dyâb." In *Arabic Varieties: Far and Wide; Proceedings of the 11th International Conference of AIDA—Bucharest, 2015*, edited by George Grigore and Gabriel Bițună, 223–30. Bucharest: Editura Universității din București, 2016.

———. "Ecriture et conscience de soi: Récits de voyage et accès à la modernité chez Bûlus ez Zaïm et Hanna Dyâb." Presented at the Kiev colloquium "Sous l'oeil de l'Orient: L'Europe dans les sources arabes," September 22–23, 2015.

Farḥāt, Jirmānūs. "Tārīkh ta'sīs al-rahbāniyyah al-Lubnāniyyah." In *Bidāyāt al-rahbāniyyah al-Lubnāniyyah*, edited by Jūzīf Qazzī, 111–78.

Gagliardi, Isabella. "'Ave maris Stella': Il santuario mariano di Montenero presso Livorno." In *Dio, il mare e gli uomini*, edited by Luciano Fanin, E. Ferrarini, and A. Galdi, 185–213. Verona: Cierre edizioni, 2008.

Galland, Antoine. *De l'origine et du progrès du café*. Paris: Poisson/Lance, 1836.

———. *Les mille et une nuits: Contes arabes*. 3 vols. Edited by Jean-Paul Sermain. Paris: Éditions Flammarion, 2004.

———. *Le journal d'Antoine Galland (1646–1715)*. Edited by F. Bauden and R. Waller. Leeuven, Belgium: Peeters, 2011–15.

———. *Voyage à Constantinople (1672–1673)*. Edited by Charles Schefer. Paris: Maisonneuve et Larose, 2002.

Gemayel, Nasser. *Les échanges culturels entre les Maronites et l'Europe: Du collège Maronite de Rome (1584) au collège de 'Ayn-Warqa (1789)*. Beirut: L'imprimerie V. & Ph. Gemayel, 1984.

Gerhardt, Mia. *The Art of Story-Telling: A Literary Study of the Thousand and One Nights*. Leiden, Netherlands: Brill, 1963.

Ghobrial, John-Paul A. "Stories Never Told: The First Arabic History of the New World." *The Journal of Ottoman Studies* 40 (2012): 259–82.

———. "The Secret Life of Elias of Babylon and the Uses of Global Microhistory." *Past and Present* (2014): 51–93.

———. "The Life and Hard Times of Solomon Negri: An Arabic Teacher in Early Modern Europe." In *The Teaching and Learning of Arabic in Early Modern Europe*, edited by Jan Loop, Alastair Hamilton, and Charles Burnett, 310–31. Leiden, Netherlands: Brill, 2017.

Gibb, H. A. R. *The Travels of Ibn Battuta in Asia and Africa, AD 1325–1354*. 5 vols. Cambridge, UK: Cambridge University Press, 1958.

Göçek, Fatma Müge. *East Encounters West: France and the Ottoman Empire in the Eighteenth Century*. New York: Oxford University Press, 1987.

Görner, Florian. "Das Regulativ der Wahrscheinlichkeit: Zur Funktion literarischer Fiktionalität im 18; Jahrhundert." PhD diss., Universität Köln, 2011.

Gossard, Julia M. "Breaking a Child's Will: Eighteenth-Century Parisian Juvenile Detention Centers." *French Historical Studies* 42, no. 2 (2019): 239–59.

Graf, Georg. *Geschichte der christlichen arabischen Literatur.* Vols. 3 and 4. Vatican City: Biblioteca Apostolica Vaticana, 1949–51.

———. *Verzeichnis arabischer kirchlicher Termini.* Louvain, Belgium: Imprimerie Orientaliste L. Durbecq, 1954.

Hayek, Michel. "Al-Rāhibah Hindiyyah (1720–1798)." *Al-Mashriq* 9 (1965): 525–646, 685–734.

Heyberger, Bernard. *Hindiyya: Mystique et criminelle 1720–1798.* Paris: Aubier, 2001. English translation: *Hindiyya, Mystic and Criminal, 1720–1798.* Translated by Renée Champion. Cambridge, UK: James Clarke, 2013.

———. *Les chrétiens du Proche-Orient au temps de la réforme catholique (Syrie, Liban, Palestine, XVIIe–XVIIIe siècles).* Rome: Ecole française de Rome, 2014.

———. Introduction to *Hanna Dyâb: D'Alep à Paris; Les pérégrinations d'un jeune syrien au temps de Louis XIV; Récit traduit de l'arabe (Syrie) et annoté par Paule Fahmé-Thiéry, Bernard Heyberger et Jérôme Lentin,* 7–47. Paris: Actes Sud, 2015.

Horta, Paulo Lemos. *Marvellous Thieves: Secret Authors of the Arabian Nights.* Cambridge, MA: Harvard University Press, 2017.

———. "Tales of Aladdin and Their Tellers, from Aleppo to Paris." *Words without Borders,* April 16, 2020. Accessed October 7, 2020. https://www.wordswithoutborders.org/dispatches/article/tales-of-aladdin-and-their-tellers-from-aleppo-to-paris-paulo-lemos-horta.

Ibn al-Ṣāyigh, Fatḥallāh Ibn Anṭūn. *Riḥlah ilā bādiyat al-Shām wa-Ṣaḥārā l-ʿIrāq wa-l-ʿajam wa-l-Jazīrah al-ʿArabiyyah.* Edited by ʿAbdallāh Ibrāhīm al-ʿAskar and Muḥammad Khayr Maḥmūd al-Biqāʿī. Beirut: Jadawel, 2012.

İnalcik, Halil. *An Economic and Social History of the Ottoman Empire, 1300–1914.* Vol. 1, 1300–1600. Cambridge, UK: Cambridge University Press, 1994.

————. "A Note on the Population of Cyprus." *Journal for Cypriot Studies* 3, no. 1 (1997): 3–11.

Jennings, Ronald. *Christians and Muslims in Ottoman Cyprus and the Mediterranean World, 1571–1640*. New York: New York University Press, 1992.

Juillien (professor of botany at the Royal Garden). Undated memorandum to Paul Lucas. *Correspondance et papiers de Paul Lucas, voyageur et antiquaire français*. Richelieu Collection, Monnaies et Médailles, carton 1, dossier 27. Bibliothèque Nationale de France, Paris.

Kahane, Henry Romanos, Renée Kahane, and Andreas Tietze. *The Lingua Franca in the Levant: Turkish Nautical Terms of Italian and Greek Origin*. Urbana, IL: University of Illinois University Press, 1958.

Kallas, Elie. "The Aleppo Dialect According to the Travel Accounts of Ibn Raʿd (1656) Ms. Sbath 89 and Ḥanna Dyāb (1764) Ms. Sbath 254." In *De los manuscritos medievales a internet: La presencia del árabe vernáculo en las fuentes escritas*, edited by M. Meouak, P. Sánchez, and Á. Vicente, 221–54. Zaragoza, Spain: Área de Estudios Árabes e Islámicos, 2012.

————. "Gerboise: L'entrée du terme arabe ğerbūʿ à la cour de Louis XIV." In *Approaches to the History and Dialectology of Arabic in Honor of Pierre Larcher*, edited by Manuel Sartori, Manuela E. B. Giolfo, and Philippe Cassuto, 342–61. Leiden, Netherlands: Brill, 2017.

Kilpatrick, Hilary, and Gerald J. Toomer. "Niqūlāwus al-Ḥalabī (c. 1611–c. 1661): A Greek Orthodox Syrian Copyist and His Letters to Pococke and Golius." *Lias* 43, no. 1 (2016): 1–159.

Krimsti, Feras. "The Lives and Afterlives of the Library of the Maronite Physician Ḥannā al-Ṭabīb (c. 1702–1775) from Aleppo." *Journal of Islamic Manuscripts* 9 (2018): 190–217.

————. "Arsāniyūs Shukrī al-Ḥakīm's Account of His Journey to France, the Iberian Peninsula, and Italy (1748–1757) from Travel Journal to Edition." *Philological Encounters* 4, nos. 3–4 (2019): 202–44.

Al-Labbūdī, Tūmā. "Sīrat al-ḥibr al-ṭayyib al-dhikr ʿAbdallāh Qarāʿalī al-Marūnī al-Ḥalabī." In *Bidāyāt al-rahbāniyyah al-Lubnāniyyah*, edited by Jūzīf Qazzī, 75–105.

Larzul, Sylvette. "Further Considerations on Galland's *Mille et une Nuits*: A Study of the Tales Told by Hannâ." *Marvels and Tales* 18, no. 2 (2004): 258–71. Reprinted in *The Arabian Nights in Transnational Perspective*, edited by Ulrich Marzolph, 17–31. Detroit, MI: Wayne State University Press, 2007.

———. "Les Mille et une nuits de Galland; ou, L'acclimatation d'une 'Belle étrangère.'" *Revue de littérature compare* 3 (1995): 312–18.

———. *Les traductions françaises des "Mille et une nuits": Études des versions Galland, Trébutien et Mardrus*. Paris: Harmattan, 1996.

Lentin, Jérôme. "Recherches sur l'histoire de la langue arabe au Proche-Orient à l'époque moderne." PhD diss., Université de la Sorbonne Nouvelle—Paris III, 1997.

———. "Middle Arabic." In *Encyclopedia of Arabic Language and Linguistics*, edited by Lutz Edzard and Rudolf de Jong. Leiden, Netherlands: Brill, 2011. http://dx.doi.org/10.1163/1570-6699_eall_EALL_COM_vol3_0213.

———. "Note sur la langue de Hanna Dyâb." In *D'Alep à Paris: Les pérégrinations d'un jeune syrien au temps de Louis XIV; Récit traduit de l'arabe (Syrie) et annoté par Paule Fahmé-Thiéry, Bernard Heyberger et Jérôme Lentin*, 48–51. Paris: Sindbad/Actes Sud, 2015.

Lucas, Paul. *[Premier] Voyage du Sieur Paul Lucas dans le Levant: Juin 1699–juillet 1703; Présenté par Henri Duranton*. Saint-Étienne, France: Publications de l'Université de Saint-Étienne, 1998.

———. *Deuxième Voyage du Sieur Paul Lucas dans le Levant: Octobre 1704–septembre 1708; Présenté par Henri Duranton*. Saint-Étienne, France: Publications de l'Université de Saint-Étienne, 2002.

———. *Troisième Voyage du Sieur Paul Lucas dans le Levant: Mai 1714–novembre 1717; Présenté par Henri Duranton*. Saint-Étienne, France: Publications de l'Université de Saint-Étienne, 2004.

Luterbacher, Jürg, Daniel Dietrich, Elena Xoplaki, Martin Grosjean, and Heinz Wanner. "European Seasonal and Annual Temperature Variability, Trends, and Extremes since 1500." *Science* 3, no. 5 (2004): 1499–1503.

Madsen, Peter. "'Auf, Auf, ihr Christen': Representing the Clash of
Empires, Vienna 1683." In *Empires and World Literature*, edited by
Piero Boitani and Irene Montori, 83–95. Milan: Albo Versorio, 2019.

Martin, Maurice. "Souvenirs d'un compagnion de voyage de Paul Lucas en
Égypte (1707)." In *Hommages à la mémoire de Serge Sauneron. Tome
II: Égypte post-pharaonique, 1927–1976*, edited by Jean Vercoutter,
471–75. Cairo: Institut Français d'archéologie orientale, 1979.

Marzolph, Ulrich. *101 Middle Eastern Tales and Their Impact on Western
Oral Tradition*. Detroit, MI: Wayne State University Press, 2020.

———. "The Man Who Made the Nights Immortal: The Tales of the
Syrian Maronite Storyteller Ḥannā Diyāb." *Marvels and Tales* 32, no. 1
(2018): 114–29.

Marzolph, Ulrich, with Anne E. Duggan. "Hanna Diyab's Tales, Part II."
Marvels and Tales 32, no. 2 (2018): 435–56.

Masters, Bruce. *Christians and Jews in the Ottoman Arab World: The Roots
of Sectarianism*. Cambridge, UK: Cambridge University Press, 2001.

Matar, Nabil. *In the Lands of the Christians: Arab Travel Writing in the
Seventeenth Century*. London: Routledge, 2003.

Mattern, Joseph. *A travers les villes mortes de Haute Syrie: Promenades
archéologiques en 1928, 1929, 1931*. Beirut: Imprimerie Catholique,
1933.

Al-Mawṣilī, Ilyās. "Riḥlat awwal sāʾiḥ sharqī ilā Amirkah. [Taḥqīq Anṭūn
Rabbāṭ.]" *Al-Mašriq* 8, no. 2 (1905): 821–34, 875–86, 931–42, 974–83,
1022–33, 1080–88, 1118–1028.

May, Georges. *Les "Mille et une nuits" d'Antoine Galland, ou, Le chef-
d'oeuvre invisible*. Paris: Presses universitaires de France, 1986.

McKenzie, Judith. *The Architecture of Alexandria and Egypt, 300 B.C. to
A.D. 700*. New Haven, CT: Yale University Press, 2007.

Morison, Antoine. *Relation historique d'un voyage nouvellement fait au
Mont de Sinaï et à Jerusalem*. Paris: A. Laurent, 1704.

Omont, Henri. *Missions archéologiques françaises en Orient aux XVIIè et
XVIIIè siècles: Documents*. Paris: Imprimerie Nationale, 1902.

Ong, Walter J. *Orality and Literacy: The Technologizing of the World*.
London: Routledge, 2002.

Ott, Claudia. "From the Coffeehouse into the Manuscript: The Storyteller and His Audience in the Manuscripts of an Arabic Epic." *Oriente Moderno* 22, no. 2 (2003): 443–51.

Özay, Yeliz. "Evliyâ Çelebi's Strange and Wondrous Europe." *Cahiers balkaniques* 41 (2013): 61–69.

Pamuk, Sevket. *A Monetary History of the Ottoman Empire.* Cambridge, UK: Cambridge University Press, 2000.

Patel, Abdulrazzak. *The Arab Nahḍah: The Making of the Intellectual and Humanist Movement.* Edinburgh: Edinburgh University Press, 2013.

Peucker, Brigitte. "The Material Image in Goethe's *Wahlverwandtschaften.*" *The Germanic Review: Literature, Culture, Theory* 74, no. 3 (1999): 195–213.

Pitou, Spire. *The Paris Opéra: An Encyclopedia of Operas, Ballets, Composers, and Performers.* Westport, CN: Greenwood Press, 1983.

Pococke, Richard. *A Description of the East and Some Other Countries.* London: W. Bowyer, 1743.

Qarā'alī, 'Abdallāh. "Mudhakkirāt." In *Bidāyāt al-rahbāniyyah al-Lubnāniyyah*, edited by Jūzīf Qazzī, 23–71.

Qarā'alī, 'Abdallāh et al. "Qawānīn al-rahbāniyyah al-Lubnāniyyah." In *Bidāyāt al-rahbāniyyah al-Lubnāniyyah*, edited by Jūzīf Qazzī, 179–210.

Qazzī, Jūzīf, ed. *Bidāyāt al-rahbāniyyah al-Lubnāniyyah.* Kaslik, Lebanon: Markaz al-Nashr wa-l-Tawzī', 1988.

Raymond, André. "An Expanding Community: The Christians of Aleppo in the Ottoman Era (Sixteenth–Eighteenth Centuries)." In *Arab Cities in the Ottoman Period*, edited by André Raymond, 83–100. Aldershot, UK: Ashgate, 2002.

Redhouse, James W. A. *Turkish and English Lexicon.* Istanbul: A. H. Boyajian, 1890.

Reynolds, Dwight, ed. *Interpreting the Self: Autobiography in the Arabic Literary Tradition.* Berkeley, CA: University of California Press, 2001.

Russell, Alexander. *The Natural History of Aleppo.* Vol 1. Revised by Patrick Russell. London: G. G. and J. Robinson, 1794.

Sadan, Joseph. "Background, Date and Meaning of the Story of the
Alexandrian Lover and the Magic Lamp: A Little-Known Story from
Ottoman Times, with a Partial Resemblance to the Story of Aladdin."
Quaderni di Studi Arabi 19 (2001): 137–92.

Sbath, Paul. *Bibliothèque de manuscrits: Catalogue.* Vol. 1. Cairo: H.
Friedrich, 1928.

———. "Les manuscrits orientaux de la bibliothèque du R. P. Paul Sbath
(Suite)." *Échos d'Orient* 23 (1924): 339–58.

Schwab, Raymond. *L'auteur des "Mille et une nuits": Vie d'Antoine Galland.*
Paris: Mercure de France, 2004.

Seale, Yasmine, trans. *Aladdin: A New Translation.* Edited by Paulo Lemos
Horta. New York, NY: Liveright Publishing, 2019.

Stephan, Johannes. "Von der Bezeugung zur Narrativen
Vergegenwärtigung: Fokalisierung im Reisebuch des Syrers Ḥanna
Dyāb (1764)." *Diegesis* 4, no. 2 (2015).

———. "Spuren fiktionaler Vergegenwärtigung im Osmanischen Aleppo:
Narratologische Analysen und Kontextualisierungen des Reisebuchs
von Hanna Dyāb (1764)." PhD diss., Universität Bern, 2016.

Teissier, Octave, ed. *Inventaire des archives historiques de la Chambre de
Commerce de Marseille.* Marseille: Barlatier-Feissat, 1878.

Thompson, Ian. *The Sun King's Garden: Louis XIV, André le Nôtre and the
Creation of the Garden of Versailles.* New York: Bloomsbury, 2006.

Touati, Houari. *Islam et voyage au Moyen Âge: Histoire et anthropologie
d'une pratique lettrée.* Paris: Seuil, 2000.

Van Leeuwen, Richard, and Ulrich Marzolph, eds. *The Arabian Nights
Encyclopedia.* Santa Barbara, CA: ABC-CLIO, 2004.

Vasari, Giorgio. *The Life of the Artists.* Translated by Julia Conaway
Bondanella and Peter Bondanella. Oxford, UK: Oxford University
Press, 2008.

Wahrmund, Adolf. *Handwörterbuch der neu-arabischen und deutschen
Sprache.* Beirut: Librairie du Liban, 1974.

Warner, Marina. *Stranger Magic: Charmed States and the Arabian Nights.*
London: Vintage, 2012.

Winter, Stefan. "Shiite Emirs and Ottoman Authorities: The Campaign against the Hamadas of Mt Lebanon, 1693–1694." In *Archivum Ottomanicum*, edited by György Hazai, 209–45. Wiesbaden, Germany: Harrassowitz, 2000.

Zotenberg, Hermann. "Notice sur quelques manuscrits des *Mille et Une Nuits* et la traduction de Galland." *Notices et extraits des manuscrits de la Bibliothèque nationale et autres bibliothèques* 28 (1887): 167–235.

FURTHER READING

The literature on Ḥannā Diyāb's travelogue and its textual environment is still rather scarce. Due to its conspicuous features and history, *The Book of Travels* will always remain connected to at least four fields of scholarship. The first and most important of these involves studies related to the *Arabian Nights* and the orphan stories, which are Ḥannā Diyāb's contribution to world literature. The second involves research on travelers and travelogues during the early modern period. The third involves studies related to historical linguistics of Arabic. Finally, in recent years scholarship has emerged on the mobility and the textual production of Eastern Christians in the early and middle Ottoman periods, which includes Diyāb's book and similar narrative literature. Autobiographical artifacts such as *The Book of Travels* have yet to be included in the vast research on the history of the early modern Ottoman world and its entanglement with Western Europe.

In the 1990s, *The Book of Travels* drew attention from the field of linguistics, notably in Jérôme Lentin's dissertation, "Recherches sur l'histoire de la langue arabe au Proche-Orient à l'époque moderne," and in other studies of his. In the past seven years, Ruth Bottigheimer and Ulrich Marzolph have published important work regarding Ḥannā Diyāb's connection to the *Arabian Nights*. Bernard Heyberger's introduction to the French translation (2015) and some of his other works, as well as John-Paul Ghobrial's research on the traces of Middle Eastern Christians around the globe, have helped place Ḥannā Diyāb's book in the social context of the Christians of the Ottoman Empire and their entangled histories.

Selected works from these research areas that are not already mentioned in the bibliography to this volume are listed below.

Literary and Cultural History of the Levant in the Early Modern Period

'Ānūtī, Usāma. *Al-Ḥarakah al-adabiyyah fī Bilād ash-Shām khilāl al-qarn al-thāmin 'ashar.* Beirut: Manshūrāt al-Jāmi'a al-Lubnāniyya, 1971.

Dakhlia, Jocelyne. *Lingua franca.* Arles, France: Actes Sud, 2008.

Hanna, Nelly. *In Praise of Books: A Cultural History of Cairo's Middle Class, Sixteenth to the Eighteenth Century.* Syracuse, NY: Syracuse University Press, 2003.

Kilpatrick, Hilary. "From *Literatur* to *Adab*: The Literary Renaissance in Aleppo around 1700." *Journal of Eastern Christian Studies* 58, nos. 3–4 (2006): 195–220.

Masters, Bruce. *The Arabs of the Ottoman Empire, 1516–1918: A Social and Cultural History.* Cambridge, UK: Cambridge University Press, 2013.

Sajdi, Dana. "Decline, Its Discontents and Ottoman Cultural History: By Way of Introduction." In *Ottoman Tulips, Ottoman Coffee: Leisure and Lifestyle in the Eighteenth Century*, edited by Dana Sajdi, 1–40. London: I. B. Tauris, 2007.

———. *The Barber of Damascus: Nouveau Literacy in Eighteenth-Century Ottoman Levant.* Stanford, CA: Stanford University Press, 2013.

Van den Boogert, Maurits. *Aleppo Observed: Ottoman Syria through the Eyes of Two Scottish Doctors, Alexander and Patrick Russell.* Oxford, UK: Oxford University Press, 2010.

Antoine Galland and the Orphan Stories

Akel, Ibrahim, and William Granara, eds. *The Thousand and One Nights: Sources and Transformations in Literature, Art, and Science.* Leiden, Netherlands: Brill, 2020.

Bauden, Frédéric, and Richard Waller, eds. *Antoine Galland (1646–1715) et son journal: Actes du colloque international organisé à l'Université de Liège (16–18 février 2015) à l'occasion du tricentenaire de sa mort.* Leeuwen, Belgium: Peeters, 2020.

Bottigheimer, Ruth B., and Claudia Ott. "The Case of the Ebony Horse: Part 1." *Gramarye* 5 (2014): 8–20.

Bottigheimer, Ruth B. "The Case of the Ebony Horse: Hannâ Diyâb's Creation of a Third Tradition; Part 2." *Gramarye* 6 (2014): 6–16.

———. "Reading for Fun in Eighteenth-Century Aleppo: The Hanna Dyâb Tales of Galland's *Mille et une nuits*." *Book History* 22 (2019): 133–60.

Marzolph, Ulrich. "A Scholar in the Making: Antoine Galland's Early Travel Diaries in the Light of Comparative Folk Narrative Research." *Middle Eastern Literatures* 18, no. 3 (2015): 283–300.

EARLY MODERN TRAVEL LITERATURE

Elger, Ralf. "Arabic Travelogues from the Mashrek 1700–1834: A Preliminary Survey of the Genre's Development." In *Crossing and Passages in Genre and Culture*, edited by Christian Szyska and Friederike Pannewick, 27–40. Wiesbaden, Germany: Reichert, 2003.

———. "Die Reisen eines Reiseberichts: Ibn Baṭṭūṭas Riḥla im Vorderen Orient des 17. und 18. Jahrhunderts." In *Buchkultur im Nahen Osten des 17. und 18. Jahrhunderts*, edited by Tobias Heinzelmann and Henning Sievert, 53–98. Bern: Peter Lang, 2010.

Göçek, Fatma Müge. *East Encounters West: France and the Ottoman Empire in the Eighteenth Century*. New York, NY: Oxford University Press, 1987.

Heyberger, Bernard and Carsten Walbiner, eds. *Les européens vus par les libanais à l'époque ottoman*. Würzburg, Germany: Ergon, 2002.

Kallas, Elie. "Aventures de Hanna Diyab avec Paul Lucas et Antoine Galland (1707–1710)." *Romano-Arabica* 15 (2015): 255–67.

———. *The Travel Accounts of Raʻd to Venice (1656) and Its Aleppo Dialect According to the MS. Sbath 89*. Vatican City: Biblioteca Apostolica Vaticana, 2015.

Kilpatrick, Hilary. "Between Ibn Baṭṭūṭa and al-Ṭahṭāwī: Arabic Travel Accounts of the Early Ottoman Period." *Middle Eastern Literatures* 11, no. 2 (2008): 233–248.

Muhanna, Elias. "Ilyās al-Mawṣilī." In *Essays in Arabic Literary Biography: 1350–1850*, edited by Joseph E. Lowry and Devin J. Stewart, 295–299. Wiesbaden, Germany: Harrassowitz, 2009.

Salmon, Olivier, ed. *Alep dans la littérature de voyage européenne pendant la période ottomane (1516–1918)*. Aleppo: El-Mudarris, 2011.

Walbiner, Carsten-Michael. "Riḥlat 'Ra'd' min Ḥalab ilā al-Bunduqīya." In *Mélanges en mémoire de Mgr Néophytos Edelby (1920–1995)*, edited by Nagi Edelby and Pierre Masri, 367–83. Beirut: Université St. Joseph, 2005.

Yirmisekiz Çelebī Efendi, Meḥmed. *Le paradis des infidèles: Relation de Yirmisekiz Çelebi Mehmed efendi, ambassadeur ottoman en France sous la Régence*. Paris: François Maspero, 1981.

Near Eastern Christianities

Ghobrial, John-Paul A. "The Ottoman World of 'Abdallah Zakher: Shuwayr Bindings in the Arcadian Library." In *The Arcadian Library: Bindings and Provenance*, edited by Giles Mandelbrote and Willem de Bruijn, 193–231. Oxford, UK: Oxford University Press, 2014.

———. "Migration from Within and Without: In the Footsteps of Eastern Christians in the Early Modern World." *Transactions of the Royal Historical Society* 27 (2017): 153–73.

Heyberger, Bernard. "Livres et pratique de la lecture chez les chrétiens (Syrie, Liban) XVIIe–XVIIIe siècles." *Revue des mondes musulmans et de la Méditerranée* 87–88 (1999): 209–23.

Khater, Akram Fouad. *Embracing the Divine: Gender, Passion, and Politics in the Christian Middle East, 1720–1798*. New York, NY: Syracuse University Press, 2011.

Walbiner, Carsten-Michael. "Monastic Reading and Learning in Eighteenth-Century Bilād al-Šām: Some Evidence from the Monastery of al-Šuwayr (Mount Lebanon)." *Arabica* 51, no. 4 (2004): 462–77.

INDEX

§10.9, §10.11, §11.162, 330, 361n226; Book of Genesis, §4.32; *Book of Travels*, xi–xii, xvii–xix, xxi, xxiv–xxv, xxvii–xxxi, xxxiv–xxxvii, 318–19, 322–25, 328–30, 332–38, 350n111, 358n198, 362n236; *Book of the Ten Viziers*, xxv; *Book of Sindbad*, xxv; booklet, §1.2; Holy Book, §4.29, §4.52; notebook, §§5.126–27; prayer book, §1.16

Bosquet de Marais, 352n137

bottarga, §11.150

Bourbon monarchy, 346n71, 350n116

Bourbon, Françoise Marie de, 352n134. *See also* Madame d'Orléans

Bourgogne, §8.12

Bourgogne, Duke of, §9.13

Bourgogne, Madame de, §§9.13–15, §9.21

branding (punishment), xiii, §6.72

bread, xiii, §§2.2–3, §3.8, §4.51, §4.65, §5.12, §5.26, §5.33, §7.2, §8.9, §8.11, §9.71, §9.74, §9.113, §9.119, §§9.154–55, §10.2, §§10.6–8, §§10.37–38, §11.49, §11.71, §11.78, §§11.145–53, 354n155; riots, 328, 331

breaking (punishment), §§9.143–44

Brémond, Capitaine, §6.12, §6.17, §§6.22–24, §6.27, §6.29, §6.42

brokers, §§7.12–13, §9.133

broth, §§11.75–77

Bsharrī, §§1.15–16, §1.24, 340n12, 340n14

bsīsa, §5.12

buildings, §§1.34–35, §3.9, §3.19, §4.12, §4.23, §4.75, §5.79, §5.91, §5.94, §5.106, §6.73, §6.117, §6.121, §6.123, §7.12, §§8.1–2, §9.3, §§9.66–67, §9.82, §9.84, §10.1,

§10.25, §11.50, 344n42; building stones, §5.74

Būlāq, §4.24

bull-pizzle whips, §7.3, §9.55, §9.145

butter, §1.36, §3.8, §5.8, §5.12

cabinets of curiosities, 327

cabins, §5.9, §6.33, §§7.1–2, §11.7, §11.12, §11.15

Cairo, xvii, §4.14, §4.17, §§4.23–25, §4.31, §4.33, §4.44, §§4.46–47, §4.80, §9.2, 333, 344n45, 345n53, 345n55, 362n231; New Cairo, §4.28; Old Cairo, §4.28, §4.51, §4.80, 345n58, 362n231

calendering, §11.43, 356n174; calenderer, §11.60

Callimeri, Antonio, §3.9, 343n40

calpac, xii, §2.7, §5.62, §5.65, §9.2, §9.16, §11.68

camel, §4.48, §5.13, §10.25, §11.168; *ashrāwī*, §4.48

cannons, §§5.35–36, §5.37, §6.1, §6.9, §§6.51–52, §6.73, §6.75, §6.111, §6.121, §§7.1–2, §7.5, §9.35, §9.112, §§10.67–68, §10.75, §11.9, §11.11, §11.50, §§11.52–53, 349n105

Capuchins, §2.4, §5.105, §6.41, §11.5

caravans, xviii, §§1.27–28, §§1.30–31, §1.34, §2.16, §5.90, §§5.95–97, §11.6, §11.43, §11.46, §11.57, §11.60, §§11.109–10, §11.111, §11.133, §11.135, §§11.138–39, §11.144, §§11.146–50, §§11.154–55, 333, 335

caravansary, xxxvii, §2.16, §4.23, §4.34, §4.47, §5.90, §5.95, §5.98, §11.24, §§11.60–61, §§11.80–81, §§11.97–98, §§11.101–2, §11.105. *See also* hostels; inns; markets

prisoners, §§5.28–29, §§5.32–34,
§5.38, §§5.43–45, §§5.47–48,
§5.63, §5.105, §5.108, §5.111, §6.2,
§§6.11–12, §§6.14–16, §6.20, §6.33,
§6.99, §9.141, §10.30, 11.1, §11.55
Prophet Muḥammad, §5.82, 342n28,
353n143
Provence, §8.11, 350n116, 351n118,
351n121, 351n123; Provençal, xi,
351n118
Province of the Islands, §5.36, §10.8,
§11.11, §§11.54–55, 347n78
public baths. *See* bath
pulse, §1.5, §11.73, §11.88, §11.93
punishments, §6.87, §§7.7–8,
§9.39, §9.55, §9.123, §9.154.
See also branding; breaking;
decapitation; drawing and
quartering; galleys; hanging; hard
labor; imprisonment; paraded in
disguise; slashed nostrils
purgatives, §§11.73–75, §11.79, §11.140;
purged, §11.76
pyramids, §4.39, 345n58

qablūjah. See hot springs
qinṭār, §4.3, §6.50, 344n47
quarantine, §6.3, §6.18, §6.22, §6.36,
349n97. *See also* lazaretto
Qulayʿah, §11.178
Qurṭ Qulāq, §11.152

Ramliyyah Square, §4.25
ransom, §6.2
rapiers, §6.15, §6.74, §§10.71–72,
§11.29, 355n165. *See also* swords,
weapons
Rās al-Nahr, §1.19, 340n13
rationing (of food), §10.6

raṭl, §5.9, §6.37, §10.8
rayyis, §§5.2–3, §5.5, §5.14, §5.16,
§5.19, §§5.22–24
reading, xi, xxvi, xxxiv, xxxvi,
§1.6, §2.18, §4.54, §5.50, §6.26,
§§6.71–72, §6.120, §9.19, §9.145,
§11.20, 321, 329, 334, 355n164
refectories, §§1.5–6, §1.13
Rémuzat, *khawājah*, §1.27, §1.38,
§2.17, §11.37
reptiles, §4.8
rhubarb, §6.49
rice, §11.71, §11.77, §11.150
Rimbaud, *khawājah*, §§7.17–19,
§11.37, §11.39, §11.121
rings, §1.36, §2.8, §6.28, §6.30, §6.32,
§§6.59–62, §6.66, 335, 342n25,
343n34, 349n104, 349n107,
362n234
riverboat (*maʿāsh*), §4.14, §4.17,
§4.24, §4.51, §§4.53–54, §4.80
riyāl, §§4.31–32, §6.8, §6.17
robbed/robbery, §1.34, §5.60, §6.25,
§9.141, §9.143, §10.73, §11.2,
§§11.64–65, §11.147
robbers, xiii
Roman, *khawājah*, §1.38
Rome, xix, §5.47, §5.56, §6.49, §6.50,
§7.12, 339n4
Rosetta, xii, §4.17, §§4.22–23,
§§4.42–43, §4.80, 345n53
Rouen, xx, §8.16, 332
Roux, *khawājah*, §7.20
rowboat, §4.5, §5.3, §5.6, §5.11, §5.16,
§5.22, §§5.26–27, §6.8, §6.10, §6.12,
§§6.17–18, §10.63, §10.67, §11.1
Royal Library in Paris. *See* libraries
royalty, §6.112, §7.7. *See also* king;
princes; princesses

stagecoach, §10.35, §10.37, §10.42. *See also* coach; diligence

starvation, §5.74, §10.6

statues, §3.19, §4.58, §6.95, §7.15, §§10.3–4

storms, xiii, §5.3, §5.17, §5.79; windstorm, §4.39

Sudan, §5.11; Sudanese lands, §4.49

Sultan Aḥmad, §9.86, §10.71, §11.50, §11.53

Sultan of France, xx, §1.29, §1.33, §§1.38–40, §2.17, §4.24, §4.38, §4.40, §5.98, §5.132, §6.16, §6.19, §6.25, §6.32, §6.118, §§6.122–23, §9.13, §9.86, §11.52, 341n20. *See also* Louis XIV of France, King

Sunday school, §9.108

Sweden, §11.56

sweets, §11.13, §11.32

swelling, §§4.20–21, §11.86, §11.90, §11.93

swindle, §9.112, 326

swindlers, §6.80, §§6.86–87

swords, §2.6, §5.10, §6.15, §6.74, §6.86, §9.23, §9.25. *See also* foil; rapiers, weapons

Syriac (sect), §6.48, §6.78

Syriac language, §4.31, 345n59

tar, §4.1. *See also* bitumen

taxes, §2.6, §3.21, §4.1, §4.4, §6.37, §6.80, §6.83, §6.86, §11.51, §§11.133–34, 340n14, 342n30, 344n41

theatrical effects, §9.103

thieves, xxxix n6, xl n16, §1.35, §9.82, §9.137, §9.147, §11.63, §11.70, §11.155, 324. *See also* "ʿAlī Bābā and the Forty Thieves" (tale); robbers

Thousand and One Nights, xvii–xviii, xxiv–xxix, xxxvi–xxxvii, xxxix n6, xli n26, *§10.9,* 318–25, 328, 330–32, 334, 336–337, 354n157, 357n190

thulth, §2.8, 343n32

tobacco, xii, §1.32, §4.19, §4.64, §§6.37–38, §11.119

toilets, §§7.9–10. *See also* chamber pots; latrines

tombs, §§1.35–36, §4.39, §9.29, 276, 341n23; tombstones, §11.143

Torah, §§4.31–32

translation/translated, xvii, xxiv–xxv, xxvii, xxix–xxxi, xxxiii, xxxvii–xxxviii, xli n51, §4.58, §4.62, §5.106, §10.9, §§10.15–16, 318, 320–21, 330–31, 344n45, 357n183, 358n202, 359n212, 360n219, 361n228, 361n230, 362n232, 362n236

translators, xi, xvii–xviii, §1.33, §4.37, §4.57, 318–23, 325, 328, 330, 334, 347n82, 353n150, 354n157. *See also* dragoman

travel papers, §4.4, §6.116

treasury, §§4.38–39, §5.107, §6.37, §6.82, §9.131, §11.25, §11.104

trees, §3.7, §4.64, §5.11, §5.79, §5.87, §6.8, §6.106, §7.12, §§9.37–38, §§9.76–77, §9.87, §9.92, §9.97, §§10.1–2, §11.63, §§11.141–42, §11.145, §11.150, §11.154, 352n137. *See also* citron; cypress; lemon; mulberry; olive; orange; palm

trials, xiii, §6.27, §§6.35–36, 341n15, 350n113. *See also* courthouses; judge/judgment; tribunal

tribunals, §6.27, §6.91, §8.1

trinket (sail), §5.2, §5.23

About the NYU Abu Dhabi Institute

The Library of Arabic Literature is supported by a grant from the NYU Abu Dhabi Institute, a major hub of intellectual and creative activity and advanced research. The Institute hosts academic conferences, workshops, lectures, film series, performances, and other public programs directed both to audiences within the UAE and to the  worldwide academic and research community. It is a center of the scholarly community for Abu Dhabi, bringing together faculty and researchers from institutions of higher learning throughout the region.

NYU Abu Dhabi, through the NYU Abu Dhabi Institute, is a world-class center of cutting-edge research, scholarship, and cultural activity. The Institute creates singular opportunities for leading researchers from across the arts, humanities, social sciences, sciences, engineering, and the professions to carry out creative scholarship and conduct research on issues of major disciplinary, multidisciplinary, and global significance.

About the Translator

Elias Muhanna is Associate Professor of Comparative Literature and History at Brown University. He is the author of *The World in a Book: al-Nuwayri and the Islamic Encyclopedic Tradition* and translator of Shihāb al-Dīn al-Nuwayrī's fourteenth-century encyclopedia, *The Ultimate Ambition in the Arts of Erudition.*

The Library of Arabic Literature

For more details on individual titles, visit www.libraryofarabicliterature.org

Classical Arabic Literature: A Library of Arabic Literature Anthology
 Selected and translated by Geert Jan van Gelder (2012)

A Treasury of Virtues: Sayings, Sermons, and Teachings of ʿAlī, by al-Qāḍī
 al-Quḍāʿī, with the *One Hundred Proverbs* attributed to al-Jāḥiẓ
 Edited and translated by Tahera Qutbuddin (2013)

The Epistle on Legal Theory, by al-Shāfiʿī
 Edited and translated by Joseph E. Lowry (2013)

Leg over Leg, by Aḥmad Fāris al-Shidyāq
 Edited and translated by Humphrey Davies (4 volumes; 2013–14)

Virtues of the Imām Aḥmad ibn Ḥanbal, by Ibn al-Jawzī
 Edited and translated by Michael Cooperson (2 volumes; 2013–15)

The Epistle of Forgiveness, by Abū l-ʿAlāʾ al-Maʿarrī
 Edited and translated by Geert Jan van Gelder and Gregor Schoeler
 (2 volumes; 2013–14)

The Principles of Sufism, by ʿĀʾishah al-Bāʿūniyyah
 Edited and translated by Th. Emil Homerin (2014)

The Expeditions: An Early Biography of Muḥammad, by Maʿmar ibn Rāshid
 Edited and translated by Sean W. Anthony (2014)

Two Arabic Travel Books

    Accounts of China and India, by Abū Zayd al-Sīrāfī

        Edited and translated by Tim Mackintosh-Smith (2014)

    Mission to the Volga, by Aḥmad ibn Faḍlān

        Edited and translated by James Montgomery (2014)

Disagreements of the Jurists: A Manual of Islamic Legal Theory, by al-Qāḍī al-Nuʿmān

    Edited and translated by Devin J. Stewart (2015)

Consorts of the Caliphs: Women and the Court of Baghdad, by Ibn al-Sāʿī

    Edited by Shawkat M. Toorawa and translated by the Editors of the Library of Arabic Literature (2015)

What ʿĪsā ibn Hishām Told Us, by Muḥammad al-Muwayliḥī

    Edited and translated by Roger Allen (2 volumes; 2015)

The Life and Times of Abū Tammām, by Abū Bakr Muḥammad ibn Yaḥyā al-Ṣūlī

    Edited and translated by Beatrice Gruendler (2015)

The Sword of Ambition: Bureaucratic Rivalry in Medieval Egypt, by ʿUthmān ibn Ibrāhīm al-Nābulusī

    Edited and translated by Luke Yarbrough (2016)

Brains Confounded by the Ode of Abū Shādūf Expounded, by Yūsuf al-Shirbīnī

    Edited and translated by Humphrey Davies (2 volumes; 2016)

Light in the Heavens: Sayings of the Prophet Muḥammad, by al-Qāḍī al-Quḍāʿī

    Edited and translated by Tahera Qutbuddin (2016)

Risible Rhymes, by Muḥammad ibn Maḥfūẓ al-Sanhūrī

    Edited and translated by Humphrey Davies (2016)

A Hundred and One Nights

    Edited and translated by Bruce Fudge (2016)

The Excellence of the Arabs, by Ibn Qutaybah
   Edited by James E. Montgomery and Peter Webb
   Translated by Sarah Bowen Savant and Peter Webb (2017)

Scents and Flavors: A Syrian Cookbook
   Edited and translated by Charles Perry (2017)

Arabian Satire: Poetry from 18th-Century Najd, by Ḥmēdān al-Shwēʿir
   Edited and translated by Marcel Kurpershoek (2017)

In Darfur: An Account of the Sultanate and Its People, by Muḥammad
   ibn ʿUmar al-Tūnisī
   Edited and translated by Humphrey Davies (2 volumes; 2018)

War Songs, by ʿAntarah ibn Shaddād
   Edited by James E. Montgomery
   Translated by James E. Montgomery with Richard Sieburth (2018)

Arabian Romantic: Poems on Bedouin Life and Love, by ʿAbdallah
   ibn Sbayyil
   Edited and translated by Marcel Kurpershoek (2018)

Dīwān ʿAntarah ibn Shaddād: A Literary-Historical Study,
   by James E. Montgomery (2018)

Stories of Piety and Prayer: Deliverance Follows Adversity, by al-Muḥassin
   ibn ʿAlī al-Tanūkhī
   Edited and translated by Julia Bray (2019)

*Tajrīd sayf al-himmah li-stikhrāj mā fī dhimmat al-dhimmah: A Scholarly
   Edition of ʿUthmān ibn Ibrāhīm al-Nābulusī's Text*, by Luke Yarbrough
   (2019)

*The Philosopher Responds: An Intellectual Correspondence from the Tenth
   Century*, by Abū Ḥayyān al-Tawḥīdī and Abū ʿAlī Miskawayh
   Edited by Bilal Orfali and Maurice A. Pomerantz
   Translated by Sophia Vasalou and James E. Montgomery
   (2 volumes; 2019)

The Discourses: Reflections on History, Sufism, Theology, and Literature—
Volume One, by al-Ḥasan al-Yūsī
Edited and translated by Justin Stearns (2020)

Impostures, by al-Ḥarīrī
Translated by Michael Cooperson (2020)

Maqāmāt Abī Zayd al-Sarūjī, by al-Ḥarīrī
Edited by Michael Cooperson (2020)

The Yoga Sutras of Patañjali, by Abū Rayḥān al-Bīrūnī
Edited and translated by Mario Kozah (2020)

The Book of Charlatans, by Jamāl al-Dīn ʿAbd al-Raḥīm al-Jawbarī
Edited by Manuela Dengler
Translated by Humphrey Davies (2020)

A Physician on the Nile: A Description of Egypt and Journal of a Plague Year,
by ʿAbd al-Laṭīf al-Baghdādī
Edited and translated by Tim Mackintosh-Smith (2021)

The Book of Travels, by Ḥannā Diyāb
Edited by Johannes Stephan
Translated by Elias Muhanna (2 volumes; 2021)

Kalīlah and Dimnah: Fables of Virtue and Vice, by Ibn al-Muqaffaʿ
Edited by Michael Fishbein
Translated by Michael Fishbein and James E. Montgomery (2021)

Love, Death, Fame: Poetry and Lore from the Emirati Oral Tradition,
by al-Māyidī ibn Ẓāhir
Edited and translated by Marcel Kurpershoek (2022)

The Essence of Reality: A Defense of Philosophical Sufism, by ʿAyn al-Quḍāt
Edited and translated by Mohammed Rustom (2022)

The Requirements of the Sufi Path: A Defense of the Mystical Tradition,
by Ibn Khaldūn
Edited and translated by Carolyn Baugh (2022)

The Doctors' Dinner Party, by Ibn Buṭlān
  Edited and translated by Philip F. Kennedy and Jeremy Farrell (2023)

Brains Confounded by the Ode of Abū Shādūf Expounded: Volume One, by
  Yūsuf al-Shirbīnī (2019)

Brains Confounded by the Ode of Abū Shādūf Expounded: Volume Two,
  by Yūsuf al-Shirbīnī and *Risible Rhymes*, by Muḥammad ibn Maḥfūẓ
  al-Sanhūrī (2019)

The Excellence of the Arabs, by Ibn Qutaybah (2019)

Light in the Heavens: Sayings of the Prophet Muḥammad, by al-Qāḍī
  al-Quḍāʿī (2019)

Scents and Flavors: A Syrian Cookbook (2020)

Arabian Satire: Poetry from 18th-Century Najd, by Ḥmēdān al-Shwēʿir
  (2020)

In Darfur: An Account of the Sultanate and Its People, by Muḥammad
  al-Tūnisī (2020)

Arabian Romantic: Poems on Bedouin Life and Love, by Ibn Sbayyil (2020)

*The Philosopher Responds: An Intellectual Correspondence from the Tenth
  Century*, by Abū Ḥayyān al-Tawḥīdī and Abū ʿAlī Miskawayh (2021)

Impostures, by al-Ḥarīrī (2021)

*The Discourses: Reflections on History, Sufism, Theology, and Literature—
  Volume One*, by al-Ḥasan al-Yūsī (2021)

The Yoga Sutras of Patañjali, by Abū Rayḥān al-Bīrūnī (2022)

The Book of Charlatans, by Jamāl al-Dīn ʿAbd al-Raḥīm al-Jawbarī (2022)

The Book of Travels, by Ḥannā Diyāb (2022)

*A Physician on the Nile: A Description of Egypt and Journal of the Famine
  Years*, by ʿAbd al-Laṭīf al-Baghdādī (2022)